The Bible Speaks Today

Series Editors: J. A. Motyer (OT)
John R. W. Stott (NT)
Derek Tidball (Bible Themes)

The Message of
Ezekiel
A New Heart and a New Spirit

Titles in this series

OLD TESTAMENT

Genesis 1—11
David Atkinson

Genesis 12—50
Joyce G. Baldwin

Deuteronomy
Raymond Brown

Judges
Michael Wilcock

Ruth
David Atkinson

Chronicles
Michael Wilcock

Nehemiah
Raymond Brown

Job
David Atkinson

Proverbs
David Atkinson

Ecclesiastes
Derek Kidner

Song of Songs
Tom Gledhill

Isaiah
Barry Webb

Jeremiah
Derek Kidner

Ezekiel
Christopher J. H.
Wright

Daniel
Ronald S. Wallace

Hosea
Derek Kidner

Amos
J. A. Motyer

Joel, Micah &
Habakkuk
David Prior

NEW TESTAMENT

Matthew
Michael Green

Sermon on the Mount
(Matthew 5—7)
John R. W. Stott

Mark
Donald English

Luke
Michael Wilcock

John
Bruce Milne

Acts
John R. W. Stott

Romans
John R. W. Stott

1 Corinthians
David Prior

2 Corinthians
Paul Barnett

Galatians
John R. W. Stott

Ephesians
John R. W. Stott

Philippians
J. A. Motyer

Colossians & Philemon
R. C. Lucas

1 & 2 Thessalonians
John R. W. Stott

1 Timothy & Titus
John R. W. Stott

2 Timothy
John R. W. Stott

Hebrews
Raymond Brown

James
J. A. Motyer

1 Peter
Edmund P. Clowney

2 Peter & Jude
Dick Lucas &
Christopher Green

John's Letters
David Jackman

Revelation
Michael Wilcock

BIBLE THEMES

The Cross
Derek Tidball

The Living God
Peter Lewis

The Resurrection
Paul Beasley-Murray

The Message of Ezekiel

A New Heart and a New Spirit

Christopher J. H. Wright

International Ministry Director,
Langham Partnership International

Inter-Varsity Press
Leicester, England
Downers Grove, Illinois, USA

InterVarsity Press
P.O. Box 1400, Downers Grove, IL 60515-1426
World Wide Web: www.ivpress.com
E-mail: mail@ivpress.com

Inter-Varsity Press
38 De Montfort Street, Leicester LE1 7GP, England

InterVarsity Press®® is the book-publishing division of InterVarsity Christian Fellowship/USA®, a student movement active on campus at hundreds of universities, colleges and schools of nursing in the United States of America, and a member movement of the International Fellowship of Evangelical Students. For information about local and regional activities, write Public Relations Dept., InterVarsity Christian Fellowship/USA, 6400 Schroeder Rd., P.O. Box 7895, Madison, WI 53707-7895.

Inter-Varsity Press is the book-publishing division of the Universities and Colleges Christian Fellowship (formerly the Inter-Varsity Fellowship), a student movement linking Christian Unions in universities and colleges throughout the United Kingdom and the Republic of Ireland, and a member movement of the International Fellowship of Evangelical Students. For information about local and national activities write to UCCF, 38 De Montfort Street, Leicester LE1 7GP, England.

USA ISBN 0-8308-2425-1
UK ISBN 0-85111-548-9

Typeset in Great Britain by The Midlands Book Typesetting Company. Printed in the United States of America ∞

British Library Cataloguing in Publication Data
A catalogue record for this book is available from the British Library.

Library of Congress Cataloging-in-Publication Data
Wright, Christopher J. H., 1947-
    The message of Ezekiel/Christopher J.H. Wright.
      p. cm.—(The Bible speaks today)
    Includes bibliographical references.
    ISBN 0-8308-2425-1 (alk. paper)
    1. Bible. O.T. Ezekiel—Commentaries. I. Title. II. Series.
BS1545.53 W75 2001
224'.407—dc21
                                                                    2001024421

18 17 16 15 14 13 12 11 10 9 8 7 6 5 4 3 2
16 15 14 13 12 11 10 09 08 07 06 05 04 03 02

For
Catharine and Andy

Contents

General

preface

THE BIBLE SPEAKS TODAY describes three series of expositions, based on the books of the Old and New Testaments, and on Bible themes that run through the whole of Scripture. Each series is characterized by a threefold ideal:

- to expound the biblical text with accuracy
- to relate it to contemporary life, and
- to be readable.

These books are, therefore, not 'commentaries', for the commentary seeks rather to elucidate the text than to apply it, and tends to be a work rather of reference than of literature. Nor, on the other hand, do they contain the kind of 'sermons' which attempt to be contemporary and readable without taking Scripture seriously enough.

The contributors to *The Bible Speaks Today* series are all united in their convictions that God still speaks through what he has spoken, and that nothing is more necessary for the life, health and growth of Christians than that they should hear what the Spirit is saying to them through his ancient – yet ever modern – Word.

ALEC MOTYER
JOHN STOTT
DEREK TIDBALL
Series Editors

Author's preface

The date at the top of a rather dog-eared essay records my awakening to the riches of biblical theology. It reads 'April 1969' and the title of the essay was simply 'The theology of Ezekiel'. I was in the third term of my theological studies at Cambridge and had covered much in the way of critical and historical issues. Suddenly, however, I was being asked to think about Ezekiel as a theologian, as a person with a mind of his own and a distinctive theological agenda. Up to then, for me 'Ezekiel' was just a book in the Bible. Theology and theologians were what came *after* the Bible. I had never thought of the biblical writers as theologians in their own right. I remember well the growing sense of excitement that welled up within me as I did the preparation for that essay (an emotional state not commonly associated with undergraduate essay writing). I was fascinated by this strange character emerging from the pages of his book. I marvelled at the wildness of his behaviour, and the matching wildness of the pseudo-psychological theories purporting to explain it. I was moved by the touching poignancy of the reference to his precious wife and her tragic death. I wrestled with the massive contours of his interpretation of Israel's judgment and his glorious vision of Israel's ultimate restoration. In short, I was hooked by the sheer fascination of hearing the living voice of a man whose theology was born in the pain and passion of his own and his people's suffering. Biblical theology came to life for me, thanks to an essay on Ezekiel.

Around the same time I came across the books of John Hercus, the Australian psychiatrist who produced wonderfully engaging case-studies on biblical characters, subjecting them to an imaginative mixture of interview, analysis and assessment. His second volume, *More Pages from God's Casebook*, included a chapter on Ezekiel which further stimulated my fascination with this enigmatic person, easily the most bizarre of all the prophets. Doubtless some of Hercus's imaginative reconstructions of the circumstances of Ezekiel's home and ministry fall far short of the actual historical reality (though we have very little independent knowledge of that anyway). But their great virtue, in my opinion, is that they brought the character vividly to life and set his message within a framework in which it could be grasped. I realized that by engaging the imagination, Hercus had helped his readers to make sense of, and profit spiritually from, a text that was otherwise (to say the least) fairly opaque. I remember pledging myself at the time to try to do for others what Hercus had done for me – that is, to preach and teach in such a way that would stimulate people's imagination and generate excitement about the biblical text, so that they could understand and respond to its message. I vowed, at all costs, never to let the Bible be boring in my handling of it (can there be anything more inexcusable than *boring* people with the *Bible*?). Whether or not I have always succeeded in this ambition, I owe the incentive at least, in a roundabout way, to Ezekiel and his impact on me as a student. It will be obvious to those who have read John Hercus's book that I have allowed my imagination to operate in a similar way at times, but I hope it will be accepted that my purpose in doing so has been the same as his – to bring the prophet to life in our minds so that his message can confront us with something of the same shocking power that so scorched the ears of his first listeners.

So when I agreed to Alec Motyer's invitation to write *The Bible Speaks Today* volume on Ezekiel, it was with a sense of repaying a debt to an old friend, by which I do not merely mean Alec himself. I trust that my study and understanding of the book have progressed somewhat beyond my undergraduate essay of 1969. I am greatly indebted to the wealth of scholarly books and articles now available on Ezekiel, including some fine recent commentaries. I particularly valued the stupendous treasure-chest of meticulous exegesis and clear theological reflection provided by Daniel Block's two-volume commentary on Ezekiel in the NICOT series. It will surely stand as the definitive work for many years.

Since the objective of *The Bible Speaks Today* series is not, strictly speaking, exegetical commentary, but exposition of the message of the book as a whole, I have felt free to organize the material with some degree of selection and with a division of the book into groups of related chapters. For the sake of completeness, however, I have provided in the Appendices some short notes on those chapters of Ezekiel which have not been treated in expository depth in the main chapters of this book.

I am grateful to Alec Motyer not only for the initial invitation, but also, along with Raymond Brown, for reading the first draft of the work and making a host of helpful comments which have inspired many clarifications and improvements. I also acknowledge with thanks the willingness of my colleagues on the staff of All Nations Christian College to release me from most of my duties as Principal during a sabbatical term in the summer of 1999 when I was able to complete most of the first draft. My tutorial group of that year also saw very little of me in that term and I am grateful for their understanding. And particularly I thank Mrs Jan Stafford who, in her final term before retirement, stepped in as Acting Principal for that term, enabling me to be free of most of the burden of responsibility for several wonderful weeks.

My wife, Liz, 'the delight of my eyes', knows only too well the debt I owe her for unfailing support in this as in other areas of ministry, and our family members likewise deserve all our gratitude for their constant encouragement. The book is dedicated to our eldest daughter and son-in-law, for whom, along with all God's people, we pray that Ezekiel's words on God's behalf will be a reality:

I will make my home among them. I will be their God and they will be my people. Then they will know that I, the LORD their God, am with them (Ezek. 37:27, my translation; cf. 34:30).

Chief abbreviations

ANET	*Ancient Near Eastern Texts*, ed. J. B. Pritchard (Princeton: Princeton University Press, 3rd ed. 1969)
JSOT	*Journal for the Study of the Old Testament*
JTS	*Journal of Theological Studies*
KJV	The Authorized (King James) Version of the Bible (1611)
lit.	literally
LXX	The Septuagint (ancient Greek translation of the Old Testament)
MT	Masoretic Text
NIDOTTE	*New International Dictionary of Old Testament Theology and Exegesis*, ed. W. A. VanGemeren, 5 vols. (Grand Rapids: Zondervan; Carlisle: Paternoster, 1997)
NIV	The New International Version of the Bible (1973, 1978, 1984)
NIVI	The New International Version of the Bible, Inclusive Language Edition (1973, 1978, 1984, 1995, 1996)
NKJV	The New King James Version of the Bible (1982)
NLT	The New Living Translation of the Bible (1996)
NRSV	The New Revised Standard Version of the Bible, Anglicized Edition (1989, 1995)
TB	*Tyndale Bulletin*
VT	*Vetus Testamentum*
ZAW	*Zeitschrift für die alttestamentliche Wissenschaft*

Select bibliography

Works listed here are later referred to by author's surname, with title or volume number where appropriate.

Ackroyd, P. R., *Exile and Restoration*, Old Testament Library (London: SCM, 1968)

Allen, L. C., *Ezekiel 1 – 19*, Word Biblical Commentary 28 (Dallas: Word Books, 1994)

——— *Ezekiel 20 – 48*, Word Biblical Commentary 29 (Dallas: Word Books, 1990)

Blenkinsopp, J., *Ezekiel*, Interpretation: A Biblical Commentary for Teaching and Preaching (Louisville: John Knox, 1990)

Block, D. I. (1), *The Book of Ezekiel, 1 – 24*, The New International Commentary on the Old Testament (Grand Rapids: Eerdmans, 1997)

——— (2), *The Book of Ezekiel, 25 – 48*, The New International Commentary on the Old Testament (Grand Rapids: Eerdmans, 1997)

Boadt, L., 'The function of the salvation oracles in Ezekiel 33 to 37', *Hebrew Annual Review* 12 (1990), pp. 1–21

Brueggemann, W., *Hopeful Imagination: Prophetic Voices in Exile* (Philadelphia: Fortress, 1986)

——— *Theology of the Old Testament: Testimony, Dispute, Advocacy* (Minneapolis: Fortress, 1997)

Bullock, C. H., 'Ezekiel, bridge between the Testaments', *Journal of the Evangelical Theological Society* 25 (1982), pp. 23–31

Calvin, J., *Ezekiel I, Chapters 1 – 12*, Calvin's Old Testament Commentaries 18 (Grand Rapids: Eerdmans; Carlisle: Paternoster, 1994)

——— *Ezekiel II, Chapters 13 – 20*, Calvin's Old Testament Commentaries 19 (Grand Rapids: Eerdmans; Carlisle: Paternoster, 1994)

Cooke, G. A., *A Critical and Exegetical Commentary on the Book of Ezekiel*, The International Critical Commentary (Edinburgh: T. and T. Clark, 1936)

Eichrodt, W., *Ezekiel: A Commentary* (London: SCM, 1970)

Ellison, H. L., *Ezekiel: The Man and His Message* (Grand Rapids: Eerdmans, 1956)

Fishbane, M., 'Sin and judgment in the prophecies of Ezekiel', *Interpretation* 38 (1984), pp. 131–150

Greenberg, M., *Ezekiel 1 – 20*, The Anchor Bible 22 (New York: Doubleday, 1983)

Joyce, P., *Divine Initiative and Human Response in Ezekiel*, Journal for the Study of the Old Testament Supplement 51 (Sheffield: JSOT Press, 1989)

Levenson, J. D., *Theology of the Program of Restoration in Ezekiel 40 – 48*, Harvard Semitic Mongraph Series 10 (Missoula: Scholars, 1976)

Luc, A., 'A theology of Ezekiel: God's name and Israel's history', *Journal of the Evangelical Theological Society* 26 (1983), pp. 137–143

McKeating, H., *Ezekiel*, Old Testament Guides (Sheffield: Sheffield Academic Press, 1993)

Taylor, J. B., *Ezekiel: An Introduction and Commentary*, Tyndale Old Testament Commentaries (Leicester: IVP, 1969)

Vawter, B., and Hoppe, L. J., *A New Heart: A Commentary on the Book of Ezekiel*, International Theological Commentary (Grand Rapids: Eerdmans, 1991)

Wevers, J. W., *Ezekiel:* New Century Bible Commentary (Grand Rapids: Eerdmans, 1969)

Wright, C. J. H., *God's People in God's Land: Family, Land and Property in the Old Testament* (Grand Rapids: Eerdmans; Carlisle: Paternoster, 1990)

——— *Knowing Jesus Through the Old Testament* (London: Marshall Pickering; Downers Grove: IVP, 1992)

——— *Living as the People of God: The Relevance of Old Testament Ethics* (Leicester: IVP, 1983) = *An Eye for an Eye* (Downers Grove: IVP, 1983)

Zimmerli, W., *Ezekiel 1: A Commentary on the Book of the Prophet Ezekiel Chapters 1 – 24*, Hermeneia: A Critical and Historical Commentary on the Bible (Philadelphia: Fortress, 1979)

——— *Ezekiel 2: A Commentary on the Book of the Prophet Ezekiel Chapters 25 – 48*, Hermeneia: A Critical and Historical Commentary on the Bible (Philadelphia: Fortress, 1983)

——— *I Am Yahweh*, ed. and introduced by W. Brueggemann (Atlanta: John Knox, 1982)

Introduction

1. Ezekiel and his times

'May God strengthen him.' This was the prayer with which Ezekiel's parents launched their newborn son into the world when they named him.[1] It was an appropriate prayer and God would have to answer it in ways they could never have envisaged in the year of his birth. It was 622 BC[2] – an auspicious year to be born, from the point of view of the family of priests in Jerusalem into which Ezekiel arrived.[3] It was the year in which the book of the law was discovered in the temple, adding urgency and impetus to the reforms which King Josiah was already instigating in the kingdom of Judah.[4] By that date, Josiah had been king for about eighteen years, since 640 BC, and had already been engaged in a programme of religious reforms for some five years.[5]

Josiah's religious reforms, which included the destruction of all pagan places of worship and the purging of priests who had served them, need to be set in the context of the political and international circumstances of his reign. For more than a century the small kingdom of Judah had been dominated by the great empire of Assyria. In fact it was technically a vassal state, and had been since the time of King Ahaz. Ahaz was the king who, in 735 BC, much against the advice of Isaiah, had put Judah under the protection of Assyria in exchange for Assyrian help against his own enemies at the

---

[1] His name, *y'ḥezqē'l*, 'May God strengthen', is almost identical to the name of an earlier godly king in Judah, Hezekiah, except that the latter is formed using the abbreviation of Yahweh at the end, rather than 'El.
[2] This date for the birth of Ezekiel depends on the assumption that the phrase 'In the thirtieth year' in 1:1 refers to the thirtieth year of his own life. That year, the year of his vision and call by the Kebar Canal, is also identified as the 'fifth year of the exile of King Jehoiachin' (1:2), which was 593–592 BC.
[3] It seems very likely that Ezekiel's father, Buzi, was a priest in Jerusalem, given the detailed knowledge of Jerusalem that Ezekiel shows in his visions. He may well have belonged to the dominant Zadokite lineage, though we have no further details of his genealogy.
[4] 2 Kgs. 22.   [5] 2 Chr. 34:3–7.

17

time – an alliance of the northern kingdom of Israel with Syria.[6] Now, however, a century later, Assyria was beginning to weaken and creak at the seams. Many of the smaller states on its western edges, including Judah, began to stir restlessly for restored independence. Josiah's reforms then, though undoubtedly motivated by religious sincerity and a desire to cleanse Israel of the accumulated idolatries of Manasseh, also heralded a revival of nationalistic hopes in Judah. The people of Yahweh and the city of David must once again be free!

So the earliest years of Ezekiel would have been spent in the exciting days of what may have seemed like a new dawn. Reform was in the air, and it produced massive religious and social turmoil. Not that everything in the country was changed for the better overnight. From the preaching of the young Jeremiah, who was called to be a prophet in 627, the thirteenth year of Josiah's reign and about five years after Josiah had begun his reforms, we get the clear impression that it was one thing for Josiah to eradicate idols from the high places, but it was another thing to remove idolatry from the hearts and minds of the people. The land was still awash with false gods and groaning under all kinds of social evil. Yet all this went alongside the appearance of flourishing worship of Yahweh in the temple in Jerusalem. The contradiction was too much for God and Jeremiah. With incredible boldness on one occasion Jeremiah preached in the temple itself against the perverted effrontery of those who spent the week breaking all God's covenant laws and then came to the temple on the Sabbath to claim safety there on the grounds of God's past promise to dwell there for ever and protect his people there. On the contrary, Jeremiah said, unless there was radical change in the ways of the people, God would abandon his city and the fate of the temple would be the same as what happened to Shiloh – an early site of the tabernacle in the days of Eli and Samuel, which had been totally destroyed many centuries before Jeremiah's day.[7] The threat went unheeded.

In spite of all his reforming zeal and good intentions, the reign of Josiah came to an untimely end when, in 609 BC, he marched out with his small army to try to intercept the Egyptian Pharaoh Necho who was heading north to help Assyria against the newly rising power of Babylon. The Judean army was defeated in a battle at Megiddo, and Josiah was killed. For a brief period Judah fell under

---

[6] 2 Kgs. 16; Is. 7.
[7] The message is recorded in Jer. 7. Probably Jer. 26 refers to the same occasion, and narrates the sequel, which was that Jeremiah only narrowly escaped a lynching for what seemed *prima facie* false prophecy – the very idea that Yahweh would destroy his own temple and city was unthinkably blasphemous.

the power of Egypt, who, after deposing Josiah's successor Jehoahaz (referred to as Shallum in Jeremiah 22:10–12), and exiling him to Egypt, installed another son of Josiah instead – Jehoiakim.[8]

Jehoiakim not only pursued a policy of subservience to Egypt, for which he paid heavily in tax and tribute, but also seems to have reversed the reforms of Josiah, much to the consternation of Jeremiah. Some of the bitterest conflicts in Jeremiah's ministry were between Jehoiakim and himself. Jeremiah ruthlessly and unfavourably compared Jehoiakim with his godly father, Josiah, and accused him of blatant greed, arrogance and injustice – predicting that he would die unmourned.[9] The hostility culminated in the notorious burning of Jeremiah's scroll of prophecies by Jehoiakim as they were read to him in his palace.[10] This event took place in 605 BC, when Ezekiel would have been about seventeen years old. He must have heard about it. It is very possible that he even witnessed the first reading of the scroll in the temple itself. Ezekiel's own recorded prophecies make it clear that he knew and made good use of the prophetic words of Jeremiah.

Back on the international scene, Egypt was vying with Babylon for the carve-up of the collapsing Assyrian empire. The eventual winner was Babylon. Under their energetic new leader, Nebuchadnezzar,[11] they utterly crushed the Egyptians at the battle of Carchemish in 605 BC. Immediately, Nebuchadnezzar set about bringing Judah and other smaller states to heel. After taking some of the nobility as hostages to Babylon,[12] he imposed vassal status on Jehoiakim. Jehoiakim, however, was not inclined to sit easily under Babylonian rule, and in 598–597 BC he rebelled. Nebuchadnezzar set out to besiege Jerusalem, and early on, Jehoiakim himself died.[13] His successor, Jehoiachin (also referred to as Coniah), surrendered the city after three months. On this occasion, Nebuchadnezzar was relatively merciful. He did not destroy the city, though he did plunder some of the temple treasures.[14] In an attempt to forestall future rebellions, he carried off into exile Jehoiachin and the royal

---

[8] 2 Kgs. 23:29–37.   [9] Jer. 22:13–19.   [10] Jer. 36.

[11] Or more properly, Nebuchadrezzar.

[12] 2 Kgs. 24:1. This earlier deportation, not mentioned in 2 Kings, is referred to in Dan. 1:1, and included Daniel and his three friends along with other 'Israelites from the royal family and the nobility' (Dan. 1:3).

[13] The precise circumstances of Jehoiakim's demise are uncertain. Jeremiah prophesied an unmourned death and unceremonious burial (Jer. 22:18–19). 1 Chr. 36:6 records that he was captured, though some suggest this may mean that he was kidnapped by a pro-Babylonian party in Jerusalem and handed over to the Babylonians. He must have died or been executed, since his son Jehoiachin was installed in his place on the surrender of the city after a three-month siege.

[14] 2 Kgs. 24:8–17.

family, along with a substantial number of the significant people in Jerusalem, 'all the officers and fighting men, and all the craftsmen and artisans – a total of ten thousand'.[15] This event is usually called the first deportation. It took place in 597 BC. And it included Ezekiel, a young trainee priest aged twenty-five.

So that is how it happened that, five years later, 'in the fifth year of the exile of King Jehoiachin', Ezekiel found himself 'among the exiles by the Kebar River' in far-off Mesopotamia, many hundreds of miles from his homeland. For it was then, five years after the first deportation, that God intervened dramatically in Ezekiel's life, commissioned him to speak his word and sent him to his own people there in exile.

Meanwhile, back in Jerusalem, even though Jehoiachin was still regarded as the rightful king and the years continued to be counted in terms of his reign, his uncle Mattaniah was installed by Nebuchadnezzar as puppet king in Judah, and was renamed by him Zedekiah. During the reign of Zedekiah, Jeremiah's ministry as the prophet of Yahweh in the city continued, but grew increasingly painful and dangerous as the anti-Babylonian party in the city gained ascendancy. Eventually, in spite of all Jeremiah's warnings, Zedekiah instigated yet another rebellion against Babylon in 599. Nebuchadnezzar's patience was at an end. He threw the whole weight of his army against Jerusalem. A short respite when he had to deal with a paltry attempt by Egypt to come to Judah's aid soon ended, and the siege dragged on for eighteen terrible months of famine and disease. All hopes, both for the besieged inhabitants in the city and for the anxious exiles in Babylon, slowly died and in the end the walls were breached. The army fled, but were cut down in the countryside. The temple, the palace, and much of the city were burnt down. The walls were demolished. King Zedekiah was forced to watch the execution of his sons, before being blinded and carried off in chains to Babylon. The bulk of the remaining population, all but the poorest, were carried off in humiliating defeat and disgrace to join the exiles who had been in Mesopotamia for ten long years already. The year was 587, the beginning of the most traumatic event in Israel's whole biblical history.[16]

For Ezekiel, the event marked the end of the first five years of his prophetic ministry – five agonizingly tough years among people who could not believe that this unthinkable event would ever happen. With the news of the final fall of the city (33:21–33) and the influx of new exiles, Ezekiel's ministry (which went on for another fifteen years), took a new turn as he struggled to bring some kind of

---

[15] 2 Kgs. 24:14.   [16] 2 Kgs. 25:1–12.

meaning, comfort and hope to this shattered, decimated and totally demoralized rump of God's people, Israel.

2. Ezekiel and his mission

'Son of man, I am sending you to the Israelites ... 'go now ... and speak my words to them' (2:3; 3:4). Ezekiel was a man with a mission. He did not, of course, have to *go* anywhere in a geographical sense, since he had already come all the way from Judah with the exiles. He was being 'sent' to the people he lived among. Indeed, it would have been easier for him, as God ironically comments, if he had been sent to a foreign people, for they would at least have listened to him even if they did not understand his language, whereas his own people Israel would understand his language but would refuse to listen to his message (3:5–7). Ezekiel's mission may be surveyed at various levels. First we may look at the preparation he unwittingly underwent even before being called as a prophet. Secondly, we shall observe the context in which he carried on his ministry. Thirdly, we shall portray the character of his ministry both in terms of the image he himself used – a watchman, and also in the more contemporary images of evangelist and pastor. Finally, we shall raise our sights to the wider missiological context of Ezekiel's vision – the knowledge of Yahweh in Israel and among the nations.

a. The preparation: Ezekiel as a priest

i. His education
Ezekiel's mission began on the day God appeared to him by the Kebar Canal, but in God's providence the earlier years of his life had been a time of preparation – as is usually the way when God calls people for special tasks. Ezekiel was the son of a priest, most probably from Jerusalem itself. The whole of his education throughout childhood and youth and into his young adult years would have been thorough training for the day when he would enter on all the varied professional duties of Israel's priesthood. These included not only all the tasks involved in the sacrificial rituals (which meant skill in animal anatomy and butchery as well as familiarity with all the levitical regulations and categories), but also the responsibility to teach and administer the law – Israel's Torah.[17]

---

[17] This double role of the priesthood in handling the sacrifices and in being teachers of the law is indicated in quite a number of texts, positively and negatively (in the latter case because of failure); e.g. Lev. 10:10–11; Deut. 33:10; Neh. 8:7–8; Jer. 18:18; Hos. 4:1–9; Mal. 2:1–9.

Although we have no way of knowing for sure exactly what such education would have included, or how faithfully it was being passed on in the Jerusalem priesthood of Ezekiel's youth, we may assume that Josiah's reforms and the discovery of the book of the law in the temple gave it a boost. What we can see from the evidence of Ezekiel's own book is that he was certainly a man with a profound command of Israel's history, literature and traditions. Furthermore, his training in the law seems evident from his skill in constructing case-studies – presenting situations with carefully marshalled and detailed evidence, and then either drawing inevitable conclusions, or inviting his listeners, like a jury, to do so.[18] The breadth of his education is also evident in his wide knowledge of international affairs, including remarkable awareness of the politics and economics of surrounding nations. He was also familiar with the mythology and imagery of the ancient near-eastern world, and could weave such material into his own messages.

ii. His priestly worldview
More important, however, than the sheer breadth of Ezekiel's intellectual learning as a trainee priest is the whole worldview that he must have imbibed as a member of the priestly élite in Jerusalem. Three elements in this priestly worldview are significant in understanding Ezekiel as a prophet.

1. *God at the centre.* Central, in the first place, to this worldview was God himself. The priesthood existed in order to represent Yahweh to the people, and the people to Yahweh. The reality of Yahweh was thus the defining fact of their existence and the paramount focus of their life and calling. There are many characters in the Old Testament, of course, of whom it could rightly be said that their lives were centred on God. But few can match the sheer uncompromising singularity of Ezekiel's passion for Yahweh. Absolutely everything in his life and understanding was dominated by Yahweh as God: the mighty hand of Yahweh; the word of Yahweh; the Spirit of Yahweh; the name of Yahweh; the holiness of Yahweh; the presence (or absence) of Yahweh; and especially, the glory of Yahweh.

---

[18] This priestly legal training probably accounts for a feature of Ezekiel's style which readers may find tedious – his somewhat verbose and repetitive attention to detail. 'The exercise of pronouncing and interpreting the law had trained him to express his ideas with extreme precision of thought and terminology, and had also taught him to present his views in an architectonic construction ... In expressing his thoughts he likes to make use of the scholastic lecture, enumerating each different case and the conclusions resulting from it, which gives his manner of speech the slow repetitious flow of the pedagogue and educationalist.' Eichrodt, p. 22.

We may, of course, trace this characteristic of Ezekiel to the impact of his phenomenal vision by the Kebar Canal, when he was overwhelmed by 'the appearance of the likeness of the glory of the LORD' (1:28). Even for a trained priest, familiar with the theophanic[19] ambience of the temple, the experience left him shattered and virtually paralysed for a week (3:15). However, when God touched and summoned Ezekiel through that amazing vision, he was breaking powerfully into a life and an intellect already thoroughly shaped by the centrality of Yahweh that was intrinsic to Israel's covenant faith and the very *raison d'être* of Israel's priesthood. We may be sure that the encounter at the water's edge transformed what may have been for Ezekiel a matter of intellectual worldview and professional training into the most intensely personal and experiential core of his whole life and identity.

2. *God's point of view.* Secondly, this 'radical theocentricity' of Ezekiel, as it has been called,[20] meant that he saw other things in the sharp white light of his passion for Yahweh. On the one hand, it meant seeing, and speaking of, *sin* from God's point of view. The Old Testament has a rich vocabulary of sin. All the prophets found ways to characterize and expose its nature and effects. None of them, however, surpassed Ezekiel in the depth and extent of his portrayal of sin in all its horror. As a trained priest he frequently uses cultic language to express it, falling back on the crucial priestly distinctions between the holy and the profane, the clean and the unclean. We should not imagine, however, that Ezekiel's frequent use of ritual language to portray sin from God's angle meant that he had a 'merely ritual' understanding of sin itself. A glance at his ethical case-study in chapter 18, or at his survey of the social and economic oppression and sexual debauchery of Jerusalem in chapter 22, will quickly show that Ezekiel had as broad an inventory of human wickedness as any of the prophets.

Ezekiel spares no sensitivities in his use of metaphor[21] and allegory.[22] Sin is an abomination, it is detestable. Sin offends God, it stinks, it is grotesque, gruesome and disgusting. It perverts and

[19] 'Theophany' is the term used for an appearance of God, or the manifestation of his presence. It is used to describe, for example, his many appearances to characters in the Old Testament, or more remarkable phenomena such as the fire and cloud of his presence guiding the Israelites in the wilderness; the earthquake, fire and thunder of Sinai; the cloud of his glory in the temple; and even the 'still small voice' to Elijah.
[20] Joyce. 'The radical theocentricity of Ezekiel' is the title of his ch. 6, p. 89.
[21] E.g. his comparison of Israel's sin to menstrual bloodstains and the ritual uncleanness thus caused (36:17).
[22] E.g. his horrendously graphic portrayals of the sins of the two kingdoms of Israel and Judah through extended allegories of sexual promiscuity, with shockingly explicit visual imagery, in chs. 16 and 23.

pollutes. And in the end it provokes Yahweh, 'the compassionate and gracious God', beyond all patience or pity. Above all, the ultimate sin from a priestly perspective is the sin of idolatry. And such was the range and depth of the idolatries taking place even within the temple itself that the glory of Yahweh could no longer bear to reside there. This is the terrible awareness that comes from Ezekiel's visionary tour of Jerusalem and the temple area in chapters 8 – 11. The worst that Israel's sin can do is that it drives God himself from his chosen home. The departure of the glory of God from the temple marks the lowest point of Ezekiel's whole ministry – compensated for only by the ultimate return of the glory in his final visions of restoration in chapters 40 – 48 (see 43:1–5).

Then, on the other hand, Ezekiel saw *salvation* from God's point of view. What motivated God eventually to restore Israel from the 'death' of exile to new life and future hope in the land? What motivated him to offer 'life' to Israelites who would 'turn from their wickedness' in repentance? What motivates God to save human beings? The question is important since the answer will affect the motivation with which we who now claim to be the people of God fulfil our calling of bringing God's salvation to others. Our motivation for mission must flow from God's own.

Most answers to the question 'What motivates God's saving action?' would focus either on human need or on divine emotion. *Human need* includes the facts that we are lost and need to be found; we are enslaved and need to be freed; we are condemned and need to be pardoned; we are alienated and need to be reconciled; we are in darkness and need light; we are oppressed and need justice; we are sick and need healing; and many other comparable assessments of our condition. God is motivated to respond to these dimensions of human need, and therefore so must we be similarly motivated. *Divine emotion* includes the wonderful biblical affirmations that God loves us, pities us, has compassion and mercy on us, grieves over our wilful waywardness, longs for our return, rejoices in our restoration, celebrates our homecoming. If this is how God feels towards his fallen human creation, then such emotions should likewise permeate our own mission motivation. All of these truths about human need and divine emotion are thoroughly biblical – and thoroughly Old Testament too. The classic illustration of both is of course Israel's own foundation redemption story – the exodus. God describes his redemptive motivation: 'I have indeed seen the misery of my people in Egypt. I have heard them crying out because of their slave drivers, and I am concerned about their suffering. So I have come down to rescue them …'[23] This passage expresses God's emotional response to

[23] Exod. 3:7–8.

the crying need of human beings in slavery. It would not be difficult to amass a long list of verses from the Psalms and the prophets and elsewhere bearing witness to both dimensions of motivation.

Undoubtedly, Ezekiel knew these truths intimately from his familiarity with the traditions and scriptures of Israel. But for him, almost the sole issue, and certainly the overwhelming motivation, was what the salvation of Israel would mean *for Yahweh himself*. Ezekiel would not have denied that obviously it would meet the terrible needs of Israel at a human level. He certainly also acknowledged that the divine emotions were profoundly engaged in that God could say, 'I take no pleasure in the death of the wicked, but rather that they turn from their ways and live' (33:11). But what ultimately mattered was that Yahweh's name and reputation should be vindicated and that Yahweh should be universally acknowledged as God. Ezekiel could not bear the thought of the name of Yahweh being mocked ('profaned') among the nations – in addition to the abuse it was getting in Israel itself. Yahweh's honour and glory must be restored to full visibility in the world. Only the salvation of his people would achieve that. This, then, is the context in which we must set the theocentric motivation expressed in 36:22–23. Needs and emotions are not excluded; but what matters most is the glory of God and the honour of his name. This acts as a salutary corrective to much that passes for mission motivation today.

This is what the Sovereign LORD says: It is not for your sake, O house of Israel, that I am going to do these things [sc. gather, cleanse, save and renew you], but for the sake of my holy name, which you have profaned among the nations where you have gone. I will show the holiness of my great name, which has been profaned among the nations, the name you have profaned among them. Then the nations will know that I am the LORD.[24]

3. *Priest v. prophet.* A third dimension of Ezekiel's priestly upbringing and worldview is perhaps less obvious. We know Ezekiel, of course, as a prophet. We read of his call vision, we hear the familiar 'This is what the LORD says', we witness the prophetic actions and signs – more bizarre than those of earlier prophets, but still the recognizable tools of the prophetic trade. What we may fail to appreciate is the abrupt disorientation and massive reorientation that it must have taken for one brought up as a priest to suddenly find himself called to be a prophet. The disjunction between the two roles was both theological and professional. Ezekiel's theological

[24] See the discussion of Ezek. 36 in ch. 8 below, 'The gospel according to Ezekiel'.

INTRODUCTION

worldview was shaped by the great traditions of Zion and the temple. Jerusalem was the city of Yahweh, the place where he had caused his name to dwell. Professionally, he was training to serve in the temple, the very navel of the earth, the sanctuary built and dedicated by Solomon nearly four centuries ago. He was heir to the lineage of Aaron, and possibly that of David's high priest, Zadok. His ministry as a priest would sustain the moral and spiritual fabric of the universe by preserving the essential distinctions inherent in all of life – the holy and profane, the clean and the unclean. He would sustain all this through the grand rituals of blood sacrifice, standing as a priest at the very fulcrum of interaction between God and humanity. Above all, he would have intimate access to the place of Yahweh's eternal dwelling.

But as a prophet he was called to identify with the voices of those who had dared to call in question this whole massive edifice of theology, tradition and ritual. There were of course establishment prophets (now conveniently labelled 'false prophets', but the distinction was not so obvious to everybody at the time) who acquiesced in the complacency of a corrupt priesthood. But the most scandalous things were being said by Jeremiah – who also came from priestly stock and incurred the hatred of his family for his treacherous message. Jeremiah was preaching that the wickedness being perpretrated in Jerusalem and even within the temple was such that Yahweh would not only abandon his dwelling-place but also give it over to destruction. He was denouncing the priests for their moral and educational failure.[25] Such was the enmity between the priestly establishment and prophets of that calibre, that on one occasion a senior priest, Pashur, had Jeremiah beaten and put in stocks.[26] Others tried, and only just failed, to have him killed, like Uriah, another prophet with the same message, about whom we know nothing except that Jehoiakim had him killed for his boldness.[27]

As mentioned above, it is very possible, if not indeed probable, that Ezekiel heard Jeremiah's temple sermon.[28] What he made of it at the time is impossible to know, but he may well have been torn between the challenge of what Jeremiah said and all the weight of his own priestly assumptions about the inviolability of the temple and Jerusalem. However, it was one thing to evaluate a prophet's message from within the secure framework of his own worldview. It would be entirely another for him, the son of Buzi the priest, to have to raise his voice, and articulate exactly the same prophetic message that many of his family would certainly have denounced as

[25] Jer. 2:8.   [26] Jer. 20:1–9.   [27] Jer. 26:20–23.   [28] Jer. 7 and 26.

wildly heretical to the point of blasphemy. It would be even more painful to endure the visionary tour of the temple precincts and be made to witness the appalling idolatries going on there, some of which were so secret that he may never have known of them in his youth (ch. 8). And it must have been unbearable to have to report all this to his fellow exiles and describe to them the horrific fiery judgment that would fall on his and their beloved city and temple. He, Ezekiel son of Buzi, the priest from Jerusalem, was now bringing the same message as the despised prophet from Anathoth.

So while we can value all the positive contributions that Ezekiel's education and training as a priest brought to his prophetic ministry, we must also appreciate the immense personal, professional and theological shock it must have been to him when, in his thirtieth year, the year he ought to have entered on his ordained priestly career, God broke into his life, wrecked all such career prospects, and constrained him into a role he may himself have viewed with considerable suspicion – the lonely, friendless, unpopular role of being a prophet, the mouthpiece of Yahweh. No wonder the anger and bitter rage to which he honestly confesses disorientated and overwhelmed him for a full week (3:14–15). God would use all that he had built into Ezekiel's life during his years of preparation, but he would use it in radically different ways from anything Ezekiel had ever imagined. Such is sometimes the way of God with those whom he calls to his service.

b. The context of Ezekiel's mission

It is time to turn from the background of Ezekiel's times and the preparation of his early priestly training to consider the context in which he lived and spoke. This can be viewed first from the perspective of his own people, 'the house of Israel' among whom he ministered, and secondly in relation to the Babylonian religious world within which he was called to conceptualize and articulate the reality of Yahweh.

i. Among a displaced people

Ezekiel lived among a people suffering dislocation, loss and trauma, with all the attendant emotional and spiritual reactions. He himself was an exile among the exiles of Judah. We need to recall perhaps some of the horrors of recent events in the Balkans, or the massive destruction of whole peoples by floods in Honduras, India or Mozambique, to get a glimmer of their experience. For those who came with Ezekiel in the deportation of 597, there was the physical stress of being far from home and loved ones. But it was tempered by the shallow optimism that Ezekiel struggled so hard to dispel – the belief that Jerusalem could never be destroyed. When finally it was, and the earlier exiles were joined by waves of survivors, there was all the added trauma of meeting people emaciated after the months of siege, starvation and the horrendously long journey from Jerusalem to Babylon. There was the gradual realization of the extent of national bereavement as every family must have counted the relatives who had died of hunger, disease, or in the final slaughter inside and outside the city.

Then there was the psychological horror and shock as the people were hurled into the abyss of disbelief over the fate of Jerusalem and the temple. And there was the theological bafflement that followed. Where was Yahweh in all this? Had he been defeated by the Babylonian gods? Or had he really done this to his own people? Was he now as disgraced in defeat as Israel? Or was he still in control of events? In either case, was there any future for Israel now? And if not, then what would become of Yahweh's wider purpose among the nations? Ezekiel, then, was called to serve God in the midst of a shattered and shell-shocked people, a context not far removed from many contexts of mission today.

ii. Surrounded by pagan religion
As an Israelite living in Babylonia, Ezekiel lived as an alien in the midst of a culture whose religious manifestation exuded power and supremacy. From what we may judge of its effect on the Israelite exiles from Isaiah 40 – 55, it was probably quite overwhelming and oppressive. Those chapters expend great energy in unmasking the glittering claims of the Babylonian gods in order to liberate the Israelites from their psychological and spiritual hold. How then, in such circumstances could a prophet generate a renewal of the ancient faith in Yahweh's universal power and supremacy? Isaiah 40 – 55 does it by reviving Israel's soaring doxology combined with a fresh use of the familiar prophetic lawsuit imagery in which Yahweh takes on the gods of the nations and routs them in open court, as it were. Ezekiel is more daring. He hijacks the Babylonian juggernaut and turns it into a vehicle for conveying the sovereign glory of Yahweh. His famous call vision combines elements of the storm theophany and the throne theophany, drawn in part from ancient Israelite traditions.[29] But his description of the four-headed, winged cherubim would have been familiar to any inhabitant of ancient Mesopotamia surrounded by the great statues of tutelary deities guarding temple entrances and other polymorphous[30] sky-bearing creatures that

[29] Cf. 2 Sam. 22:9; Job 38; Is. 6; etc.
[30] 'Polymorphous' refers to creatures with multiple forms: e.g. animal legs, human trunk and arms, wings, different heads, etc.

supported the thrones of the deities.[31] Ezekiel has taken the static Mesopotamian imagery and transformed it, mainly by the addition of wheels, hands, eyes, and the prevailing Spirit of Yahweh, into a dynamic portrayal of the sovereign, roving freedom of Yahweh. Yahweh's presence, power and glory were in Babylon, could take on and yet transcend Babylonian symbolism, and could be even more overwhelming in effect than all the Babylonian statuary put together (3:17)! Ezekiel's call vision in itself provides a fascinating case-study of cultural contextualization and of its boundaries with religious syncretism. This too is an important area in missiological reflection, since the biblical message constantly has to be expressed and understood within the varied forms of human culture, yet without mere absorption into the fallen beliefs and values of those cultures.

c. The character of Ezekiel's ministry: the prophet as a 'watchman'

Twice in the book Ezekiel is commissioned to be a 'watchman' for Israel (3:16–27; 33:1–20). The first is in the context of his original call, the second in the context of the news of the final fall of Jerusalem (33:21ff.) by which Ezekiel's prophetic credentials were confirmed and his ministry established. This choice of metaphor for his prophetic role was a powerful one. To be a watchman (a sentry, or lookout) was a huge responsibility. It meant being posted on a wall or high place in a town or military camp in time of war in order to give clear warning of the approach of an enemy. Provided that the watchman gave loud and prompt warning, responsibility passed to the hearers for whatever action they took in response. Failure to give the warning would mean that the watchman would be held responsible for the fate of those killed by the enemy.

The terrible challenge of the task as it was laid on Ezekiel lay in the identity of the enemy he was to warn against. It was Yahweh himself. The phrase translated 'give them warning from me' (3:17; 33:7), could more correctly be translated 'warn them *against* me'. It was *Yahweh* who was the attacker, coming in judgment upon his own people, not merely the human foreign armies who were his agents. The traditional expectation of Yahweh as the defender of Israel against their enemies has been reversed. He is now the enemy they face. This was the bleak and unwelcome message that dominated Ezekiel's communication especially in the early years.

This picture of the messenger of God as a watchman has been a suggestive metaphor for Christian ministry in general and the

---

[31] Cf. Allen 28, pp. 20–45, including fascinating illustrations of religious art and statues from the ancient Near East.

awesome words of responsibility in Ezekiel 3 and 33 have been a powerful motivation in some quarters for the evangelistic dimension of Christian mission. Those in danger must be warned! The image has also challenged many a pastor, charged with the responsibility of interpreting the ways of God to his or her own people and applying warning or comfort as appropriate. The long ministry of Ezekiel combined the roles of pastor and evangelist as he struggled to disturb the comfortable and comfort the disturbed and to build a community of repentance, faith and obedience out of the ruins and trauma of the exile. 'In short, he combined in a unique way the priest's sense of the holiness of God, the prophet's sense of the message that had been entrusted to him, and the pastor's sense of responsibility for his people.'[32]

i. The work of a pastor

As mentioned above, Ezekiel lived among a people suffering all the terrible effects of catastrophic dislocation. He faced every conceivable human reaction to such massive trauma. There were those who were angry and rejected the faith of Israel altogether.[33] There were those who still managed to sustain a complacent bravado and false optimism.[34] Some accepted that it was the work of Yahweh, but protested that his punishment was unjust and unfair, complaining that they were being made to suffer for the sins of previous generations.[35] Others fell into a broken acceptance and utter despair. Yahweh's deserved judgment had fallen and there seemed to be no possible future for Israel except through some miracle of his grace.[36]

Faced with everything, then, from backsliding, through bravado and bitterness, to brokenness, it was Ezekiel's pastoral mission to bring such people to a right understanding of their situation, and to a right response to God in the midst of it. At first that required almost unremitting severity, but later, under the impact of the news of the final fall of Jerusalem, his pastoral tone changed to one of comfort in the present and hope for the future. It was a sequence we might trace as follows:

1. *The reality of judgment.* Ezekiel had to disillusion the facile optimists, both in Babylon and in Jerusalem. The exiles would *not*

---

[32] Taylor, p. 29.
[33] E.g. those who reverted to the worship of the Queen of Heaven, in Jer. 44:15–18.
[34] Jeremiah warned the exiles not to listen to such futile hopes in his correspondence recorded in Jer. 29. Ezekiel had harsh words for the false prophets who were peddling these doomed dreams in Ezek. 13.
[35] Ezekiel faces the debilitating effects of this victim mentality in Ezek. 18. See ch. 5 below, 'Who then can be saved?'
[36] E.g. Ezek. 33:10; 37:11; Is. 40:27; 49:14; Lam.; Pss. 79; 80; 137.

soon be going home; Jerusalem *would* finally be destroyed; the people would be decimated by the ravages of siege, famine, disease and battle. In short, 'The end has come' (7:2). All this was the burden of his graphic acted sermons in chapters 4 – 5, and the similar preaching of chapters 6 – 7 and 12. It was essential to get Israel to face the reality of their situation, because until they understood the full scale of the judgment they faced there was no likelihood of true repentance and restoration.

2. *The logic of judgment.* Ezekiel repeated and amplified the message of the earlier prophets: Yahweh's judgment was not something inexplicable, arbitrary, or unfair. Rather, it was the logical outcome of the covenant relationship in the light of Israel's history. Sin *deserves* punishment; and Yahweh *will* punish the wicked. God had said as much about the Canaanites at the beginning of Israel's history, and had said he would treat the Israelites with the same moral consistency if they rebelled in the same way.[37] In fact, as Ezekiel mercilessly pointed out, Israel had behaved even worse than other nations (5:5–7; 16:46–52). Most earlier prophets made some use of Israel's history to prove the validity of God's case against his people. Ezekiel raises this theme to a new level with three chapters of incredible rhetorical power (16, 20, 23), using historical allegory and schematic sequencing to make the point that Israel deserved everything she was now suffering.[38] Indeed the judgment was long overdue.

3. *The limits of judgment.* Ezekiel's pastoral heart for his people could not leave them without hope, even in his severest moods. Even in the early chapters of almost unremitting doom, there are shafts of hope. Some in Jerusalem are marked out for salvation because of their mourning over the sins of the city (9:4). The glory of Yahweh leaves the temple and city, but seems to remain suspended to the east, as though awaiting the possibility of return – which is indeed promised. The historical sequence of chapter 20 is left open-ended, and issues in a sovereign work of Yahweh to change and restore his people. However, it was after Jerusalem had fallen that Ezekiel faced especially those whose despair can be felt in their laments: 'Our offences and sins weigh us down, and we are wasting away because of them. How then can we live?' (33:10); 'Our bones are dried up and our hope is gone; we are cut off' (37:11). To such broken and repentant people, Ezekiel brought incredible visions of hope and encouragement. These are to be found primarily in chapters 34 – 37 (although obviously the whole portrait of restoration of people,

[37] Gen. 15:16; Lev. 18:24–28; 20:22–23; Deut. 9:5.
[38] See ch. 4 below, 'History with attitude'.

temple and land in chapters 40 – 48 is also part of this re-visioning work). In these chapters God promises to bring his people out of anarchy, into security, back from disgrace, up from the grave and together out of division. The emphasis on newness is overwhelming: a new shepherd, new hearts, a new spirit, new breath, new unity. Ultimately only the language of resurrection (37:1–14) can really do justice to the river of hope being poured out over the languishing dead bones of the exiles.

ii. The work of an evangelist

But who could enter into such hope? Certainly not those who persisted in their wickedness, even in the midst of judgment, or those who complained that the judgment was not fair and thus exonerated themselves from blame. Thus there was another side to Ezekiel's mission which can legitimately be described as evangelistic. As a watchman he was there to give warning, but the point of the warning was to galvanize action. And the action called for was genuine repentance and change. If, and only if, such turning back to God took place, could there be the promise of life. But that was indeed the longing of God's heart, and it produces some of the most moving preaching in all the impressive range of Ezekiel's rhetoric. Again, this sequence can be traced in the following way:

1. *Conviction of sin.* As we saw above, Ezekiel is ruthless in his exposure of sin in all its gruesome abhorrence. Reading his language from the comfortable distance of those not directly targeted by his rhetoric, we may at times wince at the coarseness of his imagery or query the one-sidedness of his portrayal of Israel's whole history (e.g. in chs. 16, 20 and 23). Once we recognize, however, that Ezekiel was engaged, not in a detached academic debate, but in passionate evangelistic persuasion, we can understand his tactics. He was faced with people who refused to acknowledge their own sin,[39] who had a self-congratulatory view of their own history, who assumed a kind of benevolent blindness on the part of their covenant Lord, Yahweh, and who believed they had an absolute and eternal right to the privileges of land, city and temple. Such armour-plating could only be pierced by some high-grade explosive. Ezekiel's tirades against Israel's sin was necessary to bring at least some of his listeners to a more realistic assessment of their condition, and thereby to a genuine repentance.

---

[39] With regard to Israel's complete failure to fulfil their covenant obligations, Eichrodt comments, 'In face of facts such as these, the passionate protest [sc. by Ezekiel's contemporaries] against the message of judgment, as if it were a godless blasphemy against the solemnly guaranteed saving acts of Yahweh, had to be unmasked as the grandiose piece of self-deception that it was.' Eichrodt, p. 28.

2. *Apologetic (theodicy)*.[40] Evangelism sometimes takes place among those who are disgruntled with life, the universe and everything, and who place the blame squarely on God himself. Such, in part, was also Ezekiel's situation. Apparently there was a common attitude among the exiles which belligerently declared, 'We are not to blame, and God is not fair!' This viewpoint was encapsulated in the famous proverb about parents and children, sour grapes and sore teeth (18:2). If such people were ever to be brought to saving repentance (which was the desire of both God and Ezekiel), then such misconceptions had to be thoroughly dealt with. The evangelist must be an apologist. There was a work of theodicy to do, and Ezekiel went to it with all the skill of the priest that he had trained to become. He sets up an elaborate moral and legal case-study; he argues the point on either side; he denies the validity of the proverb and the assumptions behind it; and he affirms (with multiple repetition) the justice of God's ways. The whole exercise in chapter 18 is repeated again with further elaboration in 33:12–20.[41]

3. *Divine grace*. Just as Ezekiel is unsurpassed in his portrayal of the horror of sin, so he is hard to equal in declaring the amazing grace of Yahweh. It is unmistakably clear that no hope for Israel's future will be found in Israel themselves. Their whole history is one of innate rebellion. But Yahweh remains sovereign, and his sovereignty includes his will that they should live and not die, and that they will be forgiven, cleansed, revived, 'resurrected' and restored. In chapter 20, for example, the incorrigible rebellion of Israel is expressed in their continued desire to 'be like the nations' in their idolatry (20:32). Yet God simply turns that option down: 'What you have in mind will never happen.' And then with a mighty echoing of the divine 'I will' of Exodus 6:6–8,[42] Yahweh declares his gracious purpose of renewed redemption, even though it will paradoxically take place through judgment (20:33ff.). Likewise in chapter 36, the promises of God's grace are stupendous and

---

[40] 'Apologetics', in its technical sense, means explaining and defending the key affirmations of biblical faith. 'Theodicy', as a part of the apologetic task, means providing justification for those ways and actions of God which on the surface appear to be unjust or inexplicable.

[41] The argument is expounded in depth in ch. 5 below, 'Who then can be saved?'

[42] It is very likely that this is an example of Ezekiel's familiarity with Israel's existing scriptural traditions. It can be argued that this passage in ch. 20 indicates Ezekiel's familiarity with the written text of Exod. 6. Cf. M. Fishbane, *Text and Texture: Close Readings of Selected Biblical Texts* (New York: Schocken Books, 1979), p. 132. I am indebted on this point also to the work of John F. Evans, '"You shall know that I am Yahweh": Ezekiel's recognition formula as a marker of the prophecy's intertextual relation to Exodus' (unpublished MTh dissertation, presented to Covenant Theological Seminary, St Louis, Missouri, 1995).

breathtaking. For his own name's sake, i.e. out of consistency with
his own being and nature, Yahweh will gather and cleanse his people,
do some radical heart surgery, and grant his own Spirit to enable full
obedience. The great gospel language of the New Testament is
hardly more inspiring, and indeed owes some of its most precious
imagery to Ezekiel's eloquence.[43]

4. *Appeal for repentance.* Once conviction of sin has been driven
home, objections to God's ways put aside, and the gracious promises
of God portrayed, then the evangelist must take the next step and
call for repentance. For those who are prepared to acknowledge their
wickedness and turn from it, the good news is that God offers the
possiblity of a free transfer from the camp of the wicked who will
die to the community of the righteous who will, by divine
pronouncement, live. Repentance, however, must be practical and
life-changing (18:21; 33:14–15). Such true repentance is also purging
– the past is wiped out by the amazing declaration of God that the
repentant sinner's wicked past will not 'be remembered against him'
(18:22). This too is pure gospel. And above all, the repentance of the
wicked is what most pleases God himself (18:23). Jesus' portrayal of
the joy in heaven over one sinner that repents has its roots in the
message of Ezekiel the evangelist. His great evangelistic appeal at the
climax of chapter 18 is surely as relevant to mission now as it was
in sixth-century BC Babylon.

5. *Assurance of life.* Again, the radical theocentricity of Ezekiel
comes to the fore in his evangelistic assurance to repentant sinners.
There is no hint that God's forgiveness is a grudging concession,
reluctantly offered. Rather, it flows from the very nature and grace
of God. Yahweh is the Lord and giver of life. Israel will survive and
return, not because of any innate capacity for survival, but solely
because of Yahweh's will to life. In fact, it is not really a question
of survival, for the exile was a kind of death. Only resurrection
would suffice. Yahweh would 'open the graves' of Israel and bring
them back to the land of the living (37:12–14). So, although God's
moral character and justice necessitate judgment on the wicked, that
remains, as Luther put it, his 'alien work'. Judgment satisfies the
justice of God but it brings him no pleasure. There is a profound
redemptive theology in the divine emotion several times repeated:

> Do I take any pleasure in the death of the wicked? declares the
> Sovereign LORD. Rather, am I not pleased when they turn from
> their ways and live? ... For I take no pleasure in the death of
> anyone, declares the Sovereign LORD. Repent and live! (18:23, 32).

[43] See ch. 8 below, 'The gospel according to Ezekiel'.

So, faithful to his commission as a watchman for his people, Ezekiel fulfilled an evangelistic and pastoral role among them, leading them into and eventually, in vision at least, up and out of the valley of the shadow of death. God's purposes would continue. Israel was not finished. There was a future and a hope as Jeremiah had promised. That future, of course, lay beyond the lifetime of Ezekiel and most of his fellow exiles. It would be the next generation that would return to the land. And at another level, the complete fulfilment of all the depths and dimensions of Ezekiel's prophecy lies ahead of us still.

d. The wider horizon: Yahweh and the nations

Physically and geographically, Ezekiel's mission was confined to his fellow exiles in a small community near some irrigation works in Mesopotamia. Theologically, however, his horizon was much wider. Ezekiel's vision encompassed the nations, and not just the nations immediately involved in the contemporary history of his own people, but 'many nations', 'all the nations'. And his great passion was that, ultimately, through all that Yahweh had done in Israel and would yet do for them, the nations would come to know that Yahweh is God. In this respect he stands within the strong tradition of Israel's faith that the election of Israel was ultimately for the purpose of the blessing of the nations. That was the climactic bottom line of God's promise to Abraham, that through him and his descendants all the nations of the earth would find blessing.[44]

This fundamentally missiological understanding of Israel's existence, identity and purpose, however, was thrown into serious question through the exile – both in terms of what future there could be for the nations if Israel, the supposed means of their blessing, were destroyed, and also in terms of the disgrace that the exile had brought on the name of Yahweh in the sight of the nations. Could the nations ever come to know Yahweh, given the failure of Israel herself to know him? This question lies behind one of Ezekiel's most characteristic expressions.

The expression 'Then you will know that I am Yahweh' is virtually the signature of Ezekiel. Most often it refers to Israel, but it is frequently expanded in several contexts to include the nations, in the form 'Then they will know that I am Yahweh'. This central expression, then, declaring the clear purpose of God that lies behind historical events, is the most significant key to a missiological reading of Ezekiel. It occurs more than seventy times in the book and has been the focus of much scholarly study, especially since the *magnum*

---

[44] Gen. 12:1–3.

opus of W. Zimmerli in the 1950s.[45] Describing the phrase as the
'recognition formula', Zimmerli subjected it to detailed form-critical
and traditio-critical study. He argued that it arose from deep within
Israel's cultic and prophetic traditions (early prophetic indications of
its use go back to 1 Kgs. 20:13, 28), and carries immense theological
weight as the self-revelatory declaration of Yahweh.

As Ezekiel uses it, the predicted recognition of Yahweh is always
linked to some specific historical action on Yahweh's part and has the
effect of reinforcing his sovereignty both within Israel and in the
international world of nations. When Yahweh acted, people would
know his identity through his action. Furthermore, the certainty of
the future recognition ('You/they will know') generates an
imperative thrust. Knowledge must lead to response. To know and
recognize that 'I am Yahweh' carries the demand for appropriate
attitudes and behaviour, whether that be repentance, shame,
acknowledgment of God's justice and/or mercy, and consequent
obedience in covenant restoration. All this is certainly expressly
stated in relation to what it would mean for *Israel* to know that 'I
am Yahweh'. Whether the same responses and consequences were
anticipated from *the nations* is not so clear, as we shall see, though
some scholars would argue that they must be at least implicit.

Now, the divine intention that Israel and the nations would 'know
that I am Yahweh' is clearly linked to another strong theme in
Ezekiel which we have already noted above: that is, Yahweh's
concern and action for the sake of his own name. As can be seen in
the schematized historical review in chapter 20 and the vision of
future hope in 36:16–38, the broad outline of Ezekiel's perception of
this divine passion is as follows. All through Israel's past history, the
only thing that had kept Yahweh from wiping Israel out in response
to their repeated rebellions was his fear of what such a total
destruction would do to his reputation among the nations. Yahweh
had brought Israel out of Egypt in full international view in the first
place. To then destroy them would 'profane his name among the
nations' – that is, the name of Yahweh would be held in dishonour,
or regarded as merely one among many relatively powerless deities.
This consideration reflects very precisely the grounds on which
Moses is presented as appealing to God in his great intercessions on
Israel's behalf at Sinai and Kadesh Barnea.[46] Yahweh must protect his
own reputation among the nations. This, then, is the motivation for
the divine forbearance in Israel's past, as expressed in 20:9, 14, 22.

The repeated and incorrigible rebellions of Israel, however, had

[45] Zimmerli's wide-ranging work on this matter has been helpfully collected in his
I Am Yahweh.
[46] Exod. 32:12; Num. 14:13–16.

meant that the axe had finally fallen and the exile had now scattered Israel among the very nations whose opinion Yahweh paid such attention to. The effect was exactly what he feared – the profaning of his name (36:20–21). The name of Yahweh had become a laughing-stock among the nations. Then come the miracle and the paradox. Yahweh will restore and gather back his people, as an act of pure grace, motivated not so much by pity for Israel, as by the determination to demonstrate the holiness of his own name among the nations (36:22–23, 36). In this way the nations will come to know the identity of Yahweh, when he acts on behalf of Israel in mercy and restoration (37:28; 39:7). Indeed, the nations will come to understand the rationale for the exile and for the return from exile in the same terms as these events had been explained to Israel itself (39:21–29). The climax of the mysterious narrative describing the fate of Gog from Magog and his hordes is unfortunately often overlooked by those who become obsessed with identifying the figures and dating the events. God's purpose in the whole eschatological scenario is simply that the name, the greatness, the holiness and the glory of God will be universally acknowledged among all nations (38:23; 39:7, 21–23).

How are we to interpret this 'education of the nations' in Ezekiel's thinking? Did he have a positive hope that, in coming to know Yahweh as God, the nations would be drawn to salvation? Did Ezekiel, in other words, share the universal vision of Isaiah 40 – 66? Some scholars do affirm such a positive implication of Ezekiel's 'recognition' theme.[47] They detect an implicit hope for the nations that, in coming to know Yahweh, they will also be brought to the kind of saving, restoring knowledge of him that is explicit in the case of Israel.

It has to be said, however, that all the texts which apply the recognition formula to the nations (as distinct from Israel) do so either in relation to the anticipated punishment of the nations in the oracles directed against them, or in relation to the predicted restoration of Israel in their midst. There is no clear text that expresses the expectation that the nations would know Yahweh as a result of his delivering or saving *them* in any way that parallels the deliverance of Israel.[48]

However, before we jump to the conclusion that Ezekiel was unconcerned about the salvific destiny of the nations and compare him unfavourably with Isaiah 40 – 55, we should recall again the desperate

[47] Among those who argue for a positive interpretation along these lines, cf. H. Graf Reventlow, 'Die Völker als Jahwes Zeugen bei Ezechiel', *ZAW* 71 (1959), pp. 33–43; Eichrodt, pp. 44–45; Ackroyd, pp. 115–117.
[48] This point is carefully argued by Joyce, pp. 89–97. A similarly negative view is taken by K. P. Darr, 'The wall around Paradise: Ezekielian ideas about the future', *VT* 37 (1987), pp. 271–279. See the further discussion of the issue in the final section of ch. 7 below.

situation Ezekiel ministered into, compared with the eager hope of Isaiah's chapters. As David Williams points out, the huge difference between the context of Ezekiel's ministry and the context presupposed in Isaiah 40 – 55 helps to explain the difference in their perspectives on the nations. The prophecies of Isaiah can speak of the universal salvation of God going to the nations because they can also speak of the restoration of Israel as though it had already taken place.

Ezekiel stands a step further back than Isaiah, showing how the restoration of Israel is possible, rather than assuming that it has already taken place. Ezekiel's prophecy speaks to Israel's most extreme moment of national and theological crisis. So while Isaiah looks to the restoration and beyond, Ezekiel looks to the events that will lead up to the restoration. Yet within Ezekiel's prophecy the foreign nations are not ignored. Yahweh's honour and reputation before the nations lie at the heart of the theological problem that the exile creates. Ezekiel is true to the broad thrust of the Old Testament in developing a concern for the foreign nations that depends upon a covenantally obedient Israel. Ezekiel's apparent ambiguity regarding the nations is, therefore, explained by the context. Ezekiel can only offer hope to the nations through the restoration of Israel, a restoration that itself seems almost impossible. Ezekiel stresses the importance of Yahweh's reputation in the sight of the nations, and then points towards the restoration of Israel as the means by which Yahweh's reputation in the eyes of the world will be restored. Within this context, Ezekiel witnesses to the universality of Yahweh with the same vigour as Isaiah. Yahweh is portrayed as sovereign over the nations, deeply concerned that the nations should know and acknowledge that sovereignty ... Ezekiel echoes the broad sweep of the Old Testament in pointing towards the restoration of Israel as Yahweh's means of honouring his name amongst the nations.[49]

[49] D. A. Williams, '"Then they will know that I am the Lord": the missiological significance of Ezekiel's concern for the nations as evident in the use of the recognition formula' (unpublished MA dissertation, All Nations Christian College, Ware, 1998), p. 62. In agreeing with this interpretation, I take issue with Block's somewhat unfavourable comparison between 'the universalism and cosmic interest of Isaiah' and 'the parochialism of Ezekiel' (Block (1), p. 47). Block states that in Ezekiel, '[Yahweh] is indeed concerned that all the world recognizes his person and his presence in their affairs, but his agenda is always focused on Israel'. What he fails to note is that the focus on Israel was utterly necessary in Ezekiel's context, for only through the restoration of Israel could there be any hope for the nations, and furthermore, the blessing of the nations was precisely the purpose of the 'focus on Israel' in the first place. A missiological perspective at this point helps to hold the two parts of God's agenda together in their proper theological relationship.

3. Ezekiel and his book

a. Authorship and editing

The book of Ezekiel itself gives us no definitive statement of its authorship, but the fact that it is entirely written in the autobiographical first person, with the exception of a single verse,[50] strongly points to Ezekiel himself as having played a major part in the collection of prophetic words that bears his name. Until the early twentieth century, critical scholarship generally accepted the unity of the book of Ezekiel and his substantial authorship of it, in contrast to the way the books of Jeremiah and especially Isaiah had been subjected to increasing subdivision into different authors and editors. Then for several decades it was fashionable to fragment Ezekiel partly on the basis of dubious criteria of literary style, and partly on the assumption that some of the book must have originated in Jerusalem itself and the rest of it in Babylon. However, more recent scholarship is generally much more inclined to accept the authenticity of virtually all of the material in the book and to believe that Ezekiel himself most probably recorded and dated his own prophecies.[51]

Ezekiel may well also have initiated the process of editing which produced the chronological format of the final book. This would not rule out, of course, the probability of some continuing editorial work later on. However, the fact that the book at no point refers to the return from exile as a historically accomplished fact, or even anticipates it in the immediate future, suggests that the book was substantially complete and edited by the second generation of exile – i.e. soon after Ezekiel's own life.

> No long period of time seems to have elapsed in the composition of the book ... While Ezekiel ministered in person to the pre-587 prisoners of war and to the first generation of post-587 exiles, the later adaptations that appear in the book seem to have been made among the second generation of exiles ... The edited book invites

---

[50] Ezek. 1:3 is an editorial note giving the date and location of Ezekiel's call in the third person.

[51] For helpful summaries of scholarship on Ezekiel, see Taylor, pp. 16–20, and, with greater and more up-to-date detail, Block (1), pp. 17–22. Greenberg, in advocating a 'holistic interpretation' has some scathing comments for the spurious methods used by those who fragmented the text into alleged original units and many later additions. He lists criteria such as 'original simplicity', 'thematic uniformity' and 'psychological improbability', and comments: 'such prejudices are simply *a prioris*, an array of unproved (and unprovable) modern assumptions and conventions that confirm themselves through the results obtained by forcing them on the text and altering, reducing, and reordering it accordingly'. Greenberg, p. 20.

its readers to look back at the prophet's ministry and to apply its challenge and assurance to their own hearts and lives.[52]

This, of course, is precisely the invitation we are taking up in our exposition.

Among the factors which point to a unity of authorship and the likelihood that Ezekiel himself edited his own oracles are the following:

1. The consistent first-person reference throughout the book.
2. The frequent inclusion of dates for key oracles and the careful chronological ordering, suggesting that Ezekiel himself wrote and kept his prophetic words in a kind of personal journal.
3. The necessity for Ezekiel to be known as a true prophet, which required that there be no doubt that his predictions of the fall of Jerusalem had been made before it took place; this would have been best served by having written and dated records of his own prophecies.
4. The visionary eating of a written scroll at the time of his call (2:8 – 3:3), which is consistent with the expectation that the words he would speak from God would also be written down.
5. The precedent already set by Jeremiah, who arranged for several years of prophetic preaching to be collected in written form, through dictation to his scribe, Baruch.[53]
6. The unity of style[54] and coherence of theme and structure in the whole book, which point to a singular originating and organizing mind behind it.

We can have a strong confidence, then, that in reading the words of this book we are standing very close to overhearing the words of Ezekiel himself coming to us out of the mixture of grief, anger, brokenness and despair that shrouded the little community of Judean captives in the baking plains of Babylon in the early sixth century BC.

b. The chronological sequence

Ezekiel's book is unique among the prophetic books of the Bible by being arranged in almost perfect chronological order. By attaching dates to several of his oracles, some of them at pivotal points in his career, Ezekiel enables us to follow the course of his long ministry through the book. The fourteen date references are arranged as follows:

[52] Allen 28, pp. xxv–xxvi.   [53] Jer. 36.
[54] Ezekiel has a very distinctive style of writing, a fondness for detail, great skill in imagery and symbolic forms, a large repertoire of favourite vocabulary and expressions, and some very effective rhetorical techniques. For an excellent survey of all Ezekiel's characteristic methods and literary skills, see Block (1), pp. 23–41.

First, there are those which come in the first five years of his ministry, between his call in 593 BC and the beginning of the siege of Jerusalem: 1:1; 1:2; 8:1; 20:1; 24:1.

Secondly, there are those connected with his oracles against foreign nations, all coming in the central section: chapters 25 – 32: 26:1; 29:1; 29:17; 30:20; 31:1; 32:1; 32:17.

Thirdly, there are two final dates: the date of the news of the fall of Jerusalem, 33:21, and the date of his great vision of the restored temple, land and city, 40:1.

Of these, only one comes chronologically later than the last date recorded in the book, and that is 29:17, relating to the collapse of Nebuchadnezzar's siege of Tyre and his redirection to Egypt in 571 BC.

One might attribute this distinctive feature of Ezekiel's book to his priestly background, with a characteristic tendency to precision and accurate detail. Another purpose that it served, however, was to ground his prophetic utterances in unmistakable historical time. There could be no accusation later that Ezekiel had merely interpreted history after the event. The word of God through him had come well in advance and Ezekiel's carefully dated file of messages could prove it. Thus, not only was he eventually vindicated as a true prophet, according to fulfilment criteria, but also the sovereign power of Yahweh to predict, control and interpret events was demonstrated. As so many of Ezekiel's oracles, whether dated or not, ended: 'I am Yahweh. I have spoken. I will do it.'

c. The structure of the book

The chronological sequence of the prophecies also works effectively alongside the broader structuring of the book. This is because the ministry of Ezekiel itself falls into two clear phases: his first five years between his call and the fall of Jerusalem; and the remaining fifteen years after that event. Chapters 1 – 24 come from the first period and are predominantly oracles of judgment, pointing to the coming catastrophe and justifying it on the basis of the accumulated wickedness and rebellion of Israel. Chapters 33 – 48 come from the latter period, and the dominant theme is hope for the future through God's promise of restoration. In between these two major sections are gathered together a selection of the prophecies of Ezekiel against foreign nations. Most of them were delivered during the siege of Jerusalem, or very shortly after the destruction of the city, so it is appropriate that they are grouped together filling the space between the announcement of the beginning of the siege in chapter 24 and the news of the fall of the city in chapter 33.

Thus, at its broadest level the book has a very simple and symmetrical arrangement.

1. Chs. 1 – 24   Oracles of judgment prior to the fall of Jerusalem in 587.
2. Chs. 25 – 32   Oracles against the foreign nations.
3. Chs. 33 – 48   Oracles of hope after the fall of Jerusalem, between 587 and 571.

Within each major section there are further sub-sections, which are reflected in the chapters of our exposition. Apart from this broad pattern, there are other signs of careful structuring. The opening vision of the glory of Yahweh that dominates chapters 1 – 3, is matched and surpassed by the closing vision of the glory of Yahweh returning to his temple, people and land, in chapters 40 – 48. The commissioning of the prophet to be a watchman occurs at the beginning of his ministry in chapter 3, and is then repeated at the fresh start heralded by the news of the fall of Jerusalem in chapter 33. In chapter 6 Ezekiel addresses the mountains of Israel with words of coming judgment, desolation and desertion. In chapter 36 he addresses the same mountains, but with words of coming restoration, repopulation and renewed fertility and abundance. Chapter 7 proclaims that 'the end has come', bringing death to the whole community. Chapter 37 proclaims that even dead bones can live when the powerful breath of God breathes on them, and promises Israel resurrection from the grave itself.

It is perhaps some relief that a book which for so many people is somewhat inaccessible, because of the tone and intensity of its language and imagery, at least has a structure which is easy to grasp. It is a structure which reflects not only the chronological career of the prophet himself with its two major phases, but also the core theological truth of biblical faith: judgment precedes grace. As it was for Israel in exile, so it is for us and all people: we have to hear and accept the bad news about the reality of our sin and the terribleness of God's just reaction to it, before we can respond with joy and gratitude to the good news of God's incredible mercy, grace and purposes for ourselves and for his world. This is the message of Ezekiel to which we now turn.

1:1 – 3:15
1. Wheels within wheels: Ezekiel's call vision

Introduction: Who, when and where? (1:1–3)

As birthday treats go, Ezekiel's thirtieth birthday[1] experience is unsurpassed. He was spending it by the riverside, a location chosen perhaps for prayer and ritual cleansing.[2] He may have gone alone, or with his wife, but before it was over he had a visionary experience of the glory of God himself – an experience that left him stunned and shattered for the whole of the following week (3:15).

The place was *by the Kebar River*, which was probably a canal, part of a complex irrigation system bringing water from the Tigris and Euphrates into the city and region of Nippur. The Judean exiles had been settled in this region, possibly initially in slave camps in abandoned towns, such as Tel Abib (3:15, see below). We have no sure knowledge of the fate of the exiles once they reached Babylon, but some of them may well have had to work in such irrigation projects, toiling in the sticky heat of the Mesopotamian plain far from the hills of Judea. And Ezekiel was *among the exiles*, a phrase which describes his social, geographical and historical situation. Their suffering, their questioning, and quite possibly their angry complaints (cf. 3:14) were all shared by him. God did not send them a prophet from outside; God took one of their own number and stunned him into a costly but utterly crucial ministry among them.

The date is given with calendrical precision in verse 2, a date which, by external verification, can be fixed as 31 July 593 BC. It was *the fifth year of the exile of King Jehoiachin*, the king who had reigned only a few weeks in Jerusalem before his surrender to Nebuchadnezzar.[3] Even though he was a deposed and deported king,

---

[1] It is most likely that the expression *In the thirtieth year* refers to the prophet's own age, though several alternative reference points have been suggested, e.g. thirty years since the discovery of the book of the law in the temple in 622. Cf. Allen 28, pp. 20–21.

[2] Cf. Lydia in Acts 16:13.   [3] 2 Kgs. 24:8–17.

the people of Judah continued to date events by his reign. This particular date comes exactly five years after the first deportation, and five years before the final destruction of the city in 598/597 BC.

For Ezekiel, however, the personal significance of the day was far greater than its place in the exiles' forlorn royal calendar.[4] It was his thirtieth birthday, and he was *the son of Buzi*, the priest.[5] According to Numbers 4, Levites were eligible for their sacred work between the ages of thirty and fifty. Ezekiel would have grown up for twenty-five years in Jerusalem and known the workings of the temple and its priesthood intimately. He had probably trained for the day when he would enter that holy service himself – perhaps on his thirtieth birthday. Now that birthday had come, but where was he? Not in the temple in Zion, but on the other side of the world. Not in the focal point of the holiness of Yahweh's presence among his people in his own land, but in an unclean land, surrounded by idolatry and polytheism, mocked by his captors. No birthday-party songs were sung by the side of the canal that day. More likely he sang something like Psalm 137:

> By the rivers of Babylon we sat and wept
>   when we remembered Zion.
> There on the poplars
>   we hung our harps,
> for there our captors asked us for songs,
>   our tormentors demanded songs of joy;
>   they said, 'Sing us one of the songs of Zion!'
>
> How can we sing the songs of the LORD
>   while in a foreign land?

And yet, by the end of this day when he should have become a priest, Ezekiel had been called (if that is not too weak a word for the awesome experience) to be a prophet.

Four expressions highlight the powerful nature of Ezekiel's experience. *The heavens were opened* (1) can describe torrential rain,[6] which may be linked to the onset of the approaching storm (4). But more metaphorically the expression describes a parting of the invisible barrier between earth and heaven such that the observer can see what is going on in the very presence of God.[7] *Visions of God,*

---

[4] Notice that v. 1 is in the first person – Ezekiel's own account of the event – whereas v. 2 is an editor's clarification of the calendar date, given in the third person.
[5] *The priest* probably refers to Buzi, not Ezekiel himself, since Ezekiel would not yet have been actually 'ordained' into the priestly office.
[6] Gen. 7:11.   [7] Cf. Luke 3:21; Acts 7:56; Rev. 4:1.

or perhaps better, 'divine visions', describes not merely the appearance of God's glory that was already winging and wheeling its way across the horizon, but the whole experience of seeing divine realities behind the everyday, canalside perspective on events. *The word of the LORD came to Ezekiel*; this standard expression for the prophetic gifting completes the audiovisual experience. For Ezekiel it was not merely a word that he heard, but one that he absorbed into his whole being (2:9 – 3:3). Finally, *the hand of the LORD was upon him*. This speaks of overpowering pressure and compulsion, which in Ezekiel's case seems to have involved physical as well as psychological and spiritual manifestations. He uses the expression seven times in the book.[8]

A single word, however, captures the amazement of the moment more than any other. It is the simple expression *There* (3). Emphatic in its position, it focuses on the contrast between *what* is being described (or about to be), and *where* it is all happening. Yahweh, the God of Israel, is appearing, is speaking, is putting forth his mighty hand, *there*, in the land of exile, uncleanness and despair. Ezekiel, with his fellow exiles, most probably believed that God was far away, or to be more precise, that they were far away from God's presence in the Jerusalem temple. The exiles felt despised and rejected by those who had been left behind in Jerusalem (11:15). Yet even there, in remarkable similarity to Psalm 139:7–12, the powerful presence of Yahweh in all his glory was about to be revealed. God is *there* in Babylon! What comfort! And yet, as the storm clouds rush in over the plain towards Ezekiel, he knows that God is coming in judgment, terrifying judgment as it will turn out. No wonder he was scared witless for a week (2:15).

God is there. There are times when our doctrinal conviction of God's omnipresence needs to become an experienced reality again. Whether through geographical distance, like Ezekiel's, or through more spiritual or emotional alienation, the experience of exile from the presence of God can be dark and terrible. We may not be privileged with an overwhelming vision like Ezekiel's, and most of us will be grateful to be excused the privilege, but we can certainly pray for the reassurance of the touch of his hand reminding us that God is there, even there.

1. The vision of God's glory (1:4–28)

'If someone asks whether the vision is clear, I confess it is very obscure

[8] Ezek. 1:3; 3:14, 22, 8:1; 33:22; 37:1; 40:1. It is used of other prophets: e.g. 1 Kgs. 18:46; Is. 8:11; Jer. 15:17. Cf. J. J. M. Roberts, 'The Hand of Yahweh', *VT* 21 (1971), pp. 244–251.

and I do not profess to understand it.' Such was Calvin's humble opinion,[9] shared by many before and since. With the help of vastly increased knowledge about the cultural context of Ezekiel's ministry, unavailable to Calvin, we may fare better in understanding it, though we will do well to follow his example in avoiding some of the wilder attempts to give meaning to all its details – attempts which, as he put it, are 'better buried immediately than rebuffed at great effort'.

a. The broad structure

Although it is possible, as we shall see, to follow a broad sequence in Ezekiel's description of his vision, we are dealing here with an account that bears all the marks of an excited eye-witness. Fourteen months later Ezekiel was able to write some clearer explanations of the things he saw (in ch. 10), but this account is full of hasty, disjointed and ungrammatical language, tumbling along as the words struggle to cope with an overwhelmingly awesome confrontation with the majesty of God.

The vision begins with a storm (4) and ends with a throne (26). It has thereby combined two very powerful theophany[10] traditions that are found in Israel's worship. One describes Yahweh as 'riding on the wings of the storm', and includes such features as strong wind and lightning.[11] The other describes him as 'enthroned above the cherubim', or simply as seated on a throne above a heavenly platform.[12] The combination of both kinds of theophanic imagery into one massive multimedia experience must have been virtually beyond description. Whereas the throne imagery spoke of static power and authority, the storm imagery transformed it into dynamic movement and freedom.

At the start of the vision, Ezekiel may have thought he was simply observing the approach of yet another normal thunderstorm across the sweltering Mesopotamian plains (4). But as it rushed closer he could see that it was far from 'normal', with its pulsating, flashing core, and its brilliant effulgence. Once it was close enough

---

[9] Calvin 18, p. 22.

[10] 'Theophany' means 'the appearance of God'. There is a widespread theophanic tradition within the Old Testament. Although it was believed that human beings could not, in any literal sense, see God, nevertheless there were remarkable occasions when God appeared or displayed his glory in some form, to individuals and to the whole nation: e.g. various appearances to the patriarchs; the burning bush; Mount Sinai; the glory in the tabernacle/temple; appearances to Moses, Gideon, the parents of Samson, Elijah, Isaiah, etc. An excellent discussion of this tradition is to be found in T. E. Fretheim, *The Suffering of God: An Old Testament Perspective* (Philadelphia: Fortress, 1984).

[11] E.g. Pss. 18:7–14 (= 2 Sam. 22:8–15); 68:4; 104:3–4; Deut. 33:26; Is. 19:1; Job 38:1.

[12] E.g. Exod. 24:10; Pss. 18:10; 80:1; 99:1; Is. 6:1.

to see the details, there were three things that took his attention in turn, providing some structure for our analysis of his vision: the four living creatures (5–14); the wheels beneath them (15–21); and the platform and throne above them (22–27).

b. The four living creatures (1:5–14)

Starting in the middle of the storm vision, Ezekiel sees in its fiery heart four upright living creatures. Their appearance is, for many of us, the stuff of bizarre fantasy movies, but in the world Ezekiel had been forced to inhabit – the heart of the Babylonian empire – they were a kind of mutated variation on images he would have seen in religious painting and statues all around him. In 10:20 he explains that these *living creatures* were in fact *cherubim*, though that term is not used in the immediate description of them in chapter 1. 'Cherubim' in western art have been portrayed as cute flying babies hovering around scenes of religious devotion. Nothing could be more removed from the biblical picture, where they seem to have been related to the massive statues of guardian creatures that stood outside Mesopotamian temples, or were portrayed in paintings as holding up the sky, as the home of the gods. Solomon had installed two in his temple,[13] though their appearance differs from Ezekiel's vision. Ezekiel's description has features that were common in such paintings and statues: the upright humanoid form (5), but with multiple heads or *faces* and *wings* (6); the *legs* and/or *feet* of a bull (7); the particular animals whose heads were included along with the human one (*lion*, *ox* and *eagle*, 10). Such composite, winged 'bullmen' are found in various postures over a wide spectrum of ancient near-eastern cultures and historical eras. Typically they are seen in several main roles, either supporting the throne of a god, or guarding his temple or the palace of a king. They were the attendants of deity, supporting his majesty and defending his empire.[14] From his cultural surroundings, Ezekiel would have recognized such creatures as indicating the presence of deity, even if it did not immediately dawn on his terrified mind that it was indeed Yahweh they were attending (not until v. 28 is this identification made).[15]

Closer inspection gives an idea of the posture and relationship of the four creatures. They were vertical, with one of their two pairs

[13] 1 Kgs. 6:23–28
[14] Descriptions, with helpful line drawings, of several of these ancient near-eastern paintings and statues are provided by Allen 28, pp. 27–31.
[15] On the missiological significance of the way that Ezekiel here makes use of, but transforms, the religious imagery of his surrounding culture in order to express the transcendence and sovereignty of Yahweh, the God of Israel, see the Introduction above, pp. 28–29.

of wings upraised and touching the wings of the others overhead. The only way this can be envisaged is that they were arranged in a square (not a straight line), with the human face of each creature facing outwards to each point of the compass. So they would have seemed to have their backs to each other, except that at the back of each was the eagle's head, with the lion's head facing right and the ox's head facing left.

Ezekiel notices that each creature had four wings (unlike Isaiah's vision of six-winged seraphim), but tells us little about what they did with them, except to cover their bodies with one pair and make a lot of noise with the other (25) when they moved. Nor does he tell us anything about the actions (if any) of the human *hands* he sees beneath the wings (8). Hands, however, in biblical imagery normally signify ability, power and competence.

More significant is the symbolism of the four heads or faces – those of a man, a lion, an ox and an eagle. Again it is vital to remember that what seems strange and arbitrary to us was familiar and immediately symbolic to Ezekiel and his contemporaries. Individually or in combination, these four creatures are to be found in religious art and statuary all across the ancient world, and in Israel too they had symbolic or proverbial significance.

The *lion* was renowned for its strength, ferocity, and courage (Judg. 14:18; 2 Sam. 1:23; 17:10), and served as a symbol of royalty. The *eagle* was the swiftest and most stately of birds (Deut. 28:49; Isa. 40:31; Jer. 48:40). The *ox* ... was not only the most valuable domestic animal (Prov. 14:4) but also functioned as a symbol of both fertility and divinity (cf. Ps. 106:19–20). The *human*, being created as the image of God and invested with divine majesty (Gen. 1:28; Ps. 8), is the most dignified and noble of all. But the significance of these creatures exceeds the sum of the parts. In the absence of abstract philosophical tools these images expressed the transcendent divine attributes of omnipotence and omniscience. Carrying the divine throne, the four-headed cherubim declare that Yahweh has the strength and majesty of the lion, the swiftness and mobility of the eagle, the procreative power of the bull, and the wisdom and reason of humankind.[16]

Four living creatures, four heads, four wings: the repeated symbolic use of the number four almost certainly relates to the four quarters or corners of the earth, or the four winds. The vision is declaring that the deity so awesomely attended by this fourfold

[16] Block (1), p. 96.

supporting cast is sovereign over all the earth, in all directions. His all-seeing presence can be anywhere, almost literally in a flash.

What is amazing is that Ezekiel was able to describe these creatures at all, since they were in almost constant motion. Here is one of the key points of contrast with the ancient near-eastern religious art. Cherubim and their equivalents stood still, either supporting the throne of the god, or standing sentry-like to guard his temple. Ezekiel's living creatures are flashing back and forth like the fire and lightning they are mingled with – moving, yet not turning, by some mysterious dynamic of *the spirit* (12). For such a scene of fiery flux and motion, words almost failed him (13–14). But his curiosity did not. How were these enormous creatures able to move in this strange way – in any direction they liked, yet without having to turn around, like some celestial chess-board queen? Ezekiel's gaze turned downwards to find out.

c. The wheels (1:15–21)

Ezekiel has bequeathed to the English language the phrase 'wheels within wheels' as a term for something convoluted and difficult to comprehend. No doubt that is how he felt about what he saw at this point. Each living creature seemed to have one wheel *on the ground*, presumably by its bull-feet. Yet that wheel seemed to have another wheel inside it. The construction is impossible to portray in terms of modern engineering, though some have suggested a gyroscope arrangement, and others something like freewheeling castors. Remember, this was a fiery vision, not a physical model open to Ezekiel's leisurely mechanical inspection. The main point of the construction was that it enabled the four interlocked creatures to move in any direction without appearing to swivel or turn (17). Though the presence of wheels gives a chariot-like feel to the whole apparatus, the multidirectional potential seems to surpass any two-wheeled or four-wheeled chariot. Total and unrestricted freedom of movement seems to be the primary function of these wheels. Apart from that, they had their own share in the majestic splendour of the rest of the vision: they *sparkled*, they were *high and awesome*, and they were *full of eyes*.[17]

The wheels, then, provide the answer to how the living creatures were able to move as they did. For it would seem that neither their

[17] Why there should have been eyes on the wheels, when the living creatures had thirty-two between them already, is a mystery. Perhaps it simply amplifies the idea of the all-seeing deity. This is certainly the impression of the further mention of multiple eyes in 10:12. Perhaps Block is right to suggest that the word means 'eye-shaped precious stones', which were responsible for the sparkling appearance as the wheels moved. Block (1), p. 100.

wings nor their legs were actually the primary means of locomotion. The wings made a frighteningly powerful noise when the creatures moved – comparable to a mighty waterfall, or a battlefield, or the voice of God himself (24), but it is not explicit that they were being used to 'fly', since the creatures moved horizontally as well as vertically. Ezekiel's vision seems to have something unparalleled in the paintings and statues of his surroundings. Strong legs and multiple wings seem to have indicated the capacity for support and movement. Yet here movement actually comes from an unexpected source – wheels. And even then, it is not the wheels themselves that do the moving, for they in turn are empowered or driven by *the spirit* (20; cf. 12). And that spirit is further described as 'the spirit of life' (20, 21).[18] The whole dynamic scene, even before Ezekiel has been able to take it all in, is animated by the spirit that he recognized as the Spirit of the living God – the same Spirit that would be needed to revive and empower the prophet himself (2:2; 3:24).

d. The throne (1:22–28)

Having discovered how the incredible quartet was capable of such effortless movement, Ezekiel at last dared to direct his gaze back from ground level to those multiple heads – and then on to what was above them. The climax of his vision now arrives. Above the creatures was a vast crystal *expanse* or 'dome' (NRSV),[19] which sparkled with *awesome* white brightness.[20] Although above the outstretched wings of the living creatures it was not actually supported by them, since it remained in place when, for once, *they stood still* and *lowered their wings* (24). Nevertheless, their position is certainly reminiscent of the sky-bearing posture of similar creatures in ancient near-eastern art.

Being crystal, this great platform had a transparent quality, so that Ezekiel could see through it to what was higher still – *what looked like a throne* (26). In contrast to the gleaming whiteness of the platform, the throne was a brilliant, rich blue, as though constructed from one of the most precious stones of the ancient world, lapis lazuli.[21] And on the throne, with all the added brilliance of

[18] The MT reading here, 'spirit of life' (singular), is almost certainly preferable to the emendation behind the NIV's *spirit of the living creatures* (plural).

[19] The word ($r\bar{a}q\hat{i}^{\prime}a$) is used to describe the 'firmament' that separates the waters above and below in Gen. 1:6ff. In normal use it seems to mean the dome of the sky, or the heavens (Pss. 19:1; 150:1).

[20] The comparison is probably to crystal rather than to *ice* (NIV).

[21] Probably this is the stone referred to, although the Hebrew word sounds like *sapphire*. The deep-blue colour is similar. Cf. Block (1), p. 102. The same stone is used for comparison in describing the pavement beneath Yahweh in Exod. 24:10.

contrasting fiery amber in the centre and all the colours of the rainbow around the radiant edges, was *a figure like that of a man*. The climactic vision of the deity himself is in human form – though Ezekiel is careful to qualify all his descriptions here with repeated use of 'appearance of', 'something like' (NRSV). Indeed, his vision involves a fascinating reversal of the concept of 'image of God'. He uses the word 'likeness, similarity' (*dᵉmût*),which first occurs in Genesis 1:26–27, when God created human beings in his own image and likeness. Here, in anthropomorphic reversal, God appears in the likeness of a human being, albeit in glowing, fiery splendour that anticipates the transfiguration of the incarnate Son of God himself and certainly provided the imagery for John's great vision of the heavenly throne in Revelation 4.

Only now, it seems, does Ezekiel almost blindingly realize what he is looking at. This is no Babylonian deity attended by its guardian sphinxes. This is none other than Yahweh himself, very much alive and well and still on the throne. *Yahweh is here in Babylon!* The shock of the realization drains the last dregs of adrenalin from Ezekiel's trembling body and he collapses *face down*, unable to look any longer. But had he really *seen* Yahweh? No, he will not claim that. Had he then seen the *glory* of Yahweh? Even that would be too much to claim directly at this stage; later he will recognize it more easily. Nothing will ever be more significant for Ezekiel than this encounter with the living God; his whole life and message will be more uncompromisingly God-centred than any other prophet's. Yet all he can bring himself to say at this point is: *This was the appearance of the likeness of the glory of the* LORD.

2. The reality of God's presence

Pausing for a moment as Ezekiel lies prostrate, what does it all mean? Starting from the climax at the end, we know that the whole colossal phenomenon was a manifestation of the *glory* of Yahweh. The word (*kāḇôḏ*) is, of course, richly significant in the Bible, and for Ezekiel it had profound depths. His whole ministry was virtually framed on the one hand by the awful sight of this glory of Yahweh departing from the temple (chs. 8 – 10), and on the other hand by the joy of its returning there in his final vision (43:1–5). The word essentially has to do with 'weight', or 'substance'. It portrays the sense of God's majestic reality, the overwhelming power of his presence, the 'weight' of his eternal Being. At least four other dimensions of the glory of Yahweh are implied in the dynamic symbolism of Ezekiel's vision.

First, it portrays the transcendence of God. Isaiah managed to convey the same impression in far fewer words,[22] but the point is the same. Yahweh is the God who is exalted above all else – above the earth, above whatever spiritual beings the four living creatures represent, above the very heavens. There is a distance and a separation in the vision, even though the throne and the one seated there can be glimpsed through the crystal platform beneath them. This sense of enormous altitude, of cosmic exaltation, pervades the worship of Israel.[23] It does not deny his nearness – another equally precious article of Israel's faith and experience – but it does warn us against any kind of chummy familiarity that fails to acknowledge that the God who, with incredible grace, chooses to live in friendship with the humble,[24] is the transcendent occupant of the throne of the universe. Ezekiel's posture – flat on his face – is a good place to start in response to such awareness.

Secondly, it portrays the universal sovereignty of God. The image of a throne in itself speaks of authority and power, as it does elsewhere throughout the Bible. Yahweh's throne is the seat of his rule over history, through his kingship over earthly kings; it is the place of his exercise of righteousness and justice.[25] But the somewhat static image of a throne has been transformed in Ezekiel's vision into a highly mobile, dynamic scene, in which Yahweh's presence and all-seeing eye can be anywhere at any time, throughout all four corners of the earth. And that sovereign presence is directed solely by God himself, through 'the spirit' (12, 20, 21).

Thirdly, and by the very location of the vision itself, Yahweh is *here*. The place where he seemed to be absent and the place where his people seemed to be utterly rejected has been transformed by this tumultuous invasion. Even if the idea of Yahweh's omnipresence had been a vague part of Israel's faith, the exile must have shattered any expectation of it being really true any longer. As we have seen,[26] for many Israelites Yahweh was defeated, disabled, disgraced, and certainly very, very distant. There is no reason to imagine that Ezekiel would have been immune to the doubts and questions that would have settled like the dust of the Mesopotamian plains on the huts of the exiles. For five years he had mourned and wondered and questioned. Five years is a long time for a refugee. The conclusion that Yahweh had abandoned them must have been close to irresistible – until today, his thirtieth birthday. Yahweh, in all his kingdom, power and glory, has arrived in Babylon. No border

---

[22] Is. 6:1.   [23] E.g. Pss. 57:5, 11; 97:9; 108:5; Is. 33:5; 57:15.
[24] Ps. 25.
[25] E.g. Pss. 9:7; 11:4; 45:6; 47:8; 89:14; 103:19; Is. 6:1; 66:1; Dan. 7:9; Matt. 5:34; Heb. 1:8.
[26] See above pp. 28, 30.

guards can keep him out. No place on earth is barred to the throne-chariot of this God. He was *there*.

The combination of the second and third points above is important for us in holding a proper balance between our faith in God's universal sovereignty over the global realities of our world and our practised awareness of his active presence in the more local and daily affairs of our lives. God is everywhere and in charge. God is here and in action. What impact should such combined truths have on the choices and commitments that govern our lives?

But fourthly, although there must have been great comfort in realizing that Yahweh was present in Babylon, the vision made it clear that the predominant mood of his presence was one of continuing judgment. This is clear from the repeated imagery of *fire*. Fire and lightning flashed from the *windstorm* as it approached (4). The four living creatures were themselves *like burning coals* (13), or *flashes of lightning* (14), and seemed to move in a blazing fiery environment. The human figure on the throne seemed *full of fire* (27), above and below the waist. Though it is not explicit that all this speaks of the fire of God's judgment, this certainly is how the vision will develop on a later occasion (10:1–7). Furthermore, the picture of Yahweh riding on a fiery storm-chariot is certainly found elsewhere as a terrifying picture of his wrath in action.[27] And that will be the dominant theme of Ezekiel's message in the early years of his ministry. The wrath of God had indeed fallen on Jerusalem in that first deportation of 597, but it was far from exhausted. Much worse was yet to come. Ezekiel would literally strain every nerve in his body to communicate that message before he would be granted messages of hope and comfort. He would be commissioned to launch passionate evangelistic appeals at his people. He would be entrusted with words of the most incredible grace and restoration. But first he must confront the reality of the God he and his people were dealing with. Yahweh was present in Babylon in all his glory, but for now that glory was only to be felt in the blinding light and heat of his anger.

The crashing roar of the living creatures' wings had temporarily stopped (24), but the silence was short-lived. Out of it came *the voice of one speaking* (28), which could only have meant the voice of Yahweh himself from the throne. Ezekiel was being addressed, but not by name. Consistent with his posture of total humility – prostrate on his face – he is addressed here and throughout with the simple term *Son of man* (2:1). There is no significant connection between Ezekiel's use of the term and the vision of Daniel 7 or Jesus'

[27] E.g. Pss. 18:7–14; 97:3–5.

use of the term as a self-description. As addressed to Ezekiel, it simply means 'Human', 'Man', almost (as one might speak to someone whose name is not relevant), plain 'Mister'.

What follows is the narrative of Ezekiel's call and commissioning (2:3 – 3:15). But for that he cannot stay prostrate. So he is told to *stand up* (2:1), in a position ready to hear and obey the word he will hear. In the presence of a king on his throne, prostration was the appropriate posture for submission, but for service standing upright and ready for action was the correct posture.

The account has four sequential movements: First there is the primary declaration of his commissioning to be God's spokesman to the rebellious people of Israel (2:3–7). Then follows a physical or symbolic action which graphically identifies Ezekiel with the message he is to give by eating the scroll on which it was written (2:8 – 3:3). The commission is then repeated with some further explanation and hard encouragement (3:4–11). Finally, the whole vision recedes and Ezekiel is transported back to his encampment for a week's exhausted recuperation (3:12–15). From this chronological sequence of events we shall consider first of all what is said about Israel (2:1–7; 3:4–7), and then secondly what is said about Ezekiel (2:8 – 3:3; 3:8–11).

3. The hardness of God's people (2:1–7; 3:4–7)

The description of Israel in these verses introduces us to one of the commonest features of Ezekiel's prophetic style. Never say anything once if you can say it several times, preferably with multiple synonyms and repeated phraseology. Even a glance through the few verses of chapter 2 in English throws up seven occurrences of the word-group 'rebel, rebellious'. This, from God's point of view, is what most characterizes the people. Even in exile the hardened obduracy of Israel continues unabated. Out of the torrent of accusation three features stand out in the description of the people Ezekiel is being sent to.

a. Disloyalty (2:3)

The story of Israel is sometimes known as the history of the covenant, or salvation history. From God's perspective, which was to become Ezekiel's (see esp. ch. 20), it was a story of constant disloyalty to the God of their covenant and salvation. The language of 2:3 – *rebelled against me … in revolt against me* – uses two words (*mārad̲* and *pāšaʿ*) which suggest a political context. The idea of Israel as a nation in covenant relationship with Yahweh was drawn from the world of international treaties. Yahweh was the Great King, committed to the salvation and protection of his subjects; Israel was the vassal state, committed to loyalty to their overlord. By contrast, Israel had been as rebellious against Yahweh as any rebel state against an imperial tyrant.[28] They had been like that from the first generation of the exodus[29] and they were still a long way from recognizing and confessing it as sin in the language of Daniel 9:5, 9. *pāša'* is more frequently translated as 'transgress', but it also carries the idea of breaking the bounds of required behaviour through acts of disobedience and violation of agreements.[30] It was also a habit of Israel that went back to the very beginning[31] and was the particular responsibility of the political and religious leaders who should have known better.[32] In this verse, then, Ezekiel endorses the fundamental message of the prophets who preceded him – Israel's history was one of congenital proneness to disloyalty to their covenant God, Yahweh. Later (chs. 16, 23), Ezekiel will expand the point into grotesque historical allegories, but for now the main point that God is making to Ezekiel is that he needn't have any hope that the experience of exile might have induced a change of heart in a people with such a history. Sadly not. The revolt of *their fathers* continued *to this very day*. So this divine perspective on Israel combines their past history and their present state in making the implied threat of final judgment inevitable.

b. Defiance (2:4–5)

Mention of the fathers recalls the fact that Israel were not just a nation in a political sense; they also constituted a community with a strong sense of kinship identity. This family imagery comes to the fore now with the familiar language of Israel as a *house*. Here, however, the honoured title 'house of Israel' is debased into 'house of defiance' (2:5, 6, 7, 9). Isaiah illustrates the family aspect of the term (*mᵉrî*).

> These are rebellious people, deceitful children,
> Children unwilling to listen to the LORD's instructions.[33]

Ezekiel describes Israel as an ungovernable family, drawing on the picture provided by the law regarding the stubborn, rebellious and incorrigible son in Deuteronomy 21:18–21. The atmosphere is one of brazen defiance, in which no appeal, no pleading, is of any use.

---

[28] *Mārad* is used, e.g., of national rebellions in Gen. 14:4; 2 Kgs. 18:7, 20; 2 Kgs. 24:1; Jer. 52:3.
[29] Num. 14:9.   [30] Hos. 8:1.   [31] Is. 43:27.   [32] Jer. 2:8.
[33] Is. 30:9; cf. Ps. 78:8.

Rather, there is an external stoniness (*obstinate* translates a phrase which literally means 'stiff-of-face') matched only by an internal hardness (*stubborn* translates a matching phrase which is literally 'hard-of-heart').[34] These are a people who not only do not show any feelings toward their God, but also are resolutely determined not to. Their faces are as frozen as their hearts.

c. Deafness (3:4–7)

And so are their ears. It was not merely that Israel did not respond to the word of Yahweh, they were not even prepared to listen to it in the first place. Ezekiel highlights the incredible, wilful, deafness of Israel by using a technique that he will sharpen to the cutting edge of a razor in later chapters: rhetorical comparison of Israel with other nations, much to the disadvantage of Israel themselves.[35] If God had sent Ezekiel as a missionary-prophet to other nations, they would not, of course, have been able to understand him because of the language barrier.[36] But at least *they would have listened* (3:6) out of courtesy; whereas Israel, who could understand him perfectly well, would not even give him a hearing at all. Their un-responsiveness to God's word, then, was not because it was too difficult or distant,[37] but simply a matter of their wilful, deliberate refusal to listen. And that made them worse than the pagan nations who had never heard, but would listen if they could.

> The point being made here is that [the language] barrier is far easier to overcome than the mental and spiritual block for which the biblical term is 'hardness of heart'. The prophet and his public share the same language, concepts, traditions, and history, but his words to them will be unable to surmount that barrier.[38]

The body language that has so far spoken of Israel's stiff face, hard heart and unwilling ears now rounds off with a reference to their *forehead. Israel is hardened and obstinate* (NIV) is literally, 'they are

---

[34] 'Brazen-faced and tough-hearted', Greenberg, p. 60.

[35] Allen 28, p. 41, observes that in 2:3–7 there is a 'vertical' comparison of the present generation of Israelites with their ancestors, whereas in 3:5–7 there is a 'horizontal' comparison of Israel with surrounding nations.

[36] The people of *obscure speech and difficult language* referred to in 3:5 probably means the Babylonians (cf. Is. 33:19). *Many peoples* (3:6), may mean the other ethnic groups of exiles captured by the Babylonians and settled in the same region as the exiles of Judah. Israel's scorn for the language of foreigners is evident in Is. 28:7–13.

[37] Cf. Deut. 30:11–14, where such excuses are ruled out, and the reflection on this in Rom. 10.

[38] Blenkinsopp, p. 26.

strong of forehead and hard of heart'. The forehead was the place where the law of Yahweh should have been tied as a symbol of obedience.[39] Instead Israel's collective forehead had become as hard as bronze[40] and unblushingly brazen.[41]

As often in the Bible, the stubbornness of God's own people is a far worse problem than the ignorance of 'foreigners' or pagans. It would have been easier for Ezekiel to be a cross-cultural missionary than a prophet to his own people (5–6). It is still in some respects true today; the evangelist-pastor who stays at home in the calloused environment of his or her own culture may have a much tougher time and see much less fruit than the mission partner working among some distant but responsive people. It is a principle that even Jesus recognized in the people of Nazareth: 'a prophet is not without honour, save in his own country, and in his own house'.[42] The same irony is illustrated by the book of Jonah, where the foreign city of Nineveh repents under the preaching of the word of God, whereas the prophet, probably representing Israel itself, moves from disobedience to God's word to disapproval of God's ways. It is still tragically true that in some parts of the world the challenge of God's word receives a better hearing among those who have never heard it before than among established churches who have grown hard and deaf in their resistance to the movements of God's Spirit. And the warning of Jesus still confronts our complacency and our privileged theology with the disturbing thought that there will be some who have never heard the gospel of the works of Jesus at all, but who will fare better in the final judgment than some who have heard but have refused to respond with faith and obedience.[43]

4. The mission of God's prophet (2:8 – 3:3; 3:8–11)

Interwoven with this terrible catalogue of Israel's hardness comes the word of God to Ezekiel in person. It must have been as unwelcome to Ezekiel as it was to Moses and Jeremiah before him, though, unlike the call narrative of those two illustrious predecessors, there is no record of any words of protest from Ezekiel himself – although 3:14 hints that there was no shortage of such sentiments in his mind. Several elements stand out in the passage, all of them having something in common with other prophetic call narratives.

[39] Deut. 6:8; 11:18. [40] Is. 48:4. [41] Jer. 3:3. [42] Matt. 13:57, KJV.
[43] Matt. 10:15; 11:23–24.

a. He was being sent by God's Spirit

The role of the Spirit of Yahweh in the ministry of Ezekiel is one of the main distinctives of his book. Here it is the Spirit who comes into him, lifts him to his feet, and enables him to hear the voice of the one on the throne. Later the Spirit will take him back home, but only to repeat the excursion a week later (2:12, 14; 3:24). The first words that he hears, empowered by the Spirit, is that God is *sending* him. This important word (*šālaḥ*), characteristic of the call and ministry of all the prophets,[44] is emphasized by multiple repetition (2:3, 4; 3:5, 6). Some prophets came who were not sent – indeed this was the plague not only of the preceding years back in Jerusalem itself,[45] but was still apparently a confusing reality among the exiles themselves.[46] On the other hand, if a prophet were truly sent, he could not but go and speak, or pay a high cost.[47] So Ezekiel knew he was being given little choice in this matter – which may be the reason for the feelings described in 3:14.

The one consolation, if such it were, was that however unpopular his message and however resistant the audience, the day would come when he would be acknowledged as having been a true prophet (2:5). The so-called 'recognition formula' – *they will know* – which normally refers to the acknowledgment of Yahweh himself is here extended to include his prophet. Ezekiel will share in the reputation that will ultimately belong to the God on whose behalf he is being sent. Such is the honour of faithful servants of God, even if it can hardly have been a prospect of much joy for the present. Those who know themselves to be sent by Jesus Christ (which, in one way or another, means all those who include themselves among his disciples) need to remind themselves that ultimately their mission is his mission. Those who hear and accept our words on his behalf accept him, and conversely, those who reject the word of God through his servants reject the Lord himself.[48]

b. He must speak God's word

You must speak my words to them (2:7; cf. 3:1, 4, 10–11). Along with the concept of being sent, this is the fundamental prophetic task. It was what God commissioned Moses (with Aaron's help) to do.[49] It was what God promised that the prophetic successors of Moses would do[50] – a promise repeated and claimed at the call of Jeremiah.[51] Like his illustrious predecessors, Ezekiel would have no freedom to

---

[44] Exod. 3:10; Is. 6:8; Jer. 1:7. [45] Jer. 23:9–32; cf. esp. vv. 21, 32.
[46] Jer. 29:15–19; 24–32; cf. Ezek. 13, esp. v. 6. [47] Jer. 20:9.
[48] John. 20:21; Matt. 10:40. [49] Exod. 4:10–16. [50] Deut. 18:18. [51] Jer. 1:9.

decide the message he would deliver, or to choose any other audience (*to them … a rebellious house … to your countrymen in exile*, 3:4, 9, 11), or to make his obedience conditional on how they responded to him (*whether they listen or fail to listen*, 2:5, 7; 3:11). His task would be totally focused on one thing only – delivery of the words of Yahweh.

While the expression 'my words in your mouth' was already well established as the characteristic prophetic claim, Ezekiel, as is very typical of him, experiences it in a quasi-physical manner. If his mouth was not already hanging open from the vision itself, it was now summarily opened for a very strange meal. The unforgettable theophany which has so far captured Ezekiel's eyes and ears now engages his touch and taste as well (2:8 – 3:3). He is ordered to eat a proffered scroll filled with *words of lament and mourning and woe*. The idea of eating the words of God may have been suggested by the metaphor in Jeremiah 15:16: 'When your words came, I ate them; they were my joy and my heart's delight.' But for Ezekiel it becomes a real sensory experience, even though still within his 'vision'. From Ezekiel's subjective point of view, two things may be said.

First, the whole experience indicated that he was to absorb the word of God totally. He did not just taste it, but (again with typical attention to every detail) it was to 'fill his stomach' (3:3) so that he had thoroughly digested it. It was to become part of him, nourishing, energizing and empowering him. Yes, he would be God's mouthpiece, but not like a mechanical loudspeaker. The message would be God's, but it would also be integrally, distinctively, authentically, Ezekiel's own.

Secondly, he himself observes the paradox that although the content of the word he was to eat and then to speak was long and bitter (2:10), the act of obedience itself was *as sweet as honey* (3:3). Although the scroll contained words of prophecy, there may be an echo here of the psalmist's observation that the law of Yahweh is 'sweeter than honey' – when it is obeyed.[52] As it happens, Ezekiel will say some of the sweetest things ever said by any prophet, but the way to those words lies through the faithful proclamation of God's terrible severity and judgment. The task of declaring such a message would bring Ezekiel utter grief and devastation (cf. 24:15–27). Yet in that task, because it was the only way of obedience to the will of God who longed for the salvation of his people, there was an inner sweetness that only faithfulness to God's will can bring.

Objectively, we may also notice about the scroll itself, first, that it does not just hover mysteriously before Ezekiel, its source

[52] Ps. 19:10.

unknown or open to later questioning. It comes from *a hand stretched out*, which unmistakably connects it to the throne and its glorious occupant. This word comes directly from God himself. And secondly, the scroll has already been fully written upon. The word of God is not a blank page that Ezekiel is invited to fill in for himself as the mood (or even the spirit) takes him. In a sense it is already an objective reality, pre-written and now entrusted to him to deliver. This is not to suggest any kind of impersonal fatalism. Nor does it conflict with the conditional and historically contingent nature of the prophetic word – that is, the way in which it speaks directly to particular historical circumstances and appeals to the people to change their ways so that God can act in new ways, including ways different from those portrayed in the given prophetic word. Ezekiel will indulge in much evangelistic pleading and later he will comfort the people with pastoral encouragement, in response to the changing historical circumstances of his ministry. But nevertheless this image of the word as a scroll to be digested in advance does speak of the objective and non-negotiable nature of what Ezekiel was to deliver. The word of God is not a blank cheque to be filled in to the recipient's benefit, nor a draft discussion document awaiting the input of various focus-groups. Yes, as affirmed above, the word of God in *this* particular book of the Bible will be unmistakably Ezekiel's very own, shaped by his character, personality and passion, but it comes to us *through* him ultimately in the same way as it came *to* him: as the word given by the One on the throne of the universe. Like Israel, we may 'listen or fail to listen', but we are not invited to come up with alternative drafts or to argue a case for our own preferred options.

c. He would be safe with God's strength

Ezekiel's account of his call experience differs from those of Moses, Isaiah and Jeremiah in that we hear no word of response – positive or negative – from his own mouth. He does not seem to have been given much chance to say anything before the point when it became rude to speak with his mouth full anyway. It can't be easy to speak with a mouth full of papyrus, even in a vision. However, there are hints in the things that God says which suggest responses that Ezekiel was either already making in his thoughts, or that God anticipated him making aloud.

First, and most strongly, God addresses his *fear*. It is hardly surprising that Ezekiel was afraid of such a calling. To be commanded to address his own traumatized community with words that would produce yet further *lament and mourning and woe* was a daunting prospect. To be a counter-revolutionary in a band of rebels was likewise terrifying. Since, as we know, there were popular prophets among the exiles busy predicting that the exile itself would be a short, sharp shock, and that soon they would all be on their way home, it would take a lot of courage for Ezekiel to predict otherwise and tell the present generation of exiles that they would never personally return. Jeremiah had been beaten and imprisoned in Jerusalem for such talk. And worst of all, while Jerusalem itself was still standing, it would be just as dangerous for Ezekiel in Babylon to predict its destruction as it had been for Jeremiah to do it in Jerusalem itself.[53] Facing such a wretched career, when all he had ever wanted was to be a priest, must indeed have felt like being surrounded by *briers and thorns ... and scorpions* (2:6).[54] So God repeatedly tells him not to be afraid, either of his fellow Israelites themselves, or of their words – doubtless words of rejection, denial, scorn and hatred (2:6, four times; 3:9, twice). 'His determination to speak must be stronger than Israel's refusal to listen.'[55]

Secondly, God possibly stifles a momentary *protest*. Verse 8 of chapter 2 begins with the phrase *But you, son of man ...* which often introduces a fresh juncture in God's conversation. It goes on, *Do not rebel like that rebellious house*, which may possibly hint that Ezekiel was indeed on the point of protesting against the commission he was being given. Whether the stifled protest would have been words of inadequacy like Moses, of sinfulness like Isaiah, or of inexperience like Jeremiah, or whether Ezekiel up to this point shared in the generally embittered and cantankerous mood of his people, we cannot know. What is clear is that from this point on he was set apart from the rest of his people (itself a terribly painful thing in a culture where personal identity is predominantly shaped by community belonging). To the extent that the house of Israel has become the 'house of defiance', Ezekiel can no longer belong to such a house. He must not, cannot, defy Yahweh as they do. And before any word of his own can pass his lips, his opened mouth is being filled with a word from the hand of God himself.

Thirdly, God addresses Ezekiel's feeling of *weakness*. The fact that God repeats the words of commission (3:4–11) may support the hint of a moment of protest from Ezekiel, but the main point here is to

[53] Jer. 26.
[54] Traditionally these words have been understood as symbolizing the threatening circumstances surrounding Ezekiel. Block, however, suggests that they may rather symbolize the protective wall that God would place around him. Thorn bushes and scorpion-plants are sometimes used as hedges in the ancient Near East. He points out that the metaphor comes at just the point in the text where, in other prophetic call narratives, there is a promise of divine presence and protection (Block (1), pp. 121–122).
[55] Blenkinsopp, p. 26.

tackle the problem of Ezekiel's personal weakness and sensitivity in the face of an audience that has been repeatedly described as hardened in every relevant part of their anatomy. First of all God deflects the animosity away from Ezekiel on to himself (3:7). If the words Ezekiel had to speak were in fact the well-digested words of God, then in refusing to listen to Ezekiel they were refusing to listen to Yahweh himself. It was they, not Ezekiel, who would have to bear the consequences of that. This principle is further developed in the 'watchman' imagery below (3:16–21).[56] Secondly, God promises to make Ezekiel as tough in resisting the hatred of the people as they were in resisting the word of God (3:8–9). We do not know much about the personality of Ezekiel, but there are hints that he had a sensitive and caring side. Even if he was no more or less sensitive than the rest of us are to how others respond to us, there must have been a terrible psychological cost in being rendered *unyielding and hardened ... like the hardest stone, harder than flint.* And yet only by that process of divine toughening could he have endured what lay ahead.

Conclusion: Back home (3:12–15)

The massive multimedia meeting with God is drawing to a close. Ezekiel experiences something that will happen again several times – the dynamic transport of God's Spirit. The same spirit or wind that had raised him to his feet (2:2) now lifted him off his feet and deposited him back home in *Tel Abib.* The name means something like 'small town left over from the flood', which may indicate a ruined settlement on a small hill above the flood plain of the irrigation system. Not the most exhilarating place to launch a prophetic ministry; a foreign assignment might indeed have seemed more attractive. But that was where Ezekiel was. And that was where *the exiles ... were living.* And most of all, that was where he had now been sent.

But with remarkable honesty Ezekiel describes the mood with which he returned – which is more reminiscent of Jonah than of Isaiah. *I went in bitterness and in the anger of my spirit* (14). It is possible that this expresses Ezekiel's entering into the feelings of God against Israel; Ezekiel's anger would thus be against the people he will now have to confront. But it is more likely that this is anger directed *against* God himself for the appalling task that has been laid upon Ezekiel. If he had tried to protest (in 2:8), it had been ignored. The words are extremely strong. *Bitterness (mar)* was the emotion

---

[56] Cf. Deut. 18:19.

of Esau robbed,[57] of Israel enslaved,[58] of Naomi bereft[59] and of Job in agony.[60] *Anger* (*ḥēmâ*) is literally (and most often) boiling heat. It indicates hot, furious, raging, displeasure.

So Ezekiel came back from his day-trip to the river in boiling, bitter fury. It was only his thirtieth birthday after all, and all he had done was to go to the riverside perhaps to pray and to reflect sadly on the priest he would never be. As a priest he could have served his people and received their grateful thank-offerings and gifts. But now, all that stretched ahead was a lifetime of speaking impossibly harsh words to his people and receiving only their hatred and even violence. Ezekiel would have known the fate of a prophet from the experiences of his slightly older contemporary Jeremiah. Why had Yahweh picked on him? Was it not enough to have lost his career and his future? Was it not enough to have been wrenched away from the temple of his dearest dreams? Was it not enough to be suffering this appalling living death in exile along with all the other exiles? Must he now also endure the lonely unpopularity and social exclusion that would inevitably be his lot as the prophet of yet more doom to come?

We need to remember, as we read on through the terrible words that will come from the mouth of this prophet, that he speaks as one reluctant to be speaking at all, as one whose reaction to his prophetic calling was not just inadequacy or guilt, but bitterness and raging anger. Only *the strong hand of the* LORD *upon* Ezekiel restrained these emotions and held him, as in a physical vice, submissive to the divine will. The total physical, spiritual and psychological trauma of the whole experience left him *overwhelmed* – another strong word meaning stunned, horror-stricken, appalled. It would be a week before God could speak to him again.

---

[57] Gen. 27:34.   [58] Exod. 1:14.   [59] Ruth 1:13.   [60] Job 7:1.

3:16 – 5:17
2. Theatre of the doomed: Ezekiel's first year in ministry

Many of the prophets were gifted actors. In today's world they would have been exponents of physical theatre, exploiting the potential of gesture and mime, even elements of burlesque and clowning.[1] And all this was in addition to the amazing tool-kit of rhetorical techniques and verbal imagery they could draw on. None of them, however, was called upon to use visual drama in such a bizarre and sustained way as Ezekiel, at least in the early part of his ministry. It seems from chapters 4 – 5 that much of Ezekiel's first year as a prophet was taken up with two almost interminable mimes of siege warfare, interspersed with shorter and more pointed sketches of privation and suffering. Chapter 12 is similar; it may come from somewhat later, but still within the five years before the final fall of Jerusalem. This is one-man street theatre with a very powerful message – an unmistakably bleak message of imminent doom. We shall look first of all at God's preparation of the actor himself (3:16–27), then at the drama in three acts (4:1 – 5:4), and finally at the message it all portrayed (5:5–17).

1. The actor (3:16–27)

It was a week since Ezekiel's birthday encounter with the glory of Yahweh; a week, perhaps, of subsiding anger as he submitted himself to the divine compulsion (though see 3:22). Again Yahweh speaks, this time to impress upon him the life-and-death urgency of the task set before him.

---

[1] Some of Jeremiah's actions have a tragi-comic impact; e.g. his public smashing of huge pots (Jer. 19), his invasion of an international diplomatic conference wearing a huge ox-yoke with dangling ropes (Jer. 27), and his astonishing invitation of a whole teetotal community to a massive wine-festival in the temple (Jer. 35).

a. The responsibility of the watchman (3:17–21)

This is another example of the way in which the word of God to Ezekiel seems to have made use of his familiarity with the ministry and prophecies of Jeremiah. Here it seems that Jeremiah 6:17–21 is in the background. Not only does it use the image of the prophets as divinely appointed watchmen whose warning had not been heeded, but also speaks of stumbling-blocks as the means of divine judgment.[2] Jeremiah himself may have got the idea from Hosea,[3] though it is not difficult to imagine the comparison occurring independently to various prophets.[4]

The metaphor of the prophet as watchman is vivid and challenging. Picture an Israelite village or city in time of invasion, or the army encampment during a military campaign. Sentries would be posted by day and night on a tower or some elevated place, and charged with the crucial task of watching for any movements of the enemy. If they spotted any such danger, it was their responsibility to blow a trumpet or horn, or call out loudly, to awaken the rest of the inhabitants or army to the situation. Early warning could save lives. Sentry duty was thus an awesome responsibility. If the enemy attacked and people got killed, who was to blame? If the sentry had done his duty and given prompt warning, whatever happened next was not his responsibility. But if he had failed to see, or failed to raise the alarm, even if people died in battle because of their own cowardice or lack of preparation, the sentry would still bear some responsibility for his own failure to warn them.[5]

This, then, is the urgent commission that Yahweh now lays upon Ezekiel. *I have made you a watchman for the house of Israel.* It will be the defining model for his ministry, repeated later in the book in the context of the imminent fall of Jerusalem and the ongoing challenge that the event would pose for the exiles' response (33:1–9). As a model it immediately implies that Israel is in danger; they are in a war zone; there is an enemy about; they will need to be warned. There are other models for those who minister among God's people – shepherds of a flock; elders in a community; parents in a family; teachers in a school; servants in a household. But none is so fraught with urgency and a sense of life-or-death responsibility as this one. The prophet is on sentry duty and his one and only task is to give warning when it is needed. The sentry need not be a valiant

[2] Jer. 6:21; cf. Ezek. 3:20.
[3] Hos. 9:8, and cf. the trumpet warning in 5:8 and 8:1.
[4] Is. 56:10ff. exploits the comic thought of posting blind people as sentries as a metaphor for (probably) false prophets.
[5] Examples of watchmen in action, though with less urgent actions, include 1 Sam. 14:16; 2 Sam. 13:34; 18:24.

soldier himself. He is not called on to formulate the battle plans or co-ordinate the defence. His only responsibility is to stay awake, to see what is coming and to sound the alarm so that people can be ready and lives can be saved.

Give them warning, then, said God to Ezekiel. But there is another sharp point here. Warning about what, or whom? *Warning from me*, reads the NIV (17). But it is not merely that Yahweh is the source of the warning. He is also the source of the danger that Israel is to be warned about. 'Warn them *about* me';[6] 'Warn them *against* me'.[7] Yahweh himself was the enemy Israel needed to be warned about! Such a thought was alarming indeed, especially if the people were being fed a diet of popular predictions that Yahweh would soon rescue them from their enemies – Babylon – and whisk them back home. The real enemy was not Nebuchadnezzar but Yahweh.[8]

But this adds another twist to the paradox. Yahweh was coming as an enemy against the house of Israel. But who had posted the sentry to give warning? Again, Yahweh himself. What enemy would appoint a sentry in his target city to give warning of his own approach? At this point the analogy breaks down under the tension between the judgment and the grace of God. The warnings are real. The enemy is in deadly earnest. Those who refuse to take appropriate action will surely die. But the whole point of setting a watchman is to *save* life, and that is exactly what the following case-study highlights. Those who are unrepentantly wicked will die for their sin. But the desire of God's heart, implied in the very act of setting up an urgent warning, is that they should not do so. And if only they would heed his warning, they need not do so. This longing of God's heart will be explored to its depths in later chapters (e.g. 18:23, 32; 33:11). In this context the dominant note is the threat of death and the urgency of warning.

The case-study itself (3:18–21) is very typical of Ezekiel's method. He uses the same approach extensively elsewhere (e.g. 14:7–8; 9–11; 13–23; 18; 33:1–20). As modern educational method has discovered, it is a good way of engaging the minds of people and enabling them to appreciate significant principles or truths by interacting with situations that call for some decision or resolution. At All Nations Christian College, for example, weekly case-studies in the dilemmas and struggles of cross-cultural mission are a vital part of training people to meet such situations in real life. Ezekiel, drawing on his

---

[6] Block (1), p. 139, my emphasis.   [7] Greenberg, p. 82, my emphasis.
[8] Discerning the hand of Yahweh behind the actions of Nebuchadnezzar was a key insight of Jeremiah. Cf. his interpretation of contemporary international events in Jer. 27:1–11 (esp. v. 6); and his letter to the exiles after the first deportation, Jer. 29:1–15 (esp. the dual explanation of the exile in vv. 1, 4).

earlier training as a priest in handling the law, sets his cases up using the language and atmosphere of the law court. This includes the hypothetical language of case-law (*When*, *if*); the declaration of verdicts (guilt/death or innocence/life); and other echoes of the language of the Torah. There are ultimately only two categories of people, the wicked and the righteous (the terms are being used here in the forensic sense). But their destiny can be affected by whether or not they receive a warning of impending judgment, and by their response to the warning. The wicked person who refuses to repent, whether warned or not, will die (3:18–19).[9] The righteous person who, despite warning, turns to do evil, will also die (3:20).[10] But the righteous person who, though tempted, heeds the warning and does not sin, will be saved (3:21).

Since the significance of these cases will be worked over in much greater theological depth later, in chapters 18 and 33, we shall not comment further on them here. The major focus of this section is not so much on the fate of the respective parties, or on the justice of God's verdict (as it is in chs. 18 and 33), but on *the role of the watchman*. Only by doing his duty of giving warning can he preserve his own integrity. He will not share in the guilt of the wicked person, or the backsliding of the righteous one, but, if he fails to give warning to either, he will be held accountable for the judgment they will suffer. They are to blame for their own guilt. But he is to blame for his own failure. Provided he does give warning, however, he will save himself. What governs their fate is their own wickedness or righteousness. What governs the watchman's fate is simply whether or not he fulfils the duty of his posting. He is not judged by whether or not he is successful in persuading the wicked

[9] In this chapter, the case of the wicked person who *does* repent after warning is not considered. It is, however, included in the fuller discussion of the theological implications of the whole case-study, in 33:14–16. The verdict there is that such a person will not die, but will be 'transferred' to the camp of the righteous who will live.

[10] In 3:20 *I will put a stumbling-block before him* does not mean that God causes the person to sin. The first two clauses of the verse make it clear that the person, though previously living righteously (i.e. in conscientious obedience to the covenant law), has already 'turned' (i.e. away from God) and begun to do *evil*. Deliberate sin is already taking root. The *stumbling-block* (*mikšôl*) is the particular occasion of sin through which he falls into the judgment and punishment which God has warned him about. The word can literally be something that trips you up (Lev. 19:7). Elsewhere Ezekiel describes wealth (7:19) and idolatry (14:3) as things which will trip Israel up into judgment. God will punish sin; sometimes he may use the consequences of a particular sin to do so. Only in that sense is it meant that God 'put' the stumbling-block there. What God really wants is that people repent and so *avoid* the stumbling-block that their sin has laid in their path: 'then sin will not be your downfall' (*mikšôl*; 18:30).

to repent or in dissuading the righteous from backsliding – that is their own responsibility before God. He is judged solely on whether or not he has been faithful in the attempt.

There are some obvious comparisons with evangelistic and pastoral ministry. On the one hand, the warning to the wicked has an evangelistic dimension. In presenting the good news of the gospel, the evangelist must also confront people with the bad news of the reality of sin and the danger of judgment. The language of salvation only makes sense if there is something to be saved from. It was not only the Old Testament prophets who sounded warnings about wrath to come; it was the stark and unambiguous platform on which John the Baptist and Jesus also preached the good news of the kingdom of God. On the other hand, warning the righteous in order to help them avoid falling into sin has relevance to pastoral responsibility.

The task of rebuke and warning is difficult to do in a way that is sensitive and yet effective. But to avoid it for fear of hurting people's feelings is like a sentry failing to sound the alarm for fear of upsetting people by disturbing their sleep. Those of us called to pastoral ministry must not trifle with people's spiritual health if we are aware that they are in serious danger – provided of course we come to that awareness out of a deep biblical and God-centred understanding of what actually constitutes spiritual health or danger, and not on the basis of our own prejudice or the latest fashion in quasi-Christian therapy. Paul seems to have been well aware of the double-edged nature of this model of ministry, and urged it on Timothy and Titus: both to confront the wicked by doing the work of an evangelist,[11] and also to warn those who belonged to the righteous but were in danger of falling away.[12] By such careful 'watching', Timothy would save himself and his hearers,[13] which may well be an echo of Ezekiel's watchman model.

For us such a task is made even more uncomfortable in our own day with the dominant cultural atmosphere of postmodern relativism, in which people are not to be deemed right or wrong, still less righteous and wicked, but rather to be coming from different 'perspectives', all of which must somehow be affirmed lest we diminish people or threaten their personal and cultural identities. However, in real life there is still a recognized place for fire-alarms, early-warning systems, smoke detectors, night security guards, motorway hazard signs and anti-virus software. The task of the evangelist and pastor is founded on the conviction that there are

[11] 1 Tim. 1:3; 2 Tim. 4:5.   [12] 1 Tim. 5:20; 2 Tim. 2:14, 25; 4:2; Titus 1:13; 3:10.
[13] 1 Tim. 4:16.

dangers equally real and potentially more fatal in the moral and spiritual realm. The watchman's duty to give warning is based on the reality of the danger, not on the mood of those he has to warn.

b. The reality of God's glory (3:22–23)

Such an awesome responsibility needed a fresh dose of divine reinforcement. One gets the feeling that Ezekiel needed an enormous amount of persuasion and pressure from God to accept his role: first the role of having to speak for God at all, and now this additional model of what kind of speaker he was to be – a lone sentry, calling out warnings to a defiant people from the God they would not listen to. *The hand of the LORD* which had gripped him in his speechless rage all week (14) was again needed to propel him out of his stunned inertia and into action (22). God, it seems, would not take no for an answer.

So Ezekiel, under God's instruction, *got up and went out to the plain* (23). And there, to his amazement, stood the same vision of the glory of Yahweh as he had seen the previous week. This time he uses none of the circumlocution of his earlier description ('something like', 'appearance of the likeness of …'). He knows what he is looking at (lit. 'and behold, there, the glory of Yahweh, standing'), and recognizes it as the same as the vision by the *Kebar River*. Why this repeat vision? Perhaps to dispel any thought that the whole birthday experience had been a terrible nightmare or hallucination. It had not been some wild fantasy brought on by the thunder and lightning of a terrifying storm. Perhaps the change of location also reinforced the awareness that Yahweh was truly mobile in Babylon. Yahweh was no more confined to the rivers of Babylon than to the mountains of Israel. Perhaps it was simply because God knew the reluctance of this young would-be priest and would-rather-not-be prophet and needed to impress upon him once and for all the reality of his glory and his presence. This was the one who was coming in judgment; this was the one who was posting him as a sentry. If Ezekiel had spent the week in silent, angry resistance, it is now overcome as, for the second time, he finds himself flattened on his face by God's glory and then hoisted to his feet by God's Spirit.

c. The impossibility of the task (3:24–27)

What happens next plumbs the depths of paradox almost to the point of farce. Ezekiel is told that he is to be housebound, and that he will be unable to speak. Bound and gagged, hog-tied and tongue-tied – what possible way was that to be a prophet? How could God say to him, 'I am sending you to the Israelites,' and then, a week later, tell him,

'*Go, shut yourself inside your house*'? How could he tell him to raise the alarm like a good sentry and then make him dumb? The task in itself of being a sentry was hard enough just to contemplate. These unprecedented restrictions must have made it seem altogether impossible to accomplish. Whatever way we understand the exact implications of Ezekiel being tied *with ropes* and having his *tongue* stuck *to the roof of* his *mouth*, the effect would have been at least twofold. On the one hand, in the immediate future he would have to find other ways to deliver the message of warning than relying on fancy speeches in public places; his actual method of communicating through small-scale acted charades was almost forced upon him. On the other hand, whatever he would manage to say (27) would be exclusively from God with no risk of any admixture of ordinary conversational small-talk or distracting personal opinions on current affairs.

What exactly, then, is meant by this binding and dumbness? First of all, we may dismiss a whole category of older interpretation which treats Ezekiel as a candidate for psychoanalysis or pathological examination. Ezekiel has been confidently declared to have suffered from various conditions such as aphasia, catalepsy, epilepsy, paralysis and catatonic schizophrenia.[14] The trouble with this line of approach is twofold. First, such conditions are frequently difficult to diagnose accurately in living persons; to diagnose them posthumously from the very limited literary remains of someone who lived two and a half thousand years ago is mere speculation. And secondly, Ezekiel's 'handicaps' are clearly portrayed as imposed by God in connection with his prophetic ministry (and probably for a limited period at that), not as afflictions he suffered from previously or permanently. Ezekiel was a prophet, and ever since Saul, prophets had been known to behave strangely at times. Bizarre he may have been (though even that may have seemed less so to his contemporaries in ancient Babylon than to modern readers), but he was not sick. So we must look elsewhere for explanations.

In the case of his being bound by ropes, the questions are: was this literal or metaphorical, and was it forced or voluntary? In the case of his dumbness, the questions are: was this total or partial, and how long did it last? In the case of both, we have to ask: what was their significance in relation to Ezekiel's ministry and message?

i. You will be bound (3:25)
It is quite possible that this was meant, and happened, in a literal sense.[15] If Ezekiel's prophetic word to the exiles was going to meet with hardened faces, hearts and foreheads, they may well have put

---

[14] See Block (1), p. 154, for bibliographical details of advocates of such theories.
[15] Zimmerli, *Ezekiel 1*, p. 160; Allen 28, p. 61.

him under house arrest to keep him out of public view and to stop him disturbing the peace and lowering morale. Other prophets suffered worse. Jeremiah suffered restrictions, being banned from the temple complex.[16] He was put in stocks and beaten.[17] Later he was arrested and brutally imprisoned.[18] And indeed we know that there were voices in exile urging such treatment of 'mad' prophets of doom. Shemaiah's letter to Zephaniah in Jerusalem may well imply, 'Why don't you do to Jeremiah what we have already done over here to Ezekiel?'[19] So it is not out of the question that Ezekiel was, for a time at least, actually tied to some fixture in his own home.

Or it may be that the ropes or 'cords' are metaphorical, as they sometimes are in the Psalms for oppression and subjection to someone or something.[20] On this view, it may have been the hostility and revulsion of the people to Ezekiel and his message that forced him into confinement.[21] Or, still metaphorically, it may have been a voluntary, self-imposed confinement, at God's instruction, designed to reinforce the 'sign' element of his dumbness and the acted prophecies described in 4:1 – 5:4.[22] There is no way of being certain, and we may conclude, with Calvin, that 'one is free to choose'. More may be said, however, after we have discussed Ezekiel's dumbness.

ii. You will be silent (3:26)

Later we learn that Ezekiel's dumbness of some kind lasted for the first seven years of his ministry. When Ezekiel was told that Jerusalem was besieged, he was informed that his dumbness would come to an end when he received the news that the city had finally fallen. And this indeed is what happened, seven years and six months after his initial vision (24:25–27; 33:21–22).[23] However, there are

[16] Jer. 36:5, 19.   [17] Jer. 20:1–2.   [18] Jer. 37 – 38.   [19] Jer. 29:26–28.
[20] Pss. 2:3; 18:4–5; 116:3; 129:4.
[21] Calvin 18, p. 105; Greenberg, p. 102. Greenberg reckons that Ezekiel was told to withdraw to his house (a metaphorical state of being bound and dumb) because of the rejection of his message by the people. When Jerusalem finally fell, however, his prophecies of doom were vindicated and this 'gave him at once the credit he had lacked for seven years – gave him a "claim to be heard," "an opening of the mouth". And the restoration of the prophet to normal intercourse with his neighbours reflected and expressed the great turn of God toward his people, now that they were broken by the punishment; for concurrent with Ezekiel's release from "dumbness" is the second period of his prophecy – the predictions of Israel's restoration' (p. 121).
[22] Taylor, p. 73.
[23] Block (1), p. 157, suggests that the seven years of dumbness were imposed on Ezekiel in correspondence to the seven days that he had sat in angry resistance to God's call (cf. the reverse correspondence of days to years in 4:4–6). He thus became a sign of bearing punishment for being stubborn, which would be the fate of Israel. Since this is not explicit in the text, but only derived by comparison of the date notices, it seems somewhat unlikely that such significance was intended.

many accounts of oral messages given by Ezekiel during these years, beginning with his first recorded utterance in 5:5–17. How did he give these if he was totally dumb? So was he dumb or was he not?

The apparent contradiction leads some scholars to suggest that Ezekiel's dumbness was actually only during the siege of Jerusalem itself – that is, for the final eighteen months of the seven-year period, and that the account of it has been editorially transposed earlier in the book for some theological reason, with 3:27 being a rather lame attempt to overcome the contradiction thus introduced.[24] However, it seems much preferable to accept at face value the explanation that 3:27 offers. Ezekiel was commanded to be silent *except* when Yahweh gave him something explicit to say. Although this was not total dumbness in a physiological sense,[25] it was total dumbness in a social sense. In the ordinary course of everyday life Ezekiel would be saying nothing to anybody except when speaking directly in the name of Yahweh,[26] in which case it would be Yahweh, not Ezekiel, who was the real speaker anyway. Ezekiel, as Ezekiel, had nothing to say. 'From that moment onwards, Ezekiel was to be known as nothing but the mouthpiece of Yahweh. When he spoke, it was because God had something to say. When he was silent it was because God was silent.'[27]

In considering, finally, the combined significance of this double restriction on Ezekiel we need to take note of the way Ezekiel functioned as a *sign* to the people (12:6; 24:27). His actions, his circumstances and his afflictions all pointed to something – either about Yahweh, or about Israel. So, for example, in the case of his 'binding', it is noticeable that the same phrase is used when describing Ezekiel lying on his side to bear the sin of the houses of Israel and Judah (4:8). Again, it is not clear whether the ropes of 4:8 were meant literally or metaphorically, but it must be connected with what God had said to him in 3:25. Being 'housebound', whether enforced by others or as a voluntary self-imposed act, and whether in reality or symbolically, came to signify the way Israel would be confined in siege and be punished for their guilt.

[24] Eichrodt, pp. 75–77; Blenkinsopp, p. 32.

[25] The description in 3:26 need not describe total or permanent dumbness. The experience of the tongue sticking to the palate is used of the temporary silence that signifies respect for authority (Job 29:10), or a response to great suffering (Ps. 2:15). Being 'silent' may also be a chosen reaction to evil (Ps. 39:1–2; Is. 53:7).

[26] Note how the phrase of 3:27 is picked up in 5:5. Ezekiel's first utterance after his call vision, when God for the first time opened his mouth and loosened his tongue, begins with the direct summons to attention: *'This is what the Sovereign LORD says.'*

[27] Taylor, p. 74.

Similarly, Ezekiel's silence, other than when delivering the direct words of Yahweh (which until after the fall of Jerusalem would be almost entirely words of inescapable judgment), was profoundly significant. Just as all normal relations between himself and his family and neighbours would be broken off by such dumbness, so too was all 'conversation' between God and Israel. One of the key tasks of a prophet was to intercede on behalf of individuals or the people. But that will be no part of Ezekiel's task. Jeremiah had to be told to stop praying for his people, in the face of Israel's incorrigible, irredeemable rebellion;[28] Ezekiel will not even be allowed to start.

There is a suggestion that the phrase *you will be ... unable to rebuke them* (which seems odd, since that is exactly what Ezekiel seems to have done most of the time) would be better translated, 'you will be unable to act as a mediator on their behalf'. The expression (*'îš môkîaḥ*) literally means 'be a man of litigation', and most commonly implies one who rebukes or reproves. But it can be used of a neutral arbitrator or mediator in a dispute, or of one who stands up to defend the victim of injustice.[29] Ezekiel, in his dumbness, could not take such a role. He would join in no dispute with God on Israel's behalf. On the contrary, some of his most powerful theological and rhetorical efforts would be waged in precisely the opposite direction (e.g. ch. 18). Nor would he carry their complaints to God and come back with an answer. If that is what those who gathered in his house from time to time were looking for (8:1; 14:1–4; 20:1–3),[30] they were disappointed. 'His silence would represent the silence of God in response to their pleas for his intervention on their behalf against the victorious Babylonians.'[31]

How and where, then, shall we find our actor in the drama that is about to unfold in the scenes of 4:1 – 5:4? Not, like Amos, in the public arena addressing the crowds; not, like Isaiah, walking with easy familiarity among the leaders and nobles; not, like Jeremiah, in a place of worship or a potter's shop; not even, any longer it seems,

---

[28] Jer. 11:14.

[29] Job 9:33; 13:3, 15; 16:21; 1 Chr. 12:18; Amos 5:10. This reading was suggested by R. R. Wilson, 'An interpretation of Ezekiel's dumbness', *VT* 22 (1972), pp. 91–104, and accepted by Block (1), pp. 156–157. Cf. also NLT: 'and I will make your tongue stick to the roof of your mouth so you won't be able to pray for them'.

[30] These occasions indicate that Ezekiel was expected to speak aloud, even if in limited company. So his dumbness was obviously not pathological nor total. Block (1), p. 155, regards these glimpses of Ezekiel at home as evidence that he did not suffer violence or hostility. Apathy, not malevolence, was the serious problem at the heart of the people's hardness.

[31] Allen 28, p. 61.

by the riverside on the great open plain. We shall need to find an unexceptional hut in the tattered camp of exiles at Tel Abib.[32] It may help to look for a small group of anxious neighbours and fussing officials gathered around and just inside the door. Inside we shall find Ezekiel, alone except, perhaps, for his anxious wife. He sits there staring at us in dumb refusal to answer all questions; refusing also to come out and join the other exiles for his day's work. Possibly we may see in the dimness that he has even tied himself to one of the poles of his hut, or has he been tied by some frightened neighbour? For already, perhaps, he has been racked with terrible tremors and shaking (cf. 12:18), and sometimes he is groaning as though bereaved (cf. 21:6). And he has been like this for a whole week, apart from his last inexplicable trip to some forsaken spot on the plain – just sitting there speechless and burning with some inner rage.

Suddenly he moves to clear some space in the middle of the crowded room. If he can't speak, he can at least mime the appalling message forming in his heart (cf. 3:10). The drama is about to begin. The audience is small, but in a refugee encampment the whole community will know before nightfall what happened at Ezekiel's house that day – and the next day, and every day for the next year or so ...

2. The drama (4:1 – 5:4)

Charades as a party game can be great fun, with wild and exaggerated gestures and facial expressions, as a dumb actor attempts to get an audience to guess what he or she is depicting without words. I imagine that Ezekiel set about his task of portraying to the audience in his house the message God was giving him with similar emphatic zeal and gesticulation, only this was no party and certainly no fun at all. There may of course have been mockery along with the curiosity among the bystanders, but for Ezekiel every scene in his drama was deadly serious, and probably accompanied by deep anguish and tears.

As mentioned above, it was often a part of the prophetic repertoire to accompany their verbal messages with 'sign-acts' – that

[32] This may exaggerate slightly. We know virtually nothing about the living conditions of the first batch of exiles. Initially they were probably dumped in conditions that befitted their status as prisoners and virtual hostages. We don't know how soon they may have taken the advice of Jeremiah's letter to 'Build houses and settle down' (Jer. 29:5) – especially in the early years when expectations of an early return were high. Ezekiel's home had walls that could be dug through by hand (12: 5, 7), which suggests fairly lowly quarters.

ıs, actions or demonstrations which not only acted as a visual reinforcement to the message, but even in some way prefigured and guaranteed the event which the prophecy spoke of.[33] The action *signified* the message, while the message would sometimes explain and interpret the sign. Such sign-acts in the ministries of previous prophets, however, were generally short, vivid actions that only took a few moments to make their point.[34] Ezekiel produced a performance in which several central actions were repeated daily for over a year, interspersed, and then brought to a shattering climax, by shorter, more specific additional actions. Not only did this mean that by the end of the year almost everybody who cared to in the whole community could have come and witnessed the key scene simply by visiting Ezekiel's house (which must have become a virtual tourist attraction, to the despair of his wife, no doubt), but also the significance of the whole show must have become utterly clear even before Ezekiel removed all doubt when his mouth was finally opened and the desperate, damning message flooded forth (5:5–17). Although explanations are given during the actions, it is possible, in the light of what we have been told about Ezekiel's dumbness, that these are Ezekiel's own recollections of the instructions he was getting from God in his own head at the time, and of his own inner reactions to some of them. Probably he was silent throughout, relying on persistently repeated mime and gesture to get the message across, until at the end the full force of the meaning could be released in one terrible utterance.

There are clearly three major acts in this drama, each with two or three internal scenes. The three acts are identified by the threefold initial command to *take* some object: *take a clay tablet* (4:1); *Take wheat and barley* etc. (4:9); *take a sharp sword* (5:1). And the three acts relate, respectively, to the siege of Jerusalem (4:1–8), the suffering of the people in Jerusalem and in exile (4:9–17), and the final destruction of the city and the fate of its population (5:1–4).

a. Act 1: A city under siege (4:1–8)

Scene 1: Jerusalem on a brick (4:1–3)

Ezekiel gets up and finds a large Babylonian clay brick or tile lying somewhere nearby, still soft and waiting to be fired. This would not be a small brick of the western variety, but a sizeable block or rectangular slab. With a stick or fingernail he laboriously sketches out from memory a rough map of Jerusalem – so beloved and so

---

[33] E.g. 1 Kgs. 11:29–31; 22:11; 2 Kgs. 13:14–19; Jer. 32; 35; etc.

[34] Though some of them were protracted over much longer; e.g. Is. 20; Jer. 13:1–11.

familiar.[35] As the onlookers recognize what he is drawing, perhaps they think Ezekiel is nostalgically longing for home. That mood quickly dispels as they watch Ezekiel's busy hands modelling the clay or sand all around the brick into the unmistakable machinery of siege warfare – confining walls, ramps, battering-rams and enemy camps. Jerusalem besieged! That message in itself would be no great shock, though obviously serious. Jerusalem had been besieged before; it was to be expected by any who could read the times that Nebuchadnezzar might well do so again. That could mean great hardship for friends and relatives back home, but Yahweh would soon come to the rescue as he had before and scatter those enemy camps.[36] Perhaps that is what the onlookers expected Ezekiel to portray next.

So where, then, is Yahweh in Ezekiel's model? The prophet himself plays that role. He lifts the heavy *iron pan* (the broad, flat bread-making griddle), from his wife's kitchen and wields it high. Cheers perhaps greet the arrival of Yahweh to beat down his enemies. But no, Ezekiel crouches beside the city and places the iron griddle between his face and his model, with gestures and grimaces that clearly speak of hostility and attack. Slowly the shock sinks in. Yahweh is not inside the city defending it; Yahweh is outside the city attacking it! The little clay models around the city shrink into pathetic insignificance; it is Yahweh himself who is the real enemy.

Protests surround the silent actor at the monstrous charade and its unthinkable message, just as they had done when Jeremiah threatened the destruction of the city and temple a few years earlier.[37] Had not Yahweh guaranteed to protect his own city? Had he not placed his own eternal name in the temple itself? Ezekiel gestures even more firmly with the iron griddle, perhaps placing it not only between himself and his model city, but holding it defiantly between his own face and those of the protesters. It was made of solid iron, impenetrable, implacable. Yahweh's anger could no longer be averted by protests or pleas. The so-called holy city would feel the iron judgment of the holy God.

Scene 2: Bearing the sin of Israel (4:4–8)
And then Ezekiel just lay down, motionless, in stark contrast to the feverish activity and gesticulation of the preceding minutes. But not out of exhaustion. Everyone could see that this was still part of the

---

[35] Clay tablets with city maps (even one of Nippur itself) and other plans scratched on them have been found in Mesopotamian archaeology. See Block (1), p. 171.

[36] Memories of the decimation of Sennacherib's besieging army would have been particularly potent in giving people hope (2 Kgs. 19; Is. 36 – 37).

[37] Jer. 7:1–15; 26:1–9.

dramatic sign. Perhaps he wrapped some of the rope around himself to portray his immobility even more starkly (v. 8; unless the verse should be taken metaphorically). Perhaps he clutched to himself some symbolic token that identified himself as the priest he nearly was, for in this prone state he was to *bear the sin of the house of Israel* – a priestly action. So at this point, with the change of scene, there is also a change in Ezekiel's symbolic identity. In the first scene the prophet had represented Yahweh; in the second he represents Israel. It was, of course, a fundamental part of the function of priests in Israel to do both. As mediators they represented Yahweh to the people and the people to Yahweh.

Ezekiel was told to *put the sin of the house of Israel* upon his side as he lay there, and thus *to bear their sin.* The vocabulary recalls the Day of Atonement when the high priest 'placed' all the sins of the people on the head of the scapegoat, which then 'carried' them off into the wilderness.[38] However, Ezekiel does not carry Israel's sin off somewhere. He is simply to lie there bearing its weight, suffering under it. His suffering is not expiatory or vicarious – that is, he will not suffer instead of or on behalf of the rest of the people, but rather it is a symbolic or representative identification with their sin.[39]

So he just lay there. Perhaps he lay motionless until the visitors finally straggled off to their own homes in animated discussion before he finally got up, the day's prophecy in mime concluded.[40] But then the next day, there he was again, in exactly the same posture and position. And the next day. Day after day for more than a whole year: 390 days to be exact. Ezekiel himself knew the number from the start; the bystanders must have started counting somewhat later.

The explanation that it was *the same number of days as the years of their sin* would be understandable enough to people accustomed to such symbolic transference of days and years. The reverse

[38] Lev. 16:20–22.

[39] *Contra* Zimmerli, *Ezekiel 1*, pp. 164–165, Ezekiel's suffering cannot have been 'an event of substitutionary sin-bearing', since his suffering did not prevent the people of Jerusalem from suffering the punishment of their own sin. Nevertheless, Zimmerli is right to see the way the symbolic solidarity of Ezekiel in suffering the sin of Israel connects to the genuinely vicarious language of Is. 53 (esp. v. 11). 'Ezekiel, by lying bound, became a revealer of guilt, an accuser … He brings together in his symbolic bondage the guilt of Israel as a burden in his own life. We can scarcely deny that ideas are set in motion here which were to be more fully worked out in Is 53' (p. 165). Even the prophet's dumbness is echoed in Is. 53:7.

[40] It is virtually certain that Ezekiel spent only a certain period of each day lying in this way on his side next to his model of the siege of Jerusalem. Apart from the fact that, had he lain on one side day and night for a year he would have become deformed or paralysed, if he had survived at all, the instructions of 4:9–17 show that he had other things to do each day as well.

equivalence explained the forty years of the wilderness wandering in Numbers 14:33–35. And the 390 years is a very close approximation to the length of time between the building and dedication of the temple by Solomon in the early tenth century to its final destruction in 587.[41] On this understanding, Ezekiel's 390 days represent the years of the sinful rebellion of the whole nation of Israel, from as early as the reign of Solomon.

Complications arise, however, with the next paragraph. At some stage, Ezekiel was told to lie down on his other side, his *right side*, to do so for *forty days*, and thereby to *bear the sin of the house of Judah*. He was to do this with renewed gestures of Yahweh's hostility towards Jerusalem (7). Three questions need to be answered.

First, is a distinction between the house of Israel and the house of Judah in political terms intended here? At first sight this would seem obvious. And many have taken it that way, understanding the former to mean the northern kingdom of Israel and the latter to mean the southern kingdom of Judah. The difficulty is then: to what do the 390 years of Israel refer? The northern kingdom of Israel came into existence only after the reign of Solomon around 930 or 920 BC in a *coup d'état* led by Jeroboam.[42] It was finally destroyed when Samaria fell to the Assyrians in 722/721 BC. So 'Israel', as the name of the separate northern kingdom, lasted only about 200 years. However, it is only the use of the term 'Judah' in 4:6 that makes us think, retrospectively, that 'house of Israel' in 4:4–5 refers exclusively to the separate northern kingdom. Up to that point in the preceding chapters of the book (e.g. 2:3; 3:4, 7, 17), the expression 'house of Israel' clearly means the whole covenant people, without reference to the historical division into two political states. In fact, since Ezekiel was explicitly told to go and speak to the 'house of Israel', the expression obviously means, in those contexts, his fellow exiles from the kingdom of Judah, not the exiles of the northern kingdom who had been scattered by Assyria more than a century earlier. Likewise, in 4:13, 'people of Israel' obviously refers to the Judean exiles in their deprivation. It seems very probable, therefore, that the political division of the kingdoms is not in view in these verses, and that 'house of Israel' and 'house of Judah' are being used virtually synonymously (though see below for a nuance of difference).

Secondly, what did these further forty days/years symbolize? To answer this we need to be aware of the range of meaning of the word

---

[41] This seems the most likely explanation of the period intended, though others have been offered, including the suggestion of counting *forwards* from 587 to a date in the second century. Cf. Block (1), pp. 177–178.

[42] 1 Kgs. 12.

translated *sin*. In Hebrew, '*āwôn*, can mean: (a) actual sin or iniquity committed; (b) the guilt of that sin; and also (c) the punishment meted out for it. Probably, therefore, Ezekiel's forty days, equivalent to forty years, speak of the accepted round number figure for a whole generation (cf. the forty-year generation in the wilderness), namely, the generation that would suffer the exile as *punishment* for the accumulated sin of Israel. 'Thus the two phases of Ezekiel's sign-act, lying on his left and right sides, respectively, depict successive events: the long period of Israel's apostasy, and the subsequent experience of the wrath of God.'[43] We might add that this makes the subtle use of Israel and Judah more explicable also. The 390 days represent the sin of the whole covenant people of Israel without political distinctions. But the generation that went into exile, like the forty years in the wilderness, was indeed predominantly the people of Judah.[44] And Ezekiel, as one of those Judean exiles, certainly bore that punishment with them.

Thirdly, were the two periods of lying on one side and then on the other consecutive or concurrent? That is, did he turn over on day 391 and then lie on his right side until day 430 (i.e. consecutive)? Or did he spend a period lying first on one side and then on the other during the final forty days out of a total of 390 (i.e. concurrent)? The most natural sense would suggest that they were consecutive. However, the difficulty is that the next major prophetic vision of Ezekiel began fourteen lunar months later according to the precise date given in 8:1. This would be less than 430 days. So some scholars suggest that the final forty-day period was concurrent (the *total* figure is given as 390 in 4:9, though this may mean that the siege food was to be eaten only during the days he lay on his left side).[45] Others prefer to preserve the two actions as consecutive, and assume that the later vision (chs. 8ff.) overlapped with the final days of the daily siege ritual.[46] It is impossible to be dogmatic, but my own view

---

[43] Block (1), p. 180.

[44] Allen 28, p. 68. It is true, of course, that the northern kingdom of Israel also suffered exile – though it seems to have been a random scattering of the Israelite population throughout the Assyrian empire, with compensating importation of other ethnic groups into the land of Israel, rather than the collective transfer of the Judean exiles to the heartlands of Babylon. However, it still seems most likely that Ezekiel's forty days were intended to symbolize the whole generation of Judean exiles that were to suffer the explicit punishment of Yahweh.

[45] Taylor, p. 78; Allen 28, p. 67. According to Allen, this view 'allows for fourteen months to elapse … Accordingly, there is time for this period of 390 days – and … also a month's vacation before the prophet had to function again!' It would also allow, in view of the privations of 4:9–10, for a few weeks of his wife's much missed home cooking.

[46] Block (1), p. 278.

is that the concurrent theory is more likely, since it would seem rather odd and confusing to begin another whole major vision before the year-long acted drama had reached its conclusion.

So, putting all the preceding discussion together, it seems that Ezekiel lay on his left side for a period of 390 days that symbolized almost four centuries of all Israel's national history since Solomon, characterized as a history of unremitting *sin*. This same message will be portrayed in a different form through the historical allegories and schematic survey of chapters 16, 20 and 23. Then, during the final forty days, he also lay on his right side, finding some way of symbolizing that in that posture he represented Israel bearing its punishment in the form of the present experience of the exile of Judah – an exile that would last for the symbolic forty years of a whole generation.

For over a year, then, Ezekiel acted out his prostrate mime until its message was unmistakable, even if it was still unacceptable. Jerusalem, the clay model at the centre of his little domestic stage, would undergo a long and painful siege. This would be the culmination of centuries of sinful rebellion now being punished by Yahweh. It was indeed Yahweh whom the people were facing as the real enemy, no longer as defender and guarantor of their national security or covenantal privilege. And for those already in exile, and others who would join them soon, they would perish like the generation of the wilderness, a long, long way, in miles and in years, from the promised land.

b. Act 2: Bread of affliction (4:9–17)

The next act in the drama was not a mere mime, but a whole action, again performed daily, designed to depict the deprivation that the besieged inhabitants of Jerusalem would suffer. It also slides over into portraying the shame and suffering of the exiles as well.

Scene 1: Siege rations in Jerusalem (4:9–11)
Somehow Ezekiel gets hold of some supplies of grain and vegetables and mixes them in a storage jar. The process will have been repeated at various points during the year. He selects four types of cereal (wheat, barley, millet and spelt) and two types of vegetable (lentils and beans), in a mixture that would provide a reasonable balance of limited basic nutrition. Then come the shock instructions. He is to take just enough of this mixture to bake a rough loaf of bread weighing approximately eight ounces, or 230 grams. That is a fairly small loaf, even if it was possibly supplemented by an additional barley-cake (12). And that was to be his daily food for a year! And along with that he was allowed about one and a third pints,

or 0.6 litre, of water per day. This would be enough to keep a fit thirty-year old alive, but at virtual starvation level – exactly what the besieged inhabitants of Jerusalem would soon be enduring. It was just as well that he would be spending much of each day lying down, since there would be little energy to spare from such a lean diet. Apart from his own hunger and suffering, what anxiety and despair must his loving wife have gone through as, day after day, Ezekiel refused any other food from her hand and resolutely stuck to his fast, getting more and more gaunt and emaciated as the weeks went by?

Some think that this meagre meal was simply a symbolic act in the course of each day's prone 'besieging', and that Ezekiel would have had other meals as normal. However, it seems much more likely that he was indeed subjected to this emphatic entering into the suffering of his people. As other prophets would testify, personal suffering as part of the delivery of God's word was not unusual. Isaiah endured the shame of wandering around Jerusalem virtually naked to illustrate a point;[47] Jeremiah suffered exclusion from all social intercourse;[48] Hosea went through agonies of marital betrayal.[49] As Ezekiel's neighbours observed his daily ritual of pathetic precision, as they witnessed the agonizingly brief moment of eating and drinking, and as they then watched him grow daily weaker, thinner and possibly ridden with the ailments of malnutrition, they were being confronted with the most powerful prophetic word imaginable of what lay ahead for those left behind in Jerusalem. They could not have remained unmoved by it – whether moved to acceptance and repentance, or to argumentative disbelief. Only years later would the reports reach the exiles of the siege and suffering of Jerusalem when it happened and of the circumstances so well described in 4:16–17. And only then would the truth of Ezekiel's costly self-sacrificial prophecy be vindicated.

Scene 2: Defiled food among the nations (4:12–17)
Verse 12 literally reads: 'And a barley cake, you shall eat it, and on bits of human excrement you shall bake it, as they watch you.' It seems most likely that this is a separate sign-act, rather than a further description of the preceding verses (though NIV takes it in the latter way, '*Eat the food as you would a barley cake*'). The significance here is not the small amount of food but the disgustingly unclean way it was to be cooked. Barley cakes, apparently, could be baked on open coals, not even in a pan. So, if baked in that way, the food would be in direct contact with the smouldering excrement. The

[47] Is. 20.   [48] Jer. 16:1–9.   [49] Hos. 1 – 3.

symbolism is made clear in verse 13. Israel would have to eat food in the unclean lands of their exile. The extreme desecration of such an act makes Ezekiel, the would-be priest and child of a priestly family, recoil in horror (14).[50] His reaction has an intensity even greater than Peter's (who was no priest but simply a devout Jew), when he was presented in a vision with the command to eat food hitherto considered unclean.[51] So God relented and allowed Ezekiel to use dried cattle dung instead – a common form of domestic fuel (as it is still today in many parts of the world), which presumably did not inflict ritual uncleanness. But one can imagine that, if Ezekiel still remained dumb throughout, he was able through vivid mime and gesture to communicate that his little bits of dried cow manure were only substitutes for something which should have come from a very different and much more offensive source.

So Ezekiel's little daily ritual of half a loaf and a dung-baked barley cake, along with the physical toll on his own frame, spoke powerfully of two things: on the one hand, the siege rations that would soon be a matter of *anxiety* and *despair* among the inhabitants of Jerusalem as with horror they watched themselves wasting away during the siege (4:16–17); and on the other hand, the long misery of eating food in an unclean land that would be the lot of the exiles for many years to come.

c. Act 3: Final conflagration (5:1–4)

Fourteen months had passed. The little scratched map of Jerusalem must have hardened solid by now, though the surrounding siege models may have begun to crumble in the dust. Ezekiel must have been dragging his emaciated body through its daily chores and long prostration with ever decreasing strength. The end of his long siege is in sight and God plants in his mind one final climactic act that will bring this astonishing drama to an unforgettable finale. As with his visionary eating of the scroll, the word of an earlier prophet provides imagery that Ezekiel will translate into real life – not this time into a vision. Isaiah had likened the Assyrian king to a razor with which God would shave his people: 'In that day the Lord will use a razor hired from beyond the River – the king of Assyria – to shave your head and the hair of your legs, and to take off your beards also.'[52] Change Assyria to Babylon, substitute a sword for the razor, and Ezekiel had his final mime.

---

[50] On the particular forms of ritual defilement that Ezekiel claims never to have committed, see Lev. 22:8; Deut. 14:21; Lev. 7:17–18; 17:15; 19:6–8.
[51] Acts 10:9–15.   [52] Is. 7:20.

Scene 1: Shaved and shamed (5:1)

Where Ezekiel got a sharp sword from in a community of exiles is a mystery. Did he persuade a Babylonian soldier to lend him one – knowing he could be no threat in his starved condition? Or did he take an ordinary large cooking knife, and with a few unmistakable gestures turn it into a sword for the sake of his final mime? At any rate, what was held or gestured as a sword was quickly wielded as a barber's razor, and Ezekiel began to shave himself.

Now shaving a thick beard even with a modern double- or triple-bladed safety razor and a well-lit mirror takes some time. To shave head and beard, after a year's probably untrimmed growth, with a large, awkward sword or knife would be a painfully long-drawn-out ordeal. There would be time enough, certainly, for word to spread rapidly round the neighbourhood that Ezekiel was doing something different today, and for a considerable crowd to gather and wince as they witnessed the bizarre and painful process. Even the sharpest sword cannot match a razor, and Ezekiel must have gone through agonies as he hacked at himself, doubtless drawing blood in various difficult places around his head and ears. It must have been a sickeningly messy operation altogether.

But again, the physical pain must have been minimal compared to the psychological and emotional stress of the protracted action. For what did such shaving indicate? First of all, such total shaving was prohibited to priests,[53] so in Ezekiel's case it was a kind of self-defilement or defrocking. He was symbolically denigrating his own priesthood. Secondly, shaving of the hair and beard was often associated with extreme mourning, as in bereavement or military defeat.[54] So Ezekiel is adding yet another feature to his portfolio of signs of suffering. And thirdly, forced shaving was sometimes inflicted as a form of extreme humiliation.[55] So Ezekiel is inflicting upon himself terrible public disgrace and shame – as if his cup of social rejection were not full enough already.

But the symbolism of the sword adds another element that would eventually have become clear to the shocked onlookers. For this sword must be none other than the sword of Yahweh's anger. Ezekiel has changed identity again. No longer representing Yahweh alone besieging Jerusalem, no longer representing the Israelites alone – both the besieged and the exiled with their paltry and polluted diets, he now acts out both parts in a brilliant one-man double act. For the hand that wields the sword is the hand of Yahweh, but the

---

[53] Lev. 21:5. Even for ordinary Israelites, it was prohibited in relation to pagan rites (Deut. 14:1).
[54] Deut. 21:12; Is. 15:2; Jer. 16:6; Amos 8:10; Mic. 1:16; Ezek. 7:18.
[55] 2 Sam. 10:4–5.

83

body being shaved is the house of Israel. The hacked body of Ezekiel is Israel – Israel being shorn of its priestly role among the nations, Israel being shattered in the grief of national defeat, Israel being shamed before those nations among whom she should have shone (as the message of 5:5–17 makes clear). As Ezekiel's horrified neighbours stared at the apparition before them – this gaunt spectre of a starving man, shaved bald with his hair in piles at his feet, tears of pain stinging his eyes and blood trickling from gashes in his taut malnourished skin – they were looking into the mirror of their own future as a people.

But Ezekiel was not finished yet.

Scene 2: Fire, sword and wind (5:2)
Raiding his wife's kitchen yet again, Ezekiel sets up a pair of scales, and with that obsessive, characteristic precision of his, carefully divides his hair into three equal bundles – another time-consuming little process that must have added to the suspense and gained more spectators. Even that action had its symbolism, since being weighed and divided could also function as terms of divine judgment.[56] Next, he shovels up some burning fragments from the fire he had earlier cooked his daily ration on, and pours them right into the middle of his map of Jerusalem on the tile. Then he picks up the first of his bundles of hair and with terrible anguish tosses it on to the fire. Could anything have spoken more harshly of the fate of the people of Jerusalem in its final conflagration than that pile of hair flaming up in instant extinction?

Back to the second pile of hair, as the onlookers stare in transfixed horror. This one he scatters all around the floor surrounding the smouldering heap that his Jerusalem tile has become, and then, picking up his sword and summoning the last dregs of his strength, he whirls wildly around the room, scattering the audience and slashing violently at the hair on the floor – chopping, stabbing, cutting, swiping and striking, until he can see it no more for the tears and sweat in his eyes. Those who escape the burning of the city[57] will flee to the country, only to be cut down by the swords of the enemy.

Nearing exhaustion, he returns for the last pile of hair. Surely at least a third of the people will be saved, think the spectators, to whom the symbolism of the last two acts must have become excruciatingly clear. But with a couple of steps Ezekiel stumbles to

[56] Dan. 5:26–28.
[57] This did not necessarily mean that people would be burned to death in the destruction of Jerusalem. 'Fire' is both literal, in the sense that the city and the temple were indeed burnt, and also metaphorical of the famine and disease that would carry off many of the inhabitants (5:12).

the open door, the crowd parting before him, and, with one last effort and cry, hurls the hair upwards into the evening breeze which carries it off scattering in all directions, just as the survivors of the conflagration will be scattered to the nations.

Scene 3: The remnants (5:3–4)

The effort has brought Ezekiel close to collapse, but he returns to kneel by the scales, and there he begins laboriously to collect the few strands of hair that his weighing and dividing had missed. Not a great bundle; little more than a handful. But these remnants he tenderly clasps and slowly wraps up in the fold of his long robe – the little pouch at the waist by the rope where you could keep some precious belongings.[58] And then, as if on second thoughts, even a few of these salvaged hairs are pulled out again and in a final gesture of despair, thrown on the fire. Not even all those who would be saved among the remnant of the people would be truly saved. Some would continue their rebellion even in exile, and some would even perish literally in flames.[59]

The long-running drama was at last finished, the last scene played out. But there was no applause. Silence, more probably, greeted the final curtain – silence but for the crackling of the fire, the gasps and sobs of Ezekiel, and the acrid smell of burning hair. But it was a silence that did not last long. The acting was over, but the prophecy was not, for by some gesture Ezekiel signalled that he was about to speak – not, we may imagine, with the thunderous voice of Amos, but with the weak and parched struggle of a voice unused for over a year. His mouth opened, his tongue was loosened, and his first words were those given to him a week after his first vision (3:27): *This is what the Sovereign LORD says.*

3. The message (5:5–17)

This section very obviously interprets and explains the preceding record of Ezekiel's actions during the year, leaving their meaning in no doubt at all. Reading it through as a whole presents the stark picture of the final destruction of Jerusalem, with accompanying horrors of famine-induced cannibalism, disease and slaughter, all of which are on the one hand the inescapable consequences of siege warfare in the ancient world and on the other hand the effect of the implacable punishment of Yahweh on his incorrigible people. From a literary point of view, it is uneven and involves several restarts and repetitions. For this reason some doubt whether it constitutes a

[58] Cf. 1 Sam. 25:29.   [59] E.g. Jer. 29:20–23.

single utterance given all at one time, namely at the ending of the
acted siege. It may have been composed from recollections of the
prophecies given as commentary on the acts themselves, especially
that mentioned in 4:7,[60] unless one takes the view (as suggested
above) that Ezekiel was silent throughout the whole sequence, so
that even his 'prophesying' against Jerusalem in 4:7 was mimed. Or
it may be that Ezekiel's original speech on the final day of his siege
mime has been expanded by other oracles from later in his career.[61]
Whatever the detailed explanation of its rough structure, we may
recognize three strong central threads running through it: the
centrality of Jerusalem in the midst of the nations; the
correspondingly worse nature of the sin of Jerusalem in comparison
with the nations; and the public punishment of Jerusalem as a
warning to the nations.

a. Jerusalem: the centre of the nations (5:5)

The words *'This is Jerusalem'* hardly needed to be said, unless some
spectators of the year-long ritual siege had never recognized
Ezekiel's sketch map on the brick, or fondly imagined that perhaps
the whole depiction of catastrophe and destruction applied to
Babylon (and there were prophetic grounds for such hope). If
Ezekiel was actually pointing to all that was left of his model – now
a smouldering heap of manure and ashes, *'This* is Jerusalem' – then
it was an intensely bitter statement. In the context of the following
speech of indictment and the verdict handed down, it sounds like the
opening words of a court scene, in which the criminal is identified.
But Jerusalem was no ordinary defendant at the bar of God's
justice.

God identifies the city as *Jerusalem, which I have set in the centre
of the nations, with countries all around her.*[62] This description might
be considered appropriate in purely geographical terms. Jerusalem,
and the land in which it was situated, did indeed stand at the hub
of the ancient world of empires, if one considers Mesopotamia to the
east, Egypt to the west, the Anatolian empires to the north, and the

---

[60] Greenberg, p. 127, Block (1), p. 196.

[61] Zimmerli, *Ezekiel 1*, p. 174, proposes that Ezekiel's original speech consisted of
vv. 5–6a, 8–9, 14–15. Block (1), p. 196ff., divides the material into: (a) the indictment
of Jerusalem (vv. 5–6); (b) two announcements of judgment on Jerusalem, first vv.
7–10, and second vv. 11–17.

[62] The combination of 'nations and countries', or 'peoples and lands' is a favourite
expression of Ezekiel. Most often it refers to the places where God scattered Israel
in judgment (6:8; 11:16; 12:15; 20:23). Later the direction would be reversed as God
planned to gather his people back from the nations and countries of their exile (11:17;
20:34; 36:24).

Ethiopian and Arabian cultures to the south.[63] However, many nations and cultures have considered themselves to be the 'centre of the earth', including the Roman empire and the Chinese 'Middle Kingdom'. Even the commonest map of the world, Mercator's projection, depicts the great European colonial powers at the centre, and distorts latitudes nearer to, and south of, the Equator to achieve that effect. North American world maps tend to put the American continents in the middle with Europe to the east and Asia to the west. So while the claim may have been justified in the limited context of Israel's own world, it certainly has no universal geographical or cultural finality.

God's point, however, went somewhat deeper than cartography. It was certainly true that Jerusalem as the capital city of his people Israel (originally, and then of the kingdom of Judah, but that distinction is not significant here), was at the centre of the geography and history of the surrounding nations, and that its story was intertwined with theirs. It was also true that what happened in Jerusalem was visible and accessible to the ears and eyes of the other nations, for good or ill. But when we draw on the wider theology of the Old Testament tradition of Yahweh's dealings with the nations of humanity as a whole and the role of Israel within that tradition, we can see that the point of Israel's centrality is not merely geographical but theological and, in a sense, missiological.[64] Jerusalem, and the people it represents, were at the centre of *Yahweh's purposes* for the nations of the world – including the nations in immediate proximity historically and geographically, of course, but in a much wider sense also.

It was God's covenant promise to Abraham that all nations on earth would be blessed through his descendants.[65] The universality of that promise is transferred on to the Davidic dynasty as one of several connections between Abraham and David.[66] Israel was to be Yahweh's priestly people in the midst of the nations, representing him to them and being the agent of their coming to him.[67] Or, in another image, Israel would be a 'light to the nations',[68] which included a moral element derived from the ethical righteousness of

[63] It is often pointed out that, although the term is not used in this verse, it is similar in meaning to the phrase used to describe Israel in 38:12, 'the navel of the earth' (NIV 'the centre of the land').

[64] See Introduction, pp. 35–38, for further discussion of the missiological significance of the nations in the Old Testament and in Ezekiel in particular.

[65] Gen. 12:3, and repeated six times in Genesis.

[66] Ps. 72:17; cf. Is. 55:3–5.

[67] Exod. 19:4–6; cf. Is. 61:6; 66:19–21.

[68] Is. 42:6; 49:6. The phrase is spoken of the ministry of the servant of Yahweh, but elsewhere the servant's own identity is related to that of Israel.

Israel's laws and behaviour.[69] Indeed, if only Israel would live according to the social system given them in Yahweh's law, then they would become the object of curious admiration from the nations for their wisdom and understanding.[70]

For Jerusalem or Israel to be *in the centre of the nations*, then, meant much more than a territorial grid-reference. It was a shorthand way of expressing all the universality of God's purposes among the nations that was bound up in the particularity of Israel's election. That is, if Israel were the hub at the centre of the wheel, it was for the sake of the spokes and the rim that they were there at all. For we may note that 5:5 is not in any case simply a statement of natural fact. Jerusalem does not just happen to be at the centre as an accident of geography. No, it is in that position because of the divine will and action: *Jerusalem, which I have set in the centre* ... And if that implied a degree of exaltation as well, as it certainly does elsewhere,[71] then the ultimate purpose of that was to bring glory and honour to Yahweh himself.[72] So the centrality of Jerusalem is a statement about Israel's election.[73] What follows shows that such a privilege was matched by enormous responsibility – a responsibility in which Israel had so horrendously failed as to put even their election in serious doubt.

b. Jerusalem: worse than the nations (5:6–7)

The tragedy of Israel was that in their rebellion and sin they did not sink merely to the level of the rest of the nations who lived without the light of God's law and the history of God's redemption. They sank much lower and became far worse. Because of their election and the immense gifts of Yahweh's redemption and grace, Israel should have known and behaved better. But their privilege exposed them to even greater condemnation, as Amos had said 150 years earlier.[74]

The sin described in verses 6–7 focuses particularly on the rebellious nature of Israel, as already emphasized in chapter 2, expressed through a constant refusal to shape their social life according to the covenant *laws and decrees* of Yahweh. This phrase is used three times for emphasis (6a, 6b, 7a). It is a shorthand way of referring to the whole breadth of the Torah, and is a favourite phrase in Deuteronomy (which Ezekiel was familiar with). Later, in chapter 22, Ezekiel will provide a detailed analysis of exactly how

[69] Note how the strongly ethical dimension of light in Is. 58 flows into the attraction of the light to the nations in Is. 60:1–3.
[70] Deut. 4:6–8.   [71] E.g. Deut. 26:19; Pss. 48:2; 50:2; Jer. 4:19; Lam. 1:1.
[72] Jer. 13:11.   [73] Ps. 132:13.   [74] Amos 3:2.

the people of Jerusalem had trampled on the explicit laws of Yahweh, in social, economic, judicial, religious and personal ways. From his priestly training he knew the Torah thoroughly and could build instant case studies in righteousness and wickedness from it, as he does in chapter 18. For the moment he is content simply to speak in generalities – Israel has not 'performed the judgments (*mišpāṭîm)*' of Yahweh. For this gives him the basis for a sharp play on the word itself.

Many times in the Torah Israel was warned not to follow the ways of the nations. So one might have expected Ezekiel to accuse them of doing just that – 'you have done as the nations do'. But that would be too flattering. With crushing irony he says (lit.), 'and the laws/customs (*mišpāṭîm)* of the nations you have *not* done!' You have not lived even by the standards of justice and behaviour that are to be found among other peoples, or, with NIV, *You have not even conformed to the standards of the nations around you.*

Israel could never be just like the nations, theologically and morally speaking. Because of their election to be the vehicle of God's ultimate purpose of blessing the nations, because of their historical experience of Yahweh's redemption and their unique knowledge of Yahweh as God,[75] because of their calling to be distinct (holy) in every area of life,[76] Israel ought to have been *better*, as an example or model to be seen by the nations.[77] But for the very same reasons (namely, all those privileges and responsibilities), Israel's failure and sin were far more serious than that of the rest of the nations who had had none of them. They became *worse.* Israel's uniqueness in election exacerbated their uniqueness in disobedience. Thus, something which the psalmist celebrates as a mark of the distinction between Israel and the nations actually makes Israel's sin all the worse:

He [Yahweh] has revealed his word to Jacob,
His laws and decrees[78] to Israel
He has done this for no other nation;
They do not know his laws (*mišpāṭîm).*[79]

The nations did not know *Yahweh's* laws, but they did have their own *mišpāṭîm* – standards and codes of behaviour. Israel had sunk even below that level. In spite of the incredible privilege of their election and the priceless gift of God's law, Israel, as personified here by Jerusalem, 'has trampled underfoot its election by Yahweh and changed its honor into disgrace ... Jerusalem's sin is not something vague, but an affront to the clear,

[75] Deut. 4:32–35.   [76] Lev. 18:1–5.   [77] Deut. 4:6–8.
[78] The same pair of words as in Ezek. 5:6–7.   [79] Ps. 147:19–20.

revealed law of God.'[80] The city on a hill that stood 'at the centre' has become a sink of iniquity worse than its despised pagan neighbours. 'Instead of being a light to the world, by failing to live in the light of God's revelation, his chosen city had become the world's darkest blot.'[81]

Before Christian readers of Ezekiel's words yield to the temptation of condemning Old Testament Israel and indulging illusions of our own superiority, we need to remind ourselves that the New Testament also makes the point that sin among God's people is much worse in his sight than among those who have not had the benefit of his revelation and salvation.[82] In fact, the even greater privilege that belongs to those who have witnessed the words and works of the incarnate Son of God himself puts them under far greater responsibility to respond appropriately in repentance and obedience.[83] The failures of Israel, far from inducing any kind of smugness on our part, should function as a terrible warning not to follow their example.[84] Warnings against falling away from our true identity and responsibility are just as much relevant to churches now in the midst of the nations as to old Jerusalem 'at the centre', as John perceived after his own Ezekiel-style theophany of the glory of the risen Christ.[85]

c. Jerusalem: a warning to the nations (5:8–17)

Verse 8 really says it all. The rest of the section provides commentary and expansion. Its opening words are chilling: *'I myself am against you.'* The Hebrew sounds even more emphatic: 'Behold me – against you – even I.' The expression *against you* has the sound of a challenge to mortal combat from an enemy. Delilah used it to rouse Samson with the news 'The Philistines are *upon you!*'[86] Right here, in your face, swords drawn, ready to pounce. Used by Yahweh about himself it has a double horror. First it is the awful negation of the more familiar and comforting 'Behold, I am *with you*' that echoes through the promissory language of Israel's covenants, ever since Abraham. Israel would hear those precious words again in due course, but for the present generation they had been replaced with their bleak opposite, *'I am against you'*. Ezekiel uses the phrase fourteen times, more than half of all its uses in the Old Testament – such was the intensity of its significance in his preaching to the first generation of exiles. Secondly, it reinforces the message that Ezekiel had been miming for over a year – the real enemy of Jerusalem and

[80] Zimmerli, *Ezekiel 1*, p. 175.
[81] Block (1), p. 199. [82] 1 Cor. 5:1; 6:1–11. [83] Matt. 10:15; 11:20–24.
[84] 1 Cor. 10:1–12. [85] Rev. 1:9 – 3:22. [86] Judg. 16:9; cf. Greenberg, p. 113.

Israel was not the Babylonian army but Yahweh himself. 'I myself, the Sovereign LORD, am now your enemy' (NLT). The result of their flagrant breaking of all their covenant obligations to Yahweh meant that he, as covenant Lord, was now taking action against them as against a rebellious, treaty-breaking vassal. Far from expecting him to defend them against the Babylonian enemy, they must realize that he, the real enemy, was simply using the Babylonians as his temporary agent of retribution. There would be no rescue from them because there was no rescue from him.

Then Ezekiel allows himself another word-play on *mišpāt*. As well as meaning 'law' (6–7a), and 'standards'/'customs' (7b), it can also mean 'judgment' in the sense of *punishment* meted out in public court (8). So Yahweh tells Israel, 'Because you have not done my *mišpāt*, and have not even done the *mišpāt* of the nations, I will now do *mišpāt* among you in the sight of the nations.' The effect, even at the literary level of balancing words and phrases, is to underline the justice and appropriateness of Yahweh's punishment of Israel – a theme that will occupy much of Ezekiel's attention later.

The reason for the punishment is mentioned briefly in verses 9 and 11, namely the *detestable idols* and *practices*[87] that were abounding in Jerusalem and probably, in view of the representative nature of the term *my sanctuary*, throughout the land as a whole. These will be more fully explored and described in detail in chapter 8 – Ezekiel's next great visionary experience, which took him inside the temple itself. The form of the punishment follows closely the sequence of mime actions and fills out in words the horrific implications. The language in these repulsive verses is heavily dependent on the covenant curses listed in Leviticus 26:14–39 and Deuteronomy 28:15–68, in a way that shows clearly that Ezekiel knew those texts and could use their imagery and vocabulary.[88] The difference is that in Leviticus and Deuteronomy the curses are conditional; that is, they are portrayed as something that *could*

---

[87] The word *tô'ēbâ*, in older translations rendered 'abomination', is another term that Ezekiel uses very frequently as a way of describing Israel's sin. It speaks of something that is disgusting, repulsive or revolting (cf. Gen. 46:34 – the attitude of the urbane Egyptians to rural shepherds). 'Stomach-turning' would be an appropriate English metaphor. It thus captures the sense of almost physical as well as emotional revulsion that makes God 'shudder' when confronted with certain forms of human sin.

[88] It would be worth pausing to read those sections of Leviticus and Deuteronomy. Ezekiel will seem almost restrained afterwards! We should not imagine that God is here portrayed as *causing* or *instructing* people to sink to cannibalism, etc. All the horrors described here are well known as actual effects of prolonged siege – in modern as well as ancient times. Jerusalem would suffer national defeat and humiliation, and these would be some of the consequences of it.

happen in the future if Israel failed to live within the requirements of their covenant with Yahweh; whereas in Ezekiel they are portrayed as historical realities just about to break over the heads of the people in Jerusalem. By this means Ezekiel, like the pre-exilic prophets before him, gave his people a rationale for understanding the catastrophe that was inexorably falling upon them. It was not, as they thought, a terrible contradiction of all they believed about their special relationship with Yahweh. Rather it was the terrible confirmation that he had really meant his threats as seriously as his promises. The ruthless punishment (5:11)[89] actually demonstrated the consistency of Yahweh to his covenant – and therein lay a concealed hope, but as yet very concealed.

Finally, however, we must come back to the thread that has run through each of these sections – the nations. What Yahweh was about to do to his own people and city would not only be witnessed by the nations (8); it would also stand as a monumental warning to them. If Yahweh truly were the God of all nations (which of course was not yet acknowledged by them, but would be, according to Ezekiel's later prophecies), and if this is what he had done to the nation that was in a special, elect and redeemed, relation to him, then he was surely a God not to be trifled with. Again, Ezekiel's language gains power and volume by sheer piling up of synonyms. *I will make you a ruin and a reproach among the nations ... You will be a reproach and a taunt, a warning and an object of horror to the nations* (14–15).

In later chapters (esp. ch. 36), Ezekiel will explore in much greater depth the theological interplay of Yahweh, Israel and the nations. Here, however, it is worth concluding our study of this section by noticing that the reference to the nations in verses 5–17 is the only aspect of his verbal prophecy which effectively adds anything to what had already been so effectively portrayed in the daily dramatic performances of the previous fourteen months. It would have been difficult to get this dimension across in mime. The physical theatre had concentrated on the fate of Jerusalem and its inhabitants, and the privation of the exiles. The only representation of the nations at all was in the little clay models of Nebuchadnezzar's besieging army around the model of Jerusalem.

[89] The language of 'no pity' is drawn from the laws in Deuteronomy where those entrusted with proper execution of a court's verdict on those guilty of serious offences were warned not to give in to sentimental pity (Deut. 7:16; 13:8; 19:3, 21; 25:12). The language is harsh. In the case of Yahweh it is harsher still, pointing to the utter necessity of full and just punishment for the accumulated heinousness of Israel's rebellion and perversity. For this is the same Yahweh whose very nature is to be 'the compassionate and gracious God' (Exod. 34:6–7).

The verbal interpretation, however, does more than simply explain in words what was already fairly obvious from the mimes. It sets the whole scene of Israel's judgment in the context of the nations. There was a wider perspective on events than the mime itself could portray, a perspective that went beyond Yahweh's dealings with Israel alone. Yahweh had 'set' Jerusalem in the centre of the nations – her election therefore was of relevance to their destiny also. Jerusalem's sin was all the more heinous because it was even worse than that of the nations who knew not Yahweh. And Jerusalem's punishment would not merely 'teach Israel a lesson', but constitute a major historical object lesson for the nations.[90] As a result of it, *they will know that I the* LORD *have spoken* (13). *They* here means Israel, but as Ezekiel's prophetic ministry matures, he anticipates that God's ultimate purpose includes the nations, as well as Israel, coming to know that he, Yahweh, is truly God. That was not just Yahweh's *zeal*, it was the burning passion of Ezekiel himself, and it is introduced, though without much development yet, in this, the very first prophetic speech to fall from his otherwise dumb lips.

[90] 'The prophet Ezekiel brings the heathen nations into the picture. They are not just the admiring chorus, which Israel's pride had looked for, who now turn away in disgust and who are introduced to form a particularly bitter element in her punishment. It is much more that the prophet regards them as having been brought into a direct relationship with Yahweh ... The disgust and derision, along with profound horror, which the heathen show (v. 15), is far from being the prophet's final word about them. But all the function they fulfil here is to provide a contrast to the original blessing which it was Israel's task to bring them, but which she had refused to bring.' Eichrodt, p. 90.

Appendix 1
Notes on Ezekiel 6, 7 and 12

Chapter 6

This chapter continues the theme of God's imminent judgment upon Israel, but directs God's anger against *the mountains of Israel*. This is not simply a personification of the land in place of the people; it was appropriate because the hilltops were particularly used for the idolatrous worship at *high places*. These were shrines which littered the Israelite countryside, making use of *every high hill … and every spreading tree and every leafy oak – places where they offered fragrant incense to all their idols* (13). The chapter declares that not only will such places be destroyed, but the worshippers themselves will be slain (7), and those who survive will be *scattered among the lands and nations* (8). So there will be yet more exiles to join the first batch, and the portrayal of *sword, famine and plague* (11) reinforces the message of the acted prophecies of the previous chapters that Jerusalem will endure a long, painful and ultimately fatal siege. Verse 11 also indicates that Ezekiel was still being required to engage in a variety of gestures and actions to gain attention and reinforce his message.

At this point in the book, the message is of unrelieved judgment and doom. In the aftermath of the fall of Jerusalem, however, Ezekiel was told to address these same mountains again. This time, in chapter 36, his message is one of restoration. The hills of Judah will again be inhabited and prosperous. Both chapters, in their portrayal of judgment on the land and then of restoration to the land, strongly echo the language of Leviticus 26, which seems to have had a major influence on the theology and vocabulary of Ezekiel.

Chapter 7

This chapter also begins addressed to *the land of Israel*, and echoes throughout with the finality of its opening doom-laden toll, *The end! The end has come* (2; cf. 3, 5, 6, 7, 10, 12) The overwhelming message is that Yahweh's patience has finally come to an end. There can be no more leniency. The wickedness of the nation is such that there is no alternative any longer to the *wrath* and *anger* of God. Ezekiel is here applying to Judah the same cry of finality that Amos had raised over the northern kingdom of Israel.[1] Three features of the chapter deserve notice.

First, the coming calamity is portrayed as thoroughly deserved. God is acting with moral integrity in punishing his people. This is the message of the repeated insistence, *I will judge you according to your conduct* and *I will surely repay you for your conduct* (3, 4; cf. 8, 9, 27). There would be nothing arbitrary in the doom that lay ahead. God was about to do what had always been written into the covenant relationship. Persistent and unrepented wickedness would incur his anger and judgment, and that time had now come.

Secondly, the nature of Israel's wickedness, though spelt out in much more detail in other chapters, is here mentioned in two dimensions. On the one hand there was the ever-present idolatry (20 – much expanded in ch. 8), and on the other hand there were the social evils associated especially with violence and bloodshed (23 – much expanded in chs. 11 and 22).

Thirdly, the coming doom was inexorable. It could not be bought off with wealth, especially ill-gotten wealth; on the contrary, the whole economy will collapse (11–13, 19–20). Nor could it be deflected by the spiritual or intellectual powers of the religious professionals (26). Both prince and pauper will be powerless (27) against the justice of the LORD.

Chapter 12

This chapter records two more dramatic prophecies, similar to the great sequence of actions that filled Ezekiel's first year. Since the chapter is not dated, we have no indication whether they were linked in some way to those earlier actions, or were performed at a later date. Their message was similar to, and reinforced, the point of the previous dramatic signs.

The first dramatized message was to enact the experience of going into exile (3–16). The hasty packing and undignified exit though a hole in the wall of his house (what did Ezekiel's poor wife say?), portrayed the fate of those carried off into captivity – a fate which would engulf royalty as well as the ordinary population (10–14). The actual target of verses 12–14 was Zedekiah, the puppet king installed by Nebuchadnezzar in Jerusalem after the death of Jehoiakim and

---

[1] Amos 8:1–2.

deportation of the rightful king, Jehoiachin. Zedekiah was indeed captured by the Babylonians and blinded before being taken to Babylon, thus fulfilling Ezekiel's prediction that *he will not see it*.

The second action was to *tremble* and *shudder* (17) while eating his meals. We have to assume that Ezekiel's home had become a place to visit frequently so that even his mealtimes were observed. The message, similar to 4:9–17, was simply that the people back in Jerusalem would soon be experiencing all the fear and anxiety of prolonged siege – as indeed they did.

The chapter concludes with several short words addressed to those who were inclined to mock Ezekiel's seemingly endless charades and to point out with sarcasm that nothing he was predicting – by word or sign – seemed to be taking place (22, 27). It will, it will, was God's reply – and sooner than you think. The certainty of God's word, based on the sovereignty of God's will, is stated with crystal clarity: *'I the LORD will speak what I will, and it shall be fulfilled without delay … I will fulfil whatever I say, declares the Sovereign LORD'* (25).

8:1 – 11:25
3. Exit the glory

Introduction

They may have tied him up, but they couldn't tie him down. From the opening of chapter 8 it seems that Ezekiel was still confined to his house, though the fact that *the elders of Judah were sitting before* him may show that he was treated with some respect, even if basically his message was still not being taken seriously. On other occasions when they were sitting at home with Ezekiel their attitude was ambiguous to say the least (14:1–3; 20:1–3; 33:30–32). Whatever his physical limitations, however, Ezekiel was not captive in spirit. On the contrary, from his home in a Babylonian exile encampment he was enabled by the mysterious power of Yahweh to pay a visit to Jerusalem and have a guided tour of inspection, witnessing its worst excesses of idolatry.

Once again Ezekiel carefully records the date of this particular prophetic vision (8:1) – it was 17 September 592 BC, about fourteen months after his call vision. Recording significant dates was not simply a matter of keeping his own memoirs organized; it would be of great importance later when the final destruction of Jerusalem would confirm the validity of his claim to have truly spoken from Yahweh. Having the dates recorded meant that it could not be disputed that he had genuinely predicted these events in advance. This is explicit in 24:2 (and cf. 33:33), when Ezekiel is given prophetic information about the beginning of the siege of Jerusalem – news of which would not, of course, reach the exiles in Babylon for several months (it was almost 1,000 miles' journey from Jerusalem to Babylon).

The means of transport is described in 8:2–3a. The *figure like that of a man* is instantly recognizable as identical to the portrayal of the figure on the throne in the original vision (1:27). Similarly the *stretched out … hand* recalls the hand that had fed him the scroll (2:9). And *the Spirit* is of course the same spirit of Yahweh as had on previous occasions hoisted him upright (2:2; 3:12, 24) and provided his return journey from the Kebar River on his birthday (3:14–15). There is no need to see any distinct roles for the man, the hand, and the Spirit. Together they all point to the fact that it is Yahweh himself who transports Ezekiel and who is the figure by his side throughout the whole visionary experience, not an angelic interpreter.

Such an experience of prophetic clairvoyance – seeing actions happening at a distance from the observer or otherwise hidden to normal vision – is not unprecedented in the history of the prophets. Elisha had such gifts.[1] But nothing quite matches the scale, duration and detail of Ezekiel's vision here. He must have been 'gone' from his house guests for quite some time, though it is possible to imagine that his prostrated outbursts at 9:8 and 11:13 may have really happened physically in their presence, somewhat like sleep-talking, in a way which would have greatly heightened the suspense in the room as they awaited his 'return' and the report he gave in 11:25.

What purpose does this detailed visionary account of what was going on in Jerusalem serve?[2] For Ezekiel himself it was possibly God's way of finally convincing him that the virtually total destruction he was called on to proclaim was justified by the scale of the wickedness in Jerusalem. Ezekiel had probably trained to be a priest and would have known the temple area quite well. But he may never have seen some of the things going on there. The repeated question from his day-trip tour guide *'have you seen ...?'* suggests that the things he was witnessing were surprising and shocking to him. Is this what is *really* happening? Right in the *temple*? This would have had two effects on his future ministry and message. First, it helps us to understand the ferocity of the way he describes the sin of Israel. Ezekiel is unsurpassed in the range of vocabulary and imagery he uses to portray the sheer repugnance of Israel's active rejection of Yahweh and their wallowing in every kind of religious paganism and social corruption. After this vision he had, as it were, seen it with his own eyes, and from Yahweh's point of view. Secondly, it accounts for the strong emphasis on 'theodicy' in the preaching of Ezekiel. Theodicy means 'providing justification for the actions of God'. It seems that Ezekiel faced the constant challenge of fellow exiles that God was behaving unfairly, the punishment was too severe, they did not really deserve all this,

[1] 2 Kgs. 5:26; 6:32.
[2] In the context of the book itself, it provides a detailed exposition of the summary statement about Israel's *detestable idols ... and detestable practices*, first mentioned in 5:9, 11.

and so on.[3] Ezekiel knew differently. The judgment of God was both fully deserved and long overdue and he could now give the detailed reasons why.

1. The glory of God offended (8:5–18)

So Ezekiel takes off on his visionary flight over the desert and is deposited in Jerusalem, at a gateway on the outer northern edge of the temple courts. His tour will take him progressively closer to the more sacred areas in four stages. The precise topography of Ezekiel's visionary journey through the temple precincts is difficult to reconstruct with confidence. But it does seem clear that each stage is simultaneously closer to the holiest part of the temple and, for that reason, increasingly offensive in the idolatry being practised at each place.[4] We need to remember that this is a visionary experience and not a video documentary – although that is not an inappropriate comparison. If we read his account imaginatively, we may feel like we are watching some wildlife programme as the presenter invites the cameraman ever closer to dangerous animals being filmed unobserved, with whispered commentary for the viewer. It is not necessary to envisage all of the scenes observed by Ezekiel as actually happening simultaneously in the temple, but rather that Ezekiel's visionary tour enables him to witness the kind of idolatrous practices that were going on at different times, but all of them equally offensive to God.

On his arrival, Ezekiel is met (4) by *the glory of the God of Israel* (which had obviously got there even faster than the Spirit), unmistakably the same as the vision he had seen as part of his call. This is now his third direct encounter with this spectacular phenomenon, so he has no difficulty recognizing it and naming it directly for what it is. Here in Jerusalem, of course, is where the glory of Yahweh *ought to be* – in Yahweh's own temple and city and land. However, everything else that Ezekiel is about to see will contradict, challenge and repel the glory of Yahweh. So this opening welcome, as it were, by the divine host is a poignant prelude to his tragic exit. The whole account in chapters 8 – 11 is connected together by the theme of the slow departure of the glory of Yahweh, by several stages, from the temple and the city that bore his name (see 9:3; 10:4, 18; 11:23).

But what could induce Yahweh to leave 'home' – so reluctantly and yet so implacably? Four scenes in chapter 8 give the answer –

[3] We shall examine this bitter argument in chs. 18 and 33, in our ch. 5 below.
[4] For various reconstructions and a sketch map see Allen 28, pp. 138–141.

scenes which must have shocked Ezekiel to the core as he saw them in his vision, and which must have shattered the complacency of the elders gathered in his home when he, as he says, *told the exiles everything the LORD had shown me* (11:25).

a. Scene 1: The idol of jealousy (8:5–6)

Though Ezekiel may have noticed this before (3), his attention is now directed to it specifically. What a shock it must have been to be gazing one moment at the glory of Yahweh, and then to be redirected the next moment to the horrendous contrast of this idolatrous statue right alongside. The idol itself cannot be identified with certainty, but it is most likely that it was a statue of Asherah, or Astarte, the Canaanite goddess, consort of the high god El and mother of Baal. We read of such a statue (which probably consisted of a carved wooden pillar or image) being erected during the reign of the apostate Manasseh[5] but it was later removed[6] and subsequently burnt during the reforms of Josiah.[7] It would seem that something similar had been restored by Jehoiakim or Zedekiah. It may be that this is the figure representing the 'Queen of Heaven', whose worship seems to have become popular during Jeremiah's lifetime and went on unabated even after the destruction of Jerusalem.[8]

It is described as (lit.) 'a statue of jealousy that provokes to jealousy'. 'Jealousy' means the anger[9] that is caused by the rejection or betrayal of love. It is the proper response of a betrayed spouse.[10] It is also the response of Yahweh when the covenant obligations of loyalty to himself alone are flouted. Since he alone had redeemed his people, he alone is to be the object of their worship and obedience. Anything else provokes his jealousy.[11]

This jealousy of Yahweh can be a positive thing when it is expressed and exercised *on behalf of* his people, or in their defence, as indeed at a later time Zechariah prophesied that it would be when Yahweh returned to his rightful dwelling place.[12] But confronted with a flagrant idol in his own sacred space, Yahweh's jealousy was aroused to the extent that he could no longer stay around to tolerate it. He was leaving, but not because he wanted to; rather, because his own covenant people were doing *things that will drive me far from my sanctuary* (8:6). So who then was to blame for his departure: Yahweh himself or his own people? There is an irony here, in that in the next scene Ezekiel will hear people complaining that Yahweh

---

[5] 2 Kgs. 21:7.   [6] 2 Chr. 33:15.   [7] 2 Kgs. 23:6.   [8] Jer. 7:17–19; 44:15–19.
[9] Cf. 'a large idol that has made the LORD very angry' (NLT).
[10] Num. 5:14, 30; Prov. 6:34.   [11] Exod. 20:5; 34:15; Deut. 4:24; 32:21.
[12] Zech. 8:2ff.

has abandoned his land or accusing him of doing so (8:12). They were almost right; Yahweh had not quite left yet, but he was being driven out by those who should most carefully have cultivated his presence.

Why should the effect of this statue and all it represented have been to drive Yahweh away from his own sanctuary? First of all, his sovereignty was being challenged by this invasion of his sacred space by another, alien deity. There it was, confronting worshippers as they arrived at the very gate of the temple, worshippers who were presumably intending to worship Yahweh but were diverted, or compelled, into the worship of a rival god or goddess. Indeed, it may be that the presence of the statue by the gate itself implied that she had come to fulfil an intermediary role: in order to gain access to Yahweh you had first to pay deference to Asherah. But Yahweh will have nothing between himself and his people other than the symbols he himself ordained within the covenant itself since the days of the tabernacle in the wilderness.

Secondly, if indeed this was a statue of Asherah, then it represented all the degraded sexuality of the fertility cult associated with the worship of Baal and Asherah, which had been condemned for centuries, ever since Hosea. Yahweh was being reduced to the level of a nature god who could be reached only by the debauchery of religious prostitution and other gross rituals.[13] This was *detestable* enough, but Ezekiel is warned that he *will see things that are even more detestable*.

Detestable things. Divine *jealousy*. These are strong and unpleasant words. And in the unfamiliar world of Ezekiel's vision they may seem strange and unwelcome to us. It is important, though, to allow such words to stand up and hit us. They describe realities that we need to face as Christians – not in relation to the sinful world around us, but in relation to our own actions and attitudes. The sin of the world generates God's grief and anger. It is the sin of God's own people that produces God's jealousy. When we profess loyalty to the Lord Jesus Christ, to whose self-giving love we owe our salvation, but then live lives that are absorbed with the priorities and idolatries of the world around us, there is something detestable, ungrateful and treacherous about that. To go on doing so blatantly and without repentance is evidence of a state of heart and

[13] It has been suggested (see Blenkinsopp, p. 54) that the description of the statue as 'provoking to jealousy' can be understood to mean 'provoking to burning sexual lust'. While this may be possible as a secondary *double entendre* of Ezekiel's phrase (which would be characteristic of him), it seems certain that the primary meaning here refers not to human lust but to Yahweh's jealousy, on account of which he is taking leave of temple and city.

mind that incurs serious warnings as much in the New Testament as in the Old. Significantly Paul warns Christians against the temptations of sexual sin and debauchery with much the same abhorrence as Ezekiel had for the depraved cult of Asherah. He also uses temple imagery to sharpen his point.[14] And he is not afraid to affirm the threat of God's jealousy.[15] We need to heed such sobering warnings, especially in the midst of current moral laxness in Christian culture.

b. Scene 2: Prayers to animal deities (8:7–13)

The vision becomes surreal and dreamlike as Ezekiel first sees a hole in the wall and then is required to dig one – and finally finds a door anyway! By this strange means he gains access to an inner room in the temple precincts, and with our imaginary video camera we follow behind the prophet and his divine commentator. It is dark (12), but as the walls become visible they also seem to come alive – literally crawling with images of *all kinds of crawling things and detestable animals and all the idols of the house of Israel*. The first expression describes all creeping or crawling creatures, without necessarily derogatory intent (as the words have in English).[16] But the next two phrases leave no doubt about the repulsiveness of the scene. The *animals* portrayed are disgusting, revolting, and the *idols* are (lit.) 'droppings of excrement'. There is a strong recollection of the list of prohibited worship in Deuteronomy 4:17–18.

The room is not only dark and secret; it is filled with the smoke of incense burners, wielded by *seventy elders of the house of Israel*, who are obviously, therefore, performing worship to the gods represented by the images on the walls. The pictures are *all over the walls*, or, more correctly, all around them, probably each with its own little alcove, rather like the small side-chapels of medieval churches. Each elder seems to be worshipping at each alcove, co-ordinated by someone whom Ezekiel recognizes – *Jaazaniah son of Shaphan*.[17] So what is going on here?

Although we cannot be completely certain, it seems very probable

---

[14] 1 Cor. 5; 6:12–20.   [15] 1 Cor. 10:22; cf. 2 Cor. 6:14 – 7:1.

[16] Gen. 1:24–25; Pss. 104:25; 148:10.

[17] Almost certainly this is the same Shaphan who was the devout royal secretary involved in the discovery of the Book of the Law during the reign of Josiah (2 Kgs. 22:3–14). Three of his other sons seem to have been favourable to Jeremiah at a time when that was potentially dangerous because of his stance in opposition to current royal policy in Jerusalem: Ahikam (Jer. 26:24), Elasah (Jer. 29:3) and Gemariah (Jer. 36:10–12). Jaazaniah appears to have been 'the black sheep of a worthy family' (Taylor, p. 99). It may have been the shock of seeing a member of such a staunch family engaged in secret idolatry that led Ezekiel to name him individually.

that these were political leaders trying to invoke the support of Egyptian gods and at the same time enlist the help of the Egyptian armies. Clues to this interpretation are, first, that the ritual involved worship of animal deities, secondly, that elders were doing it, and thirdly, that it was happening in secret.

To take the first clue: deities in animal form were common in the ancient Near East, but especially in Egypt, where the worship of crocodiles, snakes and beetles ('crawling things' to a Jewish mind), among others, took place. Secondly, Jerusalem was in great danger from the threat of Babylon, and it is known that there were different parties in the city advocating different policies, some pro- and others anti-Babylon. The likelihood is that this group of influential leaders was engaged in an act of religious politics, invoking the gods of Egypt to come to their assistance by sending the armies of Egypt to attack the Babylonians.[18] We know from 17:15 that this action had already been taken on the political level. Warnings in the past about the futility of relying on Egypt as an ally against Mesopotamian powers seem to have been forgotten.[19] So there is another reminder of it in 17:17. The third clue, the secrecy of the elders' rituals, probably implies some kind of political conspiracy linked to attempted overtures to Egypt at a time when the ruling party may have been temporarily pro-Babylonian.[20] Or it may simply have been part of the pagan religious ritual itself that it required mysterious darkness.[21] The fact that they are described as *seventy elders of the house of Israel* (11) is a deliberate echo of the representative seventy elders who accompanied Moses in the ceremony of establishing the covenant at Mount Sinai in Exodus 24 and who shared a meal in his enthroned presence there. Here, by jarring contrast, are seventy elders involved in blatant breaking of that covenant, just a few partitions away from the Holy of Holies.

The reason these elders give for their outrageous behaviour in the very temple of Yahweh is whispered with superb irony in Ezekiel's ear by his divine commentator as they both watch in the hazy gloom – 'They think I can't see them!' Their precise words as reported in verse 12 are filled with ambiguity and irony, *'The LORD does not see us; the LORD has forsaken the land.'* If by the first phrase they simply thought

---

[18] We need to remember that these events lie long before the separation of religion and politics in modern western culture. In the worldview of the ancient Near East, what happened in international political and military affairs was simply a reflection, or an external manifestation, of what was happening in the world of the gods – and *vice versa*. Praying to Egyptian gods and inviting Egyptian armies were two sides of the same coin.

[19] Is. 30:1–5; 31:1–3.   [20] Cf. the similar atmosphere of Is. 29:15.

[21] Deut. 13:6; 27:15; Job 31:27.

that by hiding in an inner room they were out of sight of Yahweh, they had forgotten the sharp reminder of Jeremiah, given only a few years earlier, that even if people turned the temple into a den of robbers (i.e. a safe hideout), Yahweh was watching.[22] There are no closed doors to the eyes of the God who watches the nations,[23] the God whose eyes examine especially those in his temple,[24] and the God to whom darkness is no barrier at all.[25] Part of the irony is that they could imagine that *Yahweh* could not see them while they were engaged in praying to gods which, by definition in Israel's faith, had eyes but could not see.[26] What they said about Yahweh was actually true of the idols they were praying to.

But it is possible that the first phrase has a more sinister ring which would link it more closely to the second – 'Yahweh is no longer watching over us; he doesn't care for us any more; he has abandoned his people and his land.' Such a confession, happening in the temple itself, indicates a massive loss of confidence in Yahweh's covenantal protection of Israel and the city. This too may explain its secrecy, since the prevailing popular mood seems to have been one of buoyant optimism that Yahweh would always defend his own temple.[27] Here were men, political leaders, who sensed the game was up. Yahweh had already packed up and left.

But if that was indeed their view, namely that Yahweh had gone, what should these leaders have been doing? According to the ancestral faith, if ever the presence of Yahweh in the midst of his people were threatened, then the people should be led to repentance and confession so that Yahweh would return to them, or they to him.

'But if they will confess their sins and the sins of their fathers – their treachery against me and their hostility toward me, which made me hostile toward them ... then when their uncircumcised hearts are humbled and they pay for their sin, I will remember my covenant ... and I will remember the land.'[28]

This was what Jeremiah had called on the people to do, preaching in the very courts of the temple. He warned them, early in the reign of Jehoiakim, that if only they would change their ways, repent and return to God, it was still possible that he would continue to dwell with them in this place and allow them to do so too. Otherwise the

---

[22] Jer. 7:11.   [23] Ps. 66:7.   [24] Ps. 11:4.   [25] Ps. 139:11–12.
[26] Pss. 115:4–7; 135:15–17.
[27] Jer. 7:4. Nevertheless, it seems that something of this 'Yahweh doesn't care' attitude had permeated from the leaders to the wider population; cf. Ezek. 9:9.
[28] Lev. 26:40–42; cf. Deut. 30:1–10.

fate of Shiloh would engulf them.[29] Shiloh had been wiped out by the Philistines. It was probably already little more than an archaeological site in Jeremiah's day.

However, far from publicly leading the people in repentance and in prayer to Yahweh, pleading with him to stay with them, these men shrug their shoulders at Yahweh's presumed departure and promptly turn to alternative sources of help – foreign, pagan deities that should have turned their stomachs rather than inspired their supplication. So lightly can they discard the whole covenantal history of their faith, their fathers, their people. 'Yahweh has gone, has he?' they exclaim. 'So what? In that case, he can't see, or won't mind, what we do in this place any longer. Let's fix up some alternative protection for the present emergency.' As far as Yahweh is concerned, they think it's all over. As far as they are concerned, responds Yahweh, it is now (or very soon will be).

Again, as we seek to apply the challenge of such a posture to ourselves, the picture of ancient elders worshipping reptiles in a dark and smoke-filled room may as well be from a different planet or a science-fiction movie. Yet in principle their action is endemic to the people of God in every era. We proclaim our covenant loyalty to the living God. We put our lives under his protection and affirm his sovereign power. We sing songs about his great faithfulness and our eternal security. And yet so often in real life we act as though we had no confidence in God at all for our future. Instead, we expend enormous amounts of material and emotional resources on fixing things up for ourselves. It is well worth regularly checking where we have drawn the line between the wisdom that makes prudent provision for the future for ourselves and our families and the idolatry that builds all our hope and security on the modern equivalents of the gods and armies of Egypt.

c. Scene 3: Mourning cults (8:14–15)

Eyes blinking with the return to the daylight, Ezekiel is confronted with something his divine guide calls *even more detestable*. Closer now to the most sacred part of the temple, probably in the main forecourt in front of the temple itself, he sees and hears a group of women *mourning for Tammuz*. Though the name occurs only here in the whole Old Testament, it is probably to be identified with Dumu-zi, a name which appears in the very ancient Sumerian King List as the name of a shepherd king before the flood who is said to have reigned for 36,000 years (making Methuselah a mere youth). The story tells how he was banished by his wife, the goddess Inanna,

[29] Jer. 7:1–15.

to the underworld, where he lost his power, and was mourned by his wife, mother and sister. Thereafter, the cult of mourning for Tammuz seems to have been a popular Babylonian custom among women especially. There are probably strong links with the Greek cult of the beautiful Adonis, who was similarly much lamented among women. Tammuz gave his name to the Mesopotamian month matching June/July, when his cult was practised.[30] Since this was the heat of the summer when vegetation died, it has often been thought that he was a dying and rising nature god similar to others found throughout the ancient near-eastern fertility cults, but this is now less certain.[31]

What was so offensive about this particular form of idolatry was, first of all, that a cult of the dead was going on in the temple of the living God. In the place where the Lord and giver of life was to be celebrated, women were involved in a mourning ritual for a dead hero of pagan mythology. What made it more pointed still, secondly, was that it was a Babylonian hero at that! Ezekiel would soon have to report to Judean exiles amid the paganism of Babylon that a Babylonian cult figure was being pined for in the heart of Jerusalem – in the very temple itself. Thirdly, if the Tammuz cult did have connections with the fertility cults of dying and reviving vegetation, then Yahweh was being further robbed of his rightful place as the Lord of land, life, the seasons, and all fertility – human, animal and vegetable. Such cults were entirely contrary to the celebration and affirmation of Deuteronomy 26:1–15, which binds together the sovereignty of Yahweh in redemptive promise and historical fulfilment on the one hand with his control over all the processes and bounty of nature on the other. Instead, such a cult seeks to control nature through sympathetic magic and mourning rites, one of the marks of a paganized worldview which is still very much alive and well in the world today.

Christians are rightly recovering a creation balance in our worship and spirituality. Celtic worship has been enjoying something of a revival, even if not all of it would be immediately recognized by Patrick or Columba. However, there is a danger that what passes as allegedly 'Celtic' actually draws on pre-Christian Celtic paganism (which is very much in vogue with New Age adherents), rather than the vigorous and trinitarian Celtic Christianity which emerged after the remarkable conversion of Ireland. It is vital that our appreciation

---

[30] The fact that Ezekiel saw this vision in September need not be regarded as a problem, since, as said above, his vision was probably not meant to be contemporaneous in real time in all its parts, but a composite picture of the idolatries being practised in Jerusalem over an extended period of time.

[31] For up-to-date discussion and bibliography, see Block (1), pp. 294–296.

of creation within our worship is kept anchored to the biblical
affirmations about God himself, and not allowed to drift over into
a false kind of personalizing of nature. If creation is exalted to
excessive levels in our theology or worship, we may subtly
marginalize the person and character of the Creator and come close
to ascribing divine power and properties to natural forces and
elements. 'The earth is the LORD's, and everything in it',[32] and our
worship, like the worship of all created things, must be directed to
the Lord himself alone. The paradox is that if we worship the living
God rightly as Creator, then we shall care for creation as well, as he
commanded;[33] but if we worship the creation (in any of its
manifestations, or even by unbridled consumerism), we quickly
forget the Creator.

d. Scene 4: Sun worship (8:16)

The last scene of Ezekiel's temple tour is taking place closest of all
to the inner shrine. He is in *the inner court ... at the entrance to the
temple, between the portico and the altar.* Apart from actually
entering the building itself, this was as close as you could get to the
very presence of God. This was the place, at the very door of the
temple, where Joel summoned the priests to gather and weep before
the LORD in repentance.[34] In stark contrast, Ezekiel found *about
twenty-five men* engaged in precisely the opposite. To repent is (lit.)
'to turn to' the LORD. But these men have *their backs toward the
temple of the LORD.* The description is surely both physical and
metaphorical.[35] The temple is behind them. They have turned their
backs on the covenant God – right in front of his face. The word
backs can be used of the hindquarters of cattle.[36] In *bowing down to
the sun*, these men were literally lifting their backsides to God.
Metaphorically, sunnies to the east; moonies to the LORD. The insult
is blatant and breathtaking.

To bow down to the sun meant facing eastwards. The temple
building was aligned east-west, with the Holy of Holies at the
western end and the door and porch facing east. Such worship of
the sun, or any of the astral bodies, was utterly incompatible with
worship of Yahweh, the creator of the heavens and all their

[32] Ps. 24:1.
[33] At least, we should do so. It is still a sad indictment of so many Christian people
and churches that they can claim to worship the Creator and yet have no concern
for the needs and suffering of his created world.
[34] Joel 2:17.
[35] The expression is used, with the same heavy sarcasm, in Jer. 2:27; 32:33.
[36] In 1 Kgs. 7:25, it is used of the hindquarters of the twelve statues of oxen holding
up the great bronze laver, which were all pointing inwards.

fullness.[37] It was explicitly forbidden to Israel in Deuteronomy 4:19, but seems to have been introduced by Manasseh,[38] with appropriate horse and chariot statues at the very gate of the temple. The latter were removed and burnt during Josiah's reformation,[39] but, like the Asherah pillar ('statue of jealousy', 8:5), may have made a comeback.

What made such worship of the sun even worse in the current situation was that the sun was among the most powerful gods of the *Babylonian* empire. Astral cults were predominant in the Mesopotamian civilizations – a fact which greatly sharpens the rhetorical debunking of them in Isaiah 40:26, where the stars are portrayed as simply things created, named and numbered by Yahweh. So were these men engaged in a kind of defensive prayer tactic – pleading with the gods of Babylon to spare their city from Nebuchadnezzar's wrath? Again, what a blatant affront to Yahweh – the only true and living God, the creator of the sun itself, and the one for whom Nebuchadnezzar was nothing more than an *ex officio* 'servant'.[40]

And what a picture of utter political and spiritual anarchy in the house of the LORD! In Jerusalem's most dangerous hour, Ezekiel finds one faction in a darkened, smoke-filled room praying to the gods (probably) of Egypt, while a few metres away out in the sunshine of the inner court another faction is busy biting the dust before the gods of Babylon. And all the time, Yahweh goes unacknowledged in his own house! The accumulated affront to his holiness and sovereignty is unbearable. No wonder he is preparing to leave.

Ezekiel's guide brings the tour to a close by pointing out that although what he has shown Ezekiel is primarily a sample of ritual offences in the temple itself, that is not the full catalogue of the sins of Jerusalem, by any means. Their sin is far from merely religious – even though we must avoid thinking of anything as 'merely religious' in the context of the ancient world. As pointed out above, these particular idolatrous forms of worship had strong links with other realities of life – sexual, political, agricultural, international. Their offensiveness lay in parcelling out such areas to other deities rather than recognizing the authority and claim of Yahweh over all of them. No, the sin of Israel moves beyond idolatry in the temple and encompasses the whole social realm. Like all the prophets before him Ezekiel sees and condemns the whole range of social and economic evils that Israel wallowed in once they neglected the way of life and community that should have been theirs under the

[37] Gen. 1:14–19; Ps. 8:3; 19:1–6.   [38] 2 Kgs. 21:5.   [39] 2 Kgs. 23:11.
[40] Jer. 27:1–7.

covenant regime of Yahweh. Later, Ezekiel will list such evils in detail (18:10–13; 22:1–30). Here he summarizes this ethical dimension of their sin by declaring that they *fill the land with violence*,[41] such that the land and the city are 'full of bloodshed ... full of injustice' (9:9).

The combination of religious idolatry, social violence and injustice that has now gone on for generations constitutes such a massive offence to Yahweh that he simply cannot go on tolerating it. The imagery of the last phrase of verse 17 is obscure – *putting the branch to their nose*. It may mean some kind of obscene gesture that symbolizes defiance or insult;[42] it could mean something like 'thumbing their nose at me'; or if it should read (with some text critics) 'my nose', it may mean something like 'sticking their sins up my nose'. At any rate, it is obviously something compatible with the final word of Yahweh which we read in verse 18 – 'No mercy.' The time for all appeals is now over. Judgment must fall. Call in the executioners.

Before we move on to observe, with the stunned Ezekiel, God's terrible reaction to the idolatries that pollute his holy temple, we should pause and evaluate the relevance of this material. Already at several points we have commented that God's people in the Christian church are as prone to idolatry as were ancient Israel. We too can be infected by the seductive sexuality of our age, and pay a heavy price in the rising promiscuity even among Christian young people and the breakdown of Christian marriages through temptation and infidelity. We can labour to find our earthly security elsewhere than through trust in God, whether in expensive insurances, or even unbalanced emotional investment in positive things like family and work. We can flirt with fashionable forms of nature spirituality that subtly cross the line between affirmation of creation and syncretism with a paganized worldview. And these are just a sample of the temptations to idolatry that surround us and entice us away from the integrity of a fully biblical faith in the one living God and in the sole lordship of Jesus Christ. What kind of

---

[41] The word is *ḥāmās*, a strong word for social oppression and cruel violence. It was the particular primeval human wickedness that led to the flood (Gen. 6:11), because it is something that Yahweh hates with all his soul (Ps. 11:5). It is a particular concern of many psalmists, and becomes the focus of pre-exilic prophetic protest, north (Amos 3:10) and south (Mic. 6:12). Jeremiah found it especially something to shout about (Jer. 20:8), and like Ezekiel he saw that Jerusalem was so full of it that he pictured the people actually storing it up in great vaults to keep it fresh (Jer. 6:7). By contrast, the Servant of the Lord will do no *ḥāmās* (Is. 53:9), and the ultimate eschatological vision foresees an age to come that will be free of violence in all its forms (Is. 60:18; 65:25).

[42] Such as, in modern Britain, a 'two-fingered salute', or middle-finger insult.

disturbing video footage would be the result of a visionary tour by Ezekiel of the temple of our hearts, or the temple of the modern church as a whole? What goes on in the darkened rooms of our lives, unseen by those who only praise our outward respectability? Or in the darkened rooms of church politics, factions, corruption and power-games?

But there is another dimension to the sharpness of Ezekiel's vision in the temple. The 'detestable things' that Ezekiel witnessed there were not merely aberrations of Israel's own worship. They were gross manifestations of the religions of Canaan, Egypt, Assyria and Babylon. The temple of the one true God had become a melting-pot of religious pluralism. And the glory of Yahweh could not co-exist in genial tolerance with such a state of affairs. If Israel insisted on bringing such alien forms of worship with their fundamentally polytheistic and pagan religious foundations into proximity with the holy glory of the living God they would inevitably face first his wrath and then his departure. Yahweh simply would not stay around to be treated as one option among others. 'I am the LORD your God ... you shall have no other gods before my face.'[43]

When, as Christians, we are called upon to evaluate the claims of other religions, we may, at a human level, be rightly impressed with many aspects of the devotion and sincerity of their adherents. But in comparison with the biblical revelation of the living God and the glory of his salvation, all other religious claims are exposed as ultimately idolatrous. Ezekiel's temple vision is a sharp reminder of the incompatibility of biblical monotheism and human religions.[44] The significance for our theology of religion of the stark contrast presented in Ezekiel's vision of the idolatries in the temple is well articulated by Elmer Martens:

> In the space of several hundred square yards in the temple court, Ezekiel is confronted with multiple religions. Inside this space there is also visible the glory of God, as Ezekiel had seen it in the inaugural vision (8:4). In the presence of Yahweh's awesome might and majesty, there is no need to debate the merits of these alternate deities and worship systems. Their illegitimacy is self-evident. No attempt is made to evaluate 'from below' (from an anthropological stance), the rightness or wrongness of 'other'

[43] Exod. 20:3; this is a literal translation of the first commandment.
[44] Both the debate and the literature surrounding Christian approaches to the world of multiple human religions are enormous. An attempt to clarify and survey the many issues involved is provided by C. J. H. Wright, *Thinking Clearly about the Uniqueness of Jesus* (Crowborough: Monarch, 1997).

religions. Seen 'from above' (from a Yahwistic theology), all other religious preferences are a parody, a travesty.[45]

However, it is important to note that Ezekiel's vision is actually not directly about, or directed towards, non-Israelite followers of other religions. The wrath of God's offended glory in Ezekiel's vision is aroused not by other nations worshipping such gods and indulging in such forms of worship. Rather, it is the spectacle of Yahweh's own people, who were supposed to be committed to exclusive loyalty to their covenant God, engaging in such blatant religious promiscuity that finally breaks God's patience and calls down his judgment. It is those who did know better, those who were sinning against the light of revelation and history, those who could not claim ignorance as an excuse, who must now face the consequences of their wilful treachery.

2. The glory of God defended (9:1–11)

Enter, then, the executioners. As we return to chapter 9, we need to remind ourselves that all of this is still Ezekiel's vision. He is not now describing real human scenes like those portrayed in the sequence of chapter 8 – scenes which, although they were visionary, actually corresponded to things Ezekiel could have seen if he had been there physically. Chapter 9 is something more akin to the apocalyptic vision of Daniel or of John in Revelation, in which heavenly angelic beings are seen to carry out the divine will on earth in relation to events which, on the stage of human history, would actually be carried out by human beings. People were certainly killed in the siege and capture of Jerusalem, but the killing was done by the Babylonians, not by angels. Ezekiel's vision interprets that historical event in advance by using the symbolic language of God's own judgment being executed. At one level of reality, the swords would be in the hands of Babylonian enemies; at another level of reality, they would collectively constitute the sword of divine justice.

The indictment has been stated and all the evidence for the prosecution assembled in chapter 8, with its concluding closing words of imminent and implacable doom. So chapter 9 begins by summoning those who will carry out the divine sentence of death on

[45] Elmer Martens, 'God, justice, and religious pluralism in the Old Testament', in D. W. Shenk and L. Stutzman (eds.), *Practicing Truth: Confident Witness in Our Pluralistic World* (Scottdale: Herald, 1999), p. 51. Cf. also idem, 'Ezekiel's contribution to a biblical theology of mission', in S. Holthaus and K. W. Mueller (eds.), *Die Mission der Theologie: Festschrift für Hans Kasdorf zum 70. Geburtstag* (Bonn: Verlag für Kultur und Wissenschaft, 1998), pp. 46–57.

the city. *The guards of the city* could refer to its own armed forces, but in the vision they are clearly those who will 'visit' upon it (lit.) its fate. 'Executioners' is a good translation.[46] There is another irony here, in that such 'guardians' would normally mean angelic powers entrusted with *defending* the city, whereas here they are summoned to treat Jerusalem as the enemy of God it had tragically become. Seven figures appear. Six of them are fiercely armed to do the job.[47] The seventh, clearly the first person in history to believe that the pen is mightier than the sword, has a writing kit strapped to his side, to check the results. This last figure is dressed in linen. Linen was usually bleached white and was the customary dress of priests and sometimes of angelic visitors.[48]

Before these characters begin their work, Ezekiel notices a movement of the glory of God in his vision (9:3a). It was in its normal position *above the cherubim*, which in this context must mean the two enormous gold-plated cherubim in the Holy of Holies – the inner sanctum of the temple where the ark of the covenant rested.[49] Ezekiel could never have gone there in person, of course, but his vision gives him access to places beyond his physical reach. The glory lifts and moves just a little to the east, *to the threshold of the temple.* Apart from making it very clear who it is who is issuing the commands to the angelic executioners gathered close by, this ominous moment is the first stage in its withdrawal from the city, which will be complete by 11:23. The glory of God, which is leaving because it has been so irretrievably offended by the sin of Israel, is now defended in three ways.

a. The glory of God defended by the protection of the repentant (9:4)

Before the six armed executioners set off on their gruesome task, the priestly looking scribe is given a vital instruction – to go through the city putting *a mark on the foreheads of those who grieve and lament over all the detestable things that are done in it.* This means those who are genuinely and deeply repentant and distressed by the kinds of wickedness described in the preceding five scenes. *Grieve and lament* are strong, rhyming words[50] which portray a very real, physical grief being expressed loudly and emotionally. On one occasion Ezekiel was commanded to give vent to such groaning as

---

[46] Block (1), p. 300.
[47] The weapons are not specified, except that they were for destruction. Swords may be meant, or axes, or 'battle clubs' (NLT).
[48] Exod. 28:29–42; Dan. 10:5; 12:6–7.   [49] 1 Kgs. 6:23–28; 8:6–7.
[50] *'ānâ* and *'ānaq,* 'moaning and groaning' (Block), 'sigh and cry' (KJV).

a sign-act of the suffering of Jerusalem (21:11–12);[51] on another occasion, to hold it in, even in the face of the death of his dear wife – again as a sign (24:15–24). We may be surprised to discover that there were in fact such people in Jerusalem, people who were not in collusion with the wickedness and violence, 'those who, in the words of the Gospel, hunger and thirst after justice'.[52] When God sent Jeremiah to go through the streets of Jerusalem to see if he could 'find but one person who deals honestly and seeks the truth', it seems to have turned out to be a fruitless search.[53] Perhaps the shock of the first attack and deportation in 597 had shaken some into a change of heart and life. At any rate, we may assume that they were a minority, given that one angelic figure alone would mark them for protection while six others did the job of killing the wicked.

The *mark* was simply the final letter of the Hebrew alphabet, *taw*, or T, which in Ezekiel's day was written in the archaic Hebrew script as a simple, slightly sloping cross, like a large lower-case letter 't'.[54] To place a mark on someone or something could indicate ownership – these were the only people who truly belonged to Yahweh; but more likely it was simply meant as a protective mark when the destroying angels went about their task. It is similar, in that purpose, to the marking of the doorposts of the Hebrew homes with the blood of the Passover lamb in Egypt just prior to the exodus, to protect them from the destroying angel of Yahweh who inflicted the final plague upon their Egyptian oppressors.[55] The scene is comparable here: wicked oppressors are about to be slain by the agents of God's righteous judgment, but the innocent are to be spared by being marked for protection.[56]

Part of the glory of Yahweh as God is his commitment to utter righteousness and justice. His exaltation and his holiness are demonstrated precisely in those aspects of his character.[57] It was this conviction which led Abraham to intercede for Sodom on the basis of the affirmation 'Will not the Judge of all the earth do right?'[58] The same conviction underlies Ezekiel's exclamation in 9:8.

---

[51] The word is even used of cattle bellowing in hunger (Joel 1:18).

[52] Blenkinsopp, p. 58.   [53] Jer. 5:1–5.

[54] Early Christian interpretation, not surprisingly, saw this mark of the *taw* as a sign of the cross. Apart from the similarity of meaning at the level of protection (the cross of Christ protects us from the wrath of God), such symbolism is of course anachronistic.

[55] Exod. 12:1–30.

[56] The mark is also sometimes compared to the mark (which is not, however, called a *taw*) that God placed on Cain for his protection (Gen. 4:15). In that incident, however, the mark did not denote innocence, but God's gracious protection of Cain from the vengeance of others.

[57] Is. 5:16.   [58] Gen. 18:25.

God's judgment will be horrendously effective, just as it has been utterly deserved and long overdue. But it will also be discriminating. God sees and knows the response of every individual human heart and he will distinguish the repentant from the unrepentant. This fundamental truth, which still lies at the heart of the rationale for all evangelism, exercised the mind of Ezekiel greatly, and in later chapters he will devote much energy to arguing the case for it with the exiles and seeking to persuade them to join the protected camp of the repentant, even in their present circumstances.

When the events which are here prophetically viewed in advance from a heavenly perspective actually took place in history (that is, when the Babylonians finally captured and torched Jerusalem in 587/ 586), there was indeed a great deal of slaughter. We may be fairly sure that many relatively innocent people were killed (cf. 9:6), and that not all who would have qualified for the visionary mark of repentance were actually spared in the conflagration.[59] Conversely, not all the wicked were actually killed in the final battles, but many went off into captivity to join Ezekiel and the other exiles in Babylon – where they were faced with yet another chance to repent under the preaching of Ezekiel's later ministry. This leads to a reflection that we shall have to pick up again when we come to Ezekiel's later preaching to the exiles: what is meant by life and death in their fuller sense in terms of God's promises or warnings to this generation of his people? Some who were innocent of the national idolatry and wickedness nevertheless perished in the destruction of the city. Some who ultimately would in fact die in exile were nevertheless promised that if they would 'turn', that is repent, they could 'live' and not 'die'. If the glory of God is truly expressed in his ultimate discrimination between the righteous and the wicked, between the repentant and the unrepentant, then there must be a deeper reality to 'life' and 'death' than simply its physical circumstances or timing. For the moment, however, it is enough to note that the enthroned glory of Yahweh at the threshold of the temple did not release the executioners until the repentant had been carefully marked out and claimed as his own.

---

[59] This would seem to be the implication of 21:3–4, where the unsheathed sword of Yahweh will cut off 'the righteous and the wicked'. This cannot mean that Yahweh sees no difference between them, for such an idea would fly in the face of all the passionate preaching of Ezekiel elsewhere. Rather, it is probably a 'merism', that is, where two polar opposites are expressed simultaneously as a graphic way of denoting the totality of something (e.g. 'heaven and earth', 'from head to toe', 'land and sea', 'root and branch'). The graphic poem evokes the horror of the total wiping out of Jerusalem.

b. The glory of God defended by the destruction of the wicked (9:5–7)

At last the executioners begin their terrible task. The scene is as horrible for us to contemplate as it was for Ezekiel to witness in his vision. It is of course a picture tinged with apocalyptic, but it did happen in history when the deadly weapons of God's angelic warriors took the form of Babylonian siege machinery, swords and torches. The historical slaughter is interpreted in advance as divine judgment, in the same way as Israel's military attack upon the Canaanites in the previous millennium was interpreted as divine judgment upon them.[60] The tragedy is that Israel had in fact effectively 'Canaanized' themselves and would now be treated as the enemies of God, in line with God's warning at that time that if Israel were to behave like the Canaanites, God would treat Israel in the same consistent way. The comprehensiveness of the destruction has clear echoes of the conquest. The whole community of that generation will suffer the undiluted outpouring of Yahweh's anger – an anger that has been pent up for generations but can no longer be withheld without bringing the very character of Yahweh into massive discredit.[61]

For Ezekiel the horror is compounded with the instruction *'Begin at my sanctuary.'* Thus Ezekiel sees in his vision the fulfilment of the warning of Jeremiah 7:1–15. The place of sanctuary becomes the place of destruction. The place that should have been the focal point of God's protective presence among his people has become the focal point of their hostility to him and therefore the focal point of his judgment on them. It was a deeply ingrained tradition of Israel's faith that Yahweh would fight against his enemies *from* Zion. The awful truth is that his enemies are now *within* Zion. There is also the situational irony that the people of Jerusalem were watching out from their walls for the enemy they expected to come from afar, while all the time their real enemy was within. Indeed, there is an almost pantomime grotesqueness in the detail that the slayers began with the elders doing their sun worship with their backs to the temple. Viewers from the direction they were pointing would want to call out in warning, 'It's behind you!'

The terrible lesson of this section is that the people of God, far from being immune to his judgment, are all the more exposed to it on account of the privilege of being his covenant people and having all the benefits of his revealing and redeeming activity. This text may well have been in Peter's mind when he wrote, 'It is time for

[60] Gen. 15:16; Lev. 18:24–28; 20:22–23; Deut. 9:1–6.
[61] This is the theme of chs. 20 and 36.

judgment to begin with the family of God; and if it begins with us, what will the outcome be for those who do not obey the gospel of God?'[62] The message of Ezekiel is a constant warning to us not to take lightly the reality of God's judgment, nor to imagine that it affects only people outside the boundaries of the church.

Finally, the section is a reminder that, although it describes a particular traumatic and climactic moment in the history of Israel, it is part of a wider biblical affirmation, not at all confined to the Old Testament but shared by Jesus and the New Testament writers, that ultimately God will destroy the unrepentantly wicked in his righteous anger. This is no matter of gloating, for although it represents the triumph of God's justice and is part of his glory, it explicitly gives him no pleasure whatsoever (33:11, etc.). This too is a theme we shall return to later. Here, however, it is vitally important that we take note, theologically and missiologically, that the glory of God, which pervades this awful scene even as it slowly moves away from it (cf. 10:4–5), is fully manifested both in the protection and salvation of repentant saints and in the ultimate judgment and destruction of unrepentant sinners. We can praise him for the former, even if, like Ezekiel, we can only fall in trembling intercession in response to the latter.

c. The glory of God defended by the intercession of the prophet (9:8–10; 11:13)

> The prophet is left in the temple court alone with the angry God, while cries and shrieks can be heard from the streets of the city. The whole mass of his nation's misery overwhelms the prophet. He finds it impossible to maintain his usual attitude of dumb obedience and silent acceptance of his Lord's decisions. He is forced to utter a cry of grief, and to address a question to the judge.[63]

For all the hardness that God had embossed on Ezekiel (2:8–9), he could not remain unmoved by this searing vision. It would add to the dramatic tension of his real-life position among the exiles in his own home if he actually flung himself to the floor at this point and cried out the agonized question of 9:8. If 3:26 (see above) was in fact a prohibition on Ezekiel interceding for these people, then it is a prohibition too far. He simply cannot comply with it in silence. He must cry out in protest and challenge. In this Ezekiel stands in a long and noble tradition of prophetic intercession on behalf of Israel in the face of God's judgment. Abraham is the first instance, though his was on behalf of Sodom and Gomorrah (a relevant comparison which Ezekiel himself will pick up later in 16:44–66).[64] Moses provides the most outstanding model at the time of the great apostasy of the golden calf.[65] In briefer ways Amos and Jeremiah both pleaded with God against the judgment he was proposing, until God told Jeremiah to stop; the people had passed the point of repentance and pardon.[66]

Ezekiel's words in 9:8, however, are not, strictly speaking, intercession – except by implication. Rather, they are a challenging question to God about his intentions. And the focus is specifically on *the entire remnant of Israel*. Ever since the great pre-exilic prophets had begun to predict the judgment and destruction of Israel as fulfilment of God's covenant threats, they had also built in a word of hope through the concept of 'a remnant'. Some see this already in Amos,[67] but it certainly becomes a major part of Isaiah's message, to the extent that he named one of his sons 'Shear-Jashub' – 'a remnant will return'.[68] In the mind of the prophets, then, the future hopes of Israel thus came to focus on this remnant that would survive the purging fires of judgment and carry forward God's longstanding promise for Israel and the nations.

But now in his vision Ezekiel is witnessing what looks like a final wiping out even of that remnant. Ezekiel may not yet have come to identify the exiles (including himself, of course), with the remnant spoken of by earlier prophets. Like the rest of the exiles in those early years he would probably still have thought that the future lay with some group in Jerusalem. It would take a while for the message of Jeremiah 24 to sink in, in which Jeremiah identified the exiles as the 'good figs' who would inherit God's future for his people. So Ezekiel's agonized challenge to God effectively means, 'God, is this really the end for all your purpose for Israel? If you now destroy even this remnant left in Jerusalem, will there really be nobody left at all to carry on God's wider purpose through Israel for the nations?' How could the mission of Israel to bring blessing to the nations, by bringing the knowledge of Yahweh to them, be fulfilled if Israel itself were annihilated? The latter dimension of his question is not explicit in his cry, but it certainly exercised his thinking a lot, as we shall see in later chapters.

[64] Gen. 18:22–33.   [65] Exod. 32 – 34.   [66] Amos 7:1–6; Jer. 14:11–12; 15:1.
[67] Amos 3:12, though this is probably massively sarcastic and implies total destruction. A couple of bones and an ear is conclusive evidence that the poor sheep has been comprehensively devoured.
[68] Is. 7:3; cf. Is. 6:13; 11:1, 16; 10:20–27.

Ezekiel's intercession, then, like that of Abraham and Moses, is based not merely on heart-wrenching pity for those who were being slain, but on the ultimate purpose and glory of Yahweh among the nations.[69] In that respect, also like Abraham and Moses, it stands as a model for what ought to be the primary motivating force behind all our own intercession for the world, and especially for the church when, through hardness, disobedience and apostasy, it puts itself in the path of God's imminent judgment. It is of course entirely right to pray out of compassion for others. Jesus and Paul both did. But Ezekiel models an even deeper foundation for intercession – passion for the glory and purposes of God in the world.

The answer Ezekiel gets to his question almost seems to ignore it. God simply reasserts the utterly justified nature of the punishment (9:9), and repeats his determination to carry it through without pity, bringing chapter 9 to a close on the same note as the ending of chapter 8 (cf. 9:10 and 8:18). There will be no reprieve. No second thoughts. No appeal. All that remains is the record of the deed done (9:11). So, to Ezekiel's question, was that a yes? Yes, God *is* going to destroy the entire remnant? That must have been the implication that Ezekiel in his prostrate desperation took from such a reply. Any hope at all seems to be futile, or at least held in suspense until a second exclamation in 11:13 draws forth a different answer.

Before moving on to the climax of the vision, however, it is worth pausing again with the chilling words of 8:18 and 9:10, *'I will not look on them with pity.'* It would be easy, with all the surrounding scene of armed executioners and terrible carnage, to imagine these words being spoken with vicious coldness and implacable malice. Actually we need to remember that they were being spoken by the God who longed more than anything else to show pity, by the God who had spent centuries with this people withholding the full extent of his wrath, by the God whose very name 'Yahweh' is defined as 'compassionate and gracious'.[70] If there was steel in the voice, there were tears in the eyes and unbearable pain in the heart. For this is the same God who had cried out to his people more than a century ago,

> How can I give you up, Ephraim?
> How can I hand you over, Israel? ...
> My heart is changed within me;
>   all my compassion is aroused.
> I will not carry out my fierce anger,
>   nor will I turn and devastate Ephraim.[71]

[69] Cf. Gen. 18:18–19; Exod. 32:12; Num. 14:13–16, and note v. 21.
[70] Exod. 34:6; Ps. 103:8–10; Jonah 4:2.   [71] Hos. 11:8–9; cf. Jer. 30:20.

And yet, he had had to do so because of their unchanged rebellion, and the northern kingdom was destroyed in 721 BC. This is the same God whose mercy longs to triumph over justice,[72] whose love outlasts his punishment on a scale of 1,000 to 1,[73] who 'is slow to anger and rich in love', who is 'good to all' and 'has compassion on all he has made'.[74] For such a God to be brought to the extremity of having to utter the terrifying words we read here speaks more loudly than anything else could of the horrific, detestable and intolerable nature of human sin, and the moral necessity of its being finally and justly punished.

Rather than merely recoiling from the iciness of the words, we should reflect on what it cost the heart of the God of all love, mercy and pity to have to utter such words at all. And such reflections will drive us ultimately to the cross, for only there do we find the mystery of the infinite love and the infinite justice of God fully exposed before human gaze. For there, under the whips, swords, nails and torture of Roman rather than Babylonian enemies, God's love absorbed God's justice in God's own self, and the words *'I will not … pity or spare'* were breathed again by the Father as, for our sake, he turned his eyes away from the agony of his own beloved Son.

3. The glory of God suspended (10:1–22; 11:1–23)

The motif of the gradual departure of the glory of Yahweh from the city gathers speed throughout these two chapters. It is described as a physical rising up and moving off eastwards. But this literal suspending of the glory takes on a metaphorical dimension as well, since there are questions hanging in the air at the end of chapter 11. Where, if anywhere, does the glory go from its last observed location – the mountain east of Jerusalem? And will it ever come back? So there is a suspense about the future which is not answered fully until much later in the book. The immediate focus, however, is the role of the glory with its own undercarriage suspension in the final judgment on the city.

a. Suspended for judgment (10:1–22; 11:22–23, 1–13)

Right from the initial welcome on his arrival in the city (8:4), Ezekiel has been aware throughout his vision so far of the brooding presence of the glory of Yahweh. He had spotted its first movement eastward, from above the cherubim in the Holy of Holies to the threshold of the temple (9:3, identical to 10:4). Now, suddenly, he becomes aware

---

[72] Jas. 2:13.   [73] Deut. 7:9–10.   [74] Ps. 145:8–9, 13, 17.

of the whole original composite vision that he had seen on his birthday – complete with the *throne of sapphire* (10:1), the platform beneath it, the living creatures, the wheels underneath, and the racket of the cherubim wings. As he watches, with his ears already filled with the sound of the slaughter going on in the city, he hears the voice of the occupant of the throne again, giving further instructions to *the man clothed in linen*. Now Ezekiel further discovers the purpose for the fiery, flaming heart of the throne chariot; it is to provide fire for the final destruction of the city after the killing of the inhabitants (10:2, 6–7). The angelic figure, no longer a mere scribe but now joining the ranks of the agents of destruction, is to take *burning coals from among the cherubim and scatter them over the city*. It is an unmistakable image of the fire of God's judgment being let loose on Jerusalem – once again underlining the irony that a fire that was normally reserved for the burning up of Yahweh's enemies[75] is now being scattered on his own people. Indeed, the imagery of the fate of Sodom and Gomorrah is possibly in mind, for Ezekiel was not the first to accuse Jerusalem of being as bad as those cities, or even worse than them, and just as deserving of a similar fate (16:44–52).[76]

Most of the rest of chapter 10 is taken up with some attempted clarification of the original vision and its various details. The main point seems to be that Ezekiel now recognizes (10:20) that the living creatures he had seen by the Kebar Canal were actually cherubim – even though in physical features they seem to have been somewhat different from the cherubim statues of wood and gold that had been erected by Solomon in the temple.[77]

As the slaughter continues and the fire takes hold, Ezekiel watches the glory of Yahweh make its next movement towards departure. It moves *from over the threshold of the temple* (10:18) across the courts to the waiting cherubim chariot, all wings and wheels ready for a short taxi to the eastern gate of the temple complex (10:19) for final take-off. The glory of God cannot continue to dwell in the city that God is handing over to the fires of judgment. Finally, the glory-chariot moves again. This time (11:22–23) it lifts off *from within the city* and makes its exit as far as the *mountain east of it* – later known as the Mount of Olives.

This must have been one of the darkest moments of Ezekiel's ministry, apart from the death of his wife and its symbolic significance (24:15–24). He would have known the story of the

---

[75] Ps. 97:3; Is. 26:11.   [76] Cf. Is. 1:9–10.

[77] For helpful discussion of the details, and explanations for the somewhat different description of the creatures' four faces in 10:14, cf. Block (1), pp. 323–327, and Allen 28, pp. 152–159.

departure of the glory of Yahweh from his people when the Philistines captured the ark of the covenant – before even the temple was built – and the naming of Eli's posthumous grandson Ichabod, 'No glory', to mark that tragedy.[78] But that was centuries ago, before all the promises that Yahweh had made in relation to his temple and this city. Yet now, in his own blighted lifetime not only had Ezekiel been expelled from his beloved city, but he had also lived to witness something even worse – the glory of his covenant God, Yahweh, leaving his temple, leaving his city, leaving his people to their destruction.

At this point (11:1), Ezekiel finds himself suddenly shifted to another location to witness a remarkable scene at the eastern gate of the temple: a group of public figures discussing building projects as if nothing were happening inside the city. It may seem odd that such a group were still around in the wake of the slaughter and fire already described in chapter 9, but we need to remember that this is all part of a vision and visions do not always conform precisely to logic or chronology. Actually, placing this scene here produces a wonderful double irony. Not only is this group of pompous men engaged in planning their future apparently unaware of the mayhem in the city that will soon overtake them, but also they are doing so at the very spot (the east gate of the temple) where the glory of God had just passed on its exit from the city. There they are complacently assuming their own safety when the Lord himself, their only possible protector, has just gone and they haven't even noticed.

The *twenty-five men* whom he overhears in conversation are described as *leaders of the people*, that is, public officials, who had obviously not been among those of the governing class who had been carried off into exile in 597 BC. Ezekiel recognizes two of them from his own pre-exile acquaintances in the city, Jaazaniah[79] and Pelatiah. Their discussion is described as *plotting evil* and *giving wicked advice* (11:2). When taken with the rather enigmatic proverb that follows, this almost certainly means that they were giving false hope to the inhabitants (or at least to their own landed and privileged class), in the expectation of a safe delivery from any possible siege. Such advice was 'evil and wicked' because it led the people into complacent optimism when they should have been engaging in deep repentance and radical change of heart and life. But in the absence of such repentance, their doom was already sealed, as Jeremiah and Ezekiel both made clear. To reassure the unrepentant is to share in their wickedness.

[78] 1 Sam. 4:18–22.
[79] Not to be confused with the other Jaazaniah, apparent ringleader of the elders worshipping the Egyptian deities in the darkened room in 8:11.

The basis of their optimism seems again to be the expected inviolability of the city of Jerusalem. *This city is a cooking pot, and we are the meat* (11:3) may not sound to our ears like a proverb describing a safe place to be, yet that is what it is, as God's contradiction of it in verse 11 makes clear. In ancient Israel the best cuts of meat were cooked in a pot on the fire (probably boiled), whereas poorer pieces and offal would be fried over the open fire, or discarded altogether. These leaders, therefore, are expressing a double arrogance: on the one hand they see themselves as the choice pieces, the prime cuts, of the meat – the ones who will therefore not only survive, but survive with their privileges intact; on the other hand they still regard Jerusalem, with its covenant guarantees, as being as impregnable as an iron pot,[80] in which they will be safe from the fire of the enemy's attacks.

Who then were the offal? In the minds of these new leaders, the offal that would be thrown out of the pot referred probably both to the former leaders, who had been taken off into exile and were now being gleefully written off by those left behind in Jerusalem, who could profiteer in their absence (cf. 11:15), and also to the poorer, ordinary people of the city and countryside who were suffering violence and dispossession because of the greedy land-grabbing tactics of such men (11:6–7). God reverses both prejudices. Those who have gone into exile will eventually experience a reversal of fortune and they will be the ones to inherit the future (11:16–21, see below), and those who have been the victims of injustice and violence in the city will be the ones whom Yahweh will vindicate and treat as the best meat (11:7).

These considerations help us to interpret the difficult saying in 11:3a. They were saying (lit.), 'It is not near for the building of houses.' This may be a negative statement: 'It is not time now to be building houses', which could mean either 'Consolidate, defend and hold on – don't embark on new investments,' or 'We don't need to be worried about our building projects; we'll be safe.' Some, however, read it as a question: 'Is it not time to build houses?' This turns it into a positive statement which would imply, 'There is nothing to fear from this attack; it will soon be over and we can get back to business as usual.' Whichever is correct, it seems certain that it was a complacent attitude, and it is also quite possible that the

---

[80] Block (1), pp. 331–332, suggests that the *pot* may not be the iron cooking-pot, but could be the crockery storage pot in which the prime cuts of meat would be salted and sealed securely and then stored for future use. This would be a fitting image for their expectation that they would survive the present troubles and emerge with their land and wealth intact. But most other uses of the term in the Old Testament seem to refer to a cooking or stewing cauldron (e.g. 2 Kgs. 4:38–41).

connection with building projects reflects the ruthless tactics of seizure of land and property being practised by the Jerusalem élite over a century earlier that was so hateful to Micah.[81] These powerful few, and the class they represent, were taking full advantage of the national distress to line their own pockets (a well-known phenomenon in war-time), and they were going so far as to murder for their greed (11:6–7).

God's word of judgment on these men – reported by Ezekiel to the elders back in Babylon, but having direct and shocking effect in Jerusalem itself (11:13; see below) – rebutts the proverb and turns it upside down (or inside out, to prolong the pot image). Those who think themselves safe inside the pot will be thrown out to face the fire and sword. Far from being safe in the city, they will be driven out to be slain at the very extremities of the land – *the borders of Israel*, where some of them have probably never set foot before. They will be treated like offal, in the same way as they have treated the poor and dispossessed, whose bodies they have stacked in the streets in their atrocities of greed. In a wider sense also, it will mean they will be treated with the same contempt that they no doubt had for the pagan nations banging at the walls of Jerusalem – nations with whom they have already been compared unfavourably (11:12b; cf. 5:5–7). But most of all, this act of judgment will vindicate Yahweh (11:12a) – the God who characteristically acts to uphold the victimized and put down the mighty in the imagination of their hearts.[82]

At this point Ezekiel suddenly sees *Pelatiah*, one of the men in his vision, drop down dead (11:13). The shock of this juxtaposition of visions of angelic judgment with the death of a real-life acquaintance forces another exclamation out of Ezekiel. It is not so much a question as an astonished affirmation, 'Then you really do intend to destroy completely the remnant of Israel!' Whereas Yahweh's answer to the question in 8:8 had been virtual agreement that, yes, that is what he was doing, this second outburst from Ezekiel leads to a response from Yahweh which, for the first time, injects a note of hope into the otherwise horrendous darkness of the scene all around Ezekiel in his vision. So we turn, finally, to the hope with which the whole vision comes to an end.

b. Suspended in hope (11:14–21)

In 11:14–15, one final piece of Jerusalem gossip is revealed to Ezekiel

---

[81] Mic. 2:1–2, 8–9; 3:1–4 – a passage which may even have suggested the cooking-pot metaphor.

[82] Ps. 146; 1 Sam. 2:1–10. In Dan. 4:37 the point is acknowledged even by Nebuchadnezzar himself, after a word of authentic prophetic warning in 4:27.

before the end of his vision. What was the word on the street in Jerusalem regarding the exiles in Babylon? Not very flattering. Whatever the optimists in Babylon were saying about a rapid return, the people left behind in Jerusalem were intent on making the most of their absence. If the exiles were *far away from the LORD*, then they had also lost their stake in his land. So this was yet another factor in the opportunistic profiteering that was going on in the troubled times. People were hardly out of the city before others were muscling in on their property and land. The injustices of war are nothing new. As we have seen in the recent Balkan wars, when people are displaced through ethnic cleansing or aerial bombing, the homes they leave behind are at the mercy of scavengers. When Ezekiel reported this particular piece of news back in his house in Babylon it must have added to the hapless exiles' depression and alienation. Never mind Nebuchadnezzar; the precious homes and possessions they had left behind were not even safe from their own compatriots.

Such then, was the view of the situation from the perspective of some circles in Jerusalem. But what was God's view? As often, some human perspective or opinion provides the trigger for a divine word that not only addresses the immediate issue under discussion, but goes far beyond it in scope and vision. So here, God's answer in verses 16–21 first of all simply contradicts the Jerusalem opinion. The exiles are not lost to history and the future. They are scattered, yes, but they will be kept safe. God himself will be *a sanctuary for them* – a remarkable irony in the immediate context of the destruction of the physical sanctuary in Jerusalem. In fact, there is irony in the very structure of chapter 11. In its first half, the leading citizens who are left in Jerusalem will be dragged out of the city for judgment and destruction (7–11). In the second half, the exiles who have already been dragged out of the city in judgment will conversely eventually be gathered for restoration (16–17).

Then God's answer goes on to summarize and anticipate much more far-reaching promises which will be filled out in glorious detail later – especially in chapters 34, 36 and 37. This word of hope brings a positive ending to Ezekiel's long, dark vision, even though it brought no immediate hope to his listeners. For the destruction of the city would be total, and it was indeed the end of the history of Israel for most of the people of that generation. But it was *not* God's intention, as Ezekiel's outbursts had feared, to annihilate the remnant of his people entirely. There was hope for Israel's future. But this would not be founded on the exiles' false hopes and fraudulent protests about their own righteousness and the undeserved excesses of God's judgment. There was a long road of ministry still ahead for

Ezekiel before the people could be sufficiently disillusioned of all such deceptions. For it would only be as they plumbed the depths of contrition that repentance and restoration could be possible.

Meanwhile, the glory had departed from the city (22–23). But Ezekiel has just heard that the people will eventually return. Will the glory return then also, or will God tell the people to go back but that he will not come with them – as he had once threatened Moses?[83] The glory had stopped at the Mount of Olives. Was it merely pausing on a continuing eastward journey that would take it to the exiles in Babylon, back to where Ezekiel had first seen it? Or did it intend to wait and watch from the mountain until the exiles would return and then welcome them back to the city? Tantalizing questions. They express the suspense that the closing moments of Ezekiel's vision must have engendered.

But the most important question had been answered – the one asked or implied twice in Ezekiel's fear and desperation (8:8; 10:13). Did Yahweh indeed intend to finish off even the remnant of his people finally and for ever? Praise his name; the answer was no!

Conclusion

So Ezekiel 'returns' by direct Spirit express to the exiles sitting impatiently before him in his own home (11:24–25). Probably little time was wasted as he related *everything the LORD had shown* him. In the introduction to this chapter we asked what this vision would have meant for Ezekiel. It is worth asking the same question about those to whom this first report of the vision was given. What impact would Ezekiel's report of his vision have had on that little group of guests in his home? Remember that they were 'elders of Judah' – that is, they were from the same class of people whom Ezekiel witnessed in the secret room in the temple, in the inner court, and conversing at the eastern gate. For these men it must have been an uncomfortably nasty account to have to listen to. One may imagine that the surprise over the revelation of what was happening in the temple was not as great for them as it seems to have been for Ezekiel. Some of them at least must have been engaged in some of these practices in the temple themselves before being yanked out into exile. The big shock would have been to realize that some of the more secret goings-on (e.g. esp. 8:7–13) had now been witnessed by this young uninitiated priest sitting in front of them. To the extent that they recognized the truth of the report Ezekiel gave, they were then faced with a sharp choice. Either they must accept Ezekiel as

---

[83] Exod. 33:1–3.

a true prophet (since he had reported what they knew to be true), and then be moved to grief and repentance for their past actions. Or they could brazenly deny the truth, mock the messenger, and harden their hearts against God still further in their rebellion.

It is a terribly painful and threatening thing to be faced with sins of the past, to hear or to fear their being exposed. It is a devastating encounter with reality, a ruthless wrenching away of our masks of pretence. But it is also a profoundly defining moment in one's relationship with God. At such a moment one is faced, like Ezekiel's guests, with a stark choice. One option is to fall face down before God in grief and shame, comforted only by the humility and repentance that led the psalmist to plead, 'Remember not the sins of my youth and my rebellious ways; according to your love remember me, for you are good, O LORD.'[84]

The psalmist could make such a request because he was secure in the reassurance that 'If you, O LORD, kept a record of sins, O LORD, who could stand? But with you there is forgiveness; therefore you are feared.'[85]

The other option is to continue stubbornly in sin, heedless of all warnings or pleading, and face the consequences that befall the arrogantly unrepentant.[86] That is the choice that faces us whenever we are challenged, by other people or directly by the Holy Spirit, over our sinful actions.

Perhaps even in the reading of these scorching chapters our hearts have been moved to a more profound awareness of the sin that lurks in the hidden recesses of the present or the past. Perhaps we have seen the idolatry in our drive for security, the flirtation with sexual licence that we call maturity or freedom, the arrogance, complacency and false security that feed off our relative wealth and comfort. If the Holy Spirit exposes any part of our lives, past or present, as sin, then deal with it as such. Do not, like the exiles, blame others or accuse God. Do not, like so many today, explain it, excuse it or put it in perspective. Sin is sin and when it is exposed we are left with only two mutually exclusive alternatives – repentance or hardening. 'Today, if you hear his voice, do not harden your hearts.'[87]

Such was the choice that now confronted the silent, stony faces in front of Ezekiel himself in that hot little room on 17 September 592 BC.

---

[84] Ps. 25:7. [85] Ps. 130:3–4.
[86] As illustrated by the stories of Nebuchadnezzar and Belshazzar in Dan. 4 and 5. See esp. Dan. 5:20–23.
[87] Ps. 95:7–8.

16:1–63; 23:1–49; 20:1–49
4. History with attitude

Introduction

Second only, perhaps, to the genealogies in 1 Chronicles, the lurid allegories of Ezekiel 16 and 23 must qualify as the chapters in the Bible least likely to be read aloud in church – and just as unlikely to be preached from. They are long, they are lewd, and their language in places is, frankly, pornographic. They evoke images of the most vulgar sexual depravity and the most horrendous graphic violence. They are, in short, shocking. Shocking also is what they were intended to be when they emerged from the mouth of this young son of a priest, who must himself have been utterly appalled at what he was being given to say as Yahweh's spokesman. In fact, it is difficult to imagine Ezekiel pouring out this torrent of prophetic prurience without excruciating embarrassment and abhorrence. As one who claimed that his lips had never been defiled by unclean food (4:14) what must it have felt like to have his lips defiled by such unclean language? Especially if his wife was listening. For the fact is that most English translations have to tone down the offensive coarseness of some of the original expressions of sexual lust and obscene behaviour used in these chapters. If they offend our eyes and ears today – we who are accustomed to a barrage of such language and images in the western media – what must they have done to Ezekiel's first hearers in his own language? We can be sure, therefore, that this is not a matter of gratuitous bad taste, or evidence of some sick perversion to add to the catalogue of Ezekiel's other alleged personality disorders. These are deliberate shock tactics on a scale probably unsurpassed in the whole arsenal of prophetic assault and battery weapons.

So what was the shock intended to achieve? We need to remember that in the early years of the exile, Ezekiel's contemporaries were for the most part still convinced that they were being treated unfairly. They knew the story of Israel and this was not how it was supposed to wind up. According to the story, they were the elect people of Yahweh who had given guarantees to them at several points in their glorious past that he would always defend them. What had happened now must therefore be some kind of temporary setback, a mere technical hitch, or perhaps some kind of slip-up in the divine management of affairs. Once Yahweh had got things properly back under control, then their history could continue as before. Ezekiel's ultimate purpose was to bring the exiles to recognize the truth about their situation and thus drive them to genuine repentance. That was impossible as long as they cherished false ideas about their past as well as their present. And it was doubly difficult as long as there was still hope because Jerusalem was still standing. Somehow he had to get across the certainty that Jerusalem was doomed, and to demonstrate that such a fate was utterly deserved, fully explicable and long overdue. He had acted this message out with great personal suffering for over a year. He had exposed what was going on in the heart of Jerusalem itself. But still the people clung in hope to their glorious *history*. So Ezekiel will revisit that history and retell the story in a thoroughly revisionist way.

For his retelling Ezekiel chose the literary device of allegory – that is, a deliberately constructed story in which it is clearly understood by teller and hearer alike that the language is symbolical and refers to some reality other than the characters and plot of the allegory itself. It is a tool that is well suited to both edification[1] and satire.[2] In Ezekiel's hands it becomes the dynamite necessary to explode a whole set of religious assumptions, demolishing an unsafe building and clearing the site before any reconstruction can be planned. Chapter 20 is not allegorical, but it has the same purpose as 16 and 23, that is, to go back over Israel's history and to show that it constituted one long story of Yahweh's grace followed by Israel's rebellion, followed by declared but suspended punishment. It makes its point by a very emphatic structured presentation of the story, from its earliest beginnings to the present day. Since it carries the same revisionist message as the two grand allegories, we include it in this chapter of our exposition (at section 3 below).

Finally, before we plunge into the lurid colours of the tales before us, it is worth pausing to recognize the immensity of what Ezekiel attempts here. These are not just fairy stories. What Ezekiel is daring to touch here is the grand national epic of Israel, the story above all stories by which they understood themselves and the rest of the world. As human beings we live by stories – the grand ones such as

---

[1] As, e.g., John Bunyan's *Pilgrim's Progress.*
[2] As, e.g., Jonathan Swift's *Gulliver's Travels.*

Israel's, by which we have received our cultural identity and our basic assumptive worldview, and the lesser ones that tell us who we are in our own smaller context of family and society. You don't tamper with the stories without upsetting people. The teaching of national history in schools is always a matter of sensitivity and debate because it is perceived either to reinforce or to undermine certain perceptions of the nation's identity and place in the world. Great revolutions, such as the Communist revolutions in Russia and Eastern Europe, have always involved the rewriting of history in order to vindicate the new regime. Israel knew their story more than most, for their whole sense of identity, as well as their whole understanding of the world of other nations and of the universe itself, was dependent on the way they understood Yahweh to have acted in their past. And that story of Israel, at the time of the late monarchy, had generated a worldview which took as axiomatic that Israel was indestructible, Jerusalem was inviolable, the covenant was unbreakable – all would be well, come hell or Nebuchadnezzar. But Ezekiel dares to tell the story in a way which leads to, or rather demands, a very different ending. When Jesus did the same with his parable of the tenants in the vineyard, giving the story of Israel a very different flavour and a very different ending from the official version, it galvanized those determined to do away with him altogether.[3] You can't tamper with the stories and stay out of trouble!

1. Jerusalem: My Fair Lady[4] (16:1–43)

Ezekiel's allegories in chapters 16 and 23 may possibly draw on themes that are found in fairly common folk tales – the foundling child who, by the action of some gallant rescuer, ends up as a princess or queen; tales of two or three sisters, one usually more beautiful than the others. But if so, Ezekiel has certainly 'bent' them to his own ends, and indeed, in the second allegory, he has totally inverted the traditional tale. In the first allegory (substantially

---

[3] Matt. 21:33–46. On the significance of stories as a major factor in worldviews in general, and the particular function of Israel's story in their conception of their place in God's purpose for all the world, see N. T. Wright, *The New Testament and the People of God* (London: SPCK, 1992), pp. 69–80, 215–223.

[4] The heading is taken from the title of the musical based on George Bernard Shaw's play *Pygmalion*, which tells the story of a humble flower-seller from a London market who is 'rescued' by a gentleman intent on proving that even the least promising human material can be transformed into an apparently well-bred lady. In Shaw's story, however, it is the man whose intentions and behaviour are flawed and abusive.

16:1–43),[5] he combines the possibly traditional folk tale of 'pauper to princess' (usually a 'happy ending' motif) with the theme of marital infidelity on a scale of frenzied promiscuity, to produce a very bleak and violent ending.

Ezekiel was far from the first to present the relationship between Yahweh and Israel in terms of a marriage, and conversely to present Israel's breaking of their covenant commitment to Yahweh in terms of marital infidelity or prostitution. All of these metaphors were well established and had been powerfully used by Hosea especially (through the tragedy of his own marriage as a prophetic sign of his message),[6] and also by Jeremiah.[7] However, as so often with Ezekiel, he exploits to the limit what others had merely used as a powerful metaphor. He takes the metaphor and expands it into a narrative, turning a cartoon, as it were, into a video. The message will not just hang in the air as a concept; it will assault the ears and mental vision of his listeners with a rapid succession of garish scenes, offensive vocabulary and sickening violence until it becomes unbearable to listen to.

The most repeated word in the whole chapter is *zānâ*, to engage in prostitution, and the related nouns. Again, the use of this term for Israel's worship of other gods was not new,[8] but the sheer offensiveness of calling Israel a harlot, whore or prostitute some *twenty-one times* in this one chapter, especially with sexually explicit verbal graphics,[9] is breathtaking. When combined with the repeated phrase that in all their promiscuity they were never 'satisfied' (28–29), it is clear that Ezekiel wants it to be very clear that Israel does not stand accused[10] of a single act of adultery, but of prolonged, addictively repeated, insatiable promiscuity with multiple partners. It is a terrible

---

[5] Although chs. 16 and 23 are self-contained and probably represent distinct oracles given on separate occasions, there is a definite thematic shift at 16:44, after which the content of the rest of that chapter is more closely linked thematically to the allegory of Oholah and Oholibah in ch. 23. Similarly, some parts of ch. 23 fill out in more graphic detail some aspects of the punishment described first in ch. 16. For these reasons, our exposition will take 16:44–63 in connection with the second allegory in ch. 23, in section 2 below. And at several points, we shall look at material from both chapters together.

[6] Hos. 2:1–23.

[7] Jer. 2:20–25 (with related imagery of animal sexuality); 3:1–13 (a text which may well have inspired Ezekiel's allegory of the two sisters in ch. 23).

[8] Cf. Exod. 34:15–16; Lev. 17:7; Deut. 31:16.

[9] E.g. 'spreading your legs to every passer-by' (16:25); 'Egyptians with huge organs' (16:26); 'pouring out your "juice"' (16:36). Even more obscene language is used in 23:20–21, etc.

[10] The whole chapter is framed as a prosecution speech in a court of law, with Ezekiel called upon by Yahweh to *confront Jerusalem with her detestable practices* (16:2).

indictment of 'unrestrained nymphomaniacal adventures'.[11]

The story begins, however, as such tales traditionally do, in happier days.

a. The rescue: grace and generosity (16:1–14)

Ezekiel personifies the whole nation of Israel as the capital city Jerusalem,[12] and begins the story in a surprising way. In place of the usual honourable ancestry given in some genealogical form, emphasizing the hallowed tradition of Abraham and the other patriarchs, and instead of the glorious portrayal of Jerusalem as Zion, city of David and focus of the covenant, Ezekiel shockingly gives Israel totally pagan roots. She had sprung from the soil of the *Canaanites*, from parents who were *Amorite* and *Hittite*. There may be a double point to this abrupt beginning. It may allude to the 'foreignness' of the ancestors of Israel, aliens from their own land and not yet 'Israelites'. There was a consciousness of this even in Israel's own creeds: 'My father was a wandering [or perishing] Aramean,' recited the Israelite farmer, probably referring to Jacob.[13] And it may be a reminder that of course Jerusalem had indeed been a Canaanite city, quite possibly with a mixture of Hittite and Amorite population, for centuries before it fell into the hands of David and became Israel's capital city. However, Ezekiel's point is not ethno-geographical, but theological. Israel's own origins were just as pagan as any of the nations they so despised. They had no special claim on God, no special reason for their election.

On the contrary, had it not been for the amazing generosity of Yahweh they would not have survived the day of their birth. The nation is presented to our opening gaze as an unwanted female birth, victim of ruthless intended infanticide. Picture the exposure in the open field under the hot sun of a tiny scrap of newborn humanity, straight from the womb, with the placenta still attached and none of the customary obstetric procedures being wasted on it. It would be certain to die within a few hours of wriggling in a pool of blood. Anything further removed from the glory of David and Solomon's Jerusalem would be hard to imagine. The assault on our imagination and the re-visioning of Israel's history get off to an uncompromising start.

All the more dramatic, then, is the sudden and timely appearance

---

[11] Block (1), p. 465.
[12] The distinction between the northern kingdom of Israel and the southern kingdom of Judah is not relevant at this point of the allegory. It becomes significant only with the development of the two or three sisters after 16:44 and in ch. 23.
[13] Deut. 26:5.

of the rescuer, who is also the narrator of the story, and of course represents Yahweh himself. His intervention is described in two stages. First (6–7), he delivers the infant from its bloody death and decrees that it shall live.[14] This is simply stated as the divine *fiat* that it was. 'He speaks, and, listening to his voice, / New life the dead receive.'[15] As another woman who had just given back to Yahweh a desperately wanted child had affirmed, Yahweh 'brings death and makes alive; he brings down to the grave and raises up'.[16] Israel owed its very existence to Yahweh's word of life in the past. It would owe its continued survival into the future to his will to life also (18:32; 33:11).[17] So the child survives and grows up towards puberty.

Secondly (8–14), the benefactor who had already acted with pure grace (nothing in the condition of the infant deserved or compelled the gift of life), now adds an outpouring of generosity as well. He not only marries her, but beautifies and enriches her to the status of a queen. The stages of this amazing transformation include a symbolic betrothal (*spread the corner of my garment over you*, 8);[18] a solemn marriage covenant which identified the woman as *mine*; cleansing and anointing (9); a wardrobe full of all kinds of *costly garments* (10); adornment with the finest *jewellery* (11–12); and provision of fine food (13). The climax of the whole list, not surprisingly, is that *you became very beautiful and rose to be a queen*, and internationally famous as well, though with the careful reminder that it was all owed to the gracious gift of her divine lover – *because the splendour I had given you made your beauty perfect* (14).

The allegory is not tied too closely to specific historical reference points, but if there is any sequential point in the two actions of the rescuer, then it may be that verses 6–7 allude to the original covenant with Abraham, out of which came the very existence and early survival of Israel through times of threat and danger, while verses 8–14 allude to the Sinai covenant, the more formalized 'marriage covenant' made in Israel's national 'puberty', leading on to the gift of the land with all its bounty and beauty. The climax of international fame (14), may allude to the well-known reputation of Solomon at the height of the united monarchy.[19] If this is roughly

[14] Block suggests on the basis of certain ancient near-eastern parallels that the command to live may also imply the adoption of the abandoned child as the rescuer's own; Block (1), p. 481.

[15] Hymn, 'O for a thousand tongues', by Charles Wesley.

[16] From the song of Hannah, 1 Sam. 2:6.

[17] In ch. 37 Ezekiel changes the metaphor from a victim of infanticide to the skeletons of bodies long dead, and expands even further the miraculous power of the life-giving word of Yahweh.

[18] Cf. Ruth 3:9.   [19] 1 Kgs. 10.

correct, it fits with the presentation of Israel's history in the books of Kings (which were yet to be compiled at the time Ezekiel's early ministry), in which, after the peak of Israel's glory under Solomon, their decline into disastrous idolatry began even within his reign and accelerated thereafter.

Three further points may be made on the significance of this opening of the allegory before we move on to its darker movements.

First, it is a moving and powerful description, albeit in an unusual form, of the loving grace of God and the boundless generosity which flows from it. The picture of utter human weakness, need and vulnerability that the abandoned newborn baby evokes emphasizes that the people of God – whether Old Testament Israel or the church – owe nothing of their status to their own capacity or achievement. Their very existence is dependent on the divine command *Live!* Furthermore, the emphasis on the child's pagan parentage, and the cruelty and contempt with which they behaved, underlines the point that there was nothing desirable, special or creditable in this infant. It was utterly unwanted and despicable even to those who should have loved it. The divine rescuer's action, then, sprang from totally self-motivated and unconditional love. The source, the reason and the purpose of his redeeming action all lay within himself. His action was not compelled by, or dependent on, anything that the wallowing infant might be or do or deserve.

Israel in the Old Testament needed to be reminded of this understanding of their election, namely that it was entirely due to the love and grace of God and not based on any merit in themselves – whether numerical superiority (they were a tadpole among the nations),[20] or moral superiority (they were a stiff-necked bunch of rebels).[21] God chose them for his own purpose among the nations, and because of his own mysterious love and grace, not because of any attribute they possessed.

I am sometimes asked, when teaching the Old Testament, 'What was so special about Israel that God chose them to be his people?' And my answer is always an emphatic, 'Absolutely nothing whatsoever!' – which usually surprises people, since it is not the answer they expect. But surely there must have been some reason? No. Nothing other than the self-motivated love of God, and ultimately his mission to bring blessing to all the nations through this nation whom he chose for that purpose. Without God's redeeming gift of life – an abandoned foetus. Through God's transforming generosity – a resplendent queen. Ezekiel's contrasting images paint the colours of God's grace very boldly indeed.

[20] Deut. 7:7.   [21] Deut. 9:4–6.

The New Testament, less graphically but no less emphatically, exults in the glorious transformation that the grace of God has produced in the lives of those who have turned to Christ, marvels at the generosity of his gifts to us, and reminds us of the dire state we would otherwise be in.[22] It is a healthy spiritual exercise to remind ourselves often of this truth.

> Nothing in my hand I bring,
> Simply to thy cross I cling;
> Naked, come to thee for dress;
> Helpless, look to thee for grace;
> Foul, I to the fountain fly;
> Wash me, Saviour, or I die.[23]

Secondly, the woman's beauty was meant to enhance Yahweh's own reputation. The portrayal of the transformed woman into a queen of splendour, beauty and fame echoes other passages where similar vocabulary is used about Israel. According to Deuteronomy 26:19, it was God's covenant intention that Israel should be (lit.) 'for a praise, fame and honour, high above all the nations he has made'. This, however, was dependent on Israel's obedience to her commitment to covenant holiness. The point, was not just that Israel should be famous, or 'top nation', but that her reputation would enhance Yahweh's. Indeed, the beauty of Israel would be Yahweh's pride and joy and a major source of his own fame among the nations. Jeremiah extended the metaphor to include clothing: Israel was meant to be like a beautiful new sash, worn with pride by its owner. But instead they had become like a tattered rag that had been lying in damp soil. Jeremiah uses the same three-word phrase as Deuteronomy: Israel was to have been 'my people for my renown and praise and honour'.[24] Ezekiel takes it a step further and envisages the pride and joy that a husband has in a beautiful, fully adorned wife (his own wife is described as 'the delight of your eyes', 24:16). People admire the wife and in the same breath compliment the husband.[25] Thus, the splendour and fame of Israel as Yahweh's

[22] E.g. the father's generosity to the prodigal son, Luke 15:22–24; cf. Rom 5:6–8; 1 Cor. 6:9–11; Eph. 2:1–10; 4:22–24.
[23] Hymn 'Rock of Ages, cleft for me', by Augustus Montague Toplady.
[24] Jer. 13:11.
[25] Cf. Prov. 31:23. Interestingly, the same word (ḥādār, 'splendour', 'majesty', 'dignity') is used of this model wife in Prov. 31:25 as of humanity in general (in distinction from the beasts, Ps. 8:5), of the king (Ps. 21:5), and of the elderly (Prov. 20:29!). However, it is observed that the source of the woman's dignity is not transient physical beauty but the fear of Yahweh – in which, of course, she was a model Israelite as well as a model woman (Prov. 31:29).

people should have been in effect the earthly counterpart of the splendour and fame of Yahweh himself.[26]

The word translated *your fame* (16) is *šēm*, which elsewhere is normally translated 'name'. The irony of this verse, therefore, is that the *name* of Israel *spread among the nations*, which is exactly what Yahweh wanted as long as Israel continued to reflect the beauty and glory of Yahweh himself. The tragedy that later chapters (esp. ch. 36) will explore to its depths was that the fame Israel did in fact achieve among the nations was one that sullied and polluted the name of Yahweh because of their gross sin, rebellion and unfaithfulness. The crisp new sash became a tattered rag. The jewelled wife became a painted prostitute. God could no longer 'wear' them nor bear them.

The message of the imagery for us is that as the people who claim the name of the Lord, or rather who have been claimed by him as the bearers of the Lord's name, we live in public view. Where God's people live in God's way, God's name is adorned and beautified, and something of his splendour is witnessed among them. And indeed that is God's purpose, as the New Testament shows. The very existence of the church is for the sake of the greater praise and glory of God, and especially of his redeeming grace.[27] Even the presentation of the church as a bride, cleansed, radiant and beautiful, is recycled from the Old Testament imagery.[28] Do our lives weave the kind of clothing that our Lord would want to be seen in? Do our actions so shine like jewellery that the watching world is led to give glory to our Father, as Jesus exhorted?[29]

Thirdly, some of the details of the clothing and food that are showered on the rescuer's bride are, probably deliberately, echoes of the fabrics and provisions for the tabernacle and priests.[30] The personified Jerusalem is clothed and fed with the furnishing and food

---

[26] This point is actually clearer in Hebrew. Ezek. 16:14b reads (lit.), 'because of *my* splendour which I had put upon you', not just '*the* splendour', as in NIV. Cf. NRSV. The only other use of this form of the word (i.e. '*my* splendour') is interestingly also applied to real-life (not allegorical) women who, along with their children, were being deprived of 'my splendour' by being victims of dispossession and eviction at the hands of ruthless land-grabbers, in eighth century Judea (Mic. 2:9). The glory of God and the welfare of his people are clearly very closely bound together.

[27] Note Paul's triple use of the phrase 'for the praise of his glory' in Eph. 1:6, 12, 14. Cf. also his portrait of the church as God's showcase to the heavenly powers, Eph. 2:7; 3:10.

[28] Eph. 5:25–27.   [29] Matt. 5:16.

[30] *Embroidered dress* and *fine linen* (10) were the materials most commonly said to have been used in the tabernacle and its furnishings, e.g. Exod. 26:36; 27:16; etc. Similarly, fine flour, honey and olive oil are reminiscent of the sacrifices, as also of the supernatural food, manna, in the wilderness. The observation of these echoes goes back to the Targum (very early Jewish interpretation). See Greenberg, p. 302, and Block (1), p. 485, for details.

135

of the temple, thus signifying that the most precious thing about this whole picture is the presence of Yahweh himself, dwelling with and among his people. Temple and priesthood combine in the imaging of the people as a whole. This points to the role of Israel not just to be famous among the nations for its own sake, but to be Yahweh's priesthood in the midst of the nations – the means by which the nations would come to acknowledge Yahweh. Even Israel's beauty and splendour (ḥāḏār) may be an echo of the psalmist's description of the temple,[31] in the context of calling upon the nations to ascribe proper glory due to Yahweh. Interestingly the same combination of metaphors, church as temple and as bride, is used again as Paul seeks to portray the breathtaking challenge of our calling in Christ and the transformation he has achieved in us.[32] Peter also combines imagery from temple and priesthood in calling on Christians to live out the practical and ethical implications of their status in the eyes of the nations, so that ultimately they too will come to glorify God.[33] The ethical challenge of Christian living has a strongly missionary purpose: only as the world sees any difference in the behaviour of God's people will they be drawn to acknowledge the God whose people we claim to be.

b. The response: ungrateful and unnatural (16:15–34)

The portrait of the grace and generosity of Yahweh as the one who rescued the abandoned outcast and elevated her to royal priestly status has been painted as graphically as Ezekiel's obsession with detail can achieve. Yahweh's action now moves to the background, but it must always be exactly there – namely, the background staging against which both the actions of Israel must be seen in stark contrast, and also background lighting in which the anger and punishment of Yahweh must be seen as justifiable.

The fundamental root of Israel's sin is presented with brilliant brevity in verse 15 before being fully exposed in the following verses. *But you trusted in your beauty and used your fame to become a prostitute.* The beauty which was the gift of Yahweh now became the object of confidence in herself rather than a reason for grateful confidence in God. Israel trusted in all the rich endowment that she had as a nation and a country, trading and trifling with them, in total disregard for the requirements or the reputation of the God who had given her all she possessed.

The temptation to make the gifts of God the object of trust

---

[31] 'Splendour and majesty are before him; strength and glory are in his sanctuary' (Ps. 96:6).
[32] Eph. 2:21; 5:25–27.   [33] 1 Pet. 2:4–12.

instead of trusting in the giver himself is one that has never failed to snare God's people through history, and is still a deadly trap for many of us today. In fact, the more gifted you are, the greater is this temptation. Good organizers come to trust their own ability to organize. Effective evangelists come to trust their own well-polished techniques. Brilliant teachers come to trust their mental agility and group skills. The caring pastor comes to believe that his own counselling skills are the reason people are being blessed. The church with a successful urban ministry comes to trust its own brilliant strategies and management. The successful evangelistic programme comes to measure its success by effective marketing. The college with the fine reputation comes to trust its own unchallenged ability to attract students.

In such situations, nobody actually *stops* trusting in God, of course, or stops claiming that they do. But for all practical purposes faith in God has become as irrelevant as the words 'In God we trust', so ironically printed on US dollar bills. The very things that most prove the grace of God – the gifts he has given us – become the things that we use to replace him. This temptation was recognized early on in Israel's relationship with God. Deuteronomy portrays Moses challenging Israel before their entry into the land (the land of promise and of threat, of blessing and of responsibility), and warning them against precisely this temptation – the temptation of claiming the gifts of God as somehow a credit to ourselves. The antidote is to remember where they came from:

> 'You may say to yourself, "My power and the strength of my hands have produced this wealth for me." But remember the LORD your God, for it is he who gives you the ability to produce wealth …'[34]

Paul had similar words to challenge the arrogance of the Corinthian church, probably facing temptations similar to those facing Israel: 'What do you have that you did not receive? And if you did receive it, why do you boast as though you did not?'[35]

The other side of Israel's ungrateful response to Yahweh's generosity was that she actually 'traded on her name', which is almost literally what the words mean, except that the trade in question was the shabby trade of a prostitute: *you … used your fame to become a prostitute.* Israel prostituted the name that was hers because it was the name that was Yahweh's. And that is what made it so intolerable for Yahweh. It is unbearable enough for a

---

[34] Deut. 8:17–18. [35] 1 Cor. 4:7.

well-known husband that his wife should shame him by plying the prostitute's trade. It is scandalous that she should use the fame of the very name that their marriage commitment has entrusted to her to do so. From here on, the accusation of harlotry is hurled at Israel again and again, with all the anger of a husband whose love has been betrayed, whose gifts have been plundered, whose name has been mocked in the gutters of his rivals.

'You trusted in your beauty and traded on your name.' It is a chilling accusation, which rings true in relation to the life of the church and individual Christians. Idolatrous self-trust, and self-enrichment through the exploitation of God's name or one's own: such sins are still common enough to make Ezekiel's accusation of Israel a poignant challenge to us – especially when any form of success or fame comes our way. 'Woe to you when all men speak well of you,' warned Jesus.[36] Persecution and suffering are severe tests, but there is another kind of test that comes from success and reputation. Suffering tends to drive you to God out of sheer need and desperation; popularity tends to drive you to complacent neglect of God altogether.

> The crucible for silver and the furnace for gold,
> but a man is tested by the praise he receives.[37]

The historical failures of Israel that are being summed up by this imagery are now outlined in two sections, each with a distinct focus. First of all, Ezekiel focuses on Israel's flirtations with pagan religions (16:16–22), then, secondly, on Israel's flirtations with pagan nations (16:23–34).

i. Israel's religious prostitution (16:16–22)

The main accusation of this section, until verse 19, is that Israel had taken all that Yahweh had given her – the long list of wonderful gifts that had raised her from rejection to royalty in verses 10–13 – and had used it all in the worship of other gods. There is a mixture of the allegorical with reality in these verses, in that the picture of finery, jewellery and food being used as allurements in prostitution is meant to reflect the use of the resources of Israel in idolatrous worship at pagan shrines. *High places* (16) thus speaks both of elevated prostitutes' couches, possibly for ritual prostitution before gods of fertility, and also of the 'high places' that seem to litter the whole history of Israel during the monarchy according to 1 and 2 Kings. They were places of idolatrous worship, and only the exile,

[36] Luke 6:26.   [37] Prov. 27:21.

it seems, actually accomplished their eradication, in spite of all the efforts of reforming kings like Hezekiah and Josiah. The emphatic repetition of the verb *you took* tolls through the section. Everything Yahweh had *given*, all those precious and priestly possessions, they just *took*, gave them away, used them for prostitution – whether spiritual or literal (ritual) or both, and utterly squandered them in an orgy of unfaithfulness that went on for centuries in spite of all prophetic protests.

The motif of this section is very similar to, and possibly based on, the same sense of ingratitude and shameless squandering of Yahweh's gifts before other gods that Hosea drew, not from an allegory, but from tragic personal experience with Gomer. The only difference is that in Hosea Israel actually does not even recognize Yahweh as the giver but attributes all her material blessings to the other gods. The ingratitude and offence of it lead to a similar reaction of divine anger in Yahweh, the betrayed husband. It will be some time, however, before Ezekiel comes to the message of grace and restoration that quickly follows in Hosea.[38]

But Israel had taken something else as well and used it in a form of 'prostitution' far more horrific than any abuse of material gifts – the horror of child-sacrifice. In 16:20–22 Ezekiel makes the climax of this section something which stands out on its own, again mixing the allegorical with the literal. Israelites of course had children; Israelite wives bore them to their own husbands – that was the historical reality. But at another level, they were *sons and daughters whom you bore to me*, says Yahweh, the rescuer of the foundling, the divine husband of this wanton wife. The children of the Israelites (as 'wife') were actually the children of Yahweh (as 'husband'). This extension of the metaphor of marriage between Yahweh and Israel to include the procreation of children is almost as daring as the original metaphor itself. Like the marriage metaphor, it is grounded in the covenant relationship between God and his people. From the beginning Yahweh had laid claim not only to the generation with whom the covenant was initially established but also to all succeeding generations. Circumcision was the covenant sign of this fact, as was the ceremony of the redemption of the firstborn, introduced at the time of the exodus.[39] Yahweh claimed the firstborn as the representative of the next generation in each family. Thus Deuteronomy can address the following generation as though the covenant had been made directly with them.[40]

[38] Hos. 2:5–13.   [39] Exod. 13:1–2, 11–16; 34:19.

[40] Deut. 5:3; 29:14. Note also the command that the law be read in the hearing of the children (31:9–13), and that they be thoroughly educated in the privileges and responsibilities of covenant membership (4:9–10; 6:6–9, 20–25; etc.).

139

Whatever harmed the children, therefore, directly affected this relationship with God. Micah equated the ejection of children from their homes as depriving them of Yahweh's glory (*ḥādār*).[41] How much worse, then, was the crime of actually sacrificing children! Yet we know that this horrible manifestation of the darker side of fertility religion did manifest itself in Israel in the later years of the monarchy; it is particularly referred to during the reign of Manasseh, though it seems to have infiltrated much earlier, possibly under Assyrian influence.[42] Instead of gratefully dedicating their children into all the life, joy and blessing of the covenant relationship with Yahweh, Israel had 'taken' them and *slaughtered* them as disgusting *food to the idols*. This *detestable practice*, the depth of the depravity of the Canaanites,[43] was now the height of the ingratitude of the Israelites.

By offering her offspring Jerusalem proved her Canaanite ancestry beyond doubt. She who had been abandoned by her mother as an infant now sacrificed her own children. She who owed her existence to Yahweh's call to life now danced with death. She who had benefited from Yahweh's unrestrained benevolence now cast off all restraint herself. In her intoxication with her newfound beauty and her insatiable lusts, she suffered from a severe case of amnesia. Instead of remembering her desperate beginnings or celebrating the goodness of Yahweh in rescuing her, she trampled underfoot the grace of God.[44]

It is more difficult to know how to apply such a text today (although there are parts of the world where religious rites involving human sacrifice still take place). We may not actually sacrifice babies in religious rituals, but there is certainly an appalling mountain of child suffering caused by the various idolatries of western life – the unfettered pursuit of material wealth and individual freedoms, the total selfishness that focuses on maximum pleasure now without a concern for responsibility towards those who will inherit the consequences of our actions (or inaction) in the next generation. It is forecast that 40% of the population of Britain will be over fifty by 2020. Meanwhile our birth rate is dropping, and we are aborting

---

[41] Mic. 2:9.

[42] 2 Kgs. 16:3; 17:17; 23:10; 2 Chr. 33:6; Jer. 32:35. On the place of children within the covenant relationship with Yahweh and the legal, social and educational implications of it, cf. Wright, *God's People in God's Land*, pp. 97–99, 222–238. On the historical evidence for child sacrifice, and further bibliography, cf. ibid., pp. 231–235, and also J. Day, *Molech: A God of Human Sacrifice in the Old Testament* (Cambridge: Cambridge University Press, 1989).

[43] Deut. 12:31.   [44] Block (1), p. 491.

a substantial proportion of the next generation who would have lived and worked to support in their old age those who have so thoughtlessly snuffed them out in their youth. But it is not only the appalling scale of abortion in western societies, but also the wider abuse and scarring of the lives of our children that inspired the hymn by Graham Kendrick, which draws on the imagery of Ezekiel:

> Who can sound the depths of sorrow
> In the Father heart of God
> For the children we've rejected
> For the lives so deeply scarred?
> And each light that we've extinguished
> Has brought darkness to our land,
> Upon our nation, upon our nation
> Have mercy, Lord.
>
> We have scorned the truth You gave us
> We have bowed to other lords.
> We have sacrificed the children
> On the altars of our gods.
> O let truth again shine on us,
> Let Your holy fear descend.
> Upon our nation, upon our nation,
> Have mercy, Lord.[45]

ii. Israel's political prostitution (16:23–34)

From its beginnings, Israel was always intended by God to be a nation among the nations. The great narrative of their history, the story of God's saving actions in their midst, was played out on the crowded stage of international politics in the ancient near-eastern world over many centuries. However, their relationship with the other nations was carefully constrained by the nature of their covenant relationship with Yahweh. The covenant was modelled on the international treaties, which usually demanded total loyalty to the superior power, and prohibited any counter-treaties with other powers. Yahweh demanded no less. If Israel were Yahweh's covenant vassal, then they must enter into no treaties with other powers – divine or human. Such alliances, with their inherent threat of religious compromise, were prohibited especially in relation to the Canaanites.[46] Israel was to rely on Yahweh for victory and protection, not on the size of her armies or the clout of her 'friends'.

[45] Graham Kendrick, 'Who can sound the depths of sorrow?'
[46] Exod. 34:10–16; Deut. 7:2.

Ezekiel highlights three particular instances when Israel (in this case meaning in particular the kingdom of Judah and its capital, Jerusalem) had entered into alliance with, or subservience to, external nations: Egypt (26), Assyria (28) and Babylon (29). Ezekiel continues the prostitute metaphor but intensifies the language, describing it as something public and so deliberately lewd as to maximize the sexual allurement and the corresponding sense of scandal (23–25).

The flirtation with Egypt was an on-and-off affair for many years. It was the northern kingdom's disloyal alliance with Egypt which sparked Assyria's final attack on Samaria, leading to the annihilation of Israel as a kingdom in 721.[47] Isaiah warned Judah repeatedly in the eighth century against seeking alliances with Egypt in order to resist Assyria, but his warnings seem to have gone unheeded.[48] Ezekiel likewise in his own day severely criticized Zedekiah for doing the same thing in the face of the Babylonian threat (ch. 17). Israel would do anything but trust in Yahweh, and such lack of trust in their covenant partner and Lord not unexpectedly *provoked* his *anger* (26).

Judah's *prostitution with Assyria* primarily refers to the action of Ahaz in appealing to Assyria for help against the alliance of Syria and the northern kingdom of Israel in 735 BC. This was strongly condemned at the time, again by Isaiah, and did indeed lead Judah into a period of subservience to Assyria that was disastrous and costly in religious, financial and political terms. A lot of the national substance was indeed prostituted to secure the dubious favours of Assyria.[49] The Chronicler's laconic humour comments that when Ahaz 'had been most unfaithful to the LORD, Tiglath-Pileser king of Assyria came to him, but gave him trouble instead of help'.[50] In the case of Babylon, the reference is probably to Hezekiah's foolish showing off to the Babylonian envoys, flaunting the wealth of his palace and kingdom. Again, the 'promiscuous' act drew a reprimand and a chilling future prediction from Isaiah.[51]

Ezekiel's further comment (31–34), as he gives vent to the increasing anger of Yahweh, is that not only was Israel's action despicably unfaithful to the covenant; it was also unnatural and contrary to all normal custom. Prostitutes charge for their services. Israel, by contrast, paid her clients for their favours. The reference is of course to the squandering of national wealth on all these

[47] 2 Kgs. 17:3–6; possibly referred to in Hos. 12:1.
[48] Is. 20; 30:1–7; 31:1–3; 2 Kgs. 18:21–24.
[49] Is. 7; 2 Kgs. 16.   [50] 2 Chr. 28:19–20.
[51] 2 Kgs. 20:12–19 = Is. 39:1–8.

political flirtations,[52] but the overall charge is that all that Israel possessed in any case was from the generous grace and gifting of her 'husband'. Not only had she treated his name as a squalid asset for her filthy trade, she had also treated all his priceless gifts as saleable goods to the highest bidders.

c. The repudiation: terrifying and terminal (16:35–43; cf. 23:22–49)

The charge has been stated. The sentence begins with the judicial *Therefore* of verse 35 and, after formally summing up the key elements in the accusation (36), proceeds to outline the fate of the accused. Basically it will be the statutory penalty in Israel for adultery and murder, namely judicial execution – *the punishment of women who commit adultery and who shed blood* (38, and cf. the expansion in 23:37–39, 45). Ezekiel's purpose was to get the exiles to face the fact that the sin of Israel was such as to deserve their complete eradication, in the same way as the most serious crimes within their legal system were dealt with through capital punishment. We should not be distracted at this point by our personal views on the rightness or wrongness of the death penalty in modern society; the thing to grasp is Ezekiel's purpose. Israel must be faced with the reality of how their behaviour is viewed by the judge on the throne of the universe, not by the twisted standards of their own self-justifying apologetics. He could scarcely make that point more clearly. All that is left is how the fully deserved and finally decreed execution will be carried out.

Returning to the allegory, Ezekiel portrays Israel again as the disgraced wife of Yahweh, surrounded by the mocking ex-lovers, and now stripped naked. Her nakedness had begun the chapter as the nakedness of desperate but innocent vulnerability. Then her nakedness had been flaunted in the shameless self-exposure of the nymphomaniac. Now her nakedness is enforced by the formal act of shaming through which the divorce of an adulterous wife was (and still is in some cultures) made public.[53] But this is not merely divorce, for it moves on to the execution by stoning (the

---

[52] The cost of Israel's unfaithfulness to Yahweh in terms of the tribute she paid out of the national wealth to foreign powers was enormous. The list of such tribute mentioned in the Old Testament, along with supporting ancient near-eastern documentation, is helpfully provided by Block. Payment was made: 'To Assyria by Kings Jehu of Israel (*ANET*, p. 281), Jehoahaz of Judah (*ANET*, p. 282), Menahem of Israel (*ANET*, p. 283), Hoshea of Israel (*ANET*, p. 284), Ahaz (2 K. 16:7–9), and Hezekiah (18:14–16; *ANET*, p. 288) … Later Jehoiakim had paid tribute successively to Necho (2 K. 23:34–35), Nebuchadrezzar (24:1), and Egypt (Jer. 2:18, 36). Zedekiah paid an annual tribute to Babylon (Ezek. 17:6, 13–14), and perhaps to Egypt (vv. 7–9).' Block (1), p. 498, note 206.

[53] Cf. Hos. 2:2–3.

metaphorical legal penalty) and hacking by swords and burning (the historical, military reality) (40–41). Only then will the prostitution be at an end; only then will the just anger of Yahweh be turned away (40–42).[54] Israel began in near-death destitution and, in spite of incredible grace and generosity, has ended in virtual extinction. More bluntly, her story began in the blood of foetal abandonment, proceeded through the blood of social oppression and ritual violence, and ended in *the blood vengeance of my wrath* (38) – from one degree of gory to another.

There is a kind of horrific poetic justice about the portrayal of Israel's judgment. The actions by which Israel had sought to win favour, security and a prostitute's popularity will make her scorned and pathetic in the eyes of the world around. The world she tried to woo will turn and tear her to pieces. In view of the quasi-legal form of the whole chapter, the events are described as the verdict handed down and carried out by the judge himself (*I will gather ... I will sentence you ... I will hand you over*), but they are, at another level, simply the historical outworking of a process in which those inveterate enemies of God's people, whom she had tried to appease by selling her body and soul to them, eventually revert to type and behave as the implacable enemies they really were all along. And in the process Israel pays a terrible price for her prostitution as God finally withdraws all covenantal protection and abandons her to the consequences of the path she had followed with insatiable frenzy and incorrigible persistence in spite of centuries of prophetic warning, pleading and threatening.

[54] Some modern commentators take great offence at the portrayal of Yahweh in the allegories of Ezekiel 16 and 23. The whole story loads all the wickedness and guilt on to the female character and presents the male (deity) as faultless. Worse, the male is then portrayed as an abusive husband who subjects his wife to stripping, humiliation and gang-rape – allegedly as remedial actions! To this one needs to say, first, that the imagery of Israel as wife and Yahweh as husband was already well established before Ezekiel, and could hardly have been reversed or subjected to some egalitarian reassessment of relative guilt to satisfy modern canons of marital pathology. Secondly, we should remember that the whole portrayal is allegorical and symbolic. There is no suggestion that Yahweh actually behaved like this in a literal sense, or that this story in any way sanctioned such behaviour among Israelite husbands. Thirdly, the actions which are described as expressing the anger and judgment of Yahweh were, in their historical fulfilment, actually carried out by Israel's real-life enemies, and the description here is no exaggeration of the horror involved. Fourthly, we need to be careful not to import into our criticism of the text agendas which come from a very different context and which are in some ways irrelevant to the point Ezekiel was making – which was certainly not to defend or advocate any particular actual code of practice within failing marriages. His point, to repeat, was allegorical, and designed to provide a startling theological comment on past and current history. For further discussion of this issue, see Block (1), pp. 467–470.

Jerusalem had bared her body to all passersby. Now God provides her with all the exposure she wants, and more. If she wants to be a public spectacle, he offers his aid. Naked he had found her; naked he would leave her. The hell that awaited her was not the creation of some demonic or external power, but of her own making.[55]

When the people of God woo the world and sell their soul for political power, financial profit, social influence or other temporal gains, the end result historically has always been that, at best, they become pathetic, scorned and treated with contempt, and at worst, the world turns with ferocious destructive power on the church itself. Sometimes such judgment may be purging; at other times, as Jesus warned the churches of Asia Minor, it may be terminal. As far as Old Testament Israel is concerned, we do well to remember Paul's sobering reminder 'Now these things occurred as examples to keep us from setting our hearts on evil things as they did ... and were written down as warnings for us, on whom the fulfilment of the ages has come. So, if you think you are standing firm, be careful that you don't fall!'[56] The church, with its long history of unholy alliances with the world in all its forms, has little cause for any sense of superiority over Old Testament Israel.

2. Cinderella[57] and the two ugly sisters (in reverse) (16:44–63; 23:1–49)

Structurally, 16:44–63 can be regarded as an integral part of the enormous single oracle of judgment that chapter 16 as a whole constitutes. However, at verse 44 Ezekiel not only introduces a new proverb into his allegory; he also introduces two more characters and a shift in the storyline. So it seems best to treat this section, along with chapter 23, which expands the new story with considerable extra 'local colour' and symbolic names, as a distinct item in our exposition.

a. A sordid family (16:44–46; 23:1–4)

Ezekiel returns to the starting-point of the original allegory – the heartless pagan parents who had exposed the unwanted female birth

---

[55] Block (1), p. 504.   [56] 1 Cor. 10:6–12.

[57] The famous fairy tale relates how Cinderella, the youngest and most beautiful of three sisters, but harshly oppressed, ends up, by the magic of her fairy godmother, married to a prince while her two ugly sisters suffer the rejection they had previously imposed upon her. I had been using this comparison in lecturing on Ezekiel, before discovering that Block hints at the same comparison (Block (1), p. 509). Again, it is possible but beyond proof that a similar kind of ancient near-eastern folk tale may lie behind Ezekiel's inversion of the story here.

(16:1–5). There is an added detail, significant in view of the story so far, that the mother had not only despised her children by treating them in such a way, but also *despised her husband* (16:45). It was a family riven with unfaithfulness and contempt. Such was the mother, and so was the daughter – meaning Jerusalem. However, this unworthy mother apparently had other daughters, who were thus sisters to the one who had miraculously survived. But who then were these other sisters of Jerusalem? Ezekiel, growing well used to shocking and offending his listeners, piles insult on insult.

Imagine yourself a citizen of Jerusalem, albeit in exile: Jerusalem 'the city of our God, his holy mountain; Jerusalem, beautiful in its loftiness, the joy of the whole earth'.[58] Imagine yourself hearing the next words that Ezekiel spoke, *'Your older sister was Samaria ... and your younger sister ... was Sodom'*.[59] To be told that Jerusalem had Amorite and Hittite parentage was insulting enough. To be told that despised northern Israel (which had been destroyed over a century ago and quite right too) and debauched Sodom (which was proverbial for God's righteous judgment which not even father Abraham could avert) were your sibling sisters must have brought howls of protest.[60] Jerusalem prided itself precisely on *not* being like the rebel apostates of the north,[61] and as for Sodom – even Isaiah had dared only to *compare* Jerusalem with Sodom, not to put them in the same family tree![62]

Yet that is indeed the sordid family that Ezekiel builds in his allegory. Far from singing the songs of Zion with the exiles in a way that would undergird their confidence in the uniqueness and privilege of Jerusalem, Ezekiel undermines all such assurance and dares to put Jerusalem on the same level as those they most despised. Except that he doesn't; he puts it even lower. What we have here is a rhetorical embellishment of the essential point made right at the start of his prophetic ministry in 5:5–7. Israel was indeed set in the midst of the family of nations, but instead of setting an example to the rest of the family, she had become no better than its worst members.

---

[58] Ps. 48:1–2.

[59] The expression *with their daughters* refers to the other towns and villages of the countries of which Samaria and Sodom were capitals.

[60] The language of parents and sisters needs to be understood as a literary device, part of the allegory. There is no need to discuss the question whether there were ethnic links between Israelites and the inhabitants of Sodom and Gomorrah comparable to those between Judah and Israel. Ezekiel is not interested (here at any rate) in ethno-geography, but in making a theological point by an arresting metaphor.

[61] The speech of Abijah to the northern rebels, though recorded by the Chronicler at a different time and for a different purpose, gives some flavour of Jerusalem's point of view on the northern kingdom (2 Chr. 13:4–12).

[62] Is. 1:9–10.

b. The sin of Samaria (23:5–10)

In chapter 16, Ezekiel says nothing about Samaria (other than the comparison in v. 51), but in chapter 23 he goes a lot further because he develops the idea by naming two of the sisters and then comparing them with each other. So Samaria becomes Oholah and Jerusalem becomes Oholibah (23:1–4).[63] Oholah is described as the older sister because, historically, the northern kingdom of Israel was much larger and also was the first to suffer the fate of destruction and exile. Both sisters are described as wives of Yahweh (*They were mine*), in spite of the sexual immorality that lay in their past. Ezekiel is forced to bend his allegory to historical reality here. Obviously, Yahweh's covenant was with the unity of Israel as a whole people. But in view of the historical division of the nation into two kingdoms, it was necessary to introduce this artificial element into the story. To accuse Yahweh of bigamy with sibling sisters that his own law prohibited[64] is to quibble over what is a literary detail, not a literal situation. If anything, 'bigamy' was forced upon Yahweh by the sinful rebellion and split within his covenant people.

The accusation against Samaria (23:5–8) follows the lines already laid down in 16:23–34, namely political infatuation with external powers; in this case, with Assyria. Ezekiel uses the same metaphor of lascivious prostitution for Israel's love affair with Assyria, and the same violent language for its horrific ending – the siege and destruction of Samaria and deportation of the population of the ten northern tribes, in 721 BC (23:9–10). This was all a matter of well-known historical fact among the exiles of Jerusalem, and the reasons for it were also well rehearsed among them. Even if the theological interpretation of the fall of Samaria that we now have recorded in 2 Kings 17:7–23 was not actually written yet at this early point of the exile, the reflection and sentiments expressed in it must have been the standard view of the people of Judah. Ezekiel's task was to get them to see that everything they believed about the northern kingdom was even more true about themselves.

c. The sin of Sodom (16:49–50)

Returning to chapter 16 and the third sister, Sodom, what dimensions of their sin will Ezekiel highlight as he builds his case against his primary target – Jerusalem? Ironically, the one thing for

---

[63] These two names mean, respectively, 'Her tent' and 'My tent in her'. It is virtually impossible to be certain what, if any, symbolic significance is intended. Certainly the story makes nothing of the names, and they may be more or less artificial constructions for the sake of adding to the personification necessary for the allegory.

[64] Lev. 18:18.

which Sodom is most famous in traditional Christian interpretation, the attempted violent homosexual rape in Genesis19,[65] is the one thing Ezekiel does not mention explicitly (though it is doubtless included in the broad expression *they did detestable things*), even though the sexual colouring of the rest of the allegory would have made it very much 'at home' if it had been in Ezekiel's mind at all. Rather, he lists four things which all fall into the category of social and economic wickedness. The people of Sodom and its whole surrounding culture and society were *arrogant, overfed and unconcerned; they did not help the poor and needy*. Sodom, then, was a culture of great pride, of affluent gluttony, and of complacent ease. It sounds familiar. Furthermore, in their arrogance, greed and callousness, they refused a helping hand (lit.) to the poor and needy. It sounds even more familiar. The language is that of oppression and neglect, of prosperity for some and poverty and pain for others.

The heads of the world's richest nations met in the G8 summit in Okinawa, Japan, in July 2000. The conference itself, for a few days of obscene luxury, cost over £500 million – more than the annual gross national product of Sierra Leone – to hold. Meanwhile the same rich nations have produced only minimal fulfilment of the promises made a full year ago to cancel or reduce the crippling debt of the world's poorest countries. Affluence and complacency on the one hand; shameful reluctance to help the needy on the other. Ezekiel's description of Sodom is a sharp and prophetic description of our world, of the world as it has always been – which is why Sodom has always stood as the proverbial archetype for human wickedness in the blast-path of God's judgment.

Indeed, in the original story of God's judgment on the wicked cities of the plain, Sodom and Gomorrah, the thing that drew God's attention, the thing that brought him with two angelic companions on a fact-finding mission, was the outcry that was assaulting the ears of heaven from the pain and suffering going on at the lowest point on the earth's surface – geologically and morally. 'Outcry' is the term used twice in Genesis 18:20–21 and again in 19:13, in the full narrative that encompasses Genesis 18 – 19. It is $ṣeʿāqâ$, a technical word for loud protest against cruel treatment,[66] or even the scream of a rape victim.[67] Sodom was screaming in the ears of heaven with

---

[65] To which it has given its name in the term 'sodomy'.

[66] Exod. 3:7, 9; 22:23; Neh. 5:1; Job 34:28.

[67] Deut. 22:24, 27. It is also the word used in Isaiah's dark pun in Is. 5:7, in which the divine vineyard owner, looking for 'righteousness' ($ṣedāqâ$), found only 'cries of distress' ($ṣeʿāqâ$). Isaiah, like Ezekiel, compares Jerusalem with Sodom, and it is clear that he has its social sins of injustice, corruption and bloodshed particularly in mind; cf. Is. 1:9–10, 15–16, 21–23.

the cries of those suffering there alongside the affluence, gluttony and comfort of some of its inhabitants: a microcosm, as we have said, of the global village of our world with its appalling juxtaposition of wealth and poverty. We live still in Sodom, only on a global scale. And what is worse, just as Ezekiel accused Jerusalem of being even worse than Sodom, because they should have known better with all the social and economic instructions of the Torah, so Christians who are unconcerned about the grinding contrast between western affluent power and the poverty and need of the majority world are more guilty in the sight of God than those without the blessing of his revelation. Like the people of Jerusalem in Ezekiel's day, we live, not in Zion, but in Sodom.

d. The shame of comparison (16:47–48, 51–52; 23:11–21)

The most powerful point of Ezekiel's rhetoric now comes out, like a bare-knuckle punch. Not only does Jerusalem share a family resemblance with the likes of Samaria and Sodom by the fact that she has sunk to the same level of wickedness; she has actually plumbed the depths of depravity to such an extent that she has made even Sodom look *righteous* in comparison. The first point is made in 16:47 – simply that Judah had done more and worse than the northern kingdom (twice as much in fact, 51a). This may have been suggested by a similar negative comparison between Judah and Israel by Jeremiah.[68] However, the second point in 16:51–52 really makes the insult offensive beyond belief. Yahweh is the supreme judge who adjudicates all relative claims to innocence or guilt, righteousness or wickedness. And in his scales, the desperate weight of Jerusalem's sin has tilted the balance in favour of declaring even Sodom innocent!

The idea is utterly preposterous. So much so that Ezekiel has to express it four times in two verses – possibly reflecting the protest and opposition that must have assailed him when he first voiced such an outrageous opinion. Jerusalem's sin will take up so much of Yahweh's judicial attention that by comparison he will overlook Sodom and Samaria. Thus Jerusalem has even, in a paradoxical twist, *furnished some justification* for them. Of course Ezekiel does not mean this literally. Both Sodom and Samaria had been fully judged and punished for their own sin. It is the rhetorical comparison that counts. If the well-known fate of Sodom and Samaria was what the relatively 'innocent' suffered, what on earth or heaven must God have in store for Jerusalem?[69] Similar tactics were used by Jesus to

---

[68] Jer. 3:6–10. This is the comparison (between Israel and Judah) which is carried further in Ezekiel's allegory of Oholah and Oholibah; cf. Ezek. 23:11–14.

[69] The fate of Jerusalem was indeed considered by some to be worse than the instant extinction of Sodom (Lam. 4:6).

provoke a sense of outraged shame among the people of the towns where he ministered. The privilege they had of witnessing him at work made their rejection of him much more worthy of judgment than even the sin of Sodom and Gomorrah.[70]

If we are curious to know what exactly it was about the behaviour of people in Jerusalem that could justify such shocking comparison, then Ezekiel provides us with a catalogue in chapter 22, which adds significantly to the list of ritual apostasies he witnessed in his visionary tour of the temple in chapters 8 – 11. The charge sheet includes bloodshed, idolatry, contempt of parents, oppression of aliens, orphans and widows (the landless, familyless and homeless), desecration of the Sabbath, slander, sexual perversions including adultery and incest, bribery, corruption, taking interest, dispossession and confiscation of property ('devouring people'), neglect of religious traditions, vicious bureaucracy, murder for profit, false prophecy justifying the *status quo*, extortion and robbery. We need to ponder such a chapter long enough not only to agree with Ezekiel that the action God took in judgment on a society in such a stage of advanced depravity was not 'without cause' (14:23), but also to feel the intense discomfort that comes from recognizing the face of our own society as though in a time-warped mirror and to wonder how the judgment of God upon us can be so long delayed. The words that Billy Graham is reputed to have said about his own land could be said with equal relevance over all the decadent nations of the wealthy western world: 'God must either judge America or apologize to Sodom.'

e. The surprise of restoration (16:53–63)

Ezekiel's capacity to shock knows no limits. The searing imagery of stripping, stoning, hacking and burning in 16:39–41 leaves little hope for anyone but the vultures. Surely this really is the end to end all ends. Yes and no. Certainly, it meant the end for Jerusalem for the next generation. It was the end of the temple that Solomon built. It was the end of the Davidic dynasty and Israel's monarchy. It was, for most of the inhabitants, the end of anything that could be called life – whether in actual violent death, or in the grave of exile. Yes, in all those ways and for all those people, it was the end. But it was not the end for Yahweh and his ultimate purposes for Israel and the nations. He had plans beyond the present cataclysm, plans that incredibly spoke of a restoration as unexpected as it was undeserved (16:53).

So was it, then, the end of the covenant? Again, yes and no. Yes, the present generation of Israelites would reap the consequences of

[70] Matt. 11:20–24.

the persistent covenant-breaking of past centuries. They would experience the final outpouring of the curses written into that covenant, which they had despised and broken. The covenant itself was not dead, but death was written into it for those who trampled it underfoot in persistent disobedience. The choice had been theirs, clearly and explicitly for generations: 'See, I set before you today life and prosperity, death and destruction ... I have set before you life and death, blessings and curses. Now choose life ...'[71] But they had chosen death. Their own.

But no, the covenant was not extinct, for God will always have the last word. So, the breathtaking double reality is expressed in 16:59–60 – Israel's determination to forget (cf. 23:12), and Yahweh's determination to remember: *'I will deal with you as you deserve, because you have despised my oath by breaking the covenant. Yet I will remember the covenant I made with you ...'*[72] When God remembers, there is hope. The expression goes right back to the salvation of Noah and his family in the midst of the otherwise universal judgment of the flood.[73] But it is likely that Ezekiel again has the phraseology of Leviticus 26 in mind – not only its declaration of curses for disobedience, which are manifestly coming to their climax, but also its affirmation of God's ultimate purpose of restoration, and of grace beyond judgment. Ezekiel's words are virtually a précis of Leviticus 26:43b–45, with its surrounding context:

> 'They will pay for their sins because they rejected my laws and abhorred my decrees. Yet in spite of this, when they are in the land of their enemies, I will not reject them or abhor them so as to destroy them completely, breaking my covenant with them. I am the LORD their God. But for their sake I will remember the covenant with their ancestors whom I brought out of Egypt in the sight of the nations to be their God. I am the LORD.'

Similar hope of restoration after the fulfilment of the threats and judgment inherent in the curses of the covenant is expressed even more rhetorically in Deuteronomy.[74] Such scriptural precedents, alongside the deeper theological understanding of Yahweh's ultimate long-term faithfulness to his promise to Abraham, and his purpose for the nations through the people of Abraham, make it unnecessary to be suspicious of this part of Ezekiel's great allegory of judgment.

[71] Deut. 30:15, 19.
[72] We will postpone discussion of the phrase *establish an everlasting covenant* until the later covenant-restoration passages in Ezek. 36 and 37.
[73] Gen. 8:1.   [74] Deut. 4:29–31; 30:1–10.

Some regard it as a later insertion on the grounds that Ezekiel could not have combined words of hope with such terrible words of punishment. But that is precisely what the covenant texts did do, and what some of his pre-exilic prophetic predecessors had also done.[75]

In later chapters these visions of future hope and the appeals based upon them will become much more fully expanded.[76] In this chapter, however, the words of restoration are qualified in two ways which are entirely fitted to the context. They do not make the prospect any less real or any less miraculous as a work of God's surprising grace. But they do act as a reminder of the terrible background against which such restoration will take place.

i. It will be a shared restoration

The restoration of Israel will take place alongside the restoration of Samaria and Sodom.[77] In fact, in 16:53 and 55 their restoration is mentioned first, with that of Israel almost as an afterthought! If sin is the great leveller (for all have sinned and fallen short of the glory of God, Jew and Gentile alike), then so is the gospel. Ezekiel has brutally compared Israel to those they most despised – Samaritans and Sodomites. He has accused Israel of sins that make them even worse than such paragons of vice. Now he promises them the hope of restoration in words of pure unmerited grace, but with the shocking insistence that such hope is available for all, *including* their ugly and ungodly 'sisters'. The whole sordid family can be cleansed and restored to what it was meant to be. Amazing grace, indeed!

The gospel undermines any advance claims. When truly preached, the gospel eliminates all grounds for boasting or self-serving comparisons with others. If comparisons are to be made, then those who are most in the habit of making them may well find themselves very much on the wrong side of the equation – as Ezekiel's rhetoric hammered home to Israel, and as Jesus' observation of the tax-collector and the Pharisee would do centuries later. The gospel

[75] Is. 1 – 12 is notorious for the way it oscillates between oracles of doom and visions of hope beyond judgment. Micah is similar.

[76] See especially Ezek. 34:36; 37, and chs. 8 and 9 below.

[77] How are we to understand this prophecy of the restoration of Samaria and Sodom? Clearly neither happened in a literal sense. The northern kingdom was never re-established and Sodom was certainly never rebuilt. But then we need to remember that the prophecy of the restoration of Jerusalem also, in both Old Testament and New Testament, transcends the literal fact that it was actually rebuilt, and includes spiritual dimensions of the restoration of God's people to full covenant loyalty and complete obedience and blessing in a messianic age. Other Old Testament prophecies include named nations (e.g. Is. 19:23–25; Amos 9:12; cf. Jer. 12:14–17) in similar promises of restoration in a way that was also not literally fulfilled but points to the extension of Israel to include the nations – a fulfilment that the New Testament describes through the Gentile mission of the church. Cf. also Block (1), pp. 513–514.

undermines our pride not only by removing any pathetic claim to be less of a sinner than somebody else, but also by insisting that we have no choice over who else gets saved alongside us. And this may well be even more humbling. Certainly it is bad news for our prejudices. Exiled citizens of Jerusalem might have been prepared to accept that God would restore Samaria – inhabited as it had been by people who at least bore the name of Israel and were their own ethnic flesh and blood. But Sodom? Sodom the unspeakable (56)? Yes indeed. And not just 'Sodom also, as well as you'. The deliberate order of Ezekiel's words make it clear that he is not saying, 'God will restore Jerusalem – and also, Samaria and Sodom', but rather the other way round.[78] Indeed, in the light of the preceding insistence that the sin of Jerusalem is so depraved as to make Sodom look righteous, the point being made is more like, 'If God is able and willing to pardon and restore *you*, then Sodom will be no problem to him.' Humbling, shaming, disillusioning words. Yet words that are of the very essence of the gospel. The grace of God is good news for all or it is good news for none. Saved sinners don't get to select their travelling companions.

There are no favourites before the grace of God – or else it would not be grace. This was the message that Jesus found it so difficult to get across to his own generation, accustomed to a whole cultural hierarchy of grace-beneficiaries, a rigid classification of those who could lay claim to the attention of the God of Israel when he would act to deliver them, and those who could not. No advance claims, said Jesus, except repentance and faith. Similarly Paul found that the strongest opposition to his mission to the Gentiles came from those Jewish believers who could not accept that such despised outsiders could possibly be among the saved people of God 'on the same level' as themselves. But Paul insisted that such indeed was the very essence of the gospel, and that unless such barriers and prejudices were broken, the gospel itself had been neither understood nor embraced. When Christians erect all kinds of prejudiced barriers as to who God may or may not save (on the assumption that of course *we* are), it is like passengers on the *Titanic* arguing about who they are prepared to share a lifeboat with. If Jerusalem was to be restored at all, then, the Israelites had better not object to being asked to *receive* their sisters in the same boat (61).[79]

[78] The same uncomplimentary order, putting Israel third after arch-enemies, is found in the remarkable prophecy in which Isaiah envisaged the salvation and inclusion of Egypt and Assyria (Is. 19:23–25).

[79] The phrase *not on the basis of my covenant with you* (61), is puzzling. Lit. it is 'not from your covenant', which could mean that the pagan nations will be restored, but not *apart from* the covenant with Israel; that is, they will be included within it. Or it may mean that God's new covenantal relationship with all nations, including

ii. It will be a shamed restoration

Here and elsewhere (36:31–32) Ezekiel tempers the expectation of future restoration with an anticipation that the effect of it will be to produce a great upsurge of shame and humiliation in the heart of God's people. *Then you will remember your ways and be ashamed ... you will remember and be ashamed and never again open your mouth because of your humiliation* (16:61, 63). This is not meant to sour the joy of God's grace and redemption. It is not as if God acts grudgingly and expects that his people will never really enjoy their liberation because they will be too ashamed to do so. Rather, it is that although God blots out sin from his memory when it is pardoned, and although there is a right sense in which we should 'forget the former things' also, the memory of what we have been saved from should enhance the gratitude and joy that are ours as we think of God's saving grace. Our shame is the realization that God's judgment is just and that his salvation is entirely a matter of his incredible grace, not our merits.

When seen in the light of the rest of the chapter, and of the thrust of Ezekiel's ministry, an interesting 'reversal of shame' is going on here.[80] In Israel, as in many cultures today, shame is not only something you feel for your own failings. Shame may also be the experience of a junior or inferior, who has been let down by a senior or superior in whom they have placed trust. *You* suffer humiliation because of *their* failure. David's troops felt this kind of shame because of his inappropriate reaction in the moment of their victory.[81] For this reason the psalmist prays that Yahweh would not let him down, since he has put his trust in him. If Yahweh fails or betrays the worshipper's trust, then the latter will be 'put to shame'.[82] The situation Ezekiel faced was a massive accusation by the exiles

---

Israel, will transcend the original national confines of the covenant with Israel. It is certainly preferable to read it in a positive inclusive sense, rather than the exclusive sense suggested by the NIV, partly because of the extended family metaphor (*as daughters*), and partly because Ezekiel's whole point is to deny that Israelites have any remaining privilege above and beyond their pagan neighbours. On the contrary, they will be dealt with at the end of the queue.

[80] See M. S. Odell, 'The inversion of shame and forgiveness in Ezekiel 16:59–63', *JSOT* 56 (1992), pp. 101–112.

[81] 2 Sam. 19:6–7.

[82] Pss. 22:4–8; 25:2; etc. This, of course, was a major factor in the public shame and humiliation that the cross was for Jesus. He was shamed, not for his own sin, but because it appeared to all those who watched that the God he had so publicly trusted and taught had finally let him down and disowned him. The psalmist's plea is turned stingingly against him as a humiliating insult, 'He trusts in God. Let God rescue him now if he wants him' (Matt. 27:43). How searchingly true are the words of Philipp Bliss's hymn 'Man of Sorrows!': 'Bearing shame and scoffing rude, / In my place condemned he stood.'

against Yahweh that *he* was the one who had betrayed his people's trust. In their warped opinion, *they* were being shamed and humiliated in the sight of the nations because of *Yahweh's* failure to deliver on his commitments as their champion. On the contrary, says Ezekiel, again and again. *You* are the ones who have failed and betrayed Yahweh by your inveterate covenant breaking. Yes, you feel ashamed, and so you should – but for *your own* failure, not Yahweh's.

Thus, when eventually they would be restored to the land and to a renewal of the covenant, they would fully understand that perspective, accept it, and feel shame for their previous ways. The grace of forgiveness will produce not just joy in the present, but shame over the past. As well as the cultural and theological point explained above, there is a deep spiritual and psychological truth here. There is a repentance that precedes forgiveness and salvation. But there is also an even deeper kind of repentance that comes with a maturing awareness of the grace of God in one's life. It is a repentance linked to a profound sense of shame, as one's memory recalls past sins, not morbidly and condemningly, but with infinite gratitude for the fact that they have been nailed to the cross and then buried in the depths of the sea by the grace of God. It has become a habit of my own, when blessed by words of appreciation or praise, to remind myself inwardly or aloud, 'A sinner saved by grace – nothing more.' And there is still profound value in the old saying, when observing the downfall or degradation of some other human being, however repulsive their sin: 'There, but for the grace of God, go I.' We walk, as an African Christian proverb says, on two legs: grace and forgiveness. To these, Ezekiel would simply add that our appreciation of forgiving grace should include an appropriate sense of utter shame.

> [Yahweh's] intent was that her sins should be forgiven but never forgotten. Only a sober memory of the fate from which she was rescued could keep her from ever bragging again, as in v 56, that she was not like that sinner Sodom (cf. Luke 18:9–14; Rom 3:19, 27). Instead, it would provide motivation for bearing the fruit of repentance (Matt. 3:8).[83]

3. Israel – the video: rewind and fast-forward (20:1–44)

At this point we need to remind ourselves of the overall purpose of this group of oracles, as explained in the introduction to the chapter.

[83] Allen 28, p. 246.

Ezekiel's intention is to force the exiles to look again at the history they thought they knew, the history which was giving them such a misplaced sense of confidence (while Jerusalem was still standing) and of grievance (when it finally fell). With his two repulsively pungent allegories he has painted an utterly different version of the national epic from the one they had learned in school or at home. In chapter 20 he drops the allegorical, metaphorical style and simply retells the story. But he does so in a cleverly schematic way in which a repeated sequence is left hanging and uncertain at the end, but with no doubt as to the direction in which it is pointing. It may well be that Stephen drew his inspiration for his great final speech before the Sanhedrin from Ezekiel's model of retelling the story.[84] Certainly it has the same effect: subverting the hallowed assumptions of security and pointing inexorably toward judgment. This is history with attitude.

a. The patterns of Israel's history

There is a great biblical tradition of the historical survey; that is, reciting all or parts of the story of God and Israel, in such a way as to highlight the response that Israel ought to make, or the ingratitude of the response they actually made, or Yahweh's amazing grace in persisting with such a people at all.[85] Jesus' parable of the tenants in the vineyard is a succinct example of the tradition in a genre that was all the more challenging by being so brief and parabolic. Its meaning was not lost on its hearers.[86] In Ezekiel's hands, the history of Israel is turned into a prosecution speech. (Interestingly, for Stephen it was presented by the defendant – but in such a way as to allege that his prosecutors were the ones who should really be in the dock). It was delivered on 14 August 591 (20:1), almost a year since the vision in the temple, and two years since his initial call. The city was still standing and the optimism of the exiles was probably still running high. But if the elders who came to sit in Ezekiel's house that day were hoping for a more encouraging word than his previous performances, they were again going to be disappointed. More than disappointed, they were put on trial, as Ezekiel is commanded, in courtroom language, to *judge them* and *confront them* (20:4).

The history lesson that follows is arranged in a scheme of four periods, which are not particularly equal in length, but are chosen

[84] Acts 7.
[85] Other examples include Deut. 26:4–10; Josh. 24:1–27; Amos 2:9–12; Mic. 6:1–8; Pss. 106; 107. The closest of these to Ezekiel's version is Ps. 106, which, as an undoubted exilic psalm, may even have been influenced by Ezekiel's handling of the tradition. For major points of comparison, see Block (1), pp. 615–616.
[86] Matt. 21:33–46.

simply to illustrate the main theme. They are: Israel in Egypt (20:5–9); the first generation after the exodus (20:10–17); the second generation in the wilderness (20:18–26); and the years in the land up to and including the exile (20:27–31).

Then, for each of the first three periods, Ezekiel presents a fixed sequence of four events in which, first of all, Yahweh declares some gracious intention or does some significant action. Secondly, however, this is followed by an act of rebellion on Israel's part, introduced by the word *But*. Thirdly, Yahweh then declares in his anger that he will destroy the people, beginning with an appropriate *So*. Fourthly, however, with another *But*, Yahweh witholds his judgment, for the sake of his own name. For the fourth period, the last two phrases are missing, leaving the impression that, on this occasion, there will be no suspension of judgment as before. The axe will finally fall.

This schematic nature of the chapter can best be seen from the following table.

Actions	Period			
	1. Israel in Egypt vv. 5–9	2. Wilderness: 1st generation vv. 10–17	3. Wilderness: 2nd generation vv. 18–26	4. Conquest to exile vv. 27–31
Yahweh's grace in action	vv. 5–7	vv. 10–12	vv. 18–20	v. 28a
But/Yet, Israel rebels	v. 8a	v. 13a	v. 21a	[v. 28b]
So, Yahweh's anger declared	v. 8b	v. 13b	v. 21b	[vv. 30–31]
But, Yahweh protects his name	v. 9	v. 14	v. 22	—

A brief glance at each of the periods Ezekiel sketches will reveal his subversive message. In each case, he alludes to the most important known feature of the history, but twists or inverts it into a kind of parody of the received interpretation.

i. Israel in Egypt (20:5–9)

Unusually, Ezekiel traces the election of Israel back to Egypt, not to Abraham. This cannot have been due to ignorance of the patriarchal tradition of election, so it must be seen as his deliberate skewing of the story for effect. The particular effect in mind is that something else is also traced back to Egypt – Israel's apostasy in going after other gods. Israel's election was usually located prior to Egypt, and her idolatries were usually located after Egypt (beginning with the golden calf at Sinai). By pulling them both together into Egypt itself, Ezekiel achieves maximum contrast. At the very time when Yahweh was demonstrating the strength of his electing love, Israel was demonstrating the strength of their congenital rebelliousness. With all the wonderful promise of deliverance and the idyllic prospect of the land ahead of them, would they not give up all other gods and follow the one who promised them all this on oath (6–7)? No, they would not. The Egyptian idols, though so comprehensively defeated in the land of Egypt itself, did not lose their grip on the hearts of the Israelites (8a).[87] Even the exodus, then, the supreme moment of Israel's redemptive history, the paradigm of God's redeeming character, took place against the backdrop of the knowledge that it was not just the Egyptians who deserved God's judgment. But for Yahweh's concern for his name, Israel too would have perished in Egypt (8b–9). Ezekiel has here intensified the original Pentateuchal tradition, which had at least let Israel get out of Egypt before the first of the occasions when God became 'angry enough to destroy them' – at Sinai and at Kadesh Barnea.[88] For Ezekiel, the Israelites walked out of Egypt under the suspended anger of the very God who was delivering them.

ii. The wilderness: first generation (20:10–17)
These verses refer to the exodus generation itself, which experienced the momentous revelation of the law and making of the covenant at Sinai, but which then failed to move on to the promised land and consigned themselves to perish in the wilderness. Ezekiel picks out of this period two great gifts – the law, as the source of life (note the repetition of this assertion in vv. 11, 13 and 21),[89] and the Sabbath. Both were gifts of Yahweh (*my laws* and *my Sabbaths*), and the latter is also described as *a sign between us* (12). The Sabbath was indeed a sign of the covenant, a memorial of both creation[90] and redemption.[91] The term included not only the weekly seventh day,

[87] Although there is no specific reference to the Israelites worshipping the idols of Egypt in the Pentateuchal narratives, it is hinted at in Joshua's challenge to the generation after the conquest to choose Yahweh above all the gods of their ancestors – including those of Egypt (Josh. 24:14).
[88] Exod. 32 – 34; Num. 14; Deut. 9:7–29.
[89] These texts, affirming the law as the source of life for those who obey it, is authentically scriptural, echoing both Lev. 18:5 and Deut. 30:15–20. Jesus' answer to the rich young man's question virtually quotes these texts (Matt. 19:16–17). We need to remember this positive and life-giving quality of the law in the Old Testament (celebrated in many psalms, esp. 1, 19 and 119) as the proper context from which to understand Paul's darker picture of the law as a source of death when confronted with our sin and abuse of it.
[90] Exod. 20:8–11.   [91] Deut. 5:12–15.

but also the sabbatical and jubilee years,[92] and related economic institutions concerned with the relief of debt and slaves. It therefore had a vital role in the whole ethos of Israel's social life. Deuteronomy 15 illustrates the central place that sabbatical institutions had in preserving the covenantal sense of justice and compassion in Israel's economic structures. Leviticus 26, with which again Ezekiel is probably interacting, blamed the exile on (among other things), neglect of the Sabbaths, which, in the light of prophetic accusations about the same thing,[93] meant much more than just a lack of ritual observance of one day a week. It reflected the total loss of Israel's distinctive socio-economic system in the waves of oppression and exploitation that swamped the nation during the monarchy. Again, Ezekiel telescopes history and traces Israel's rejection of Yahweh's laws and their desecration of the Sabbaths right back to the generation to whom they were first given. Furthermore, he makes this the reason for the failure to enter the promised land (15–16) – something of a twist on the original history in which that failure was due to the people's loss of nerve at Kadesh Barnea when confronted with the report of the spies about giants and skyscrapers.[94] In Ezekiel's book one form of rebellion is as bad as any other and it is no problem to substitute later forms for earlier ones.

iii. The wilderness: second generation (20:18–26)

Here Ezekiel seems to be influenced again by Deuteronomy, with his reference to Yahweh's warning of *their children* – that is, the children of those who had come out of Egypt but had perished in the wilderness. This was the generation to which the great speeches of Moses in Deuteronomy were addressed, urging them not to be like their parents, but rather to obey Yahweh, to keep his covenant and to move forward under his blessing into the land ahead of them. But tragically, though not unexpectedly by this stage of the lesson, we are reminded that they did not. They were no different from their parents and fell into exactly the same sins. The entry into the promised land, then, so gloriously described as the mighty act of Yahweh in the book of Joshua, is now also seen to have happened under the suspended anger of God, just like the exodus (21–22).

Another twist is added, again dependent on Deuteronomy but making its point even more sharply, in that Ezekiel affirms that Yahweh had declared his intention to expel Israel from the land and scatter them among the nations even before he had brought them

---

[92] On sabbatical years, see Exod. 23:10–11; Deut. 15. On the jubilee year, see Lev. 25.
[93] E.g. Amos 8:5–6; Is. 58:13 (in the context of the rest of the chapter); Jer. 34:8–16.
[94] Deut. 1:28.

into the land at all (23). Deuteronomy had foreseen this as the almost inevitable consequence of *future* disobedience which would activate the curses and threats of the covenant.[95] But Ezekiel regards it as something that was already so justified by Israel's behaviour in the wilderness itself that it was announced in advance before they even crossed the Jordan. The whole history of Israel's life in the land as well, then, the glorious and beautiful land of promise and blessing, proof of Yahweh's faithfulness to the patriarchs, inheritance for Yahweh's firstborn son, was also lived under the suspended judgment of the divine landlord.[96] The exile, on this interpetation, was not some inexplicable surprise. It was simply Yahweh blowing the final whistle after a greatly extended period of injury time.

Another example of Ezekiel's determination to shock by apparent contradiction and distortion comes in verses 25–26. The NIV has softened the literal Hebrew, which is: 'I also gave them not-good statutes and laws which they would not live by; I defiled them through their gifts by the offering of every firstborn ...' The shock is in the allegation that Yahweh actually gave bad laws and caused the defilement of human sacrifice. Early Christian interpretation seized on these verses as polemic against the Jews, claiming that they showed that the law itself was not good and not life-giving. Modern critics have seized on them as evidence that child sacrifice was once an officially accepted rite within Yahwism. Both misinterpretations ignore the fact that Ezekiel is being horrendously controversial in this whole chapter, creating a rhetorical parody of Israel's history in order to highlight its worst side. In a context of such sustained sarcasm and irony, we cannot suddenly take a verse like this as a face-value doctrinal or historical affirmation.

It is impossible to imagine, in the light of his overwhelming emphasis on the goodness and importance of God's law and on the horrific evil of child sacrifice, that Ezekiel could have seriously meant that Yahweh himself gave bad laws and commanded human sacrifice. The NIV is probably pointing in the right direction, though it is not really accurate as a translation. Israel had turned God's law upside down and rejected it, so that it *became for them* 'not-good' and a source of death, not life. They had gone in for child sacrifice *as if* God had required it, perhaps even portraying it as part of the law of Yahweh. So Ezekiel portrays Yahweh as letting them do so – ending up in their own defilement and destruction. Those actions

[95] Deut. 4:25–28 (note, 'after you ... have lived in the land a long time'); 28:64–65; 29:22–28. Cf. also the warnings of Lev. 18:24–28; 26:33–35.
[96] 'The prophet has telescoped eight or nine centuries of national history into one cryptic statement and retrojected it on Israel's desert experience.' Block (1), p. 636.

160

which people insist on pursuing against God's revealed will eventually become actions to which he 'gives them up', and in the end such persistent inversion of his actual laws and will becomes self-destructive.[97]

iv. Conquest to exile (20:27–31)

In this section the pattern begins to get blurred as the passion rises. Ezekiel is moving from the distant past to more recent history, and describing practices which his listeners in exile would have been familiar with back home. The divine action-gift is obviously the conquest by which Yahweh *brought them into the land* (28a). The rebellious response of Israel is summarized as the idolatry that was carried on for centuries at the high places – most likely either actual hilltop shrines with trees associated with the Canaanite fertility rituals, or artificial plinths and wooden poles erected for the purpose in places where no actual hill was available. They seem to have been a virtually ineradicable feature of Israel's religious life during most of the centuries of the monarchy, in spite of several royal attempts to remove them. Although it was probably carried on alongside the continuing worship of Yahweh,[98] it was fundamentally disloyal to the covenant's demand for exclusive devotion to him and was therefore tantamount to *forsaking* Yahweh altogether (27).[99]

At this point we might have expected the pattern to be followed: some announcement of God's anger followed by his decision to hold it back. But instead of that, Ezekiel suddenly leaps across the safety fence created by the past orientation of his story so far and confronts his listeners right in the present. *Therefore say to the house of Israel* (30). No longer is this an unflattering accusation against *your fathers* but a direct challenge to the present generation. Indeed, if the exiles were already getting into the habit of blaming all their own suffering on the sins of their ancestors (as they do in ch. 18), such comfortable ground is here cut right from under them. The sins of the fathers had followed the present generation right into exile, and the same sins were still being practised there. Verses 30 and 31a imply that the worst of Israel's idolatries were continued among at least some exiles, even to the point of child sacrifice. We have no other verification of this, but, given the desperation and trauma of the situation, it is not

---

[97] Cf. Ps. 81:12 (though the verb is not the same in Hebrew), and Rom. 1:24, 26, 28.

[98] Elijah challenged the people to see the inconsistency of such syncretism (1 Kgs. 18:21).

[99] V. 29 is a bitter joke. It is a divine pun playing on the Hebrew term for 'high place', *bāmâ*, as though it were derived from the reversal of similar-sounding words meaning 'What's this you're going to?' It is, of course, an artificial sarcasm, not an actual etymology.

unthinkable that some exiles may have felt that only such desperate actions could placate the anger of God. Such was the extent of their spiritual and moral darkness that they imagined they might placate Yahweh's anger by doing the thing that was actually arousing that anger more than anything else.

So this section of the historical sequence contains no word of judgment suspended. On the contrary, it is now being poured out upon them in the very fact of exile. Therefore no pleading will be entertained. Yahweh has no more answers to give (31b, which is the answer to v. 3). The case stands. The story is finished. The end.

Except that it isn't! For the present generation there would be no suspension of judgment. But in God's longer purposes, there would be a *sequel* to the judgment; it would accomplish a winnowing and a purging of the people that would enable the story to start all over again – back to the future, with a new exodus and a new wilderness, a new land and a new worship (32–44). Before we end this chapter by enjoying that prospect, however, it is worth looking back at one phrase which punctuates the preceding presentation of Israel's history – *for the sake of my name*.

b. The purpose of God's mercy

On each of the occasions that God had been about to act in destructive punishment on rebellious Israel, he had acted differently. The reason given in each case (9, 14, 22) is not mere pity, or anything to do with second thoughts or second chances. It is quite deliberate self-restraint in the light of another consideration – namely the reputation of his own name, as the God called Yahweh, among the nations. If he were to destroy the Israelites in Egypt, what would the Egyptians think of him? If he were to destroy them in the wilderness, likewise what would the Egyptians and other nations think of him? The nuance of these verses is well captured by the New Living Translation: 'But I didn't do it, for I acted to protect the honor of my name. That way the surrounding nations wouldn't be able to laugh at Israel's God, who had promised to deliver his people' (9). 'But again I held back in order to protect the honor of my name. That way the nations who saw me lead my people out of Egypt wouldn't be able to claim I destroyed them because I couldn't take care of them' (14).

Ezekiel is here echoing the Pentateuchal tradition according to which Moses pleaded with God on the basis of exactly this consideration on the two occasions in successive generations when they were most in danger of being wiped out by his anger – at the incident of the golden calf, and at the rebellion at Kadesh Barnea. On both occasions Moses not only appealed to Yahweh's covenant promises to Abraham, as well as to his covenant commitment to the people through the exodus and Sinai covenant. Moses also reminded God in remarkably bold terms that he had a reputation to think of. Whatever God would do to Israel would be seen by the nations, and they would draw conclusions that would, to say the least, not be flattering to Yahweh himself.[100] As in so much else, Moses becomes a model for intercessory prayer conducted for the sake of the name of Yahweh. In appealing to God to act in the forgiveness and restoration of his own people, Daniel and the psalmists also concentrate on this powerfully motivating factor – God's concern for God's own name and reputation.[101]

Behind this point, however, lies the more foundational understanding that *all* God's dealings with Israel were not only open to the gaze of contemporary nations, but were ultimately undertaken with all the rest of the nations in mind. The scope of God's universal purpose, the goal of his universal mission, included all the nations, not just Israel. The election, redemption and history of Israel were all part of that mission of Yahweh to the nations of the world – the mission by which, ultimately, according to a key element in the theology of Ezekiel, the nations would 'know that I am Yahweh'. Hence God's passionate concern for the honour of his name among *Israel* is all of a piece with his universal concern for the honour of his name among all *humanity*. 'To speak of the name in this context is to say that Israel exists not for itself but to fulfil the divine purpose in history. That is why Israel must on all occasions sanctify the name, a profound conviction expressed by Jesus in the first petition of the Lord's Prayer.'[102]

But 'sanctifying the name' – that is, treating the name of Yahweh with all the honour and respect owed to its uniqueness and distinctness from all other names of gods – was not something that only Israel would do. In verse 41, Yahweh himself would demonstrate the holiness of his name (in the same sense, its uniqueness and distinctness). He would do it in Israel (*among you*), but also he would ultimately do so to universal acknowledgment (*in the sight of the nations*).

The purpose of God's mercy to Israel, then, on those occasions when he would have been utterly justified in acting in exterminating justice, was as much to demonstrate his own nature and to defend his own name as any of his other acts in their history. The paradox is, as the climactic verse 44 points out, that Israel would come to know the full character of Yahweh as God, both when he chose to

---

[100] Exod. 32:11–14; Num. 14:13–16; Deut. 9:26–29.
[101] Dan. 9:15–19; Ps. 79:9–10.   [102] Blenkinsopp, p. 88.

treat them as their sins deserved, and when he chose not to. Chapter 36 will explore this paradox even further, and sharpen it by observing how Yahweh's determination to act 'for the sake of his name among the nations' was what governed both the sending into exile and the gathering from exile. It was the grateful testimony of many a psalmist that Yahweh was to be blessed and praised precisely because 'he does not treat us as our sins deserve',[103] though they knew this against the background that he was the God who 'does not leave the guilty unpunished'.[104] The two sides of this paradox would ultimately be resolved only on the cross of Jesus Christ, which stands as the simultaneous vindication of the justice and mercy of God, and to which the name of the Lord among the nations has been nailed once and for all. For there God did deal with sin as it deserved, but he did so by laying on his own Son and Servant the iniquity of us all so that we need bear its guilt and penalty no longer.

c. The persistence of God's grace

And so we come back to the concluding word of grace that is so unexpected after the historical diatribe in the first part of the chapter. There is a hope, there is grace, but it is a grace that is incredibly strong, severe and purposeful. And it is a hope that owes nothing whatever to anything on Israel's side – for on that side, as Ezekiel's placarding of their history has shown, there has never been anything other than rebellion. Nevertheless Israel must now respond in repentance. But they must know that any future they can have will be:

> ... a future which is dependent not upon man's ability to respond but upon God's willingness to act ... The possibility of a response from Israel – however improbable – is not wholly excluded. But at the same time it is expressed in such a way that the response is really no matter of human endeavour but entirely of divine grace. For the stress laid in these passages [including 34, 36, 37] is the will of God that men should live rather than that they should die.[105]

The word of grace begins in severity, however, by simply confronting head-on the determined idolatry of the people. There is something faintly comic about the brevity of verse 32. Israel with almost childish petulance whines, 'We want to be like everybody

[103] E.g. Ps. 103:10.
[104] Exod. 34:7. Cf. the similar juxtaposition of wrath and mercy in Deut. 4:24, 31.
[105] Ackroyd, p. 109.

else. We want their toys too.' And God simply replies with parental
finality, 'Never!' Israel's desire, of course, was the direct opposite of
what they were meant to be. They were supposed to be different,
holy, distinct from the nations, not merely in their religious practice
but also in all aspects of their social, economic and political life. The
monarchy had begun with a challenge to this distinctiveness and a
rejection of it, much to Samuel's and Yahweh's despair.[106] In echoing
that request from the very beginning of the monarchy – a monarchy
that was now in its final hours – Ezekiel shows just how incorrigibly
persistent was Israel's determination to go the way of crass idolatry
(*wood and stone*). But Israel's persistent sin is met and will be
overcome by Yahweh's persistent grace. '*What you have in mind will
never happen!*' God will not be defeated by Israel's stubbornness. He
will fulfil his purpose for them and for the world through them, in
spite of all resistance. One might add that there is great hope for the
world in this. For if the world were dependent for its salvation on
the spiritual and moral purity of the church and its evangelistic
obedience, rather than on the indefatigable persistence of God's
longing for its redemption, it would be doomed to disappointment.
For the stubbornness, corruption and apathy of the church in many
generations, and its determination to be like the world rather than
to win the world, have not lagged far behind Old Testament Israel's.

This divine persistence is then highlighted by the repeated *I will*
of the following verses, which describe a new version of Israel's
history that will be played out in the future. It is like a video being
rewound, and then rerecorded with a revised version of the old story.
There will be a new exodus, but it will take place in the context of
great wrath (33–34). There will be a new wilderness experience,[107]
but it will be for the sake of executing a purging judgment. Just as
those who experienced the first exodus did not all reach the
promised land, so those who have the new opportunity to respond
to God in exile will be 'sorted' with the purpose of excluding from
future blessing those who continue in rebellion (36–38). And when
the return to the land eventually happens, things will be very
different from before, for '*there the entire house of Israel will serve
me, and there I will accept them*' (40). And then, through the entire
experience of judgment, purging, restoration and acceptance, Israel
will finally *know that he is the* Lord 42, 44). For this, more than
anything else, is the central burning passion of Ezekiel's ministry.
The world must know that Yahweh is truly God, but that will be
possible only when the people of Yahweh truly know it first.

[106] 1 Sam. 8.
[107] *The desert of the nations* (35) probably means the experience of exile in the midst
of the nations – specifically in the Mesopotamian desert.

Conclusion

It may be that we come to the end of this survey of Ezekiel's lurid and scathing presentations of the history of Israel feeling somewhat uncomfortable. If so, Ezekiel would doubtless be pleased, for that was his intent. But the question remains: did he go too far? Has he not engaged in distortion of the story? Who got it right, the great epic narratives, which at least include some glorious and positive periods alongside the more negative ones, or Ezekiel, with his unrelieved picture of rebellion, depravity and betrayal? Two considerations may help to answer these questions.

First, we must bear in mind both the terrible task that Ezekiel faced and the rhetorical tools he chose to use. He was faced with the onslaught of the most traumatic catastrophe that had ever hit his people – a people who were no strangers to trauma and catastrophe in their history. And he was faced with people who were obsessed with a totally wrong interpretation of that catastrophe: namely, that it was not really deserved at all, and Yahweh was being unfair or incompetent or both. Some of them were also gripped by a disastrously naïve optimism about their own situation: namely, that it would soon be over and they would return to a Jerusalem that had yet again been delivered by Yahweh's mighty power. The only way to counter such utter misconceptions was to shatter them ruthlessly on the hard rocks of reality – the reality of their long history of ceaseless offence to Yahweh and heedless breaking of their covenant obligations to him. Having seen the size of his task, we can then appreciate his rhetorical method, which was to use deliberate parody, scathing allegory, grossly distorted caricature imagery and schematic arrangement of materials for maximum impact. Ezekiel was not writing a dispassionate chronicle of Old Testament history from the patriarchs to the exile that might later do service as a class textbook in some rabbinical school. He was embroiled in fierce argument with hostile or apathetic opponents, who, we recall, had stiff faces, hard hearts and brazen foreheads. His rhetoric had to be strong and shocking enough to pierce through armour-plated resistance.

Secondly, it will help to remember that there is always more than one way to tell the story about the same historical event or period. Even in the Old Testament traditions themselves there are variant ways of looking at the same period. The Pentateuch, for example, portrays the wilderness period as substantially a time of grumbling, unbelief, and wasted opportunity.[108] Hosea similarly saw it as a time of inexplicable betrayal of Yahweh's love.[109] Jeremiah, on the other hand, for a different rhetorical purpose, could liken it to Israel's

---

[108] As summarized in Deut. 1:26–46.   [109] Hos. 11:1–4.

honeymoon period with Yahweh.[110] The story of Israel could be written in a way that highlighted the mighty acts of Yahweh on behalf of his people; in that sense it was indeed their 'salvation history'. Ezekiel knew that story well and does not question it. But the same story could be told from the perspective of Israel's constant failure, and how that was seen from heaven's point of view. And the latter presentation is just as true, for all that we might say that in comprehensive terms it is selective.

But then all history telling is selective. What you select depends on what you want to say and what your reason is for telling the story at all. How many biographies of great Christian leaders and missionaries leave you wondering what has been left unsaid? The official biography, perhaps with the laudable intention of inspiring praise to God and imitation by lesser mortals, will concentrate on the great achievements, the mighty moments, the long struggle perhaps, and the triumphant conclusion. Another story could be told in every case, of the petty failures and sad betrayals, of times of doubt, depression and disobedience, of sexual misdemeanour and lack of integrity, of overwhelming ordinariness as well as transient greatness. The famous 'red book' in the television programme *This Is Your Life*, we can be sure, tells the former story and not the latter – and quite appropriately. It is selective, but we do not necessarily accuse it of falsification.

And what of the history of the Christian church as a whole? Most of us know the broad outlines of the great tale of the spread of the gospel, of the missionary expansion of the church, of the great triumphs of the faith all over the globe – from Celtic and Nestorian mission in the early centuries, through the prolific mobilization of the Moravians, to the staggering statistics of multinational church and mission growth in the twentieth century. But if it were appropriate, in the kind of situation Ezekiel faced, we know that an entirely differently flavoured story could be told, a story of Christianity which could spin an unending list of atrocities and perversions of the gospel which have assaulted the gates of heaven and brought grief and wrath to the heart of God.

What allegory might Ezekiel devise that would do justice to the horror and obscenity of the Crusades, the pogroms, the Inquisition, the conquistadores, the drowning and burning of Anabaptists, the Holocaust, apartheid, religious bigotry in Northern Ireland, genocide in Rwanda and ethnic cleansing in the Balkans? Sometimes that other story of Christian doings is told with lurid malice in the media, by secular opponents of the faith. Perhaps, rather than always

[110] Jer. 2:1–3.

reacting so defensively to the way the world sees us, we should listen for the echoes of Ezekiel's voice and turn again in repentance to the severe but persistent grace of God – grace which will ultimately work God's saving will for humanity in spite of the wretched failures of those whom he has called to be God's people.

Appendix 2
Notes on Ezekiel 15, 17 and 19

Having marvelled at Ezekiel's capacity for constructing complex and multilayered allegories in chapters 16 and 23, we have in chapters 15, 17 and 19 somewhat lesser examples of the same skill in verbal imagery. The common element in all three chapters is the use of the vine as a metaphor for Israel.

Chapter 15

Vines were such a key element in Palestinian agriculture that it is not surprising that, like the olive tree, they could be used as a metaphor for Israel itself. So, in Psalm 80:8–19, Israel is a choice vine that Yahweh brought out of Egypt and planted in Canaan, where it flourished. The psalm is written, however, from exile and first bemoans the fact that the vine has been broken down and burned with fire, and then appeals to God to rise up to protect and restore it. Isaiah likened Israel to a vineyard in which Yahweh had invested a great deal of care and effort, only to be rewarded with the bitter grapes of injustice and oppression.[1]

Ezekiel here subverts the whole metaphor by diverting attention from grapes and wine to the *wood of the vine*, which, he argues, is worthless in comparison with all other kinds of wood. The devastating implication seems to be that Israel has no intrinsic worth anyway, even as a vine in good health. But when the wood of a vine is burned, it is even more useless than ever. So, in the aftermath of the fiery judgment to come upon Israel, what will be left of any value at all? The short piece of imaginative comparison is bleak and haunting, and would certainly have brought no comfort to the exiles. If the main stem of Yahweh's vine was to be burned up, what possible future could there be for those branches which had already been lopped off in exile?

[1] Is. 5:1–7.

Chapter 17

Here we have a deliberately constructed allegory designed to illustrate specific historical events. The allegory is set out in verses 3–10, and then the explanation is immediately given in verses 11–21. This is then followed by another smaller allegory whose purpose is to point to a brighter future initiated by God himself (22–24).

The events referred to are the first deportation in 597, when Nebuchadnezzar took Jehoichin and the top people of Jerusalem off into exile and installed Zedekiah as regent, and then Zedekiah's futile flirting with Egypt for support against Babylon, which ultimately led to his demise.

So, in the allegory, the first *great eagle* is Nebuchadnezzar, and the *topmost shoot* refers to Jehoiachin and the first exiles. *The seed of your land* refers to Zedekiah, whom Nebuchadnezzar *planted* in Jerusalem. Like a *low, spreading vine*, Zedekiah professed loyalty to the king of Babylon, but secretly spread his roots towards the second *great eagle*, namely Egypt. The result, however, was that the vine withered and eventually perished altogether. Such would ultimately be the fate of Zedekiah. The allegory thus also becomes a prediction, since it comes from the period before the final rebellion of Zedekiah and the fall of Jerusalem. At that time, says Ezekiel, Pharaoh will prove a useless ally, as always, and Zedekiah will suffer a humiliating fate.

It is not entirely clear what purpose the allegorical presentation of events serves, though the predictive element obviously strengthened Ezekiel's credentials when eventually his words came true.

The final section, verses 22–24, makes the point that ultimately the security and fruitfulness of Israel will come, not from either of the two great eagles – human empires which are intrinsically fickle and transient – but from God himself. And when God intervenes to reverse the fortunes of his people, then the world (*All the trees of the field*) will know who has done it. In comparison with the truly great eagle, Yahweh himself, Nebuchadnezzar and Pharaoh are very small birds indeed. And in comparison with all the other trees, the redemptive work of God for his people will result in a tree of truly cosmic dimensions.

Chapter 19

Here we have another rare example of Ezekiel's poetic gift. He composes *a lament concerning the princes of Israel*, that is, a funeral dirge that would normally be sung after the death of those it names. Like chapter 17, the song has historical reference. It describes two or possibly three of the last kings of Israel and their fate. Unfortunately Ezekiel does not provide us with a key to the riddle, as in chapter 17, so divergent identifications have been offered.

The *lioness* refers to Israel,[2] or more specifically, the tribe of Judah,[3] as the *mother* of the kings. The first king (3–4) is undoubtedly Jehoahaz, or Shallum, who was carried off to Egypt in 609 BC by Pharaoh Necho after the defeat and death of Josiah in the battle of Megiddo.[4] The second king (5–9) may be Jehoiachin (skipping over Jehoiakim), who surrendered Jerusalem to Nebuchadnezzar after the first short siege in 597. He was then carried off into captivity in Babylon. Or it may be Zedekiah, who had more time to establish the kind of reputation portrayed in verses 6–7. Zedekiah too was captured and taken to Babylon.[5]

In verses 10–14 Ezekiel shifts his imagery again and describes Judah as a vine which grew to excessive heights through the forest canopy, until its arrogance was overthrown, cut down and burned. The fate of Judah's kings would soon be the fate of the nation itself – no longer planted in God's fertile land, but *planted in the desert, in a dry and thirsty land* (13). For the time being, no songs could be sung but the songs of *lament*. 'The exiles are hereby reminded that they, who now wallow in the misery of Babylonian exile, represent the pathetic remainder of this once proud plant.'[6] What is clear is that the song proclaims in the language of funeral lament the demise of the Davidic dynasty, for *No strong branch is left on it fit for a ruler's sceptre* (14). The lioness would produce no more natural-born cubs for the throne. Only the intervention of Yahweh himself would produce another 'David' – but that was a song for another day (see 34:22–24).

---

[2] Cf. Num. 23:24; 24:9.

[3] Gen. 49:8–9. It seems that Ezekiel is drawing on the imagery of this portrayal of Judah as a lion.

[4] 2 Kgs. 23:33; cf. Jer. 22:10–12.

[5] Block (1), pp. 604–606, makes out a case for identifying this second lion with Jehoiakim, the actual successor to Jehoahaz.

[6] Block (1), p. 610.

14:12–23; 18:1–32; 33:10–20
5. Who then can be saved?

Introduction

'Scratch where they itch' has always been a sound motto for pastoral and evangelistic ministry. It's no good answering questions that people are not asking, or leaving unanswered the questions they do ask. Though 'scratching' may be a severe understatement for the way Ezekiel tore the skin off his hearers, it is nevertheless an appropriate metaphor for his ministry. He faced not only the kind of false and dangerous assumptions that we looked at in the last chapter, but also a barrage of questions from his fellow exiles. They were questions that arose from widely different emotional and psychological states of mind, but Ezekiel tackles them all in his usual robust way. In this chapter we shall look at the answers he gave to three questions. Two of them are explicit questions found in the text itself, along with Ezekiel's handling of them. The first, however, has to be inferred from Ezekiel's own words.

1. *Anxious hope.* First of all, in the years before the final fall of Jerusalem, the exiles certainly entertained the hope that the city would yet be spared. We have seen that a major part of Ezekiel's efforts hitherto had been directed at trying to get them to realize that this was a forlorn hope, and that the city was doomed. Nevertheless, it seems that some of them were asking, 'Will God not spare the city for the sake of at least the few righteous people that are still there?' This hope was probably linked to a particular anxiety that the exiles would have had for their relatives, and especially their children, who were left behind in the city. It is this mixture of hope and anxiety that Ezekiel addresses in 14:12–23

2. *Bitter complaint.* Then there were those, possibly a majority, who reacted to the exile with a sense of bitter unfairness. Their question was, 'Why is God punishing us for all the sins of past generations? We do not deserve this! Yahweh is acting unfairly.' This question had crystallized itself into a popular proverb: 'The fathers

have eaten sour grapes and the children's teeth are set on edge.' This may have been tinged with a sense of fatalistic resignation as well: 'Since that is how things are, there is nothing we can do about it anyway.' Ezekiel tackles the whole mindset expressed in the proverb and the question in 18:1–32 and 33:12–20.

3. *Deathly despair.* Finally, there were those who had given up hope altogether. This may have included some who had been convinced by Ezekiel's message that the city was doomed, even before they got news that it had actually fallen. But certainly after 587 BC, their number must have swelled enormously as people realized the awful truth. They would probably never see Jerusalem again in their own lifetime. Their question was whether it was worthwhile or even possible to go on living with such a prospect: '*Our offences and sins weigh us down, and we are wasting away because of them. How then can we live?*' This is the opening question of the section in which Ezekiel begins his answer (33:10–20), though he has even more wonderful news for such despairing folk in chapter 37.

Let us join our prophet again, then, as he tackles these questions with a brilliant ability to shatter false hopes that had been built on flawed reasoning, and yet at the same time to offer a true hope that would be built on genuine repentance. In this chapter we shall see something of Ezekiel's evangelistic skill. We shall also feel the pulse of his heart beating with God's own passionate longing for people to turn from the road that leads to destruction and find the narrow gateway to life.

1. Only the righteous will be saved (14:12–23)

There is just a chance that Ezekiel may have been somewhat to blame for fuelling the particular expression of hope that some of the exiles came up with. In his great vision of what was going on in Jerusalem, Ezekiel had described how one of the angelic figures had gone around the city instructed to place a mark on the forehead of those who lamented over its wickedness (9:3–4).[1] In Ezekiel's vision, such people were to be spared God's wrath when the destroying angels went about their task. Ezekiel did not report how many such people were marked – or indeed if any were found at all. But suppose at least some were found? If they were to be spared judgment, then they could be presumed to be righteous in God's sight, even though they were not explicitly described as 'righteous' in the vision of chapter 9. So if some were to be spared, could God not be persuaded to spare the whole city for the sake of even a few

[1] See above, ch. 3.

righteous people within it? Maybe the representatives of the exiles had come to ask Ezekiel to intercede with Yahweh along those lines. And they doubtless quoted Scripture at him as well. After all, Abraham had pleaded with God on behalf of Sodom and Gomorrah on exactly those grounds: namely, that Yahweh was a just God and would not destroy the righteous with the wicked. One can imagine them earnestly pleading with Ezekiel and quoting Genesis 18:23–33. Even if there were only a few righteous people left in Jerusalem, they could form a kind of 'human shield' against God's anger, rather as unscrupulous dictators have been known to place innocent civilians in and around military installations as a way of deterring enemy attacks. At a more trivial level, during my own years as a parish minister, when visiting families who had no active connection with the church, I was sometimes amused to hear tales of this or that brother, son, grandfather or uncle who had 'gone into the church' (that is, was ordained), as though it somehow guaranteed some divine favours on the rest of the family.

Added to this apparently scripturally justified hope, there was another particular anxiety among the exiles in Babylon. It seems that some of them had children who had been left behind in Jerusalem. These are referred to in 24:21 and 25, and may be implied by the references to *sons* and *daughters* in 14:16, 18 and 20. This unhappy situation may have been intentionally caused by the forced splitting up of families by Nebuchadnezzar. Such ruthless action would have acted as a disincentive to rebellious action at either location. He could say to one group, 'If you revolt here in Babylon, think what I can do to your children in Jerusalem'; and to the other group, 'Before you consider another rebellion here in Jerusalem, remember your parents in slavery in Babylon.'

So the argument among the exiles ran, 'Maybe Yahweh will spare the city in spite of all its wickedness, for the sake of the righteous who are still there. And maybe our children are among the righteous – or at least, will be spared along with them.' Did Ezekiel not agree? Would he not please intercede with Yahweh for their children, as Abraham did for the sake of his nephew? It would have been a passionate and heart-rending request.

Yet again, in order to resist their pleas, Ezekiel needed the bronze forehead Yahweh had given him, as well as the instruction that he was not to act as an intercessor for them (3:26).[2] But, for the form of his answer, he drew on his priestly background in setting up case-studies. This one comes in the form of a four-part narrative, with a shocking climax.

[2] See above, ch. 2, pp. 71–73.

a. No proxy salvation, in general (14:13–20)

First of all, Ezekiel calls on his hearers to imagine a general case – *a country*, any country. This country has sinned against God *by being unfaithful.* This particular verb (*mā'āl*) is virtually a technical term for breaking the covenant by acting treacherously or faithlessly. So although the subject is any nation, and we need to give full force to the general point Ezekiel is making about Yahweh's moral sovereignty over all nations,[3] the vocabulary gives a hint already that the kind of sin in mind is that which is typical of Israel. So we are to envisage any nation engaging in sin to the extent that God decides to *stretch out my hand* – another regular term for God's acting in judgment. God's hand then delivers four strikes, which are described in four successive paragraphs, each given to one of the most feared disasters that can befall nations: *famine* (13); incursions of *wild beasts* (15); military defeat through *the sword* (17) and epidemic disease, or *plague* (19). This is a familiar list of catastrophes well known in the ancient Near East, and often associated with divine judgment in the Old Testament. Ezekiel has already spoken of the triad of famine, sword and plague in 5:12, and here he adds a fourth – wild beasts. Again, the language itself recalls the covenant curse vocabulary,[4] even though the case being set up refers to any nation in general.

Then, secondly, Ezekiel asks for a further stretch of imagination. Who, he asks, are the most righteous people you can think of? Three proverbial figures spring to mind, namely *Noah, Daniel and Job*, all of them famous for their moral integrity and approval by God. Now suppose, says Ezekiel, painting a remarkable mental picture, that all three of them lived in that one country, miraculously transported to the same time zone. Would their combined righteousness ward off God's striking hand and *save* or deliver the country? No, counters Ezekiel; they alone would be saved because of their own righteousness.

A word on the hypothetical righteous brothers is needed. Noah is well known for the righteousness of his character, for we read that 'Noah was a righteous man, blameless among the people of his time, and he walked with God.'[5] Job, likewise, is described even more warmly, first by the narrator: 'This man was blameless and upright; he feared God and shunned evil';[6] and then by God himself: '... my servant Job ... There is no one on earth like him.'[7] So if salvation

---

[3] This is more than a 'façade of universalism' (Allen 28, p. 217). A similar affirmation of Yahweh's moral governance of all nations is found in Amos 1:2 – 2:3 and Jer. 18:1–10. In both those cases the rhetorical tactic is similar: namely, the final accusation of Israel itself.   [4] Esp. Lev. 26:22–26.   [5] Gen. 6:9.   [6] Job 1:1.   [7] Job 1:8.

comes through having a good reserve of transferable moral credit, this country has enviable assets already. Daniel is more of a problem. The biblical character of that name, of course, had just as polished a reputation for righteousness, integrity, trustworthiness and excellence,[8] alongside a remarkable capacity for political and personal survival. The trouble is that, whereas Noah and Job were characters of antiquity and legendary fame, pre-dating Israel's own historical emergence, the Daniel whose stories are told in the book of Daniel was a contemporary of Ezekiel. He was probably somewhat younger in fact, and, according to Daniel 1:1–6, had been brought to Babylon as a youth in the first batch of early hostages taken by Nebuchadnezzar in 605 BC. This means that he had been in Babylonian society only about fifteen years before his name appears in Ezekiel's mini hall of fame, alongside legendary figures of the distant past. It is possible, of course, though somewhat unlikely, that he had become a youthful hero whose name stood for exceptional integrity even by then. Most scholars, however, believe that the name here in Ezekiel 14 does not refer to the biblical character (there is a slight difference in the Hebrew spelling anyway), but perhaps to an ancient king of Syria, known to us from the Ugaritic texts as the father of Aqhat, about whom there is an epic narrative. Dan'el, as he is called, was also apparently renowned for his wise, just and compassionate rule. His name may have been legendary for these qualities in Israel as well.[9]

Coming back to the case-study, Ezekiel insists that the presence of even such famously righteous men, and even all three of them together, would have no effect on the judgment of God upon the rest of the sinful society. They themselves would be *saved*, or delivered,[10] but their righteousness would not avail for the salvation of others, including children.[11] And by his rhetorical strategy, Ezekiel manages

---

[8] Dan. 6:3–4.

[9] Although most scholars now take this view, Block resists it and argues a case for the biblical Daniel as the model of righteousness that Ezekiel refers to – thus drawing on both ancient stories and one of their own contemporaries, for added dramatic effect (Block (1), p. 448). One wonders, then, however, why the name appears as the middle of the three.

[10] The verb *nāsal* is regularly used for God's delivering his people from their enemies, e.g. at the exodus.

[11] The NIV interprets the phrase in vv. 16 and 18 as *their own sons or daughters*. The assumption that the text refers to the actual children of Noah, Daniel and Job has produced problems, since of course Noah's children were in fact saved along with him, and, though Job lost his in his calamity, others were restored to him. It *might* mean that, if Noah were here today, even he could not save his children – i.e. Jerusalem is even more wicked than human society before the flood. But the Hebrew does not have the suffix for 'their', and it is more likely that the statement is general: 'They could not save sons and daughters – or anybody else but themselves.' Cf. NRSV and NKJV.

to spin the point out to four times its possible length. Rather than just listing the four strikes of Yahweh's hand all at once, he repeats the whole case-study for each one, so that there is a kind of tolling bell of *They alone would be saved.* It's a quadruple thumbs down. The people who asked the question have their answer, and it's no, no, no, no. There will be no 'beneficial solidarity'[12] for all the inhabitants of Jerusalem on the backs of those who may be righteous there. 'Ezekiel's message is that there are no party-tickets to deliverance.'[13] 'There is no salvation by proxy.'[14] The only hope for salvation is for those whose lives and actions prove their own righteous standing before God.

b. No privileged exemption for Jerusalem, in particular (14:21)

Having established his general point by fourfold repetition, Ezekiel turns on the real object of the exercise. If what he has said is true for *any* country, how much more will it be true for Jerusalem? And indeed, *How much worse will it be* when God acts with the same fourfold work of judgment upon them (21). If they thought they might have some privileged exemption from the moral laws of Yahweh by which all nations are judged, they were terribly wrong. Furthermore, of course, there is an undoubted echo here of the nasty comparison that Ezekiel has already drawn between Israel and the rest of the nations in chapter 5: 'in her wickedness she has rebelled against my laws and decrees more than the nations and countries around her' (5:6). So, if there would be no hope for other nations on the basis of a few hypothetical righteous resident heroes, there would be even less for Jerusalem anyway. If the people's question had relied for biblical precedent on Abraham's intercession for Sodom, then there is an added irony here, which looks forward to chapter 16. Just maybe God would have spared Sodom for the sake of a few righteous people, if his visiting angels had found any, other than the family of Lot whom they rescued. But in any case, Jerusalem is far worse than Sodom ever was (16:47–52), so there was absolutely no hope for them.

One of the more difficult tasks of preaching and teaching the Scriptures is to help people to recognize that contexts affect the message – that is, both the message to be found in any particular section of Scripture, and also the message that is needing to be preached in any particular situation. And one of the dangers of systematic theology is the temptation to formulate a doctrine that is thought to be valid in all circumstances regardless of the context in which it is believed or the response it generates. Ezekiel's preaching

[12] Allen 28, p. 218.   [13] Taylor, p. 128.   [14] Blenkinsopp, p. 74.

here is compelled to stress one scriptural truth about God's work in salvation against people who had twisted another scriptural truth into a form of self-serving insurance policy. At another time and in another context God had indeed spoken of the way in which successive generations are included in the covenant of grace. The love of God which had given such gracious promises and achieved such great redemption for those who first entered into covenant relationship with him was extended to future generations. But this was on the assumption of careful teaching and faithful obedience by parents and children alike. Those who were exhorted to trust and obey Yahweh on the basis of his love and promise needed the reassurance that their families were included and the future was secure. That was the explanation that a father could give his son about 'our righteousness' in the context of obedience, fear of the Lord and continued prosperous life in the land.[15] In such a context of covenant obedience, the love of God could be promised to 'a thousand generations of those who love him and keep his commands'.[16]

But Ezekiel was precisely *not* addressing such covenant-faithful families. He was confronted with people whose lives were a total denial of the grace and redemption of Yahweh. These were people who for generations had lived in disobedience and rebellion, but who still hoped that they could somehow profit from somebody else's residual righteousness which they thought might impress Yahweh and persuade him to spare them all. 'The exiles hold to wrong doctrine and therefore to a vain hope.'[17] To such people the message had to be the other side of the coin. Each person is responsible before God for their own life and behaviour, and especially for the way they have responded to the grace and the demands of God's covenant. This is not some new doctrine of individual responsibility, introduced for the first time by Ezekiel (see further discussion below), but a stark highlighting of something which had always been true, but now needed the kind of exclusive emphasis that would

[15] Deut. 6:20–25. It is important to be clear that 'our righteousness' here does not mean some kind of 'works righteousness' by which people could in some way earn God's salvation or blessing. Rather it speaks of that 'right response' to the saving grace of God *already experienced*, the response of personal and moral commitment to obeying God's covenant commands. Righteousness in this sense means being in right standing with God on the basis of a trusting and obedient response to what he has already done for us.

[16] Deut. 7:9. It is interesting that the following verse not only lacks an equivalent multiplication of generations, but speaks in individual terms of God repaying to their face those who hate him. The second half of Deut. 7:10 is singular (cf. NKJV). It implies the individual responsibility of those who reject God's covenant and are punished with destruction. [17] Greenberg, p. 261.

counteract the people's false hopes based on wrongly used scriptural promises and precedents. Only the righteous[18] will be saved, and their righteousness is not available to third parties under some collective credit accumulation and transfer scheme.

c. No more protest at God's justice (14:22–23)

Yet there will be some survivors …! One wonders how Ezekiel got away with such amazing shock tactics. Four times he had told these enquirers, anxious parents among them, that there was absolutely no hope that their children in Jerusalem would be spared the coming calamity, no matter whose righteousness they quoted or claimed. Yet here he suddenly says that there will be some survivors – including *sons and daughters*. Is he simply contradicting himself? No, for two reasons.

First, this prediction that there would be a few survivors from the final conflagration of Jerusalem is consistent with what Ezekiel had said on other occasions.[19] It was not a novel or contradictory point. His basic, and underlined, point was that Jerusalem as a city would not be spared but finally be destroyed. Secondly, these survivors are not said to be 'saved', in the same way that Noah, Job and Daniel are repeatedly described as having been saved because of their righteousness. They are merely survivors, who will have been *brought out of it*. And even that survival is certainly not based on their own or anybody else's righteousness.[20] On the contrary, their *conduct and their actions* will continue to be wicked enough to furnish walking visible proof of why the city had to be destroyed. The survivors have no soteriological significance, but only didactic – to teach the other exiles a lesson about the justice of God.

So, with a masterly, though desperately cruel, stroke of rhetorical power, Ezekiel tells the exiles that they may indeed see sons and daughters again, but the comfort they provide will not be, as they hoped, the comfort of having their relatives spared, but the cold comfort of coming to recognize the rightness and justice of God's judgment on the city. 'Ironically, the very children who had been the focal point of theological hope for their worried parents would turn out to be agents of a different truth, witnesses to divine necessity.'[21]

---

[18] In the sense of note 15 above.

[19] Ezek. 5:3; 6:8; 7:16; 12:16. In this also he was following the same line as his 'control text', Lev. 26:36–39.

[20] 'This escape from the devastation is not to be confused with deliverance, the saving of one's life (cf. v. 20), or being saved (vv. 14, 16, 18). These are not exceptions to the principles enunciated earlier, but random survivors, like Amos's "two legs or a piece of an ear" (3:12), or Isaiah's "two or three olives on the topmost bough" (17:6).' Block (1), p. 451.   [21] Allen 28, p. 219.

Both the report (presumably) of what had been happening in Jerusalem, and the continued behaviour of the new batch of exiles,[22] would be such a revelation to the existing exiles that they would be compelled to admit that Yahweh's wrath was justified – all his punitive actions had not been *without cause* (23). Far from being arbitrary or excessive or unjustified, Yahweh's action against his people in Jerusalem would not only be justice done, but justice being seen to be done, even by those whom it most affected.

Indeed, says Ezekiel, they would not merely admit it, but in a strange way they would *be consoled* by it. The verb, *nāḥam*, implies being able to breathe deeply as tension is relieved, and thus to experience comfort, consolation or reassurance. In this context it implies a lessening of the feeling of grievance or protest by a recognition that God was right to do what he had done. Various translations bring this out: 'You will breathe easier over the disaster that I have inflicted';[23] 'You will not feel so bad about the disaster';[24] 'You will feel better about what I have done' (NLT). It would be cold comfort, but none the less real.

There is indeed a grim consolation that comes from seeing justice done. It is important to distinguish such comfort from gloating or the ungodly sweetness of revenge. I remember seeing on the news an interview with the relatives of a rape and murder victim whose attacker had at last, after many years, been apprehended and successfully prosecuted and convicted. They spoke of the comfort it brought them. Their daughter could now 'rest' at last. The doing of justice would of course not bring her back to them, but there was some consolation and relief that her loss had now been recognized through justice having taken its course. 'Now we can sleep easily at last,' they said – which seems to express what *nāḥam* is getting at very well.

When raised to the cosmic level of divine justice in relation to the staggering and unimaginable mountain of human wickedness and evil, there is, it seems to me, a similar and appropriate comfort that comes from the certainty that 'the Judge of all the earth will do right', that ultimately all persistent and unrepented wickedness will be appropriately punished. There ought to be no pleasure in such a prospect, for there is none for God himself, as we shall see emphatically below. But if it were not so, we should be lost in the abyss of the endless victory of evil. So we can draw comfort and

---

[22] The phrase *when you see their conduct and their actions* (22) seems to assume that the new arrivals would continue with the outrageous behaviour which had been going on in Jerusalem, to such an extent that even the earlier exiles would be shocked at it, and would acknowledge that God was justifiably angry.

[23] Block (1), p. 440.   [24] Allen 28, p. 210.

ultimately enormous hope from the chilling biblical affirmation of divine justice, even as we rejoice in the overwhelming triumph of divine love in the grace of redemption.

2. Only the wicked need die (18:1–29; 33:12–20)

In chapter 18 Ezekiel has given us one of the most profound, moving and influential reflections on the relationship between God's justice and human freedom, combined with one of the most powerful evangelistic appeals in the Old Testament. It is a rich and complex chapter, with several levels of meaning related to different aspects of the questions the exiles were raising. With its sharp interjections of things the people were saying (initially in v. 2, and then in vv. 19 and 25), it probably reflects an actual disputation that Ezekiel had with his hearers, possibly on more than one occasion. In this chapter we find Ezekiel exercising his robust evangelistic skill, along with a passionate pastoral concern for his contemporaries. And it all begins with a popular slogan, a saying that was common not only among the exiles in Babylon, but also back in the homeland.[25]

a. The unacceptable proverb (18:2–4)

> 'The fathers eat sour grapes,
> and the children's teeth are set on edge.'[26]

Like most popular proverbs, the brevity and metaphorical form of the saying allow it a breadth of possible nuances when we ask exactly what it was meant to imply. Why did people go around saying this, in exile or back in Jerusalem? Probably there are two ways of understanding it. First of all, as a general expression of 'the way things are', it encapsulates an assumption about life based on observation. Children do suffer because of the sins or stupidity of their parents. One generation's wickedness affects the quality of life for the next. We do reap what others have sown before we arrived, and future generations will reap what we sow now.

But, secondly, since Yahweh was believed to be in charge of 'the way things are', this particular outworking of his ways was being

---

[25] Jer. 31:27–30.

[26] NIV has mixed gender-specific and gender-inclusive language. In Hebrew it is 'fathers' and 'sons'. But it implies generations as wholes, so it would be better to use inclusive terms in both halves: 'Parents eat sour grapes; but their children's teeth feel rough' (Allen 28, p. 263). It is also best to translate with a present tense, in the form of a proverbial saying (the Hebrew uses the imperfect characteristically for this), rather than the past tense ('have eaten'), which was more appropriate to Jeremiah's slightly different citation of the proverb.

regarded as unjust. The present generation (the exiles) believed that they were being made to suffer on account of the sins of their parents and even earlier ancestors. Most commentators, ancient and modern, have assumed that the second interpretation of the proverb is the dominant (or only) one. Fundamentally, it expresses theological objections by the exiles to the assumed injustice of the way God was treating them. However, both Allen and Block[27] give more weight to the first, more general, interpretation, without denying that it was shading over into the kind of self-justifying complaint against God's justice which the chapter certainly tackles later.

The difference between the two ways of reading the proverb can be expressed merely by whether one translates the conjunction in the centre as 'and' or 'but' (both of which are possible in the Hebrew). The first way of reading it (with a simple 'and' in the middle), makes it a general observation: 'One generation makes mistakes and the next generation suffers the consequences. *That's the way things are.*' The second way (with 'but' in the middle), makes it a complaint: 'It's the past generation that committed the sins, but the present generation who are being punished for them. *That's unfair.*' It will be worth examining the implication of each of these approaches, since it is very likely that something of both of them was indeed afflicting the mindset of the exiles and seriously hindering them in making the right response to God in their situation.

i. No to fatalism
If the exiles were using the proverb simply as a statement of observed fact, it probably indicates that they had succumbed to a kind of fatalistic resignation: 'We happen to be the generation who are having to pick up the pieces after our predecessors. They made the mess; we are suffering for it; there's nothing we can do.' Such an attitude would have had a terribly debilitating effect upon the morale and the morals of the people. 'If we can't change the past (which we can't), then we can't change the present or the future either, so why bother to try?' So there would be no motivation to change, no hope of any relief from the relentless operation of a principle that seemed inevitable, no incentive to respond to the prophet's appeal for a change of heart. Allen puts it like this:

> The slogan gave expression to practical nihilism. The exiles saw the present through the prism of the past ... Overwhelmed by that recent catastrophe [the fall of Jerusalem], they saw their

[27] Allen 28, pp. 271, 280–281; Block (1), pp. 558–561.

whole lives doomed and devoid of purpose. Life was like that, and nothing they did could alter it ...

[The slogan] gave expression to a negative syndrome contaminating the exilic community. A spirit of fatalism was causing moral and social degeneration. The mushroom cloud of God's retrospective wrath had drifted over their lives. So nothing would change and there was no point in virtue.[28]

Block argues even more strongly that the exiles had adopted a kind of 'cosmic fatalism'. '[The proverb] reflects a materialistic fatalism, a resignation to immutable cosmic rules of cause and effect, an embittered paralysis of the soul, that has left the exiles without hope and without God.'[29] It seems doubtful to me, however, that the exiles would have articulated something akin to modern atheistic determinism and detached their philosophy of events from the direct control of Yahweh in the way Block implies. Even if the proverb were only an observation about life, it would still have been life as directed by Yahweh's sovereignty. But if the proverb generated resignation and paralysis in relation to the proper response they ought to be making to Yahweh, that was just as damaging as any loss of faith in his ultimate control of events. The main point was that, as long as they thought in this way, they felt no need or motive for repentance and thereby closed the only door to salvation.

Today, of course, we find that a similar kind of deterministic fatalism in a variety of forms also afflicts many people and stands as a major hindrance to their response to the gospel. In some cases it may be, as in the case of the exiles, a belief about our captivity to past generations – whether in terms of genetic 'programming' or behavioural and attitudinal 'baggage' that we inherit from our forebears. Or it may be a religious belief such as *karma* in Hinduism, which binds us inexorably in the present to the consequences of deeds committed in our own past lifetimes. Or it may be the various New Age and neopagan perspectives, which see us all as merely parts of the great single earth-force, in which manipulation of power, rather than morality or penitence, is seen as the answer. Or it may just be a world-weary sense of personal impotence in the face of global forces that seem beyond any influence we may have or any action we may take. It really doesn't matter what you do, 'they'll get you in the end'.

All such views – from sophisticated religious or psychological philosophies, to popular cynicism – have a double negative effect. Not only do they lead to apathy and a passivistic approach to life

[28] Allen 28, pp. 271, 280.   [29] Block (1), p. 561.

in which nothing seems terribly worth doing; they also provide a seemingly plausible foundation for such irresponsibility. And if the future seems to be nothing more than the inexorable continuation of the impersonal laws of space-time physics, or simply the recycling of the past, then personal responsibility is easily denied, and repentance becomes meaningless. What is there to repent of, if everything is fated or beyond my control? 'When they said, Repent, Repent, I wonder what they meant,' sings Leonard Cohen in his sharply perceptive song about postmodern dissolution and disillusion, 'The Future'. But without repentance, there is no gospel, no salvation, no hope. That was the bad news that Ezekiel, as all true evangelists, had to get across before any word of hope could be uttered.

The beginning of Ezekiel's answer to such an attitude expressed through the proverb comes in the opening affirmation of verse 4. After summarily denying any continuing validity to the proverb, Yahweh makes a definitive statement about human life which is sweepingly universal in its scope and yet inescapably individual in its challenge: *'For every living soul*[30] *belongs to me, the father as well as the son – both alike belong to me.'*

The claim of this text is, first of all, that all human persons, all human lives, belong to Yahweh. That in itself is a staggeringly universal affirmation. It is comparable in its massive implications to the opening claim of Psalm 24:1: 'The earth is the LORD's, and everything in it'. The Hebrew construction is similar.[31] It means, then, that human beings, far from living in the grip of fatalistic and impersonal laws, actually live in relation to the personal God Yahweh, to whom all lives belong.[32] Human life is relational. History is relational. Yahweh is not the quasi-personal name of some distant

---

[30] It is regrettable that the NIV translates by 'soul' here the Hebrew word *nepeš*, which has a much wider meaning than the English 'soul' usually conveys. It does not suggest some immaterial part of the human person, but simply means the whole living person as a unity of flesh and enabling spirit or breath (Gen. 2:7). It would be better translated here by 'person'. In other contexts it can mean 'a life', or 'an individual'. *Nepeš* is not something that humans *have*; it is essentially what we *are*. For a helpful discussion of the range of meaning of this Hebrew word, and other dimensions of human life in the Old Testament, see, H. W. Wolff, *Anthropology of the Old Testament* (London: SCM, 1974).

[31] As also, Lev. 25:23: 'the land is mine'.

[32] There is a further implication, which is not really part of the argument in the text but is an equally important and polemical point to make: every human life on earth belongs to *Yahweh*, the personal God of Israel, not to any other god or gods of the nations. Human beings who live in contexts where allegiance is paid to other gods are living under usurped sovereignty. They actually belong to Yahweh and indeed are morally accountable ultimately to him. This is more clearly and explicitly affirmed in Ps. 33:13–15 and is turned into a powerful appeal in Ps. 96.

and impersonal divine force. He is the personal owner of every human person who has ever lived, lives or will live on the planet. Literally, 'All the lives [plural], they belong to me.' What an enriching and affirming anthropology! All human life is related to the personal ownership of Yahweh, not abandoned to impersonal forces.

This is a foundational and reassuring truth for all those engaged in the struggles and ambiguities of evangelistic and pastoral ministry. The lives of all those to whom we minister already belong ultimately to Yahweh, the God and Father of our Lord Jesus Christ. Our task is to help them to find, or return to, or relate to, their rightful owner. Similarly, this truth is a major theological underpinning of all Christian effort for social, economic and political justice and compassion in the world of human need. In caring for people, just as in caring for the earth itself, we are caring for God's property – a humbling and sobering perspective on all our relationships.

Then, secondly, the universal claim is individualized to make it apply equally to every person, regardless of generational priority or otherwise. The Hebrew reads (lit.), 'As the life of the father, so the life of the son, to me they [belong].' This actually implies more than simply that they *both* belong to Yahweh. It implies that each belongs to Yahweh in the same way, on the same conditions, with the same demands, as the other does. The relation of either to Yahweh is not mechanically determined by the relation of the other. 'The son's relationship to me is no different from the father's relationship to me.'[33] Again, this is a powerful affirmation of the value of individual human life and the moral significance of personal choices and actions. It counteracts all forms of nihilism and fatalism by insisting not only that the whole of humanity belongs to the personal God, Yahweh, our creator and redeemer, but also that every individual human being stands before him in direct personal relationship and moral accountability. The universality and particularity of God's involvement in human life could hardly be more succinctly stated.

As far as Ezekiel's immediate hearers were concerned, they could no longer excuse their own apathetic or stubborn lack of response to Yahweh's word on the grounds that it would make no difference, that they were simply chained to the deeds of previous generations. Not so: they stood before Yahweh on their own two feet and their own choices would govern their own destiny.

---

[33] Allen helpfully translates: 'Every person stands in relation to me. The parent as a personal entity [sc. *nepeš*] and the child as a personal entity relate to me in the same direct way.' Allen takes the construction 'to me' (*lî*) to imply 'relates to me' rather than the more normal sense of ownership, 'belongs to me' (Allen 28, pp. 263, 265). However, it seems to me that both are included.

As far as contemporary ministry is concerned, the text reminds us of the importance of insisting that people must take responsibility for their own choices and actions – past, present or future. Evangelism certainly involves confronting people with this unpalatable fact, and pastoral care often involves helping people to venture fearfully out of the protective caves in which we seek shelter from the cold wind of personal responsibility. Ezekiel's message has a stark pastoral severity at this point because that was the only basis on which the glorious evangelistic good news could be proclaimed at the end of the chapter. It is an example and a strategy well worth pondering.

ii. No to blame-shifting

If, as seems likely, the exiles were widely quoting this proverb to give vent to their feelings about their own situation, then it most probably is more than just a general observation about life, but a specific complaint about how things had turned out for themselves. There is one very clear implication of their complaint, and one probable implication. First of all, it implies, 'We are not the ones to blame for all this suffering that has come upon us; it is all our ancestors' fault. We are suffering the punishment that their wickedness incurred.' The second aspect is somewhat more subtle, since it relates to how this view then affected their attitude to Yahweh. Did they actually *blame* Yahweh for this, or simply *accept* that this was the way he dealt with sin, even though it seemed unfair to them, now that it had actually fallen on them?[34]

The problem is complicated by the fact that certain Old Testament texts do speak of God punishing successive generations for sins committed by parents and grandparents. Indeed, it is written into the second commandment in the Decalogue itself.[35] However, it is important to grasp the meaning of such passages carefully. They are talking about the effect of serious sin committed by one generation in a family upon the generations immediately below. The consequences of sin, perceived as Yahweh's punishment, would certainly affect more than just those who commited it. If, for example, parents were to turn away from the covenant obligation to

---

[34] Some suggest that Ezekiel himself may have contributed to the theological argument that would have been used to bolster the complaint, by his strong portrayal of the accumulated sins of Israel's whole history in chs. 16, 20 and 23 (see above, ch. 4). However, although those chapters do indicate that punishment had been deferred by God for his own reasons, 20:30ff. makes it very clear that there could be no complaint that the innocent were being punished: the exiles were as guilty as all previous generations. Cf. Allen 28, p. 271.

[35] Exod. 20:5; Deut. 5:9. Cf. also Exod. 34:7; Num. 14:18.

worship Yahweh alone and started to use idolatrous images (the issue in the second commandment), then such apostasy would undoubtedly affect their children and grandchildren in the extended family. The whole family (which could include up to four generations of living relatives) would become infected by idolatry. So whatever judgment fell on the parents would afflict the rest of the family. In Hebrew idiom that is expressed as God 'visiting the sins of the parents upon the children to the third and fourth generation'. This does not mean that God deliberately and arbitrarily punishes children for sins they have not committed. It does mean that human beings are not isolated in their actions, but inevitably involve others and especially their family, in the consequences of their sin.

Already within Israel's law, human courts were prohibited from inflicting punishment upon children for offences committed by parents, or *vice versa*. 'Parents shall not be put to death for their children, nor children put to death for their parents; each of you will die for your own sin.'[36] This fundamental principle of individual responsibility before the law (which stands in probably deliberate contrast to some ancient near-eastern legal practice)[37] was to govern the ordinary *human*[38] process of court cases. As a principle of legal procedure, it was not in conflict with the moral and social principles that operate in relation to sin and punishment within and between the generations of society as a whole. Children and grandchildren do in fact suffer the consequences of parental *sin*. But courts of law were not allowed to inflict punishment on them for parental *crimes*.[39]

---

[36] Deut. 24:16, NIVI.

[37] The biblical law was very probably designed to prevent the kind of vicarious punishment which sometimes happened elsewhere. In the laws of Hammurabi (a law code from ancient Babylon), for example, if a builder built a house which later collapsed and killed the son of its owner, then the son of the builder was to be put to death (Code of Hammurabi, 230) Deut. 24:16 would have prohibited such forms of legal penalty. 2 Kgs. 14:5–6 provides an example of the application of the law in Israelite history, when Amaziah refrained from executing the children of those who had murdered his father, in obedience to this law. On the position of children in judicial proceedings in Israel, cf. Wright, *God's People in God's Land*, pp. 222–238.

[38] In rare and exceptional cases of direct divine judgment for major apostasy and rebellion (Korah, Dathan and Abiram, Num. 16), or the execution of someone whose offence had threatened the whole community's welfare (Achan, Josh. 7), whole families were judged together as one. But this was not normal legal practice.

[39] The distinction between general social connections and specific judicial process is well pointed out by S. R. Driver: 'There [in the second commandment] the reference is to the providence of God, operating naturally through the normal constitution of society: children are linked to their parents by ties, physical and social, from which they cannot free themselves; and they suffer, not because they are *guilty* of their fathers' sins, but because by the self-acting operation of natural laws their fathers' sins entail disgrace or misfortune upon them. Here [in Deut. 24:16] a law is prescribed for *human action*, and a principle is laid down for the

Innocent people do suffer as a result of other people's wickedness. But that does not mean that courts can punish the innocent for the sins of the guilty.

What Ezekiel does in the famous final phrase of 18:4 is to insist that the principle which already governed Israel's law[40] also operates in God's justice. The law stated, 'Each person shall be executed for his own sin.' The prophetic expansion simply makes it exclusively clear: 'it is the person[41] who commits the sin who shall be the one to be executed.[42] This has the effect of leaving untouched that element of truth which lay behind the proverb (namely, that children do suffer because of the sins of their parents), but of denying the self-excusing use that was being made of it by the exiles (namely, blaming their parents for their own suffering). 'If the descendants are punished, it is not because of the family connection but because they reproduce and perpetuate *freely* the conduct of the parent.'[43] For what the affirmation means, when reversed, is: 'If someone is executed under God's judgment, it is because he or she is the one who has sinned.' God is no less just than the standard he demands of human courts. So Ezekiel confronts the proverb-spinning exiles with this response: 'Yes, you *are* suffering the final consequences of

---

administration of justice by the State: the family of the criminal is not be punished judicially with him. The two cases are thus altogether different: it is one thing that, in virtue of the physical and social conditions in which they live, children should suffer for their fathers' sins; it is another that, by the deliberate intervention of human authority, they should be punished for criminal acts which they have not committed.' S. R. Driver, *A Critical and Exegetical Commentary on Deuteronomy* (Edinburgh: T. and T. Clark, 1895), pp. 277–278.

[40] It is important to reject the popular belief that Ezekiel here *innovates* the idea of individual responsibility: that is, the idea that Ezekiel replaces a previous assumption of collective, trans-generational liability with this new emphasis on individual guilt and punishment. This hoary opinion has been challenged widely by scholars and is now regarded as fundamentally mistaken both in what it attributes to Ezekiel and also in its assessment of Israel's pre-exilic legal culture. Unfortunately, the idea still circulates as one of the few things people 'know' about Ezekiel: he 'invented' individual responsibility. Far from it. Cf. J. R. Porter, 'The legal aspects of the concept of "corporate personality" in the Old Testament', *VT* 15 (1965), pp. 361–380; J. W. Rogerson, 'The Hebrew conception of corporate personality: a re-examination', *JTS* new series 21 (1970), pp. 1–16.

[41] *nepeš* again (4). As in the first part of the verse, it is a pity that NIV translates as *The soul who sins* ... This gives the impression of some kind of 'sin of the soul' distinct from the physical realm. In this context the word is being used, as frequently in the legal texts, simply to mean 'the individual who ...'

[42] 'Be executed' is used here because the phrase used is a technical term from the legal context. It refers not simply to death in general, but to death inflicted as an act of duly authorized judicial penalty – i.e. execution. The same forensic colouring affects the rest of the chapter's use of 'righteous' and 'wicked', 'he shall live', 'he shall die', etc.   [43] Blenkinsopp, p. 82, his italics.

many generations of sin; but no, you are *not* being wrongly punished as innocent victims of somebody else's guilt, because, far from being innocent, you yourselves are just as guilty of the same sins as your forebears. If you are being "put to death" (in exile), it is because you yourselves are persons who have sinned. Stop trying to shift the blame.'

Contemporary application of this dimension of the exiles' complaint is not hard to identify. It seems to encapsulate two fundamental human tendencies which have been apparent in fallen humanity ever since the garden of Eden: to blame somebody else and to blame God – anything but accept personal responsibility for sins committed. These tendencies still constitute another huge barrier to evangelism.

First of all, if someone or something else is really to blame for the mess I have made, then I can dismiss (or at least diminish) my own personal responsibility. And if I am not really responsible, then I am under no constraint to apologize or repent. But without repentance there can be no forgiveness and salvation. Thus, shifting the blame not only provides a specious sense of security from one's conscience, or God's wrath (or at least the press); it also roadblocks the only way to salvation that the gospel offers.

Secondly, if God is unfair in the way he punishes people, then, to the extent that any of my misfortunes are being inflicted by him, I am not so much a sinner as a victim. And the victim mentality is also a major barrier to the gospel, for it provides the perfect defence: 'I should not be the one being accused here; I am the injured party. *God* is the one who needs to repent and change so that I can forgive *him*.' It is the gospel stood on its head.

Both of these tunes are played very loudly in modern and postmodern society. We are not to blame – it is always someone else's fault, directly or indirectly. So we lay the consequences of our personal and collective wickedness at the door of our genes, or our environment, or government failures, or market forces, or global trends, or psychological stress, or anything else that is sufficiently vague and removed from uncomfortable proximity to our own choices and actions. And of course, we blame God. That is, if God exists. And paradoxically, furthermore, all the things that we blame God for are a kind of proof that he does not exist anyway. So we encounter that popular perversity of people blaming the God they don't believe exists for allowing or causing things that he should have stopped if he did.

Such blame-shifting tactics were unacceptable to Ezekiel then, and unacceptable to God then and now. So God simply repudiates the proverb that expressed it. Every generation and every individual needs to face up to responsibility for their own sin, and to recognize that in God's justice, only the wicked will ultimately perish under his wrath and judgment, whatever the appearances to the contrary.

b. The ethical case-study (18:5–18)

Yet again Ezekiel's priestly training comes to his assistance as he seeks to establish his argument by setting up a detailed case-study and involving his listeners in drawing conclusions from it. We shall look first of all at the specific point that Ezekiel is making through his case-study, and then survey also the wider ethical significance of its actual contents.

i. The debating-point

Ezekiel invites us to imagine three generations of a family – father (5–9), son (10–13) and grandson (14–18). The father is *a righteous man who does what is just and right* (5). He is then described in glowing terms until verse 9. The divine verdict upon his life is that *That man is righteous; he will surely live.* This needs to be recognized as being couched in the language of a courtroom decision based on the evidence presented. The account begins and ends with the affirmation that the man is *ṣaddîq* – in the right, one whose life and behaviour vindicate such a declaration and who, rightfully under the covenantal provisions, is granted life.

The son, however, turns to wickedness and becomes a man of violence and bloodshed, as well as doing the opposite of all that his father had done. Leaving nothing to the already demonstrably faulty memories of his hearers, Ezekiel repeats most of the father's good points in reverse about the son (10–13). The question *Will such a man live?* could be quickly answered solely on the basis of the evidence – the court must decide on his execution and it will be his own responsibility (*his blood will be on his own head*). If there had been any thought that his father's righteousness or reputation would avail for his reprieve, then 14:12–20 would already have aborted it – the righteous save only themselves. In any case, this is the divine courtroom, not some corruptible human court where nepotism and bribery might prevail.

The grandson, however (the critical generation), learns his lesson from his father's behaviour and fate, and changes back to be like his grandfather. Out comes the list of behaviours again, and in comes the righteousness of the original hero – give or take a few points. What should be the divine verdict on the representative of the third generation? *He will not die for his father's sin; he will surely live.* He is declared to be as righteous as his grandfather, on the same grounds, and without prejudice from the intervening generation.

What was the relevance of all this to the exiles? The point seems to be that they would, if asked, have imagined themselves to be generation three – that is, the heirs of wicked parents. And further, they imagined that they were actually suffering the punishment that was really deserved, not by them, but by the previous generation. But Ezekiel insists: 'No, you are actually generation two – suffering the penalty of your own sins. Previous generations (in historical reality, not in the case-study), have also been wicked and come under God's judgment, but you are certainly not righteous sons! Your punishment is because of *your* sin, not that of your ancestors, on the principle, repeated for emphasis (20), that it is the one who sins who bears the punishment.'

This would seem to be the best way to understand what the people say in verse 19: *'Yet you ask, "Why does the son not share the guilt of the father?"'* Some commentators find a contradiction between this and the alleged complaint of the proverb in verse 2. It is said that there (in v. 2), the people *complain* that God punishes the children for the sins of the parents, whereas suddenly here (in v. 19) they *demand* that he should do so and protest that he doesn't![44] However, it seems preferable to read verse 19, not as protest or demand, but as *surprise*, and to read it strictly in relation to the model Ezekiel was setting before them. When Ezekiel gives God's favourable verdict on the grandson, the listeners exclaim, 'What? Why does your model not have him suffering for the sin of his parents? That's what's happening to us. That's what happens in general. Haven't you heard, "Parents eat sour grapes and the children's teeth are set on edge"?'[45] But Ezekiel insists on his strict segregation of the generations in God's moral verdict upon them. The rewards of righteousness can't be bequeathed. The punishment on wickedness need not be inherited. The verdict depends on each generation's own response to God's law. So if the exiles have come under the death sentence, then they must look to their own behaviour and stop blaming their ancestors.

[44] Block (1), p. 580, solves the contradiction by arguing that the proverb in v. 2 was not actually a complaint about divine injustice, but simply a secular observation about cosmic laws of cause and effect, which had produced fatalism. However, I think he too rigidly excludes the complaint and injustice element that the rest of the chapter seems to imply was also inherent in the proverb.

[45] Greenberg, p. 332, suggests this solution: 'The question seems rather a provocative one: how is it that your model does not conform with the reality that innocent children do bear their parents' punishment, as we attest from our own experience! ... The answer is: the son in the model – unlike you – was really innocent!'

ii. The ethical content

Turning now to look at the content of Ezekiel's ethical portrait of
model righteousness (and its opposite), it provides us with a
fascinating insight into Old Testament ethics, and much food for
thought as regards wider ethical relevance.

Ezekiel begins by defining the righteous man of his case-study in
archetypal terms. He is one who *does what is just and right*.
Literally, 'he does justice (*mišpāṭ*) and righteousness (*ṣᵉdāqâ*)'. This
ancient pairing of words expresses fundamental Old Testament
convictions first of all about Yahweh himself. 'The LORD loves
righteousness and justice',[46] and indeed they are the very foundation
of his throne – the principles on which he governs the universe.[47] But
they are not just principles; they are a matter of delight to him, as
all who claim to know him should understand.[48] At a human level,
the very reason for the election of Abraham, according to God's own
reflection on the matter, was so that he would initiate a community
who would 'walk in the way of the LORD by doing righteousness
and justice' – and would do so precisely in contrast to the kind of
community characterized by the screams of oppression and injustice
coming out of Sodom and Gomorrah.[49] As God's demand upon
Israel, the doing of righteousness and justice was especially looked
for in their kings, successfully in the case of David,[50] optimistically
at first in Solomon,[51] and with woeful failure in their later
successors.[52] Fundamentally, the one who does justice and
righteousness is the one who, out of faithful loyalty to Yahweh as
redeemer and covenant Lord, seeks to live in obedience to his laws
and in conformity to the whole ethos and guidance of his word. The
author of Psalm 119 is a particularly earnest example.

We should not confuse ourselves with questions about whether
this is some kind of 'works righteousness' or an alleged attempt to
earn legalistic status before God. Such ideas are decidedly
anachronistic and not part of the Old Testament faith. Righteousness
describes the right response of the person who chooses to live as
befits his or her membership of the covenant community of Yahweh.
It does not mean moral perfection, but it certainly implies moral
commitment. It is the characteristic of the person who takes

[46] Ps. 33:5.   [47] Pss. 89:14; 97:2.   [48] Jer. 9:24.   [49] Gen. 18:19, my translation.
[50] 2 Sam. 8:15.   [51] 1 Kgs. 10:9; and cf. Ps. 72.
[52] Jer. 21:11 – 22:5; though notice the exception of Josiah: Jer. 22:15–16. Block 1,
pp. 568–569, suggests that Ezekiel may even be drawing on a codified list of standard
conduct required of royalty and royal administrators, in the light of similar
requirements in ancient near-eastern documents and alluded to elsewhere (e.g. Deut.
17:14–20; Prov. 29:4; 31:1–9). Since many of the first batch of exiles were drawn from
the ruling strata of Jerusalem, such a reminder of the standards they *ought* to have
maintained would be particularly pointed.

192

seriously the command to love the Lord your God with all your heart and soul and strength, and who does so in grateful response to the prior redeeming love of God.[53] 'It is a term of allegiance and obligation, not of achievement.'[54]

The character of this model of righteousness is then portrayed in a kind of Identikit format. The list includes ten statements, grouped in five pairs (v. 6–8), followed by a summarizing conclusion in verse 9a. This little cameo is very similar in form, and in some of its content, to other portraits of ethical righteousness that we find in the Old Testament. They are fascinating insights into the ethical worldview of ancient Israel when it was seeking to express the moral outworkings of faith in Yahweh, in both personal and social terms. It would be well worth reading through the following passages and comparing the moral values and standards that surface repeatedly: Psalms 15 and 24; Job 31; Isaiah 33:14–16; Leviticus 19.[55]

The first pair (v. 6a) states that the man has kept himself free from idolatry, particularly the sort that was practised at the mountain shrines – probably again a reference to fertility cults. The second pair (v. 6b) moves on to sexual offences and combines something which was fundamentally a criminal offence in Israel (adultery) with something which simply caused ritual uncleanness as well as being personally insensitive.[56] The third pair (7a) moves to the economic realm and describes the man as a responsible and 'merciful creditor' (NLT). He does not use his position as a lender as a means of oppression, and he is scrupulous to observe the law about returning any pledges taken as collateral once the loans had been repaid, or earlier in cases of extreme need.[57] The fourth pair (v. 7b) interestingly combines a negative statement that one might expect, *He does not commit robbery*, with a positive extra: the man is given to active generosity and care for the needy, in fulfilment of many such exhortations in the law.[58] The fifth pair (v. 8) returns to the economic sphere with the frequent Old Testament mark of righteousness – the refusal to demand interest[59] – and combines it with judicial integrity, which was another major concern of Old Testament law.[60] Economic and judicial corruption went hand in hand in Israel's degeneration during the monarchy, as those who most exploited the poor also

---

[53] Cf. Deut. 6:5, 20–25.   [54] Allen 28, p. 273.

[55] Cf. the discussion of these models of individual ethics in Wright, *Living as the People of God*, ch. 9: 'The way of the individual'.   [56] Lev. 18:19–20.

[57] Exod. 22:25–27; Deut. 24:6, 10–13.

[58] Deut. 10:18–19. Cf. Is. 58:7; Job 31:16–20; Prov. 14:31; 17:5; 19:17; 31:20 (showing that such marks of righteousness should characterize women as well as men).

[59] Exod. 22:25; Lev. 25:35–38; Deut. 23:19; cf. Ps. 15:5; Neh. 5:1–13.

[60] Exod. 23:1–9; Lev. 19:15–18; Deut. 16:18–20; 24:17.

gained the economic power to manipulate the courts in their own favour.

What is striking about the overall portrait is that, without being comprehensive in every area of life, it manages to touch on several major domains of ethical choice. It ranges from religious rituals, through private and intimate sexual behaviour, to the public arena of social, economic and judicial activity. It is also careful not to define righteousness merely in negative terms. It is not enough simply not to be a robber. The righteous person is actively generous. It is not enough to say, as one often hears in situations of bereavement, 'He never did anyone any harm.' The question one is tempted to ask is, 'Yes, but did he ever do anyone any good?' When combined with the many similar ethical passages in the Old Testament, the sensitive reader gains a remarkable impression of the scale and depth of the way in which the faith of Israel sought to inculcate an ethos of personal moral behaviour in a socially caring community that is still very fruitful in its relevance and power.

Coming back to Ezekiel, it is also worth noting that, although he was a priest and used imagery and concepts from Israel's religious life more than any other prophet, and although in his visit to the temple in chapters 8 – 11 he focused (naturally enough) on the religious perversions that were happening there, he did not define righteousness in exclusively, or even predominantly, ritual terms. Ezekiel would have been familiar with every detail of the sacrificial system, but he would also have fully agreed with the scale of priorities so succinctly expressed in Proverbs 21:3: 'To do righteousness and justice is more acceptable to [Yahweh] than sacrifice.' His list of what counted as righteousness in the sight of Yahweh here fully endorsed the perspective of the pre-exilic prophets who had argued – some in the most shocking language – that social integrity and justice were far more important to Yahweh than the whole religious system he himself had instituted.[61] Ezekiel's own perspective on what constituted the wickedness of Jerusalem is contained in chapter 22, and it is interesting to compare its negative list of evils with the positive description of righteousness here.

What, then, has Ezekiel accomplished through his repudiation of the unacceptable proverb, and his carefully structured ethical case-study and its implications? Effectively he has removed all shelter from the exiles. They cannot shrug off their plight as yet another illustration of a proverb about the general unfairness of life. Nor can they shift the blame for their punishment on to the previous generation. They are being punished because they themselves fit the

---

[61] Amos 5:21–24; Hos. 6:6; Is. 1:10–17; Jer. 7:1–11, 21–23.

paradigm of wickedness, and the divine verdict on their behaviour is thus identical to that on the plundering and murdering wicked son in his case-study: 'They will surely be put to death and their blood will be on their own head.'

How did they react to such a comprehensively damning case, argued out in the face of all their questioning and surprise? Some continued to argue (18:25, 29), and we shall look at their comment and Ezekiel's answer below. But there were certainly some, perhaps the first in Ezekiel's ministry so far, whose defences were at last pierced by the word of God through the prophet. The conviction of their sins at last bore in upon them and extinguished all the pretences, false hopes and bravado. For them, the effect of realizing the truth of Ezekiel's message was as overwhelming as the vision of God's glory had been on him. They were shattered. They felt completely crushed by the weight of their sins. They felt deprived of even the will to go on living.

In chapter 33, in a context which recalls this disputation in chapter 18, and significantly puts it alongside the news of the fall of Jerusalem, we read of the response of this group of exiles in the words Ezekiel now addresses to them: 'This is what you are saying: "Our offences and sins weigh us down, and we are wasting away because of them. How then can we live?' (33:10). Notice carefully – *Our* sins. No longer our parents' sour grapes, but our own sins. That is what is causing us to be burdened and perishing. 'Ezekiel had carried his point.'[62] This acceptance of the terrible truth about themselves, which did not of course deny the guilt of previous generations,[63] is the first glimmer of accepting responsibility, accepting guilt, accepting the justice of God's verdict. On such a fragile foundation, hope can be built at last. For only to those prepared to make such a contrite declaration can the words of repentance and life be offered. And that indeed is what follows.

Before we explore Ezekiel's equally rich portrayal of what repentance would mean and could enable, it is worth once again stressing the importance of what Ezekiel has done here. The severity of his case-study and its implications for the exiles may seem cruel

[62] Greenberg, p. 341.

[63] There is further evidence of a dawning awareness among the exiles that it was not a case of '*either* our parents are to blame *or* we are', but in fact that both were true. Cf. Lam. 5:7 ('Our fathers sinned … and we bear their punishment') with 5:16 ('Woe to us, for we have sinned!'). Similarly, the great confessional prayer of Dan. 9 stresses repeatedly that the sin for which Israel is being punished in exile must not be attributed only to the fathers, but to the exiles themselves as well: 'we are covered with shame … in all the countries where you have scattered us because of our unfaithfulness to you. O LORD, we and our kings, our princes and our fathers are covered with shame because we have sinned against you' (Dan. 9:7–8).

or lacking in pastoral sensitivity. But in fact it is the opposite. Pastoral duty requires that we attend to people's deepest need and most urgent danger, not that we shore up their self-excusing defences. The ultimate goal is to lead people to a restored relationship with God through the grace of forgiveness. But without repentance there can be no forgiveness. And without the acceptance of responsibility there can be no true repentance. Tragically, so much in modern culture militates against people assuming full responsibility for their own choices and behaviours and all the consequences that flow from them. We are solicited on all sides by attractive alternatives to personal responsibility. The need to find someone or something else to blame is matched by a limitless supply of convenient scapegoats: the inadequacy of parents, of schools, or of employers; the inequity of our social status or economic opportunity; the inevitability of our genetic inheritance; our personality type (now conveniently classifiable); society; poverty; mental or emotional stress – the list goes on. Any or all of these factors and many more, of course, can have profound influence on our lives for good or ill. But when people allow themselves to be 'protected' by such walls of external factors from accepting personal responsibility, they are locked into a world where repentance has no meaning. *I* am not the one who needs to say sorry, and in any case, in the absence of any transcendant personal moral authority, to whom or to what should such repentance be addressed? The evangelistic and pastoral task in such a culture is increasingly difficult, yet Ezekiel shows us that there is no other way out of exile. What, then, is Ezekiel's understanding of repentance?

3. Only repentance makes the difference (18:21–32; 33:10–20)

The word 'radical' is so overused that it has become almost a meaningless word added for cosmetic effect. Used properly, it means something which goes to the roots of an issue and faces hard realities. To be radical means to be prepared to examine the deeper dimensions of a situation and to be willing to face the challenge of real change. It seems the most appropriate term to describe the scope of what Ezekiel now holds out to the exiles and to us as he moves from accusation to hope, from problem to solution, from certain death to promised life.

a. Radical choice (18:21–24)

There is a very significant shift in Ezekiel's argument at verse 21. Up to that point he has been talking about successive generations – fathers and sons – and separating them with moral firewalls of distinct responsibility. Suddenly he moves to considering individual lifetimes – *a wicked man* (21–22), and *a righteous man* (24). And he affirms that the same choice that faced the son when he reflected on the behaviour of his father (between generations, v. 14) also in principle faces each of us when we reflect on our own behaviour (within our own lifetimes). Three things may be said about this proffered choice.

i. Real choice and real change are possible

You can choose to change! It is a powerful affirmation of the reality of human freedom and the seriousness of the choice that God has placed in our hands. Just as, in the preceding argument, Ezekiel was at pains to insist that the action of one generation did not lock the next one into an unbreakable chain of consequences, so here he presents each individual with the same truth – which is simultaneously liberating and challenging. It is liberating because a wicked past need not imprison the present and future; the wicked man can choose to turn *away from all the sins he has committed* (21). But it is also challenging because a righteous past does not guarantee the end of the journey; the hitherto righteous man may choose to turn *from his righteousness* and embark on the same life direction as the wicked (24). But the main point to be stressed is the sheer power of this affirmation. You can *choose*, and you can choose *again*. The choice is always open. We are not mechanically determined beings, locked into the consequences of our own or anybody else's past. We are human persons entrusted by God with moral freedom of choice. Choice is real and change is possible.

ii. Moral choice is a matter of life and death

Like the word 'radical', the word 'choice' has also become almost deprived of significant meaning today. It has been elevated into one of the gods of the consumer culture, as we are told that we must have choice in every area of life – no matter how trivial. We not only insist rightly on choice in major areas such as education and careers, in politics and social priorities, or religious convictions and moral values. We must have almost infinite multiplicity of choice in everything from computer fonts and screen colours, to breakfast cereals and phone companies. With such a plethora of constant choosing to be done, contemporary people suffer from a condition identified in the USA as 'option paralysis'. For which condition, of course, a whole new lucrative brand of consultancy has been developed; we are bombarded with offers from all kinds of advisors who will help us choose the best option for ourselves, from gas bills to Internet service providers, from garden design to healthy living.

It becomes increasingly difficult to insist that there are some choices in life that matter in an ultimate sense. Evangelists were once accustomed to calling people to 'choose Christ' – meaning the call to make a life-time commitment that rejected all alternatives and affected our eternal destiny. Today such a call, within our consumerist cultures, may be understood to mean little more than 'Give Christ a try for a while and see if he works for you; you can always try something else later if you aren't satisfied.' And in the market-place of old denominations and new Christian movements, you can have a conveniently customized Christ, tailored to suit your particular religious consumer needs.

No such trivial understanding of choice exercised Ezekiel's mind. He calls people to recognize that their choice of commitments and behaviour, in response to the known will of God, is literally a matter of choosing life or death. With such language he takes on, possibly consciously, the mantle of Moses, who had so forcefully presented exactly that choice to the people:

> See, I set have before you today life and prosperity, death and adversity. If you obey the commandments of the LORD your God that I am commanding you today, by loving the LORD your God, walking in his ways, and observing his commandments, decrees, and ordinances, then you shall live and become numerous, and the LORD your God will bless you in the land that you are entering to possess. But if your heart turns away and you do not hear, but are led astray to bow down to other gods and serve them, I declare to you today that you shall perish; you shall not live long in the land that you are crossing the Jordan to enter and possess. I call heaven and earth to witness against you today that I have set before you life and death, blessings and curses. Choose life so that you and your descendants may live, loving the LORD your God, obeying him, and holding fast to him; for that means life to you and length of days, so that you may live in the land that the LORD swore to give to your ancestors, to Abraham, to Isaac, and to Jacob.[64]

Ezekiel echoes, not only the crucial language of life-and-death choice, but also the evangelistic appeal at the end: 'Choose life!'

It is worth pausing to ask what Ezekiel and the exiles would have understood by 'life' and 'death' in this context. At one level of the discourse, life and death refer to judicial sentencing: either someone is declared innocent and leaves the court alive, or is declared guilty and is executed (that is the initial meaning of the affirmation in v. 4:

[64] Deut. 30:15–20, NRSV.

'The person who sins is the one who shall be put to death', (my translation). In another context also, we have already seen (in ch. 3 above) that life and death meant literally that: many would physically die in the siege and destruction of Jerusalem. Yet it was not so simple, since doubtless some who were among those who grieved over the sin of the city were also killed in the catastrophe, while many of the guiltiest survived the destruction physically but went off into the 'death' of exile. A further twist is now added: those addressed in exile are among the 'dead' (which is how they describe themselves in 37:11), and yet they can be offered 'life' if they will repent and change their ways. Later it is clear that 'life' meant the eschatological hope of return to the land and to the life of settled fullness and blessing there under the good will of Yahweh. This will be the burden of the great chapters of hope, 34, 36 and 37, and of course the vision of renewal in 40 – 48.[65] But for Ezekiel's immediate generation of hearers (as for Ezekiel himself, of course) that was a life they would never personally enjoy. The majority of those who went into exile would physically die in exile, and it would be the next generation who would return. If the offer of 'life' to such people meant anything, it must have been more than simply the promise that their children would see the promised land again (though we should certainly not minimize the importance of such hope for those who had come to think that God was finished with Israel for ever).

It would be anachronistic to attribute to Ezekiel a full understanding of the promise of eternal life in all the fullness of its New Testament revelation in the light of the resurrection of Jesus. But it would also be wrong to deny that Israelite believers in the Old Testament era had any hope of life in relation to Yahweh beyond death. It seems clear that there is a dimension to 'life' in the promise of Ezekiel (and also reflected in some of the Psalms) which transcends either mere avoidance of physical death (since death happened for most if not all of Ezekiel's generation in exile), or the hope of national restoration to the land (since that did not happen for most of Ezekiel's contemporaries). 'Life' must have signified a restored and blessed relationship with Yahweh at a personal level, which the righteous and the wicked who repented could enjoy, and that would somehow transcend physical death. Even the wickedest among the exiles, who were doomed to the virtual death of exile itself, and who faced actual personal death before the restoration, are

[65] Allen 28, pp. 269–270, 279–280, sees the burden of Ezekiel's ministry in relation to this point as the attempt to prepare the people for return to 'life' in the land, by the necessary purging and repentance that would make them spiritually and morally fit for the life of the new community of restoration.

challenged to repent and change, with the promise that they could then 'live'. What would it mean to be given such life from God? Perhaps Ezekiel the pastor would have turned such repentant people to the words of Deuteronomy itself in explaining to them what such life meant, in the passage quoted above: 'loving the LORD your God, obeying him, and holding fast to him; for that means life to you'. And he may have reinforced this definition with words such as these from the Psalms:

> For you do not give me up to Sheol,
>   or let your faithful one see the Pit.

> You show me the path of life.
>   In your presence there is fullness of joy;
>   in your right hand are pleasures for evermore.[66]

iii. Choice can be in either direction

Ezekiel's words in 18:21–24, expanded in 33:12–14, are, as mentioned above, both liberating (for the repentant) and challenging (for the righteous). He is not only concerned to urge the wicked to repent. He is also concerned to warn the presently righteous not to be complacent. In this, of course, he is carrying out to perfection the ministry of being a watchman – the sentry called to give due warning to all inhabitants. Doubtless this is why chapter 33 has the repetition of his appointment as watchman linked immediately to precisely the double challenge of these verses (33:7–9 followed by 10–20).

The challenge to the righteous is sobering. 'The righteous are warned of the truth that, in John Bunyan's parlance, "there was a way to hell even from the gates of heaven."'[67] It reminds us that no matter what our doctrine of eternal security, it should never become an excuse for complacency or something to be traded on as a divine insurance policy against our misdemeanours. Such was the tragic error of those who trusted in the (equally biblical) assurance of God's protection of Jerusalem and then behaved as if it were a licence to kill and indulge in all the other excesses listed in Ezekiel's chapters of accusation. If there is no peace for the wicked, there is also no false peace for the righteous. 'Watch yourselves,' warned Moses.[68] 'Watch and pray so that you will not fall into temptation,'

---

[66] Ps. 16:10–11, NRSV. Other passages in the Psalms which speak of life in ways that seem to transcend a merely physical reference point include Pss. 34:12, 22; 36:9; 56:13; 63:3; 80:18; 133:3. There is also the repeated plea of the author of Ps. 119 that God would renew, restore, protect, revive his life, in the single Hebrew appeal ḥayyēnî!, 'cause me to live!' (cf. Ps. 119:37, 40, 50, 88, 107, 149, 154, 156, 159).
[67] Allen 28, p. 279.   [68] Deut. 4:9, 15, 23.

warned Jesus.[69] 'If you think you are standing firm, be careful that you don't fall!' warned Paul.[70] We never grow beyond the need to continue making the active decision to love and serve God in righteousness of life and behaviour. It was to those who had grown old with him, after a lifetime that included the wonders of the conquest of Canaan, that Joshua issued the memorable challenge: 'choose for yourselves *this day* whom you will serve'.[71] Choices matter all through life.

Just as the Bible gives examples of those who, after a lifetime of wickedness found God's mercy and grace through repentance (such as Manasseh),[72] so it gives examples of those who, after a years of faithfulness fell into grievous sin in later life (such as David himself[73] and Uzziah[74]). Perhaps the thief on the cross, who in his dying moments made the choice to turn from his violence and murder (not that he had much choice to return to them), and place his trust in the one crucified next to him, illustrates *par excellence* the life-and-death issues that can hang on even such a final choice. He also proved the willingness of God, in the person of his dying Son, to respond to such a choice with instant mercy. Tragically, the other thief illustrates the harsh reality of those who choose to persist in rebellion and rejection.

b. Radical consistency (18:25–29; 33:17–20)

The people's objection in verse 25 is translated in many ways.[75] The NIV *'The way of the Lord is not just'* is probably too strong. The phrase, *lō yittāḵēn*, has more the sense of something that does not add up, or is not consistent. Certainly, as the people use it, it seems to imply unfairness, but mainly they seem to be saying that they can't make sense of Yahweh's actions, if they are as Ezekiel has just described them. The idea that the children of wicked parents would *not* be punished for their parents' sins, or the idea that wickedness and righteousness and their consequences could be exchanged by human decision and divine response, was too much to cope with. Or, perhaps, the objection was in part yet another ploy to avoid the sheer power of the case against themselves. It is always easier to berate heaven for unfairness or inconsistency than to accept one's own guilt. Both the justice and the mercy of God have been targets of complaint.[76]

[69] Matt. 26:41. [70] 1 Cor. 10:12. [71] Josh. 24:15, italics added.
[72] 2 Chr. 33:1–20. [73] 2 Sam. 11. [74] 2 Chr. 26:16–23.
[75] E.g. 'The Lord's action is unscrupulous' (Block (1), p. 584); 'The way of the Lord does not conform to rule' (Greenberg, p. 326); 'The Lord's policy is inconsistent' (Allen 28, p. 264).
[76] The latter, for example, in Jesus' famous parable of the workers hired at various points in the day to work in a vineyard, and then all paid the same (Matt. 20:1–16).

Ezekiel's response to this accusation of divine inconsistency is very forceful. He repeats his claims again and again and refuses to accept the charge – but rather reverses it and throws it back at the objectors. But his defence of divine consistency is also radical, in the sense that we can see how it goes to the roots of Yahweh's character as God. Specifically, it goes to the roots of the following great truths.

i. Yahweh's consistent covenant promises
We have already seen that Ezekiel is deeply indebted to the covenantal theology of Leviticus 26 and Deuteronomy. And here he shows that Yahweh is acting out of profound consistency with those great texts. Not only is he fulfilling the threats of judgment upon the nation for its long history of rebellion and covenant-breaking, but also now he is willing to act on the promises of restoration beyond judgment for those who would turn and seek his face again. The individualized offer of 18:21–22 and 33:14–16 is nothing more than the personal outworking of the great promises of Leviticus 26:40–45 and Deuteronomy 4:29–31; 30:1–10. God is radically consistent from the national to the individual level. The person or the nation that seeks his face in repentant turning from wickedness, however prolonged, will find Yahweh to be the God who is committed to forgive and forget. Other gods may have other ways, but this is the covenantally consistent way of Yahweh.

ii. Yahweh's consistent will to life
Ezekiel 18:23 (with 33:11) must rank among the most wonderful affirmations about God in the Bible: *'Do I take any pleasure in the death of the wicked? declares the Sovereign Lord. Rather, am I not pleased when they turn from their evil ways and live?'* The rhetorical questions of course expect the answers 'No' and 'Yes' respectively, and therefore constitute an emphatic declaration that God wills life, not death. But by putting the point in the form of these questions, our view of God is uncomfortably challenged. For in the light of the stark denunciations of the wicked elsewhere in the book, and the raw and terrifying descriptions of the wrath of God in action against them, one might have been tempted to answer the first question (*'Do I take any pleasure in the death of the wicked?'*) with a 'Yes': the wicked are such an offence to God that it is as much a pleasure to him to destroy them as it is a relief to us to swat that infernal mosquito.

But it is not so! God must and God does punish the wicked on the basis of his utter and cosmic justice. The moral integrity of his universe cannot ultimately remain fractured by the presence of deliberate sin unrepented and unpunished. But the exercise of punitive justice gives the Almighty no pleasure at all. What pleases him is that moment of repentance and genuine turning on the part of a sinner which liberates God to exercise his unique and greatest divine capacity in the granting of life. *Life* is God's gift. Life is his creation. Life is his desire. Life is his pleasure. And so, as we saw in the paradox of the watchman metaphor, the very God who is coming as the enemy against his people himself sets the sentry in their midst to warn them of his approach, so that they can heed the warning and save their lives. Likewise here, the whole point of this great disputation with the house of Israel has been to bring the wicked to recognize their desperate plight and to turn around. In their wickedness they face the God who decrees with no pleasure that the one who sins will die. In repentance they will face the God who decrees with pleasure that the one who repents will live. Such is Yahweh's radical consistency, in judgment and in compassion.

c. Radical repentance (18:30–32)

So at last we are able to come to the point of the whole chapter. On the twin bases of the reality of the choice that can be made, and the rock of God's consistency, Ezekiel can make his great appeal to the people, brilliantly addressing both the community as a whole and every individual listener: *'Therefore, O house of Israel, I will judge you, each one according to his ways, declares the Sovereign* LORD. *Repent! Turn away from all your offences'* (18:30; cf. 33:11).

Ultimately there are only two categories of people before Yahweh – the righteous and the wicked. By argument, illustration and case-study, Ezekiel has insisted (the bad news) that only the righteous can be saved, but also (the good news), that only the wicked need perish. Only repentance can make the difference, but it truly can and will make all the difference in the world for those who respond. So Ezekiel works and weaves and pushes and pulls to achieve that response. Ezekiel too seems to face only two categories of people. On the one hand, there are those who think it's all unfair. It is not. It is the sublime justice and mercy of God. And they will get no fairer deal elsewhere, for there is nowhere else to run to. But on the other hand, as we see at 33:10, there are those who think it's all over. It isn't yet, for with God there is always time to turn, always space for grace, always scope for hope. God offers a free transfer from the camp of the wicked to the community of the righteous. God offers a free pardon and a new life. But the offer is open only to those who truly repent.

Leaving nothing to misunderstanding, Ezekiel makes it abundantly clear what that required repentance will mean.

i. Repentance which is practical (18:21, 30b–31; cf. 33:14-15)
Ezekiel would have known Hosea's beautiful litany of repentance; indeed, in 18:30 he alludes to its second line:

> Return, O Israel, to the LORD your God.
> Your sins have been your downfall!
> Take words with you
> and return to the LORD.
> Say to him:
> 'Forgive all our sins
> and receive us graciously,
> that we may offer the fruit of our lips.'[77]

Words would matter, but words would not be enough.

Ezekiel would probably also have known the poignant confession in Psalm 51, and, even though he would later speak of the restoration of the sacrificial system, he would have agreed with the psalmist's sentiment:

> You do not delight in sacrifice, or I would bring it;
> you do not take pleasure in burnt offerings.
> The sacrifices of God are a broken spirit;
> a broken and contrite heart,
> O God, you will not despise.[78]

Sacrifices alone would not be enough either. The repentance that would prove that Israel really had got *a new heart and a new spirit* (31) would have to be thoroughly practical. It would involve both negative and positive aspects.

First of all, negatively, it would mean a total rejection of former ways. *'Turn away from all your offences ... Rid yourselves of all the offences you have committed'* (30–31). These are strong words. 'Turn away from' is the basic Old Testament word for repentance (*sˇûb*), very familiar especially from the book of Jeremiah, where it was the burden of Jeremiah's ministry. The same word could be used for returning to the LORD,[79] but turning *to* God must involve turning *away from* all that offends him, namely, the sins which, by incurring his wrath, cause our *downfall*. So there has to be a radical change of direction which deliberately rejects the former ways and practices – something which would be utterly revolutionary for Israel, in the light of the description of their endemic and ingrained waywardness described in other chapters. *Rid yourselves* speaks of the very decisive

---

[77] Hos. 14:1–2.   [78] Ps. 51:16–17.   [79] Jer. 3:12, 14, 22; 4:1–2; Hos. 6:1; Joel 2:12.

action of throwing something away as totally unwanted and unwelcome. *Offences* is a little weak; the word has the sense of 'acts of rebellion and treachery'. Israel must recognize the loathesomeness and betrayal involved in their persistent evil ways, and in throwing them away they must return to submissive and wholehearted loyalty to Yahweh.

But was such change actually possible? Only if it was genuinely internal as well as external. It would require a whole new attitude and mindset, virtually a new 'person' within. In short, they would need to *get a new heart and a new spirit* (31). Later that expression will become the focus of some major reflection and rhetoric. In 36:24–27 (cf. 11:19), it is described as something that Yahweh will give to Israel in the process of restoration and regeneration that can be his work alone. Yet here it is something that Israel must do themselves. There is no real contradiction. The grammatical construction of two successive imperatives (*Rid yourselves ... and get*), often implies that the second is the consequence of the first, not a separate independent command (cf. *Repent and live!*, 32. It's rather like 'Work hard and get promotion!'). And furthermore, the Old Testament recognizes the mysterious interaction between what humans are required to do, and what God alone can do for them. The same paradox is found in Deuteronomy 30:1–10, where turning to God and loving him with 'all your heart and with all your soul' is both the command and the condition that Israel must fulfil (2 and 10) and the gift that Yahweh will give as part of his restoring grace (6). Similarly here, the new heart and new spirit are something Israel must 'get' as part of the genuineness of their repentance, yet ultimately something that God alone can give them.

Secondly, such new attitudes will be manifested positively in very different behaviour. Fundamentally, it means that the wicked man must return to the way of life that characterized the righteous father of verses 5–9, that is, he *keeps all my decrees and does what is just and right* (21). Yet again it is important that we exclude all suspicion of legalism and 'works righteousness' here. Nothing is further from Ezekiel's mind than that Israel (or anybody) could somehow earn their salvation by works of the law that could outweigh the sins previously committed. The next verse removes that idea, as we shall see. No, what is meant here is that only faithful obedience to God in practical reality is the proof of the genuineness of repentance and faith in God's promise. The New Testament insists on exactly the same truth.[80]

What will such practical repentance mean? Ezekiel gives an example in 33:14–16, when the offer made in 18:21–22 is repeated.

---

[80] Luke 3:7–14; 1 John 3:7–10.

Genuine repentance will cause the wicked man to return to economic integrity and compassion after having been an exploiter of other people's need, as illustrated by the return of pledges taken for loans. Not only is repentance not merely a matter of words; neither is it merely a spiritual or emotional attitude. It involves putting things right even if it costs. It affects one's financial affairs and relationships. Indeed, given the hold that money has over us, it is likely that until repentance and conversion does affect that part of our lives, it is premature to talk about a new heart and a new spirit. The heart is not changed if our pockets have not felt the difference. Interestingly, when he was asked for his advice as to what exactly repentance should mean, John the Baptist gave answers which Ezekiel could have written for him: sharing food and clothing with the needy; an end to exploitation of others by official power; no extortion; no abuse of the courts; financial contentment.[81] And it was precisely the evidence of just such radical change that led Jesus to pronounce that salvation had come to the house of Zacchaeus and that he was restored to his heritage as a true child of Abraham, committed to the way of the Lord by doing righteousness and justice.[82]

ii. Repentance which is purging (18:22; 33:16)

True repentance wipes out the past! This is the incredible message of verse 22: *'None of the offences he has committed will be remembered against him.'* This does not mean that the man himself will totally forget his wicked past. As we have seen in 16:61 (amplified in 36:31–32), Israel is told that in the time of restoration they will remember the past with shame, as a counterfoil to the amazing grace of Yahweh's forgiveness. There is for all of us as sinners an appropriate and salutary remembering of our sin. It is a remembering which prevents us ever losing the precious joy of forgiveness. No, it is *God* who will not remember the wicked person's sin *against him* – that is, will not take any further action on it. The charges will be dropped. The slate will be wiped clean. The guilt is gone. The debt is cancelled. When the accusation of the past is brought up, by the sinner himself or by any more sinister accuser, God's voice will intervene with finality: 'Forget it!' Repentance has purged the divine memory.

But what is this? This is the man who committed idolatry and adultery (18:11)! It will not be remembered against him, says God. But this is the man who lived in callous oppression of the poor, committing robbery and extortion (18:12–13)! That too will not be

---

[81] Luke 3:11–14.   [82] Luke 19:1–10.

held against him, says God. Repentance means change, and repentance produces change – change in God's own attitude and action towards the repentant: *'if a wicked man turns ... None of the offences he has committed will be remembered against him.'* What incredible words of immediate, amazing grace, words that only God could utter, words that express in stark simplicity the glorious liberating truth of the biblical gospel!

The immediate, present, nature of God's response to the repentant wicked, as well as to the previously righteous person who reverts to wickedness (18:24; 33:12–13), may well have been what sparked the people's objection about Yahweh's inconsistency. We want to weigh God in the scales of our own distorted sense of fairness. And in our self-righteousness it doesn't seem right that people should just be let off for their sins when they repent. The gospel affirmation that repentant sinners are instantly forgiven is, and always has been, offensive to those who weigh themselves in their own scales and are rather impressed with the result. When Jesus called sinners to repentance and declared that they were forgiven when they responded in faith, without insisting that they go by the prescribed route of the temple, priesthood and sacrificial system, he caused such offence too. When Paul preached that we are justified by grace through faith and not through works of the law, he likewise caused offence and was accused of giving people licence to sin. When we preach that God's saving mercy towards us is entirely unmerited but entirely available to the guiltiest sinner only on the grounds of repentance and faith, we will likewise meet the offended response of hurt pride or sheer incredulity. If we never do meet such response, we need to check if we are preaching the truly biblical gospel of God's grace.

Conversely, if somebody has been living in a respectable manner for a long time, but then goes off into serious moral wickedness and spiritual backsliding, shouldn't God take all their previous righteousness into account and let them off in the end? In thinking thus, we betray the hold that self-righteousness still has on us – as if we were ever saved by our deserts in any case. Behind all such thinking lies the very ancient conception that our eternal destiny depends on some kind of divine or angelic calculation in which, at the end of life, all our good deeds and all our bad deeds will be weighed up, and the decision made then about whether we have done enough good to be saved, or so much evil that the scales must tip into damnation. This kind of calculus affected medieval Christianity and led to the kind of abuses by which one could buy indulgences to stock up on the credit side in advance – a crass distortion of the gospel, which the Reformation attacked so

207

vigorously.[83] It is still, in a different form, the basis on which judgment will be made on the destiny of sinners and saints in the thinking of Islam. Only on judgment day will you know for sure what the verdict is. In the meantime you can only do your best and say your prayers.

But against all such postponed-calculation views of our standing before God, this text affirms that God deals with us in the here and now. The question is not one of quantity, but of direction. It is not a matter of asking how much wickedness or how much righteousness there is in our past, but what direction are you facing now? Are you turned towards God or away from him? God relates to each human being in the living, personal present – not as if we were walking bank statements. Neither wickedness nor righteousness is a commodity that can be stored up or counterbalanced. After repentance, the wicked man is not required to achieve a balancing amount of righteous deeds to cancel the past before being granted the verdict of life. No, the glorious immediacy of the divine declaration is breathtaking. He has turned to 'do righteousness' and so *he will live.*

Having mentioned Islam, it is also worth noting that this verse stands squarely against one of the fundamental pillars of Hinduism also: the iron law of *karma*, according to which nothing can ever cancel the past – not only the past in this life, but in all previous existences and incarnations. Everything is carried forward. Everything will 'be remembered' against you or for you – including what you have no chance of ever remembering yourself. Except that it is not really a matter of anything being 'remembered' or 'forgotten', for it is an utterly impersonal cosmic law. So there is no personal grace, and no God of judgment and grace to whom you can turn. *Karma* governs everything. *Karma* rules, until it is confronted and obliterated by the gospel – the liberating gospel of the grace of the biblical God.

This is the gospel that we as Christians know through the cross of our Lord Jesus Christ, the gospel so richly celebrated in many New Testament texts. But Old Testament believers celebrated it in advance. Even if they did not yet know the means, they knew the character of Yahweh their God: that he is 'the compassionate and gracious God, slow to anger, abounding in love and faithfulness, maintaining love to thousands, and forgiving wickedness, rebellion and sin'.[84] This was the fundamental truth that fuelled the

---

[83] And so beautifully at times as well: Cranmer captured in two phrases the whole thrust of Ezekiel's gospel in his post-communion prayer which asks God to accept our worship, 'not weighing our merits, but pardoning our offences' (from the *Book of Common Prayer*, Order for Holy Communion). [84] Exod. 34:6–7.

intercession of Moses[85] and Nehemiah[86] and inspired Joel to lead his people to repentance.[87] For the psalmist it was sheer joy that such a God 'does not treat us as our sins deserve or repay us according to our iniquities', but rather that 'as far as the east is from the west, so far has he removed our transgressions from us'.[88] The metaphors of forgiving grace begin to pile up: God does not keep a record book of sins;[89] on the contrary, whatever record there was can be blotted out because 'I, even I, am he who blots out your transgressions, for my own sake, and remembers your sin no more.'[90] The decisiveness and finality of God's forgiveness are perhaps most memorably, and most reassuringly, captured by Micah: 'You will tread our sins underfoot and hurl our iniquities into the depths of the sea.' No wonder Micah exclaimed, in echo of his own name,[91] 'Who is a God like you, who pardons sins and forgives the transgression of the remnant of his inheritance?'[92] Who indeed? Praise his name!

iii. Repentance that is pleasing to God (18:31–32; 33:11)

The closing verses of this great chapter, Ezekiel 18, express all the heart longing of God. He has no pleasure in anyone's death; all he longs for is that people should repent and live. This is the great evangelistic appeal that Ezekiel has been working up to all through the chapter. The question is urgent, and rhetorically unanswerable: *'Why will you die, O house of Israel?'* You don't have to! God doesn't want you to! Turn back to God and live, and you will please God more than your sins have ever hurt him.

We have had little enough opportunity so far in our study of Ezekiel to hear and feel the pleasure of God, so we ought to savour this moment. What is it that brings pleasure to the heart of the Almighty? What is it that puts a smile on the face of God? What is it that rings all the bells in heaven? Didn't Jesus himself give us the answer? 'I tell you … there will be more rejoicing in heaven over one sinner who repents than over ninety-nine righteous persons who do not need to repent … There is rejoicing in the presence of the angels of God over one sinner who repents.'[93] And in the same chapter Jesus portrayed the joy of the father running to welcome back the prodigal son, and ordering up a celebration feast because the one who was dead is now alive again. The parable has, of course, its individual relevance – the joy over one repentant returning sinner. But it doubtless touched the same chord in Israel as the message of Ezekiel 18 was designed to do – to urge the people of God *as a*

---

[85] Num. 14:18.   [86] Neh. 9:17.   [87] Joel 2:12–13.
[88] Ps. 103:10–12. For Jonah, the same truth, when applied to others, was an acute embarrassment (Jonah 4:2).   [89] Ps. 130:3–4.   [90] Is. 43:25.
[91] 'Micah' means 'Who is like Yahweh?'   [92] Mic. 7:18–19.   [93] Luke 15:7, 10.

whole to return from the grave of exile and rebellion against God by turning round, asking the question, 'Why should I die?' and then setting off on the road home.[94] The same call of God reaches out to us over the centuries. And if we respond to it in the same way, we will be met by the outstretched arms and beaming face of the waiting Father.

[94] Cf. N. T. Wright's corporate interpretation of the parable, relating it precisely to the challenge to Israel to repent and return, in *Jesus and the Victory of God* (London: SPCK, 1996), pp. 125–131.

24:1–27; 33:1–33
6. The turning-point

Introduction

Ezekiel was a man who remembered his dates better than any history-exam candidate. His whole book is organized around carefully recorded dates on which he received particular messages from God to pass on to the people. But there were two dates he would never forget, not just because they were recorded in his journal, but because on each of them his life changed dramatically. Both of them were charged with paralysing emotional trauma. One was his thirtieth birthday, the day he was called to be a prophet. The other was the day his wife died. On the first, he was overwhelmed by anger at a destiny he was unable to resist (3:14–15). On the second, he was overwhelmed by a grief he was unable to express (24:12–18).

The first date was 31 July 593 BC. The second, about four and a half years later, was 15 January 588, assuming that the date in the heading of chapter 24 covers the content of the whole chapter, including the final declaration of the imminent destruction of the city (24:1–14), and the tragic sign-act involving the death of his wife (24:15–27).[1] The first date marked the beginning of his ministry as

---

[1] The second date is a matter of dispute. The problem is that if we calculate the length of time between the date in 24:1, when the siege began, and that in 33:21, when the news of the fall of the city reached the exiles, it comes to three years. The siege itself is known to have lasted for about eighteen months. This would mean that it took a further eighteen months for the new exiles to bring the news to the exiles in Babylon – an inordinate length of time for a journey that is elsewhere known to have taken about four or five months (cf. Ezra 7:8–9). So scholars resolve the problem in one of two ways. Some regard the later date as a textual error, and the *twelfth year* (33:21) should be changed to 'eleventh year' on the basis of some textual variants (e.g. Zimmerli, *Ezekiel 2*, p. 191; Eichrodt, pp. 457–458; Allen 29, pp. 149, 152; Taylor, p. 216). This textual change would reduce the news delay to a more realistic six months. Alternatively, Block suggests that the earlier date at 24:1, which is in a slightly different format from the rest of the dates in the book, is actually the same

a prophet; the second date signalled the end of the first phase of that ministry – the early years in which the only messages that pierced his otherwise dumb lips were messages of judgment and predictions of the coming destruction of Jerusalem. But the second date, once it had its confirmation in the news of that terrible event (in 33:21–22), also signalled the beginning of the second phase of his ministry – the years in which, with loosened tongue, he was able to hold out hope and encouragement to a people who were shattered by the events which had vindicated Ezekiel as a true prophet. It was, in short, the turning-point of his life in personal and prophetic terms – the end of the old and the beginning of the new.

1. The end of the old world (24:1–27)

a. The fate of the cooking-pot (24:1–14)

God tells Ezekiel on the fateful day on which, by divine revelation, he is made aware that the siege of Jerusalem had begun (2), that he is to *Tell this rebellious house a parable,* or an allegory (3; cf. 17:2) – something which Ezekiel seems to have become quite renowned for (20:49). This makes it likely that what follows was a piece of verbal imagery, perhaps in the form of a cooking-song, though it is not impossible that we have here another acted parable. That is, it may well be that Ezekiel set up one final dramatic action involving his domestic kitchen (cf. 4:3, 9–12), though if he did, he sacrificed a valuable cooking-pot and risked burning his house down. That loss would have been trivial in the light of the sacrifice to come in the second half of the chapter.

The parable begins with what appears to be a cheerful cooking-song to accompany the preparation of a very special meal. People are to put the pot on the stones, put in the water, then fill it up with a large quantity of the very best cuts of meat available along with the tasty marrow bones.[2] Then the wood is arranged, the fire is lit, and the delicious cooking begins. This is a happy song of anticipation. Was Ezekiel at last singing songs of deliverance and celebration? Those who remembered his earlier use of a cooking-pot proverb

as the date in 2 Kgs. 25:1, which refers to the years of Zedekiah's reign, not the years since the first deportation. This would have the effect of dating the start of the siege a year later, thus again making the total time from the start of the siege to the arrival of the news at Babylon two years rather than three. See Block (1), pp. 772–774, for further discussion of the problem.

[2] Block (1), p. 775, suggests that the text may hint that it was a special religious feast – perhaps the meal that went along with the fellowship offering, symbolizing vertical and horizontal harmony between God and the worshipping family.

(11:3–11) might have wondered if Ezekiel had now changed his mind about his interpretation of its imagery. Were the inhabitants of Jerusalem (the 'meat in the pot') to be safely preserved as the choice cuts after all? Would there be celebration meals to give thanks for another great deliverance of Jerusalem? Was Ezekiel preparing a feast for a grand victory party?

Suddenly the song stops and the word begins (6), with the same relentless shock that Ezekiel had mastered so well.[3] *Woe to the city of bloodshed!* (6, 9). We are immediately back in the world of chapter 22, where the violence and murder going on in Jerusalem are highlighted among all their other sins. The bloodshed has become so common and brazen that no attempt is even being made to conceal it (7). Even the blood of animals ordinarily killed for food was supposed to be poured on the soil and covered.[4] But human blood was being shed 'on the open rock' – that is, in open defiance of heaven's gaze.

So, no, forget your false hopes. This is no cheerfully bubbling cauldron for the Sunday lunch. This is a pot fouled and filled with all the pollution of the people's wickedness. Ezekiel changes the focus from the meat to the pot itself. The phrases used (in the NIV, *encrusted, deposit*, 6; *impurities, deposit*, 11–12) are somewhat obscure. Based on ancient translations, some suggest 'rust', but that would be wrong since the pot was made of copper. It may refer to the build-up of food deposits that had not been previously scrubbed off and would make the pot dangerously unhygienic. Or it may even be a total reversal of the description of the meat in the pot – far from being choice cuts, it is nothing more than a mass of putrid decaying flesh. The New King James Version hints at both senses with the translation 'the pot whose scum is in it' – scum being an appropriate insult for those who regarded themselves (changing the metaphor) as the cream of society.

So the parable proceeds with the drastic action of the divine cook. The Hebrew is difficult in places in verses 6–12, but the sequence of actions seems reasonably clear. First, the contents of the pot are emptied out – all the choice pieces of meat are forked out, with no regard for their importance (*without casting lots*). The cooking-broth seems to be thrown away, and any pieces of meat and bones that are left in the pot are then dry-roasted to ashes. But the pot itself is still not cleansed of its own 'sickness', so in a final act of anger, the cook heaps up the fire, transforming it from a gentle cooking barbecue to a blazing bonfire, and puts the empty pot back on the inferno until

[3] The same tactics were used by Isaiah, who turned a happy grape-harvest song, with romantic overtones, into a sudden attack on Israel for their ingratitude and faithlessness (Is. 5:1–7).   [4] Deut. 12:15–16, 20–25.

it glows red-hot and finally melts and is burned away with all its impurities. If the parable was indeed acted out, it must have been spectacular, dangerous and totally transfixing. Even as a verbal account it would have raised the temperature of horror and fear in the listeners, as they pictured the pot as a prophetic symbol of the city.

> The city itself was to suffer devastating damage. Jerusalem was infected with life-destroying social corruption, which must lead to its own demise. The capital was attracting to itself the outworking of a self-incurred curse. It was to become no mere ghost city, waiting quietly for a kinder turn of events, but a Dresden, an inferno of destruction (cf. Lam. 2:8, 9, 15; Neh. 1:3, 17). Such was its inevitable destiny – in which Yahweh too was mysteriously involved (vv. 8, 11, 13) ... Those exiles who perversely continued to put their faith and hope in something other than God had to grasp that outside God there was no hope.[5]

The message of the cooking-pot, then, was unmistakable. Not only were the inhabitants of Jerusalem to be cast out or cremated with no regard for rank or status; the city itself was so corrupt that the only fate that was now appropriate for it was the all-consuming meltdown of final destruction. And the fire has been lit, said Ezekiel, this very day. The 'wood' of Nebuchadnezzar's siege engines is already being stacked around Jerusalem. The parable then concludes (14) with the direct address of Yahweh, a word of terrible finality that sums up and surpasses all the previous passages which express the ending of Yahweh's patience. It is all the more powerful for being so terse. There can be no further argument: 'I am Yahweh. I have spoken. It will come and I will do it. I will not be restrained, neither will I spare, neither will I relent.'[6]

b. The death of Ezekiel's wife (24:15–27)

It is impossible to be certain if this event took place on the same date as the dated parable in the first half of the chapter, but even it if did not, it must have followed quite shortly afterwards in view of its significance to the exiles in the period between Ezekiel's announcement that the siege had begun and the arrival of the news that the city had fallen.

We have here, in a few short verses, one of the most poignant moments in the rich story of Israel's prophets – comparable to, but possibly surpassing, the heartbreak of Hosea[7] and the loneliness of

[5] Allen 29, pp. 62–63.   [6] Cf. comment above on 9:10, pp. 118–119.
[7] Hos. 1 – 3.

Jeremiah.[8] It is only from this text that we know that Ezekiel had a wife at all, but the knowledge does retrospectively colour some aspects of the preceding story, as we have mentioned from time to time. She would have been carefully chosen, for the rules regarding priests' wives were strict.[9] If Ezekiel was only thirty-four by this time, she may have been only in her twenties. She is described as *the delight of your eyes*, a term of real endearment, of intense affection (cf. NLT, 'your dearest treasure').[10] God puts into this tiny phrase all the love of Ezekiel's life – possibly all the love there was in his life at all.

We can only guess at what lies behind God's acknowledgment of how precious this devoted young woman was to his prophet, but it must surely have included her care for him during that awful first year of his prophetic ministry when he virtually starved himself to death before her eyes. And at what personal cost had she come to accept the traumatic destruction of her own hopes when she had first married this young son of a priest? Once in exile, she would have known, of course, that Ezekiel would probably never be privileged to serve in the temple. But at least she had married into a priestly family. So she would have been proud to have an honoured and respected husband who would help to make her own exiled life bearable. But instead of that, she was now practically living under house arrest with a husband who was the butt of everything from mockery to hatred and whose unpredictable eccentricity made her house a virtual tourist site. Had Ezekiel's wife been as angry with God as Ezekiel himself had been at the 'hand of God' upon his life? Quite possibly, and yet, presumably, she supported, encouraged and comforted him, giving delight to his eyes in the bleak physical, emotional and theological landscape of their doubly blighted lives. Was he even able to talk to her? Or did his dumbness, apart from when speaking the direct words of God, extend even to their intimate life together? We may not know, we cannot tell what pains they had to bear. But this tiny shaft of divine recognition – *the delight of your eyes* – tells us that they had borne them together, and if nobody else loved Ezekiel, his precious young wife did.

What unfathomably bleak horror, then, must have engulfed Ezekiel when the word of verse 16 bore in upon him. *With one blow* his only precious possession would be ripped from him. The

---

[8] Jer. 16:1–9; 15:17–18. [9] Lev. 21:7–8, 13–15.

[10] The term *maḥmad* is used in the erotic appreciation of a lover in Song 5:16, in describing the desperate preciousness of newborn babies in Hos. 9:16, and in evaluating the treasures that starving people will gladly give up for food (Lam. 1:11). Elsewhere, as in Ezek. 24, it describes the treasures of the temple (Lam. 1:10; Joel 3:5; Is. 64:11).

expression suggests sudden death, unprepared for by any preceding deterioration or normal sickness. Nothing more than a day's warning – which would not lessen the pain, but only confirm to him that it was no accident but yet again the heavy hand of God in his life. And along with the warning came the knowledge that this heart-wrenching personal tragedy would be the ultimate *sign* (24, 27). It would quite literally be the last thing he could give or do that would convince those capable of being convinced that Yahweh was serious in his intention to destroy Jerusalem and the temple. But the sign would not consist merely in the death of his wife, but in the reaction he was to display to it in public. For he was not to exhibit any of the customary responses to bereavement; even his groaning was to be suppressed within himself.

Imagine, then, the scene. The precise chronology of events as described in the text is open to dispute, but this seems the most likely. One day Ezekiel receives the devastating news that his wife is to die the next day. If he was truly dumb apart from directly inspired speech, then he could not share it with his wife – even if he could have found it possible to do so. And in the same message, he is given the instructions to display none of the signs of mourning, or to receive any of the attentions of sympathizers (*the customary food of mourners*, meaning appropriate dishes that family and friends would bring for the funeral period). The next morning – just imagine the agony of this – he simply *spoke to the people* (18).[11] That is, he just went about his normal duty as a prophet giving God's word to those who turned up at his house – knowing that every minute spent in speaking to such unwittingly unwelcome guests was a minute less that he had with 'the delight of his eyes'. And then, with a heartbreaking brevity that must have been the only way he could cope with the memory of it all, he simply records: *and in the evening my wife died. The next morning I did as I had been commanded.* And that's it. Ezekiel's most treasured possession manages just two entries in his journal. In 24:16 she appears for the first time, the sparkle in his eyes. Two verses later she is gone, and the light of his life goes out for ever.

And then the awful news spreads rapidly among the community: 'Ezekiel's wife has died!' And friends, family and sympathizers flock to the house – only to receive a shock greater even than the totally unexpected and untimely death of such a young woman. Expecting to find Ezekiel giving vent to all the emotionally beneficial and

[11] Some (e.g. NLT) think this means he told them the message of vv. 16 and 17, but I think that is very unlikely. How could he have told them if his wife was there listening? And also, it seems that his behaviour after the bereavement was a complete surprise to them, not something they had been told to expect.

culturally expected signs of grief – weeping, lamenting loud and long, going bare-headed and bare-foot, and covering his lower face – they find him sitting there, or going about some domestic jobs as if nothing had happened, washed, dressed and ready for business as usual. They bring in the customary dishes of food for the bereaved, and he won't even touch them! They must have been shocked, offended and baffled, since it was probably common knowledge how much Ezekiel loved his wife and how precious they were to each other. Baffled, that is, until they noticed the suppressed pain of the unshed tears in his eyes, the wild effort of self-control that was gripping him, the total abnormality of his show of normality. This was not callous bravado, this was the awful prelude to a message that they knew was coming. So they ask him directly, knowing from years of experience now that when Ezekiel speaks it will be aimed at themselves: (lit.) 'Will you not declare to us what these things mean *to us* that you are doing?' (19). They grasp the fact that the death and Ezekiel's reaction are a sign, but a sign of what? What do they 'sign-ify'?

So Ezekiel somehow finds the voice to tell them. God had taken from him the delight of his eyes. And what was the delight of theirs, the thing they longed for most? Jerusalem, yes, but especially the beautiful temple, not to mention the children they had been forced to leave behind there. The temple especially is described in superlative terms: in relation to Yahweh it is, poignantly, *my sanctuary* – my holy place, though in view of the pollutions described in chapter 8, this was a hollow description now. In relation to the people it is their *stronghold ... pride ... the delight of* their *eyes ... the object of* their *affection ... their joy and glory ... their heart's desire* (21, 25). They could not believe that it could ever be destroyed, any more than Ezekiel could have believed that his wife would be struck dead in the bloom of life. Yet God was about to take away all those treasures – treasures in stone and in people – in a massive bereavement that would leave them as utterly overwhelmed by inexpressible grief just as Ezekiel was at that very moment. They would do exactly as he had done – mourn with a mourning too great for words and symbolic gestures. They would be paralysed with a devastating, debilitating, wasting grief (22–23). And then, if not now, they would know who was truly God and that their own sins had caused such desolation (23–24).

'And', we may imagine Ezekiel adding, or thinking in his agony, as he turned their gaze and his own to the lifeless form of his lovely young wife lying in the room in front of them, 'if *this* does not confront you with the reality of what I have been saying, if *this* does not drive you to repentance before it is too late, then nothing ever will and God alone will be your judge.'

217

And what are we to make of such a desperately costly sign? The Bible makes no secret of the cost involved in being a servant of God in a hostile world, and many faithful prophets suffered in the course of their ministry, including suffering in the intimacy of their personal lives. But the death of a young wife seems outrageously cruel. It does not seem that we can take refuge in imagining that it was a natural illness and death which was later interpreted by Ezekiel in this way. His account is too specific for that. Yahweh took his wife – with a warning, yes, but still it was Yahweh's direct action that left him desolate. We need to set this fact alongside what we know of God from 18:32 and 33:11. If God takes no pleasure in the death of anyone, even the wicked, then how much more was it an act of 'no pleasure', but rather of terrible grief, for God to take the life of this presumably believing and righteous young woman?

Only one thing seems to me to have justified it in God's eyes, and that is the assumption that its 'sign' value did actually achieve its purpose and pointed at least some people towards acceptance, confession, repentance and salvation. If there were those among the exiles who turned to the Lord and found saving grace and life in the wake of that terrible morning in the home of Ezekiel, then her death was not in vain. What measure of consolation this may have brought to Ezekiel himself is impossible to say. But he is not alone among those who have lost loved ones in the service of the word of God, and whose loss has borne mysterious fruit in the salvation of others. Nor was Ezekiel alone in paying the cost of the death of his most dearly beloved for the sake of others. His pain was in some mysterious sense a sharing in the pain of God. For the God who took Ezekiel's wife was the God who would give up his own beloved Son to death on the cross. And he did so because he so loved the world, including the exiles who crowded Ezekiel's desolate home that day. If any of those exiles are among the saved whom we shall meet in the new creation, it will ultimately be because of Christ's sacrifice, not Ezekiel's.

The only consolation that we are told about for Ezekiel comes in the personal word to him that follows in 24:25–27. His prediction will be vindicated. News will come of the final destruction of the city and the temple. And when it does, then Ezekiel's long dumbness will be over. His *mouth will be opened*, his tongue will be liberated and he will speak freely with his people. We need not quibble over the detail that, obviously, the *fugitive* would not arrive in Babylon to give the news of the fall of Jerusalem on the same day that it actually happened. There is a rhetorical element in these verses. On the one hand, they emphasize the certainty of what is being predicted. As surely as Ezekiel's treasure lies dead, so the people's treasure will be destroyed too, and they will hear the news in person. On the other hand, the repeated expression 'in that day' (NIV, *on the day ... on that day ... At that time* – it is all the same phrase in Hebrew) has an eschatological flavour. This was the expression commonly used for some future act of Yahweh associated with the Day of the Lord. It is an expression frequently linked not only to the finality of an act of *judgment*, but also to the vision of *hope* to follow. With the death of his wife, the end has indeed come. But the sign points beyond the tragedy to the faint glimmer of a new beginning that will build on the only foundation left after the fires of judgment: namely, the knowledge that Yahweh truly is God (27). No other foundation for hope would be left.

But then, no other foundation would ultimately be needed.

2. The beginning of a new world (33:1–33)

After the dated announcement that the siege of Jerusalem had begun (24:1–2), Ezekiel and the exiles had a long wait ahead of them – less painful, no doubt, but no less anxious than the waiting of the besieged inhabitants of Jerusalem itself. In fact they waited almost two years – the eighteen months of the siege itself and a further six months before the news of its terrible ending arrived among them.[12] Either Ezekiel himself or those who edited his prophecies into the shape of the present book created the sense of a gap and the suspense of the long wait by placing a whole section of oracles against the nations (chs. 25 – 32) in between the announcement in chapter 24 and the arrival of the news in chapter 33.[13] There is thus a literary as well as a chronological pause, marking the turning-point of Ezekiel's ministry.

A first glance through chapter 33 gives the impression that we have heard all this before, and indeed there are major recapitulations of earlier messages. However, the chapter does present a new context and there is a coherence among its somewhat diverse parts. It is structured rather like a see-saw: the central fulcrum is the arrival of the news (21–22). Then there are two sections balanced on each side: on one side, the renewal of Ezekiel's watchman responsibility (1–9), along with a reminder of the ways of God with the wicked and the

[12] On the probable dating, see above, note 1.

[13] Some scholars, e.g. Blenkinsopp, believe that Ezekiel's dumbness was for this period only (from the beginning of the siege to the news of the fall of the city), not from the moment of his call. The effect of such a 'highly significant silence' (p. 150) was to highlight the hiatus that the siege created in Ezekiel's ministry and the major transition from his earlier ministry of judgment to his later ministry of hope. My own view, however, is that Ezekiel's dumbness lasted throughout the years from his call to the arrival of the news of the fall of the city.

righteous (10–20); on the other side, a repudiation of the specious theology and false expectations of those left behind in Judah after the fall of the city (23–29), and a reminder to Ezekiel of the fickleness of his listeners (30–33).

a. The recommissioning of the prophet (33:1–9)

The language here clearly recalls 3:17–21, when God, a week after his original appearance to Ezekiel, had summoned him to the prophetic task with his appointment to be a watchman or sentry for his people. We need not discuss again the significance of the imagery and its powerful application to the prophetic task of warning – warning both the wicked to repent, and the righteous not to turn away into sin.[14]

The main difference is that, whereas in chapter 3 it seems very likely that we have an account of a private word from God to Ezekiel on the occasion of his call, giving him this responsibility, here in chapter 33 it is explicitly a message that he is to make public (2). And he does so in typical fashion. First of all he sets up before the people a situation for them to consider (1–6). A country is faced by an enemy (ominously) brought by Yahweh. They appoint and place a sentry, as expected. If he does his duty, then the people's fate is their own responsibility. If he fails to give due warning, then if anybody gets killed, it is their own responsibility, but the watchman too will be held accountable by Yahweh. The last two points – the fact that the man who dies *will be taken away because of his sin*, and Yahweh's own involvement (*'I will hold the watchman accountable'*) – both indicate that this is no ordinary war story, but indeed a parable that is meant to apply to the listeners themselves – sinners in the presence of Yahweh as they knew themselves to be after years of Ezekiel's preaching.

Then he goes on to explain that this was precisely the nature of the ministry he has been exercising in their midst all this time (7–9). The ironies that we noticed in 3:17–21 are still here: the sentry has been appointed, not by the people (as in 33:2), but by Yahweh himself. But it is Yahweh who is the enemy that the sentry must warn against! So, then, Ezekiel had been fulfilling his commission, warning the people and saving his own life in doing so. And he had done it in every creative (not to say crazy) way he possibly could. For, as Blenkinsopp comments, 'the task is not just to sound the prophetic trumpet blast … but to recognize and evaluate the situation and to find ways of creating an awareness that will lead to appropriate action. Not all of Ezekiel's methods may be appropriate

---

[14] See above, pp. 65–69.

today, but we cannot help admiring the variety of ways, verbal and nonverbal, in which he attempts to discharge his task.'[15]

The repetition and making public of the watchman's task, however, constitute a kind of renewal of Ezekiel's prophetic ministry. His task would certainly not be finished when the vindication of his predictions of the destruction of Jerusalem finally came true. Far from it; that was only the end of the beginning. In sheer length of time, his ministry after the fall of Jerusalem would last almost three times longer than the five-year period between his call and that event. His last dated prophecy (40:1) was almost twenty years after his call.

The context of his renewed ministry would change enormously, inasmuch as he now faced a people utterly broken by the catastrophe of 587. The burden of his message shifts from being predominantly one of judgment to being predominantly one of hope. And yet the same image is used for his role – that of a watchman, a sentry. He must still watch for the danger signs; he must still warn and plead; he must ensure that those who repent and join the camp of the righteous stay there and live accordingly; and there will always be the unrepentant who will need continuing severity.

The implications for Christian ministry seem to flow naturally: there is no sharp divide between the role of the evangelist and the pastor, for those who have been evangelized will need careful pastoring to prevent backsliding, and even those who are among the flock being pastored need the challenge of the evangelistic warning and appeal. The sentry is never off duty.

b. The responsibility of the hearers (33:10–20)

Yet again, we have repeated material, this time from chapter 18. But then what preacher can ever say he has never preached the same sermon twice? The difference, as we noted in chapter 5[16] lies in the words of the people. Whereas in chapter 18 the trigger was the proverb that seemed to shift all responsibility for the exile on to earlier generations, here the people's cry is one of penitential despair: *'Our offences and sins weigh us down, and we are wasting away because of them. How then can we live?'* (10). The immediate context makes their words all the more significant. Ezekiel has just spoken of *the wicked man* who *will die for his sin* (9). The people's confession now amazingly accepts that they are in exactly that category (note *'our* offences'). They accept the divine verdict (they are the wicked) and the divine sentence (they deserve death), and so they resign themselves to a living death, rotting away in exile.

[15] Blenkinsopp, p. 146.   [16] See above, p. 195.

But it need not be so! The watchman brings not just warning to the wicked, but also hope. They can turn around. They can turn away from sin and towards God, and in doing so they can find life. So the wonderful words of divine mercy and evangelistic appeal are sounded again (11), and are then followed up with the same meticulous argumentation that we found in chapter 18 and have come to expect from Ezekiel's sharp, priestly trained mind. Having already relished the liberating and challenging gospel that these verses contain,[17] we need not repeat the points; except to say that seeking to show the justice and consistency of God to people under conviction of sin, who could scarcely take in the mind-boggling scale of God's mercy, must have been very different from trying to demonstrate these things to people convinced of their own innocence and complaining under the scourge of God's anger. Jesus likewise found it a much sweeter task to convince self-aware sinners of God's mercy than to convict the self-righteous of God's wrath. Evangelists and pastors would bear similar testimony.

The main point of this repeated sermon, then, is to hammer home the vital responsibility that lay on the people as they listened to Ezekiel, just as Jesus repeatedly did also to his own generation: 'He who has ears to hear, let him hear';[18] 'He who hears this word of mine and does not do it is like a fool ...'[19] Ezekiel would continue to do his job as Yahweh's watchman in their midst. Now the responsibility passed to his hearers.

> [Ezekiel's] aim is to clarify once and for all Ezekiel's prophetic self-consciousness before his people. If he has denounced them as wicked, this has been Yahweh's evaluation. If he has pronounced the death sentence on them, this is the divine verdict. His role has been to alert the community to the peril of their ways, and to call them back to the path of righteousness. He has taken his charge seriously; now let them do the same.[20]

c. The vindication and liberation of the prophet (33:21–22)

But why should the exiles take Ezekiel any more seriously than they ever had? Because one day the community was shattered by news that meant they could never again deride him as one who was merely crying wolf. The wolf had come and the prey was devoured.

It was 8 January 585 BC. Probably we should not think of a solitary escapee who came only to Ezekiel's house. He was doubtless one, perhaps the first to arrive, of the great new influx of exiles who had spent the past five or six months making the same wretched

---

[17] See above, pp. 206–210.   [18] Mark 4:9.   [19] Matt. 7:26.   [20] Block (2), p. 243.

journey that Ezekiel and his community had made ten years earlier; except that this new batch of exiles had been forced to do it in an emaciated state after eighteen months of siege and starvation. We can only imagine the horror of that trail of refugee-prisoners, and guess at the number who must have perished *en route*. And we can only likewise imagine the lament that went up among the first exiles as they heard the dread words *'The city has fallen!'*

Ezekiel, however, was prepared for the news, not merely by having predicted it two years previously, but by another divine visitation the night before the messenger arrived. He describes the experience in the same way as his original call – a profound sensation of the physically overwhelming grip of God. But this time, instead of it having the effect of binding his tongue from everything but the direct utterance of God, it had the opposite effect. He was released from his dumbness. What a sense of joy and relief must be contained in the words *and he opened my mouth!* ... *So my mouth was opened and I was no longer silent.*

So 33:21–22 reports with great brevity, and in reverse order, two things: the news of the fall of the city and the ending of Ezekiel's dumbness. Each of them had a profound significance beyond their obvious surface meaning as reported events.

First of all, the news of the fall of Jerusalem vindicated once and for all Ezekiel's claim to be bringing the genuine words of Yahweh – that is, he must now be acknowledged among the exiles as a true prophet. His predictions for the past five years had been fulfilled, in spite of all the false optimism and desperate hopes of the people in Babylon or in Jerusalem. The same would have been true, of course, for Jeremiah also, after his even longer ministry of forty years predicting the coming catastrophe. We can imagine that such vindication brought no joy to either prophet. For both of them the terrible dilemma of having to bring such a word in advance, and then being reviled and disbelieved, was that the only thing that would vindicate their claim to be true prophets of Yahweh was the last thing that they actually wanted to happen – the destruction of the city and temple. So it was cold comfort when it did happen. However, now at least the people would listen to his words with greater attention. Whether they would respond with any greater practical change in their ways was another matter (33:30–33; see below).

Secondly, the release of Ezekiel from his dumbness signalled a fresh start in his prophetic ministry. Previously, he could say nothing but the words of predicted judgment and doom, along with all the lurid and detailed justification for Yahweh's intense anger. Now there could be new words of encouragement, hope and pastoral challenge.

He could finally assume the normal role of a prophet, interceding on the people's behalf before Yahweh and offering messages of hope for the future. So long as the temple and the city had stood, these basic functions had been denied him. But hereafter, though he would continue to issue diatribes (cf. e.g. 33:24–29; 34:1–10), he could begin to focus on a new day when the corrupt tenets of official theology would be replaced by authentic spirituality and Yahweh would reconstitute the nation as his covenant people.[21]

d. The extinction of false hopes (33:23–29)

Human beings seem to have a limitless capacity to reinterpret events subjectively in their own favour. Sometimes this can be admirable hope and optimism in the face of adversity; sometimes it can be perverse refusal to accept the reality of disgrace and defeat. I write this on the day President Milosević of Yugoslavia proclaimed to his people, amid the appalling devastation of his country by the NATO bombardment, that the outcome of the disastrous war in Kosovo was a victory for the Serbs and they should be proud of their heroes. It is a doubtful matter, of course, whether any side can claim 'victory' in such a conflict, but in the wake of the withdrawal from Kosovo it sounded a hollow claim to make. Likewise in the wake of Nebuchadnezzar, it seems that the fires of Jerusalem were still smouldering when the survivors left behind in Judea[22] came up with a new idea to bolster their shattered existence. Their words are recorded in yet another popular saying that Ezekiel is called upon to refute: '*Abraham was only one man, yet he possessed the land. But we are many; surely the land has been give to us as our possession*' (24).

This argument was an attempt to give scriptural, theological rationale for their hope that, having survived the fall of Jerusalem, they would now be the ones through whom God would carry forward his promise to Israel. It seems very likely that it was also being used to give a specious legitimacy to the seizure of lands vacated by the exiles. This seems to have been going on already after the first deportation (cf. 11:1–15). Like vultures tearing at a carcass, these people were taking the best pickings they could from the deserted estates of those who had been deported. Now they have the gall to put forward a biblical justification. But their saying was flawed in all kinds of ways. Abraham had not possessed the land, but

[21] Block (2), p. 255.
[22] While the bulk of the population was carried off, it is reported that the Babylonians left some of the poorest people behind to work the vineyards and fields (2 Kgs. 25:12; Jer. 52:16).

merely received and believed the promise that his descendants would. Even that level of 'possession' in advance was based upon his faith and obedience in response to God's promise – about which the people's attitude says nothing. It was never a matter of mere arithmetic, but of God's promise and gift – that was true even at the time of the conquest. When, in due course, God himself would take the gracious initiative to give the land back to his people, then the Abraham precedent would be appropriate,[23] but not until then.

So Ezekiel has to declare a very different perspective on the relative status of the exiles in Babylon and the survivors in Judah. It was a perspective that had already been expressed by Jeremiah by a visible sign (of good and bad figs)[24] and by letter.[25] The future lies with the exiles, not with those left behind in Jerusalem, whether after the first or second deportations. The mere fact that they were still left behind in the land gave them no right to claim the whole heritage of the Abrahamic covenant for themselves. They were the past, not the future. In any case, the behaviour of the survivors was identical to all the wickedness that had been going on in the land and the city, as a result of which the destruction had come as God's final judgment. So, given their unrepentant and unchanged attitude and behaviour, it was a bit rich to start quoting Abraham, the model of faith, obedience and righteousness. No, they may have survived the actual conflagration, but their fate would in the end be no different (27–29).

e. The exposure of flattering attention (33:30–33)

Most of us would rather be popular than unpopular. For the minister of God's word, each condition brings its own dangers and temptations. Right at the start of his ministry, God had warned Ezekiel of the unpopularity that he would face. That is probably too weak a word for the stiff faces, hard hearts and brass foreheads of hostility that he was going to face (2:3–7; 3:4–9). But he had survived all that with God's help, and doubtless also the support of the dear wife now departed. Now everything would change. His vindication as a true prophet would mean that people would really listen. He would be the talk of the town. In every little gathering under the shade of walls and doorways (33:30), Ezekiel, the wonder prophet whose prediction had come true, would be the name on everyone's lips. And they would come in their droves to sit and hear his every

---

[23] Similar language is used in Is. 51:1–3, but as a divine promise to a restored people being encouraged to 'pursue righteousness' and 'seek the LORD' – which is not the condition of the survivors described in Ezek. 33:23–29.
[24] Jer. 24.   [25] Jer. 29:1–19.

word. Perhaps he would no longer be confined to his house, now that he was no longer dumb either. Maybe they brought him to the place where they met for worship – the fledgling synagogues that developed during the exile. And they watched and listened, encouraging him to do his prophetic thing. Maybe they even applauded at the end. If it had been today's world, they would have had T-shirts with his name on for the kids to wear. In the sad drab life of exile he was the best entertainment around (32). He was public attraction number one. Ezekiel was, definitely, in.

Ezekiel was also human. And such popularity is dangerous. It is dangerous first of all for the prophet. The temptation to believe that 'now at last everybody is listening to me, so I am a success after all' can be a dangerous illusion. So God warns Ezekiel again. There is a significant balancing here, when we link this with the original call in chapters 1 – 3.[26] Then, God had warned of the *opposition* and promised to strengthen him against it. Here, at the point of the relaunching of his ministry for its second major phase, God warns him of the *flattery* he will receive and warns him not to be fooled by it. He must judge the success of his ministry neither by the numbers listening, nor by their enthusiasm in appreciation of his words, but only by the practical response of changed lives. Every preacher knows the frustration of hearing flattering, or even sincerely enthusiastic, comments on his or her message, but then finding no real change in attitude or action to follow. Such frustration led to one of the saddest things Jesus ever said: 'Why do you call me, "Lord, Lord," and do not do what I say?'[27] Why? Because enthusiasm has always been easier than obedience, and the wise prophet or minister heeds God's warning to Ezekiel. Don't allow yourself to be taken for an entertainer.

But the popularity of a great preacher is also dangerous for the listeners. There is the danger of imagining that just because you have gone with the crowd and attended the meetings, sung the songs, got the blessing, gone to the front, bought the T-shirt … that you have actually *done* something in response to the claim of God on your life. We so easily substitute the form of religion for the power of radical, life-changing obedience to the demands of the kingdom of God. There is the danger that some will even try to exploit the popular preacher for their own ends – even if the preacher himself or herself does not. The description of some of Ezekiel's hearers, that *their hearts are greedy for unjust gain*, may possibly indicate that some unscrupulous people were trying to make a fast buck out of

[26] Structurally, this literary/thematic 'envelope' is another indication that chs. 1 – 24, with 33, encompass the first part of Ezekiel's ministry.

[27] Luke 6:46–49; cf. Matt. 7:21.

Ezekiel's entertainment value.[28] If so, they were certainly not the last to do so. Many people have got rich by leading the band on the wagon of the megastars of the Christian circus. There is also the perennial danger of the compulsive convention-goer – that of enjoying the sound of God's word but never actually putting it into practice. James said that such behaviour was like looking in a mirror and then forgetting your own appearance.[29] Jesus, more starkly, called it life-threatening folly.[30]

3. A preview of Ezekiel's new message

Before we leave this turning-point in Ezekiel's ministry, it may be helpful to survey the road ahead. As we have seen, the fall of the city meant the final collapse of all the false hopes that the people had put in their theological assurance and insurance. The important thing now to get across was that the hope had been false, not because it had been placed in the wrong things, but because it had not been accompanied by any understanding of the necessary commitment to covenant obedience on their part. They had thought Yahweh was their covenant God. He was. They had thought they were Yahweh's people in Yahweh's land. They were. They had thought Jerusalem was his city, the temple his dwelling-place, and the Davidic kings his appointed rulers. They were. But all these beliefs had been held, not as motivations for faith, humility and righteousness, but as alleged security against the consequences of disloyalty, pride and wickedness of every conceivable kind. The only way Yahweh could penetrate the armour of false assumptions was to strip them all away utterly in the cataclysmic destruction of all those props – no more a great people, no more king, no more land, no more temple, no more city. But not no more Yahweh! The exile was not a full stop. It was a comma – a break, a pause, in the grand flow of God's story with his people. History was not at an end, but at a new beginning. There was hope for the future because Yahweh was God of the future as much as of the past.[31]

What shape, then, would such a future take? The only shape that could be envisaged by Ezekiel, in his historical context, was the shape already established by God in the story so far. If Israel's rebellion had meant the destruction of all the great realities through which their relationship with God was expressed and embodied, then

---

[28] 'As with Simon Magus (Acts 8:18), their receptivity to the word of God was distorted by the inner feeling of "what is there in this for me?"' (Taylor, p. 218).

[29] Jas. 1:22–25.   [30] Matt. 7:24–27.

[31] This was the message that Is. 40 – 55 was so concerned to impress upon the disgruntled exiles.

the restoration of Israel must involve the restoration of those same realities, in a new world order that Yahweh would bring about after the purging of Israel in exile. That indeed is what follows in the rest of the book of Ezekiel. There are, of course, still passages in which God's judgment must be expressed, whether against the depraved rulers of Israel in the past, or against other nations that would oppose Yahweh's sovereignty. But the major thrust of the following chapters is to outline God's work of restoration at every level of his relationship with Israel. In chapters 8 and 9 of our exposition, we shall look at these different dimensions.

Block helpfully summarizes the structure of Ezekiel 34 – 48 as follows:

> Although [these chapters] divide generically into two major blocks, the first (chs. 34 – 39) concerned with proclaiming the good news, and the second (chs. 40 – 48) with envisioning the good news, the focus is on Yahweh's restorative actions, for the glory of his name, according to the following grand apologetic scheme:
>
> 1. Restoring Yahweh's role as the divine shepherd/king of Israel (34:1–31)
> 2. Restoring Yahweh's land (35:1 – 36:15)
> 3. Restoring Yahweh's honor (36:16–38)
> 4. Restoring Yahweh's people (37:1–14)
> 5. Restoring Yahweh's covenant (37:15–28)
> 6. Restoring Yahweh's supremacy (38:1 – 39:29)
> 7. Restoring Yahweh's presence among his people (40:1 – 46:24)
> 8. Restoring Yahweh's presence in the land (47:1 – 48:35)[32]

However, before we can turn to those great chapters of hope and restoration, we must pause, as the book itself does, and consider the intervening chapters (25 – 32), in which Ezekiel's prophetic gazes turns away from Israel for a moment, and directs its attention to the surrounding nations.

---

[32] Block (2), p, 272. Block points out how this programme of restoration followed a pattern of expectations that would have been found widely among ancient near-eastern peoples in relation to national recovery after defeat (pp. 271–272).

25:1 – 32:32
7. 'Then the nations will know that I am the LORD'

Introduction

a. The structure of the material

Whoever organized the book of Ezekiel into its present form[1] obviously had an eye for the element of suspense. After the intense and tragic narrative of chapter 24, with its concluding prediction that a messenger would come with the news of the fall of the city, we would like to read straight on to hear of his arrival and the reaction to the news itself. But instead, like the exiles themselves, we must sit and wait. And wait. And while we wait, Ezekiel will treat us to a selection of his alternative poetry, oracles aimed in a very different direction from all that has gone before.

We have felt the heat of his anger and heard the bitterness of his sarcasm targeted at Israel. In a few months he will embark upon a very different and more positive pastoral message and ministry, but we need a breathing-space to prepare for such a transition. So into the gap he steps now with a conveniently collected little portfolio of oracles which he had spoken against various nations. Almost all the messages that have been put together in chapters 25 – 32 were delivered during or shortly after the siege of Jerusalem itself, so it is reasonably appropriate that they are inserted at this point in the book, in view of the historical context referred to in chapters 24 and 33. These were the words that filled the silence as the exiles waited in agony during the months of the siege of Jerusalem, doubtless hearing a mixture of news and rumours on the Babylonian grapevine. And so, appropriately, they fill the editorial gap between the announcement of the beginning of the siege (24:2) and the news of its terrible end (33:21).

[1] As discussed in the Introduction (pp. 39–40), it is perfectly possible that Ezekiel himself played a large part in the shaping of his own book.

Whoever organized the book of Ezekiel into its present form also had an eye for elegant structure. The collection of oracles in chapters 25 – 32 has a number of features which indicate a careful literary structuring that can hardly have been accidental.

First of all, there is a small section right at the centre of the collection which seems quite out of place at first: 28:24–26. Here we find, not condemnation of the foreign nations, but words of hope and future security for Israel. Far from being an inexplicable intrusion, however, Block is surely right to regard these verses as 'the key that unlocks the entire unit'. They make clear that the purpose of the surrounding oracles against the nations is indeed to provide 'a backhanded message of hope' for Israel. Yahweh's action against their enemies will ultimately mean that their own future will be secure, in spite of the catastrophe happening at the very time the oracles were delivered. Block further points out that these verses function as a fulcrum for the entire collection, since the rest of the material is balanced very precisely on either side: (a) 25:1 – 28:23, judgment on six nations (for 97 verses); (b) 29:1 – 32:32, judgment on Egypt (for 97 verses).[2] This precisely central position of the words of hope for Israel is again unlikely to be accidental and stresses the positive intention of the whole collection – viewed from Israel's perspective.

The second main indication of careful structuring is the triple use of sevens. Altogether, seven nations are targeted: Ammon (25:1–7); Moab (25:8–11); Edom (25:12–14); Philistia (25:15–17); Tyre (26:1 – 28:19); Sidon (28:20–23); Egypt (29:1 – 32:32). Even though there is an enormous variation in the length of treatment given to each (the section against Egypt is the same length as the other six put together), nevertheless, the use of seven named nations is a recognized feature of Israelite rhetoric. Amos, for example, condemns seven nations before turning on Israel. And the pre-Israelite nations in Canaan were listed as seven.[3] Then also the two major oracles, against Tyre and against Egypt, each break up into seven internal sections that are clearly demarcated in the text, as we shall see below.[4]

b. The point of the material

From what we know of the prophetic movement within Israel, from its earliest days, it seems that one of the fundamental tasks of the prophets was to pronounce words of woe and judgment upon the

---

[2] Block (2), pp. 4–5.   [3] Deut. 7:1.
[4] Block provides detailed tables of further comparisons of style and vocabulary between the oracles: Block (2), pp. 6–12.

enemies of Yahweh and of Israel. The narratives give us some graphic examples of this.[5] These chapters, then, are examples of Ezekiel fulfilling that role – just as many of the other prophets did. There are many similarities between these chapters and comparable collections of oracles against the foreign nations in Amos 1 – 2, Isaiah 13 – 23 and Jeremiah 46 – 51.

When we read through such chapters, however, we may be struck by how similar they sound to all the other chapters in which the prophets were attacking and condemning Israel. The same forms of speech are used, the same metaphors of courtroom justice, sometimes the same accusations of sins and crimes, the same ringing words of condemnation, the same declarations of coming doom and destruction, and above all, the same ultimate speaker: Yahweh the God of Israel. So we might be led to imagine that the oracles against the nations were simply modelled on the oracles against Israel – more of the same, but just directed elsewhere. The ironic truth is that, in fact, it was exactly the other way round. Starting probably with Amos, it became the shocking habit of those prophets who were truly speaking from Yahweh, and not merely earning a living, to turn upside down the people's expectations. They took the words and forms and language of what they were supposed to say against Israel's enemies and turned them instead upon Israel itself – effectively saying that Yahweh was now treating Israel as his own enemy.

This strategy is most clearly and simply illustrated by Amos 1 – 2. In his first great public appearance in Bethel, Amos gathered a crowd in the traditional way by hurling oracles of Yahweh's judgment against all of Israel's wicked neighbours – Syria, the Philistines, Tyre, Edom, Ammon, Moab. This would have been popular, traditional stuff, guaranteed to raise cheers and approval. Then suddenly, without a pause for breath or a change of format, he turns exactly the same indictment against Judah[6] and, in even greater detail, against Israel.[7] The other prophets then followed Amos' example, using the oracle of woe upon the enemies of Yahweh as their sharpest weapon against Israel itself.

---

[5] E.g. the vivid story of the prophets who urged Ahab to go to war against the Syrians, including Zedekiah of the iron horns (1 Kgs. 22). From a different standpoint, Balaam is an interesting example of a foreign prophet hired by Balak, king of Moab, to curse his enemies – the people of Israel. Happily for Israel, frustratingly for Balak, and unfortunately for Balaam (who lost his fee), Balaam was unable to keep his part of the contract and ended up compelled by Yahweh to bless Israel repeatedly. The richly comic story in Num. 22 – 24 illustrates precisely what prophets were expected, and often paid, to do.
[6] Amos 2:4–5.   [7] Amos 2:6–16.

In Ezekiel's case, we have already noted that this is what he does as early as his great dramatic prophecies in the first year of his ministry – acting out the message that the real enemy attacking Jerusalem was not Nebuchadnezzar, but Yahweh himself, personified in the prone body of Ezekiel, with his iron griddle, glaring menacingly at a clay model on the floor. And then we saw how he takes the language of the oracles against the nations and turns it on Jerusalem. Shockingly, Yahweh says to Jerusalem exactly what he said to Tyre, Sidon, Egypt, and all their other inveterate enemies: 'I ... am against you' (5:8; cf. 26:3; 28:22; 29:3; etc.). So the burden and balance of the matter is not that Yahweh will judge the nations just as he is judging Israel, but rather that he will judge Israel in the same way that he judges the nations. The rhetorical strategy of the prophets was deliberately as simple as it was shocking: Israel, the covenant people of Yahweh, was now to be counted among the enemies of Yahweh and must be addressed as such.

But having understood that perspective, we still must do justice to the significance of these oracles against the other nations, regarded as enemies of both God and Israel. What were they there for? Why did prophets in general proclaim such messages? And why specifically does Ezekiel include some of them here? The general point is that such negative messages of ultimate defeat and destruction for Israel's enemies were, of course, by implication positive messages of deliverance and hope for Israel itself. To know that Yahweh was acting *against* your foes gave you reassurance that he was acting *for* you. This could apply nationally, or, as many psalms illustrate, at a personal level also. In the case of Ezekiel, then, the timing of these oracles against the nations is most significant. During the siege of Jerusalem, when the people of Israel were facing their darkest hour, Ezekiel adopts the more traditional voice of the prophet and proclaims, on behalf of Israel, the mighty voice of Yahweh against their enemies. Yes, they themselves stood under the terrible judgment of God, from which there would be no rescue. But no, they were not totally abandoned to their enemies. Yahweh was still their protector. Yahweh still held the ring in the great circus of nations. Their enemies would not triumph over them for ever with impunity. Such words did not yet speak of constructive restoration for the shattered people. That task lay ahead after the full effects of the catastrophe had sunk in (see chs. 34 – 37, in ch. 8 below). But these oracles against the nations did have a positive purpose in assuring the people in their utter desolation that Yahweh was neither blind nor beaten and would yet rise up against their enemies as of old. Set against the final flames of the destruction of their city, temple and land, that must have been cold comfort, but comfort nevertheless.

When we grasp, then, how these oracles functioned for the people of Israel, it helps us move towards a more fruitful understanding of what they may have to say to us today – which is, of course, our purpose in this exposition. But of all the parts of the Old Testament that people struggle to see the relevance of, the oracles against the foreign nations in the books of the prophets are probably ranked alongside the genealogies in Chronicles and the regulations on mildew in Leviticus. For some people it is hard enough to read the words of the prophets about ancient *Israel* and find spiritual food or comfort for their souls. How much less when they read words spoken against some ancient city or nation that is virtually unknown outside the world of museums of archaeology? By the end of this chapter, we should be able to suggest a number of ways in which this unpromising material actually has much of importance to say to us.

One final point to notice, before turning to the oracles themselves, is a matter of both structure and content. It is the frequency of the expression *'Then they* [or *you*] *will know that I am the* LORD.*'* This is one of the definitive phrases of Ezekiel's whole message, but it occurs with such an intensity of repetition in these chapters that it obviously must be of considerable importance to our understanding of their purpose. It also occurs twice within the 'fulcrum' text, 28:24–26. Clearly we need to recognize, then, that we are dealing not merely with prophecies that were some kind of comfort to Israel in their loss and disorientation, but with actions of God on the stage of human history that were intended to be revelatory.[8] People would see and know something about the living God through all that is spoken of here. The purpose of these oracles was not to fan Israelite nationalism, but to envisage the next stage of God's long-term mission of being universally known among the nations of the world. Although the language and atmosphere are very different, the theological agenda in relation to current historical events is the same as that expressed in the more famous words of Isaiah 40:5:

> 'And the glory of the LORD will be revealed,
> And all mankind together will see it,
> For the mouth of the LORD has spoken.'

1. Against aggression and revenge: Judah's four nearest neighbours (25:1–17)

The first four oracles are directed against the close neighbours of Judah. All four countries could be seen by the naked eye on a clear

---

[8] 'The prophet's intention went far beyond merely satisfying nationalistic longings. [The aim of these sayings] is to announce each divine intervention in international affairs as a moment of self-disclosure for Yahweh' (Block (2), p. 12).

day from a vantage point in Jerusalem itself. The order follows a geographical sequence starting to the north-east with Ammon, then moving clockwise towards Moab in the east, Edom in the south, and Philistia in the south-west. The sequence will continue to the north-west with Tyre and Sidon in chapters 26 – 28. The kingdoms of Israel and Judah had never enjoyed stable and harmonious relations with these surrounding countries, though from time to time there seems to have been some peaceful but uneasy co-existence, due either to domination by Israel or Judah, or to alliances of convenience against larger common enemies.

a. Background

In terms of the ancient traditions, the first three (Ammon, Moab and Edom) were regarded as having kinship ties with the people of Israel, going back to the mists of their ancestry. Ammon and Moab were the sons of Lot, the nephew of Abraham, but the incestuous circumstances of their birth seem to have poisoned Israel's perception of their descendants.[9] Deuteronomy records that efforts were made to avoid conflict with them at the time of Israel's progress from the wilderness towards the land of Canaan prior to the conquest, on the grounds that they had been granted their territories by Yahweh just as much as Israel would be granted theirs.[10] However, the inhospitable response of the two nations to the needs of the Israelite migrants, along with Moab's attempt to put a curse on Israel[11] and their seduction of Israelites into idolatry and immorality,[12] resulted in their being banned from ever belonging to the sacred assembly of Israel.[13]

Edom had much closer kinship ties with Israel, since the tradition traced the ancestry of both nations back to the twin sons of Isaac – Esau (the elder) and Jacob.[14] The rivalry and hatred between the brothers (albeit with later reconciliation) in the Genesis narratives formed a microcosm of the relationship between the two nations. As with Moab and Ammon, efforts were made to avoid confrontation during the march toward the promised land, with Moses even making an appeal to the obligations of kinship. This was rebuffed,

[9] Gen. 19:30–38.
[10] Deut. 2:9–12, 19–22. It is interesting and significant that Deuteronomy here attributes to Yahweh, not to other national gods, the movements and conquests of non-Israelite nations.   [11] Num. 22 – 24.   [12] Num. 25.
[13] Deut. 23:3–6. This makes the story of Ruth, a Moabitess, even more remarkable in that not only is she adopted by conversion into the faith of Israel, but she marries into an Israelite family and becomes an ancestress of king David (Ruth 4:13–22), as well as entering the genealogy of the Messiah Jesus (Matt. 1:5).
[14] Gen. 25:21–26.

however, and the enmity remained.[15] Nevertheless, Deuteronomy remarkably called on the Israelites not to 'abhor' Edomites, since they were brothers, and to grant them permitted access to the sacred assembly if requested, by the third generation. That is, the grandchildren of any Edomite who settled in Israel would be allowed to become members of the covenant community.[16] Unfortunately, this attitude was not the dominant one throughout the stormy history of the two nations.

In Ezekiel's lifetime, and especially in the decade or so leading up to the fall of Jerusalem, relationships between all the smaller states in the Palestinian region were totally dominated by the two great world powers of the day – Babylon and Egypt. Of these, the major threat was Babylon, under the dynamic leadership of the youthful Nebuchadnezzar. After the collapse of the Assyrian empire, which had dominated the ancient Near East for 150 years, Nebuchadnezzar defeated the Egyptians at the battle of Carchemish in 605 BC[17] and took control of most of the Syro-Palestinian region. The minor states then either jostled for Babylon's favour, or banded together for defensive security. Ammonites and Moabites joined with Nebuchadnezzar in his punitive attack upon Jerusalem in 598 for the rebellion of Jehoiakim.[18] This was the attack which led to the downfall of Jehoiakim, the surrender of the city by his successor Jehoiachin, and the first deportation, which included Ezekiel and his fellow exiles.

A few years later, however, after Jehoiachin had been taken into exile and replaced by Zedekiah, Zedekiah himself initiated a defensive alliance of smaller states against Babylon. This took place early in his reign (perhaps about 595 BC), and involved an international diplomatic conference in Jerusalem, attended by ambassadors from Ammon and Moab, as well as Edom, Tyre and Sidon (i.e. all the countries listed in Ezekiel's oracles, apart from the Philistines and Egypt). We read about this conference in Jeremiah 27, since Jeremiah was commanded to gatecrash it with a dramatic acted prophecy urging the assembled nations to do exactly the opposite of what they were gathered for. He told them that they should submit to Nebuchadnezzar rather than rebel against him, because

[15] Num. 20:14–21; Deut. 2:2–8.
[16] Deut. 23:7–8. Interestingly, the same command and consideration are extended to Egyptians, on the grounds of their original hospitality towards the family of Jacob during the famine. This is a rare perspective on Egypt that skips over the oppression of the later Pharaoh to the generosity of the earlier one.
[17] After this, the Egyptians were no longer a major threat (cf. 2 Kgs. 24:7), but Judah continued to look for help from them – help which never came, or was ineffective when it did (cf. Ezek. 29:6–7). [18] 2 Kgs. 24:1–2.

Nebuchadnezzar in his position of world domination was simply acting as the servant of Yahweh, God of Israel. Needless to say, this prophetic reading of the international situation did not commend itself to any of the nations – including Judah. They continued their policy of resistance.

So it seems that when Nebuchadnezzar's patience snapped and he attacked again in 588, there was some kind of alliance in place between all these states. It was probably expected that they should collectively come to the aid of any of their number who was attacked first.[19] When the attack fell upon Jerusalem, however, far from coming to her assistance, the other states reneged on whatever commitments the alliance had arranged and stood back with relief and malicious delight to see the fury of Nebuchadnezzar falling anywhere else but on themselves. This understandable self-protection was compounded, moreover, by an aggressive vengeance against Judah which, as chapter 35 shows, included some territorial opportunism, especially by the Edomites. The Edomites also seem to have been particularly treacherous to refugees from the conflict.[20] Once the beast is down, the vultures come for the pickings. The Ammonites had similarly seized territory after the fall of the northern kingdom to the Assyrians in 721 BC.[21]

b. Content

The four oracles in chapter 25 have a very similar pattern. Each nation is accused of either words of malicious gloating over Judah's misfortune, or of actual acts of revenge in which old hatreds and ancient enmities were fully vented and old scores violently settled. Each nation is then told that they themselves will suffer destruction from some other source, even if they have escaped the sword of Babylon. In the case of the Ammonites and Moabites, they will be overrun by *the people of the East* (4; sometimes translated 'Qedemites'), meaning the constantly threatening tribes of desert peoples to the east of the Jordanian rift-valley lands. The cause of the overthrow of the Edomites and Philistines is not specified.

---

[19] The choice of which capital city among the small nations Nebuchadnezzar should attack seems to be have been somewhat arbitrary. According to Ezek. 21:18–23 his decision to take the road to Jerusalem rather than to Rabbah, capital of Ammon, was made by the ancient equivalent of tossing a coin. The prophet, however, clearly understood that even such a process, which, from Nebuchadnezzar's point of view, did not in the least involve Yahweh, was actually fully under the sovereign control of Yahweh, for whom Babylon was simply an agent of his own judgment against Judah.
[20] Obad. 14.   [21] Jer. 49:1.

Compared with oracles against these same nations in other prophets,[22] these prophetic denunciations from Ezekiel are (for him) quite short, but in the heat of the circumstances, they say all that needed to be said. The oracles against Tyre and Egypt will show us Ezekiel's more characteristic poetic expansiveness. It is likely, of course, that we have here a carefully edited selection of what may have been a larger number of actual prophecies. In the case of Edom, for example, there is another, much longer, oracle which has been included in chapter 35, for thematic and theological reasons that will be explained in our next chapter.

We noted above the frequent use in these chapters of the expression *'Then they/you will know that I am the LORD.'* It occurs in three of these four oracles (25:7, 11, 17); of the Edomites it is said only that *they will know my vengeance* (14), but in the longer oracle in chapter 35, the normal 'recognition formula' (as it is known in scholarly circles) is used three times (35:4, 9, 15) in relation to Edom. The question arises: what does it mean to say that these nations will 'know that Yahweh is God', and when will they do so? More pointedly, if they were to be destroyed, who would be left to 'know Yahweh' (acutely, in 25:7)? Does it mean no more than that the nations will know Yahweh as their 'executioner' in the final act of their destruction – in the same way, say, that a murderous criminal might be said to 'know' in his final moments that justice is on the side of the police officer who lethally outguns him? Or is there any indication of some future hope of restoration for these nations implicit in the repeated affirmation that they will know that Yahweh is God? These questions will be addressed more fully at the end of the chapter. At this point, it is probably best to say that Ezekiel leaves such questions unanswered. He is totally committed to the affirmation that the nations must know that Yahweh alone is God, and that Yahweh is universally sovereign over the international world, in its past, present and future. But what exactly that will ultimately mean for the nations outside Israel he is not prepared to speculate.

Other prophets, however, did take a more explicitly optimistic view. Ironically, it is Jeremiah who surprises us with some remarkable words of future hope for those nations. It is surprising because Jeremiah actually experienced the siege and fall of Jerusalem at first hand, not from Ezekiel's anxious but safe distance, and he might therefore have been expected to take an uncompromisingly harsh line towards the treacherous surrounding nations. First of all,

---

[22] For the sake of comparison, it may be helpful to list these. *Ammon*: Jer. 49:1–6; Amos 1:13–15; *Moab*: Is. 15:1 – 16:14; Jer. 48:1–47; Amos 2:1–3; both *Moab and Ammon*: Zeph. 2:8–11; *Edom*: Is. 34:5–15; Jer. 49:7–22; Lam. 4:21–22; Amos 1:11–12; Obad.; Ps. 137:7; *the Philistines*: Is. 14:28–32; Jer. 47:1–7.

in a short passage which must date from shortly after the fall of the city,[23] he addresses the surrounding nations who had plundered Judah, and holds out to them the possibility of restoration after judgment on precisely the same conditions that he constantly held out to Judah itself: namely, repentance and the true worship of Yahweh. On such a basis they could even look forward to being 'established among my people' – a remarkable offer of inclusion which echoes the more breathtaking affirmation that Isaiah made about Assyria and Egypt.[24] Then, in his oracles against Moab and Ammon, which actually surpass Ezekiel's in severity, he concludes both of them with words of future restoration: 'Yet I will restore the fortunes of Moab in days to come';[25] 'Yet afterwards, I will restore the fortunes of the Ammonites.'[26] We need not enquire about the literal fulfilment of such hopes, since even in the case of the northern kingdom of Israel we know that prophetic words of restoration in relation to them were never literally actualized. The point is rather the twofold affirmation that, on the one hand, God would deal with all nations in both judgment and restoration in the same consistent way as he did with Israel, and on the other hand, that the hope of salvation is broadened out to include the non-Israelite nations in God's great mission of blessing all the nations of the earth.

2. Against economic arrogance: Tyre and Sidon (26:1 – 28:19)

Tyre and Sidon were the two great trading cities of the Phoenicians, on the Mediterranean coast to the north of Israel. The name *Tyre* is derived from the word for 'rock' (Hebrew *ṣôr*, Assyrian *Ṣur[r]u*), and the city was indeed substantially built on a rocky island just off the coast of Phoenicia, about 100 miles north of Jerusalem. Part of the city was on the mainland, but the island gave it not only two excellent, safe harbours for all its maritime trade, but also virtually impregnable security from invaders and attackers. The Phoenicians were a remarkable seafaring people who had established economic dominance throughout much of the eastern Mediterranean basin, and indeed had trade contacts as far as Spain, and right up as far as Brittany and south-west Britain. One of their trading colonies, Carthage (on the coast of modern Tunisia), was a major rival to the rise of Rome until its final overthrow after several costly wars.[27]

---

[23] Jer. 12:14–17.   [24] Is. 19:23–25.   [25] Jer. 48:47.   [26] Jer. 49:6.
[27] For a helpful survey of the history of Tyre in biblical times, and a study of Ezekiel's prophecies against her in comparison with Isaiah and other prophetic texts, see T. Renz, 'Proclaiming the future: history and theology in prophecies against Tyre', *TB* 51.1 (2000), pp. 17–58.

The chapters that contain Ezekiel's prophetic denunciation against Tyre can be divided in two major ways. At the broadest level, there are four movements in two balanced halves: a prophecy against the city of Tyre (26:1–21), followed by a lament for the city of Tyre (27:1–36); then a prophecy against the king of Tyre (28:1–10), followed by a lament for the king of Tyre (28:11–19). At a more detailed level, this structure is further divided by the way the first of these sections is subdivided into four oracles, which all begin with the same expression that introduces the other three main sections: *'this is what the Sovereign LORD says'*. This produces a sevenfold list of oracles all beginning with this expression: 26:1–6 (the expression comes in v. 3); 26:7–14; 26:15–18; 26:19–21; 27:1–36; 28:1–10; 28:11–19. As mentioned above, this is doubtless a deliberate piece of literary editing. It will be simpler for us to follow the broader division into four panels.

a. Tyre is doomed (26:1–21)

Ezekiel launched into this denunciation of Tyre very soon after the fall of Jerusalem.[28] The first section (26:1–6) follows on in a very similar vein from the preceding oracles against the other neighbours of Judah. Tyre is condemned for its arrogant and opportunistic response to the destruction of Jerusalem. Far from feeling any compassion for the suffering of an old ally,[29] Tyre saw only the welcome removal of a commercial competitor (26:2). The description of Jerusalem as *the gate to the nations* (2) underlines the enormous strategic importance of the city on the trade routes that flowed through Palestine from north to south. Clearly Tyre saw the destruction of Jerusalem as her own opportunity to gain control of all that trade and to add it to her own maritime revenues. Yahweh, however, proclaims a different destiny, in general terms, but with some appropriate local colour (5).

Of the *many nations* (3) that did indeed attack Tyre over the centuries, the one that Yahweh would use as the agent of his judgment in Ezekiel's own day would be Babylon, as we see in the second section of the chapter (7–17). And specifically, it would be Nebuchadnezzar,[30] fresh from his overthrow of Jerusalem, who

[28] There are problems over the date in 26:1, which may be textually damaged, since the month is missing. Probably it needs to be squared with the date in 33:21, such that this oracle was delivered after the news of the fall of Jerusalem had reached the exiles. See Block (2), p. 35.

[29] Relations between the two nations had been generally fairly harmonious, going back to early alliances and trade contracts at the time of Solomon (1 Kgs. 5).

[30] Or more correctly, in its Babylonian spelling, Nebuchadrezzar. His title *king of kings* (7) was a popular honorific description used by Assyrian kings, and also applied to the supreme god of Babylon, Marduk.

would attack and besiege them. Ezekiel prophesies that Nebuchadnezzar would besiege Tyre. He did indeed do so. The language Ezekiel uses, however, was drawn from the stereotyped language of siege warfare for mainland cities. It would have been very familiar to the exiles themselves, especially to those who had just arrived in Babylon having endured the kinds of thing Ezekiel describes here. Some of what is described would certainly have been used against the mainland settlements on Tyre's coast, but would not have been appropriate for the siege of a rocky island.

As it turned out, Nebuchadnezzar's siege of Tyre lasted for thirteen years until everybody was absolutely worn out by it – including the hapless Babylonian soldiers, who seem to have found it almost as much of a burden as the inhabitants of Tyre. Another oracle by Ezekiel, thirteen years later at the end of Nebuchadnezzar's siege of Tyre, portrays the frustration and failure of his army, and his decision to attack Egypt instead (29:17–21).[31] That later oracle faces up to the fact that the original prediction contained in this chapter had not been literally fulfilled by the Babylonians, and gives an interesting new twist to events in response to that apparent failure. Although Nebuchadnezzar did not actually capture and destroy Tyre, there seems to have been a negotiated settlement in which the city came into submission to Babylon for some time. The eventual conqueror of Tyre was Alexander the Great. In 332 BC he built a massive causeway[32] out from the coast to the island in order to press his siege and attack. The pictures of complete destruction and abandonment in the oracles of this chapter more appropriately describe the fate of the city at the hand of Alexander.

The third section of the chapter (15–18) portrays the effect that the fall of Tyre will have on the surrounding coastlands, including, of course, the settlements on the coast that were effectively part of the city. The overwhelming atmosphere in their lament (17–18) is fear: memory of the fear that Tyre itself used to impose upon all who dealt with her, and fear at the implications of her collapse. The scenario rings bells of familiarity even in our modern world. Those who wield enormous economic power, as individuals, companies or nations, have the capacity to engender great resentment and fear in others, especially if that economic power is used to bully, oppress and exploit the weaker partners in the process. But there is an even greater fear of the consequences that can follow on the collapse of a great economic power: the feud that follows the murder of a Mafia

[31] This prophecy is discussed below in the section on Ezekiel's oracles against Egypt.

[32] Alexander's causeway remains beneath the peninsula that has silted up over it in the centuries since.

godfather; the chaos and loss that follow the collapse of a giant company or bank; the apocalyptic and potentially global effects of the collapse of a whole national economy, or of a major global political power bloc. Ezekiel 26:17–18 captures very dramatically this double terror – the terror imposed by the economic tyrant in its prime, and the terror of the vacuum created by its fall. His prophecy speaks all the more powerfully when its relevance is expanded from a small corner of the ancient Mediterranean economy to the global contemporary world of international economic giants.

The fourth section of the chapter (26:19–21) describes the final engulfing of Tyre. With appropriate imagery, Ezekiel describes it as being overwhelmed by the very sea on which it had built its phenomenal power and wealth. But the sea will act on Yahweh's command. The destruction of Tyre will not be the result of impersonal economic forces, but the direct judgment of God. This affirmation is strengthened by the phrase *when I bring the ocean depths over you* (19). The word is *t^ehôm*, usually translated 'the great deep', meaning the vast, primeval ocean that was 'tamed' at creation[33] but burst forth to engulf the word in the flood until it was restrained again by God's power.[34] Tyre would not merely disappear beneath the waves; it would be swamped in the power of God's judgment and consigned to the oblivion of the pit.

b. The lament for Tyre (27:1–36)

Again, it may have been Amos who started the fashion of singing the funeral lament in advance for the targets of his prophecy. In Amos 5:1–2, he launches into a dirge for Virgin Israel, lying dead and deserted in her own land – a shocking image and a shocking method of conveying it. Many other prophets used the idea. Here Ezekiel raises it to a new poetic art form, by combining the literary form of a lament with another of his carefully crafted allegorical or metaphorical narratives. The simple device here is that he portrays Tyre as a huge sailing-ship (4–11), laden with all the multiple cargoes of its far-flung trade (12–25a). But when the ship puts out to sea, it suffers shipwreck and sinks within sight of land (25b–29). Thereupon, in a brilliant 'lament within a lament', Ezekiel portrays all the people on the shore wracked with bitter mourning and terror at the fate of such a stately vessel (30–36).

The lament begins by quoting the words of Tyre itself: *'I am perfect in beauty'* (3). Though this is not quite the same as the massive arrogance of the king of Tyre himself or of Egypt in claiming virtual divine status (28:2, 9; 29:3), it is certainly a proud

[33] Gen. 1:2.   [34] Gen. 7:11; 8:2.

241

boast. Doubtless the expression was justified; Tyre was obviously a magnificent and beautiful city. The same phrase is used to speak of the beauty of Jerusalem before its destruction.[35] But it was very much a self-made magnificence, built on the revenues of a trading empire that seemed as limitless as *the high seas* themselves (29:4). Ezekiel describes Tyre as though she were a ship, displaying in the process a quite remarkable knowledge of marine engineering and the geography of important commodities and of mercenary soldiers (10–11). Tyre was obviously well provided for and well defended. The sheer detail with which Ezekiel embellishes his basic metaphor is rich and typical of his style, and also gives a valuable glimpse into the economic, political and military world of an ancient trading empire.

The same penchant for detail pervades the next section (12–25a). Not content with merely saying that Tyre traded with many nations, Ezekiel meticulously lists not only all her trading partners but also all the commodities that were being traded. It reads like a cargo manifest, and may well have been based on one; though how Ezekiel might have come to have such a document is beyond guessing. (Maybe he had just paid very special attention as a schoolboy in geography class.) The geographical spread of the nations mentioned in his list is remarkable. It runs from Tarshish in the far west (probably Spain), through the coastlands of the Mediterranean, to Arabia and Mesopotamia. Though the list relates to the trading empire of Tyre, the literary and theological centre remains as *Judah and Israel* (17). Here, as in 5:5, Jerusalem is at 'the centre of the nations', even when another city is the primary focus of attention. There are also strong echoes of the Table of Nations in Genesis 10, with many names in common, and similar patterning of places. The cargo manifest also gives an indication of the luxurious opulence of Tyre. 'While some of the commodities were common, most were luxury wares: precious metals, jewels, special woods, ivory, choice cloth, fine carpets, perfumes, and foodstuffs ... As a ship and as a city, Tyre is filled to the brim, basking in luxury, and capitalizing on the political power that attends her economic hegemony.'[36]

Ultimately, however, Ezekiel's purpose is not to educate us about Tyre's economy, but to reinforce the message that all her wealth and power would be useless against the sovereignty of Yahweh. In human terms it was true just as much in ancient times as today that 'she who controls the economy rules the world and accumulates vast quantities of wealth'.[37] But in Yahweh's sovereign rule over the rise and fall of nations, history, as the sea is to shipwrecks, becomes the graveyard of

[35] Lam. 2:15.
[36] Block (2), p. 82. Block provides detailed analysis of the places and commodities mentioned in this fascinating list (pp. 66–82).   [37] Block (2), p. 81.

successive economic empires. So Ezekiel's extended metaphor continues with the great ship of Tyre rowing grandly out to sea, only to be suddenly swamped or capsized by a fierce storm (26). The ship sinks, with the total loss of all its fantastic merchandise, and also of all its proud human cargo – sailors, military and business-class passengers (27). All that is left is an eerie silence (32), which quickly gives way to the terrible cries of *bitter mourning* and *lament*. The cry 'Who is like Tyre?' (cf. 32) would once have been uttered in adulation, matching the boast of verse 3. Now it echoes that boast only in the terrible negation of a city sunk and silenced for ever.

c. The fall of the king of Tyre (28:1–10)

A city, and indeed a whole empire, can be metaphorically portrayed as a ship. But the reality is, of course, that all empires are built by people and ruled over by people. God's judgments in history are not directed impersonally at abstractions or structures, but at the human beings who run them and benefit from them. So here, Ezekiel turns his attention from Tyre itself to the man who ruled over it at the time – king Ethbaal II. It may be that the exiles imagined that Tyre would be able to resist Babylon and turn the tables on Nebuchadnezzar, which would of course benefit the Jewish exiles. That delusion may have grown as the siege dragged on without success. Doubtless Tyre's ability to survive the siege for so long and to continue her maritime trade must have fuelled the arrogance of the king of Tyre, which is so much in focus in this chapter. Yahweh's word through Ezekiel is that Tyre's king is destined for the same fate as his city, in spite of the vast attributes and resources that were his partly by divine gift and partly by his own magnificent achievement.

The oracle against the king of Tyre, like that against the city, falls into two sections which may have been originally separate, but effectively complement each other thematically. The first (1–10) is a classic prophetic accusation followed by predicted judgment. The accusation is stark and damning. The king is claiming divine status (*'In the pride of your heart you say, "I am a god"'*), and divine authority to dominate the world on the word of his command (*'I sit on the throne of a god'*). It is not clear whether this was an actual claim historically made by Tyre's rulers (Egyptian kings were hailed as divinities, but it was not a common cultural feature of Canaanite or Mesopotamian politics), or whether this is the prophet's own interpretation of Tyre's arrogance, as seen from Yahweh's point of view. The king of Tyre was behaving as if he had divine power and authority. He had delusions of grandeur, invincibility, omnipotence and world sovereignty. Nations bowed to his supremacy. The destiny of so many peoples seemed to hang on economic decisions made by his government. And, as it must have seemed to him, it had all come about by the appliance of science, the skilful use of technology and economic theory, and the amassing of capital and wealth through advantageous domination of world trade (3–5). What is being described in these verses may have been an ancient empire, but it has all the factors that are also to be found in the western economic hegemony of late modernity: claims to intellectual and economic superiority coupled with massive arrogance and complacency.

God's response is to remind the human occupant of the throne of Tyre of his humanity and mortality – a lesson much needed by the occupants of today's thrones and dominions. *'You are a man and not a god'* (28:2; cf. 6, 9). In spite of his enormous power, he lived as a mere man, and he would die as such. His fate would be similar to that of Jerusalem – attack and destruction by foreign enemies. He would discover, like Nebuchadnezzar, that the only eternal dominion belongs to Yahweh, and 'those who walk in pride he is able to humble'.[38] Unlike Nebuchnadnezzar, there is no indication that he would repent and acknowledge the King of heaven; his fate would be more like that of Belshazzar.[39]

d. A lament for the king of Tyre (28:11–19)

The second oracle against the king of Tyre is called a lament, but continues the theme of God's judgment and the justification for it. Here Ezekiel makes colourful poetic use of ancient traditions regarding the creation of humanity and the garden of Eden. It is important not to read his poetry here literally. Ezekiel was not affirming that his own contemporary, Ethbaal II, was actually in the garden of Eden, or that he was a kind of 'alter-Adam', or that he was literally a bejewelled guardian cherub.[40] Rather, he is using the language of the creation stories as a metaphorical device to convey the great height from which the king of Tyre would fall. His language also indicates the enormous privilege and responsibility that are entrusted to those who wield human power and authority. The implication seems to be that there was nothing intrinsically wrong in being a king, or in being wise and wealthy. These things were gifts of God, entrusted to this king, just as much as the first human beings as described in Genesis were entrusted with all the wealth of the

[38] Dan. 4:37.   [39] Dan. 5:18–31.

[40] The rich languages draws from both royal and priestly imagery as well as the creation stories. The list of precious stones has many in common with the stones that were attached to the breastpiece of Israel's high priest. Block provides detailed analysis of all the imagery in these verses (Block (2), pp. 102–115). Their overall purpose is to show the exalted status of the king, and to affirm that it was in itself legitimately granted to him by Yahweh.

earth's resources to manage and care for with delegated dominion. 'Whatever the origin of Ezekiel's image of the king of Tyre in all his glory, the announcement that Yahweh had appointed him to his position in the garden is orthodox. The sovereign Lord of history is also behind the throne of Tyre. The king is Yahweh's officially designated signet, his guardian cherub, his gardener.'[41]

But, just like the first human family in the early chapters of Genesis, the king of Tyre had succumbed to the temptations of wickedness, pride and violence. The accusations in verses 16–18 form a triplet of double sins: violence associated with the domination of trade (16); arrogance associated with aesthetic brilliance and intellectual corruption (17); and dishonest trading practice that made a mockery of religious practice (18). Again, the list has many modern counterparts. All three pairs could be pointed descriptions of the malaise of modern western domination of the world. Likewise, God's judgment echoes the narrative of the fall: expulsion from the original privileged context (16b), and the dust and ashes of final death (18b).

Ezekiel's free use here of motifs from the Genesis stories indicates that even in his day they could be understood not only as explanatory narratives for the historical origin of the human condition, but also as prototypical of subsequent human experience. That is, the narrative of the fall was not only something that happened to Adam and Eve; it describes a reality that recurs again and again in human history. The fall of a contemporary potentate in the sixth century BC could be described in terms drawn from the story of the original fall of the primeval pair. The king of Tyre was not the first example of a massive fall from grace and privilege into judgment and destruction, and he certainly will not be the last.[42] On the contrary, these chapters force us to reflect soberly on the

[41] Block (2), p. 115.
[42] From as early as the first Christian centuries, some Christian theologians have read Ezek. 28:11–19 as a description of the fall of Satan, coupling it with Isaiah's comparable taunt-song for the downfall of the king of Babylon (Is. 14:4–23), in which similar arrogance is portrayed and similar motifs and imagery employed to depict his total perdition. However, it is important to be clear that the original purpose of these texts was first of all to depict the historical demise of contemporary historical human beings. Beyond that we may certainly see in them a pattern for God's power to topple and destroy all human pretensions, including the eschatological pictures of human rebellion found in Revelation. But the Old Testament does not engage in speculation about the origins or the 'life story' of Satan, in these texts or elsewhere. The only relevant point that we may take from reflecting on such passages is that, if the fall of those created angels whom we refer to as Satan and his hosts is in some way mirrored in the fall of human beings, then it must have likewise involved an over-reaching hubris and arrogant aspirations after divine status and autonomy.

transience of even the most powerful economic empires, including that which dominates the contemporary world. Further reflections will be gathered at the end of this chapter.

Before leaving Tyre to its watery fate, it is worth noting that Ezekiel's imagery in these chapters finds its way into at least two New Testament contexts. In Acts 12:19–23 the regal arrogance of Herod is expressed in terms that undoubtedly echo the words of the king of Tyre (and significantly some people from Tyre were present at the time): 'This is the voice of a god, not of a man.' His painful demise illustrates yet again the peril of such pathetic delusions of divinity. And in Revelation 17 and 18, the imagery of Tyre's trading empire is amalgamated under the name of 'Babylon'. She is the 'great prostitute, who sits on many waters', and she is the centre of a world-dominating trade empire, which causes catastrophic alarm when it is finally destroyed. Ezekiel's legacy of prophetic insight into human megalomania and divine sovereignty lived on, and is still powerfully relevant today.

3. Against imperial delusions: Egypt (29:1 – 32:32)

The second half of Ezekiel's collection of oracles against the nations is entirely taken up with a single nation – Egypt. Once again, the material has been carefully structured into seven distinct sections, each marked off by the title *the word of the LORD came to me*, and most of them with a date as well. These sections are as follows.

a. 29:1–16 Pharaoh, crocodile of the Nile, will be slain and his country reduced

The date (1) was 7 January 587 BC, when the siege of Jerusalem had been going on for about one year already. Hophra had been Pharaoh in Egypt since 589 BC, and had expansionist plans in Palestine. His intentions and activities seem to have given hope to the people of Jerusalem (and doubtless to the exiles in Babylon also, as they heard the news) that they could yet be saved from the hand of Nebuchadnezzar by the help of Egypt. Back in Jerusalem, Jeremiah had to disillusion the people of any such hope,[43] and in exile, Ezekiel set about the same task. For both Jeremiah and Ezekiel, Nebuchadnezzar was Yahweh's 'man of the moment', the 'servant'[44] who was carrying out Yahweh's sovereign will in international history at that point. His own time would come and Babylon too would fall, but in the meantime resistance to Nebuchadnezzar was tantamount to resistance to Yahweh himself.

[43] Jer. 37:5–8; 44:30.   [44] Jer. 25:8–11; 27:1–11.

Ezekiel uses two pictures for Egypt. First, he portrays her as the great sea-monster, elsewhere named as Rahab or Leviathan – the mythological creature that represented all that opposed Yahweh. In other texts this great creature is slain by Yahweh to symbolize his victory over all the forces of chaos and evil.[45] Here, it is combined with a more local and lowly reality – the crocodiles that do actually inhabit the river Nile. So Pharaoh is portrayed as a grand crocodile basking in the Nile, imagining that the river itself is owned and indeed created by him himself. The arrogant claim *'The Nile is mine; I made it for myself'* (3; cf. 9) expresses the pride and delusions of Egyptian imperialism. Such a claim to divine status was more at home in Egypt, where the Pharaohs were acclaimed as gods, than in Tyre. Whereas the king of Tyre boasted of divinity because his empire ruled the waves, however, the Pharaoh makes a more domestic claim: ownership of the Nile. The Nile, with its annual floods and the clever complex of irrigation projects based on them, was the great source of Egypt's agricultural prosperity and the symbol of all her cultural and imperial greatness. The claim of ownership was not in itself exaggerated – the Nile did flow through Egypt and Pharaoh was king of the land it flowed through.

However, the second half of the boast (*'I made it for myself'*) goes way beyond a merely territorial claim and inflates the Pharaoh's status to that of creator. He claims to be the source of the source; the giver of the fertility that Egypt depended on. Such blasphemous arrogance sets the Pharaoh against Yahweh just as much as when a previous Pharaoh had explicitly refused to acknowledge him as God in Egypt – and paid the penalty.[46] Ezekiel prophesies that the basking lord of the Nile will be dragged out, along with masses of fish (Egypt's people), and left to die and rot in the desert (4–5). Then the true maker and owner of the Nile will be recognized for who he is (6a).

The second picture of Egypt was also a familiar local reality – the famous reeds from which papyrus was (and is still) made, and among which baby Moses was hidden. Useful for many purposes, reeds were useless as a staff or crutch. They were not only apt to shatter under stress, but the jagged edges could lacerate hands or armpits and the fall would injure your back (6b–7). Ezekiel was not the first to use this as a metaphor for the unreliability of Egypt as an ally. The Assyrian commander used it to warn the people of Judah against expecting help from that quarter during an earlier siege in the reign of Hezekiah.[47]

[45] Pss. 74:13–14; 89:9–10; Is. 27:1; 51:9; Job 7:12; 9:13; Amos 9:3.

[46] Exod. 5:1–2.

[47] Is. 36:6. Unfortunately the Assyrian went on to tell Jerusalem not to trust in Yahweh either, which was the opposite of Isaiah's own message to his people. By the time of Ezekiel, however, Yahweh himself had become the real enemy and Egypt's help would be even more useless.

So Ezekiel prophesies not only the defeat and destruction of the Pharaoh, but the humiliating reduction of Egypt's status as a great world power. The words of limited restoration (13–16) give a ray of hope for Egypt which shines much more strongly elsewhere.[48] The destruction will not be as total as it would be for some of the other nations in the list of seven.

b. Nebuchadnezzar will plunder Egypt in compensation for Tyre (29:17–21)

This short section is actually the last recorded prophecy of Ezekiel. Its date, 26 April 571 BC, places it two years after the great visions of chapters 40 – 48. It was also about sixteen years after siege of Jerusalem, in the course of which Ezekiel had made his graphic prophecy concerning the siege and capture of Tyre (ch. 26). That siege had gone on for thirteen long years, during which Nebuchadnezzar's soldiers were exhausted by the incredible feats of siege warfare that were demanded of them.[49] But they got nothing for their pains. Eventually the city surrendered, but it seems there was no destruction such as Ezekiel had predicted, and, worse (for Nebuchadnezzar and his disgruntled veterans), no booty. If some of those veterans returned to Babylon and mixed with the exiles, their frustration may have mingled with the exiles' cynicism, and it seems that questions were raised over the apparent non-fulfilment of Ezekiel's earlier prophecy. This seems to have happened to Ezekiel more than once before.[50]

So God helps Ezekiel in two ways. First, he adjusts the prophecy in a way which illustrates in a remarkable way God's own freedom over his word. Nebuchadnezzar had been carrying out God's plans, but although he had succeeded in reducing Tyre to vassal status, it had led to no reward. So he would be granted Egypt instead.[51] Secondly, this later fulfilment of the adjusted prophecy would both indicate the certainty of God's good plans for Israel (29:21a)[52] and confirm Ezekiel's status as a true prophet.[53] It is nice to think that

[48] Esp. in Is. 19:19–25.
[49] Vast quantities of rock and soil would be moved up against the defences; enormous timbers would be hauled and constructed into siege engines; the physical slog must have been intolerable for thirteen years.
[50] Ezek. 12:22, 27.   [51] Jer. 43:8–13; 46:25–26.
[52] The *horn* here is simply a symbol of the restored national strength of Israel. It does not have any messianic significance in this context.
[53] '*I will open your mouth*' (21b) is not a reference to Ezekiel's dumbness, which was long in the past by this time. The expression (lit. 'I will give you opening of the mouth') is idiomatic for having one's words confirmed and accepted without embarrassment or contradiction.

the last recorded words of God to Ezekiel, like his first, gave him reassurance of his authenticity as a true servant of God, 'so that he might share the spirit of Isa 49:4: "My cause is in Yahweh's hands and my recompense lies with my God" (cf. 1 Cor 4:1–5)'.[54]

What then are we to make of this interesting prophetic response to an unfulfilled prophecy? Clearly in Ezekiel's own day there were those who were disturbed that his words in chapter 26 had not come true in a literal way within an acceptable (to them) time frame. We need to 'be careful not to share the woodenness of Ezekiel's contemporary critics'.[55] Several thoughts may help.[56] First, Ezekiel's language (in ch. 26 as everywhere else) shares and amplifies a feature of all prophetic communication: namely, the use of rhetoric, hyperbole, and stereotyped phraseology in relation to topics such as divine judgment and military defeat. We have already noted that some of the details of siege warfare listed in chapter 26 were standard for mainland cities, but would not have featured in the siege of an island port like Tyre. Literalism generates false expectations which easily then become accusations of false prophecy. Secondly, biblical prophecy always had a conditional element. That is, predictions of future events were made in seemingly absolute terms, but when circumstances changed, or certain responses were made by human beings, God would sometimes not do what was predicted, or would do something quite different. Jonah's prediction of the destruction of Nineveh is the most obvious example. It may be that if Tyre's policy changed and they submitted to Nebuchadnezzar (who was, prophetically speaking, Yahweh's agent at the time), God waived the threat of total destruction. Thirdly, the successful siege and destruction of Tyre did eventually take place, though not by Nebuchadnezzar, but by Alexander the Great in 332 BC.

It is ironic that the book of Ezekiel contains this little passage which serves as a warning that even in Ezekiel's own day it was clear that there need not always be a literal fulfilment of the predictions he had made with his artistic poetic rhetoric. The fact that a prediction did not quickly 'come true' in the literal terms in which it was given did not mean that the prophetic word that embodied it

<hr/>

[54] Allen 29, p. 111.   [55] Allen 29, p. 110.

[56] Block discusses seven possible ways of handling the discrepancy between Ezek. 26 and 29:17–21 (Block (2), pp. 147–149). See also the discussion of the matter by Renz, op. cit., pp. 47–52. Renz says: 'It is concluded that the prophecy was not fulfilled in the way Ezekiel and his audience would have naturally expected it to be fulfilled, yet the 'failure' of the prophetic word was not as dramatic as is often claimed. The net results of Nebuchadrezzar's campaign were his control over the Levant and the end of Tyre's commercial predominance. While Tyre and Babylon must have come to some sort of understanding, in the final analysis Tyre was the loser' (p. 50).

lost all authenticity and relevance. This could not be the only test of whether or not a prophet was truly sent by God.[57] It is ironic, since Ezekiel has probably suffered posthumously more than any other prophet from the labours of those determined to take some of his later visions with utter literalism and to predict on the basis of them all kinds of scenarios for 'the end times' – some of which have manifestly failed to materialize as their proponents predicted (though not before they had made a great deal of money and popularity out of peddling them). The fault, now as among Ezekiel's exilic contemporaries, lies not with the prophet himself, but with those who misunderstand and abuse the prophetic word.

c. Egypt will experience God's judgment on 'the day of the LORD' (30:1–19)

This oracle is not dated, but most probably it comes from the same time as the surrounding ones (apart from 29:17–21): namely, the period of the siege of Jerusalem. It seems that Ezekiel had to work hard to dispel the vain hope that salvation would come for the people of Judah from the assistance of Egypt. On the contrary, Egypt was now facing the same destiny as Israel herself: namely, *the day of the LORD* (3). This expression goes a long way back in Israel's history. Originally it seems to have been a term that summarized Israel's expectations that Yahweh would defeat their enemies and raise Israel herself up in victory and salvation. Amos, however, had turned it into a day of 'darkness, not light', because Israel herself was now numbered among the enemies of Yahweh.[58] Later prophets, including Ezekiel (7:7, 10, 12, 19), followed suit and the term became synonymous with God's expected judgment.[59] The original target of the 'day', the other nations, was not forgotten, however. Obadiah thought especially of Edom;[60] Jeremiah, whom Ezekiel so often follows, applied it to Egypt.[61]

The day of the LORD for Egypt would involve comprehensive judgment which would include military defeat and plunder (3–4), the destruction of all her allies (6–9), the destruction of Pharaoh's army by Nebuchadnezzar (10–12), and the destruction of all Egypt's idols, strongholds and cities (13–19). Ezekiel does not include even the note of future hope for Egypt that he had hinted at earlier (29:13–16), which Jeremiah also shared.[62] His purpose was to demolish any expectation among his contemporaries that any help or salvation could come from Egypt. Its geopolitical power would be smashed; there was no hope from that quarter.

---

[57] Deut. 18:21–22.   [58] Amos 5:18–20.   [59] Joel 1:15; 2:1–11; Zeph. 1:7–2:3.
[60] Obad. 15.   [61] Jer. 46:10.   [62] Jer. 46:26b.

d. Nebuchadnezzar will break the arms of the Pharaoh (30:20–26)

The date of this short word, 29 April 587, probably coincided with
the arrival in Babylon of the news that the Egyptian attack on the
Babylonian forces in Judah had been successfully repelled after a
temporary respite.[63] The siege of Jerusalem went on. Did the exiles
still think that Pharaoh could try again to relieve Jerusalem? Not a
chance, says Ezekiel. He's like a soldier with a broken arm and no
sling (21). And anyway, God has not finished with him yet. Soon he
will be as useless as a soldier with two broken arms – easy prey for
the mighty sword of Babylon. Ironically, the imagery of a strong
arm with a raised sword was common as a Pharaonic symbol in
Egyptian art of the period. This particular Pharaoh, Hophra, in his
role as the incarnation of the god Horus, described himself as
'Possessor of a Strong Arm'.[64] Not any longer, says Yahweh. Big
Chief Strong Arm will become Little Chief Broken Arm. The
language is deliberately grotesque and cartoon-like, embellished with
Ezekiel's typical verbosity. The message, however, was brutal and
clear. The Egyptian hope was a fool's optimism.

e. The felling of Egypt's cosmic tree (31:1–18)

Almost as though it was too trivial to deal with such a massive topic
in the limp language of broken arms, Ezekiel reverts in his final three
oracles to the grand metaphors of ancient near-eastern mythology.
This one likens Pharaoh and all his majestic pomp and arrogance[65]
to the great cosmic tree which, in some forms of ancient mythology,
stood for the whole inhabited world. 'The motif of the cosmic tree
… presents the living world as an enormous tree with its roots in the
subterranean deep and its top in the clouds, a shelter for every living
being.'[66] In Egyptian religion, as in Hebrew symbolism, there was
also 'the tree of life', and there may be some reflections of that idea
here too (particularly noticing the references to Eden), though the
term is not used.

The comparison with *Assyria* (3) is somewhat problematic. In
answer to the question posed in verse 2b, the Hebrew text says,
'Behold Assyria …' If this is correct, then the remainder of the
chapter actually describes the glory of Assyria and its final

[63] Jer. 37:7–8.   [64] Block (2), pp. 175–176.

[65] NIV translates the Hebrew term *hāmôn* as 'his hordes', referring to his armies.
However, the term can mean 'wealth, substance, pomp', and it is probable that this
meaning is more appropriate in these oracles which focus mainly on the Pharaoh's
pride in his own vast power (of which, of course, his armies were a significant
element).

[66] Allen 29, p. 125. The same cosmic-tree symbol is found in Nebuchadnezzar's
dream, in Dan. 4.

destruction, as a sharp object lesson for Egypt regarding her own fate. Egypt is told that her own destiny will be no different from Assyria's.[67] Many scholars, however, emend the text by one letter to produce the name of a tree, the cypress, in a kind of parallelism with the cedar of Lebanon. This would make the whole chapter refer exclusively to Egypt, which may seem preferable in view of the concluding words of verse 18.[68] In either case, the prophecy relates to the doom of Egypt – either by comparison with the fate of Assyria, or by direct prediction of her own.

The first half of the poem (2–9) describes the great height, strength, security and glory of the tree. It was unequalled among all the trees *in the garden of God* (8). Again, Ezekiel resorts to the imagery associated with Eden, and does so explicitly to highlight the fact that all the greatness of an empire such as Egypt (as of Babylon, as Daniel reminded Nebuchadnezzar),[69] came from the endowment of Yahweh himself: '*I made it beautiful with abundant branches, the envy of all the trees in Eden in the garden of God*' (9). Power and empire are not intrinsically evil; they fall legitimately within the sovereign permission of the Lord of history. It is the fact of human corruption and abuse of power which leads to hubris and nemesis. And that indeed is the fate of this imperial tree.

So the second half of the poem (10–18) describes how the tree's arrogance about its height (10) led to its being cut down, to sprawl over a vast area. The human reference point of the analogy comes to the fore as the final destiny of the tree is that it sinks to the underworld, to a place of ignominy and shame. The splendour that was Egypt is laid low. The admiring question of verse 2 becomes the astonished question of verse 18. From majesty to the mire; from the heights of perfection to the pit of hell. 'The incomparable finally meets his match in the one who has power of life and death. The greatest of trees in God's garden has the gardener to answer to.'[70]

f. The destruction of the Egyptian monster (32:1–16)

Dated 3 March 585 BC, this oracle comes some time after the news of the final fall of Jerusalem to Nebuchadnezzar had already reached the exiles. There was no longer any hope of deliverance coming from Egypt. All that was left was to signal the final demise of that great power. Starting with the comparison of Egypt to *a lion among the*

---

[67] Thus NIV, NRSV, NKJV, NLT. Also Block (2), p. 184.

[68] Thus, e.g., Zimmerli, *Ezekiel 2*, p. 149; Eichrodt, pp. 422–423; Allen 29, p. 122.

[69] Dan. 2:36–38; 4:20–22. Ironically, Nebuchadnezzar, as the great cosmic tree in his own dream, was to suffer the same fate as he himself had inflicted on Assyria and Egypt.   [70] Allen 29, p. 127.

nations, Ezekiel quickly reverts to the imagery already used in 29:3–5 and virtually republishes that oracle with some additional graphics. Egypt, the great mythological sea-monster, will be hunted down, netted and hauled out to provide food for scavenging birds and beasts. The cosmic language (32:7–10) signifies the cataclysmic effects of the destruction of this great power among the rest of the nations. There is something about the description that raises it beyond its own historical context. Yes, Egypt was conquered by Babylon on the scene of early sixth-century international politics. But, like the fall of many other empires during and after biblical times, the event foreshadowed the ultimate collapse of all vaunted human empires before the sovereignty of Yahweh. For it was Yahweh, wielding the sword of Nebuchadnezzar, who would *shatter the pride of Egypt* (12), just as, within two generations, he would wield the sword of Cyrus to shatter the pride of Babylon. And ultimately all such human pride will fall before the Lord of history.

> The LORD Almighty has a day in store
>   for all the proud and lofty,
>   for all that is exalted
>   (and they will be humbled),
> for all the cedars in Lebanan, tall and lofty,
>   and all the oaks of Bashan,
> for all the towering mountains
>   and all the high hills,
> for every lofty tower
>   and every fortified wall,
> for every trading ship
>   and every stately vessel.
> The arrogance of man will be brought low
>   and the pride of men humbled;
> the LORD alone will be exalted in that day,
>   and the idols will totally disappear.[71]

g. Pharaoh and his army descend to the underworld (32:17–32)

Two weeks later, on 17 March 585, Ezekiel conducted the funeral rites of Egypt and brought his remarkable series of oracles against that one state to a climactic ending. Basically, God instructs Ezekiel to bury Egypt (18), with words of committal that unflatteringly levelled all their self-exaltation (19). But in the thinking of the ancient world,

[71] Is. 2:12–18.

shared at least in a metaphorical sense by Israel,[72] the grave was not oblivion. It was the entrance to that murky underworld of the dead, a place where the dead 'live on' in a shadowy existence that in some way reflects not just their status in life, but also the manner of their death and especially their burial (or lack of it). So Ezekiel, with that unfailing love of detailed description, scorns the thought of merely reporting that Pharaoh and his proud armies are dead and buried. No, with the same secret video camera that pierced the darkness of the temple in his visionary tour (ch. 8) he will take us on a guided tour of the remoter regions of Sheol (*the grave*) and point out a few of the more exotic inhabitants – just so that we don't imagine Pharaoh being lonely. When the roll is called down yonder, the most significant name on the list is undoubtedly Assyria (22–23). It was still a very fresh memory in Ezekiel's own generation that Assyria *had spread terror in the land of the living*. But that's all it was now – a memory. Assyria was dead and buried. The message was ominously clear: if that was the fate of proud Assyria, nothing better could be expected for Egypt – or any of Assyria's successors.[73] Not even the honourable burial of great warriors (27) will be accorded to them. They will share the eternal shame of the uncircumcised and the unburied. The only consolation Pharaoh and his armies will have is that they are not alone in the pit. What a place, where the only comfort is the company of the already dead![74]

[72] It is important to recognize the poetic genre of this oracle and its rhetorical use of imagination. It should not be treated as if it were intended to offer doctrinal teaching on the nature of the afterlife or the geography of hell. 'This is not the chapter to turn to if one wishes to understand the Bible's teaching about the afterlife.' Taylor, p. 210.

[73] This unflattering description of Assyria in the underworld may support the view that 'Consider Assyria' is the correct reading at 31:3.

[74] There is a possibility that 32:31 means that Pharaoh will *repent* for all the death he has caused to his soldiers through his arrogant adventures. The Hebrew *nāḥam* could certainly mean that. It may seem unlikely, but Walter Brueggemann has given his support to this reading of the verse, first proposed by Ellen Davis. 'On this reading … pharaoh will at long last, at the eleventh hour, repent and become a willing vassal of Yahweh. If this reading can be accepted (and I find it persuasive), the brutal, sad tale of Egypt unexpectedly portrays even Egypt coming, at the last moment, out of the fissure of devastating punishment to new life with Yahweh.' Brueggemann, *Theology of the Old Testament*, p. 506. If this were the case, it would be the only instance in the whole book of Ezekiel of any of the nations 'knowing God' in any positive sense of repentance and restoration (a prospect which is of course envisaged in other prophets – esp. Is. 19:19–25). That Pharaoh's putative repentance is located in the shadowy post-mortem world of the grave would seem to diminish any significance we could read into it. More likely the use of *nāḥam* here means either (a) that Pharaoh is consigned to 'an eternally unassuaged sorrow over the lives he sacrificed so vaingloriously' (J. A. Motyer in a private communication), or (b) that Pharaoh is consoled by the presence of all the other armies of defunct powers. His only comfort is that he is not alone in the pit.

Finally, as we leave Pharaoh in his dismal new residence, we may notice how climactic it is that this whole section of oracles against the nations leads to this picture of death and descent into the grave and the awful world of the dead. It provides a stark and vivid memory to carry forward into the next section of the book, which will lead our imagination through various scenes of restoration and renewal, climaxing in the glorious picture of resurrection as Ezekiel witnesses the bones of an army long dead coming back to life (37:1–14). Israel will be restored from the grave of exile to their own land, the land of the living. This will be the theme of our next chapter.

4. God and the nations: the message

However, before we leave the grave and head towards the resurrection in chapter 37, we should pause to reflect on what we have been reading hitherto. In the introduction to this chapter we raised the hope that these ancient oracles against foreign nations would have something of importance to say to us today. Having surveyed the material, it is now time to see if that promise can be kept. Three dimensions of the message of these chapters seem to stand out – especially when they are set alongside the challenge of similar material in other prophetic books. First, they unquestionably affirm the sovereignty of Yahweh as God in the midst of the ebb and flow of international affairs. Secondly, they equally clearly portray the transience of all human power and glory, whether political, military or economic. And thirdly, they repeatedly affirm that the goal of all God's action is that the nations will know him, Yahweh, to be God. Ezekiel would have endorsed Habakkuk's famous vision that 'the earth will be filled with the knowledge of the glory of the LORD, as the waters cover the sea'.[75] Let us then turn to observe the sovereignty of God in the midst of human history; the transience of empires as the pattern of human history; and the knowledge of God as the goal of God's mission.

a. The sovereignty of God in the midst of human history

The overwhelming message of these chapters is the same as the one which Daniel forcibly impressed upon Nebuchadnezzar:

> The Most High is sovereign over the kingdoms of men and gives them to anyone he wishes ...

[75] Hab. 2:14.

> His dominion is an eternal dominion;
>   his kingdom endures from generation to generation.
> All the peoples of the earth
>   are regarded as nothing.
> He does as he pleases
>   with the powers of heaven
>   and the peoples of the earth.
> No-one can hold back his hand
>   or say to him: 'What have you done?'[76]

Or in the punchier language of his direct address to the then most powerful man on earth: 'Heaven rules.'[77] OK?

There are three aspects of this sovereignty of Yahweh in the international arena that are worth observing: its universality, its focus and its consistency.

i. The universality of God's sovereignty

First, Ezekiel, along with all the other prophets, affirms that Yahweh is universally sovereign over the affairs of the nations of the world *in general*. Yahweh is not a local god whose power extends only over his own people. Nor is he merely a local god who happens to be the neighbourhood bully – that is, capable of pushing his weight around among the nations that had dealings with Israel. The prophets declare that the whole world of international history and exchange is actually under the sovereign direction of Yahweh the God of Israel. His reign is universal.

This affirmation has a long history in Israel. As early as the exodus it was being proclaimed in triumphant defiance of the authority of Pharaoh.[78] In the context of Israel's impending conquest of Canaan, Deuteronomy affirmed, almost in passing, that it was Yahweh himself who had moved nations around on the chessboard of middle-eastern history long before Israel even came on the scene at all.[79] The psalmists likewise celebrate Yahweh's universal reign over the nations, whether as a matter of warning and judgment[80] or of praise and rejoicing.[81] Ezekiel makes the point through oracles which affirm Yahweh's involvement in the plans and actions of 'third-party' nations – with no direct connection with the history of Israel itself. Nebuchadnezzar's siege of Tyre, for example, did not directly impinge on God's dealings with Israel (who were already in

---

[76] Dan. 4:17, 34–35.   [77] Dan. 4:26.   [78] Exod. 15:18.
[79] Deut. 2:5, 9–12, 19–23. For comment on the universal implications of these verses (which the NIV puts in parenthesis!), see C. J. H. Wright, *Deuteronomy*, New International Biblical Commentary (Peabody: Hendrikson, Carlisle: Paternoster, 1996), pp. 35–37.   [80] Pss. 2; 33:8–11; 99:1–3.   [81] Pss. 47:7–9; 67; 96.

exile). Yet it is clearly described as happening on Yahweh's authority and for his purposes. Likewise, after the thirteen somewhat fruitless years of that siege, Ezekiel portrays Nebuchadnezzar as turning his attention to Egypt, but his conquest of that country is described as Yahweh's compensation gift to him (29:17–20). That was hardly how the matter was viewed by Nebuchadnezzar, or indeed by the Egyptians, but it is the prophetic interpretation of international affairs. Yahweh is in control.

This is a perspective of biblical faith that we need to reaffirm in our modern world. It is easily open to misrepresentation. To say that God is sovereign over world history does not mean that he directly wills everything in the sense that 'that is exactly what God wanted to happen'. Human beings make their own plans and act out of the evil of their own hearts, and we know from Scripture that God is as grieved and angry as we are – more so, rather – at the depths and extent of human evil on the international stage. Nor does it amount to sheer fatalism, as though all events were manipulated by the strings of a divine puppeteer. The Bible gives full scope to the reality of human freedom and responsibility. People and nations plan what they plan and do what they do, and will one day give account to God for the exercise of that freedom. Yet behind and above all that, the Bible unquestionably affirms that there is a mysterious freedom and sovereignty of the creator of the universe at work. His purposes will not ultimately be defeated, and even the evil that people do can be turned to good ends by his sovereign power.

ii. The focus of God's sovereignty
Secondly, again in company with the rest of the prophets, Ezekiel affirms that Yahweh is sovereign over international history with particular relevance to how events impinge upon his purposes *in and through Israel*. The scope of Yahweh's sovereignty is universal, but its focus is on Israel. In this section of chapters, the thrust of this is primarily defensive: Yahweh will defend Israel from the hatred and attacks of her enemies (esp. chs. 25 and 35). However, already we know from the first half of the book that Yahweh could also use the nations as the implements of his judgment upon Israel. This was the historic role of Babylon. Babylon was the sword in the hand of Yahweh (graphically depicted in ch. 21, and in acted symbolism in Ezekiel's early barber-shop mime in 5:1–4); just as Isaiah had portrayed Assyria as a razor or a rod in the hand of Yahweh in an earlier generation.[82] So, whether positively or negatively, God's involvement in the plans and actions of the nations is woven into his

[82] Is. 7:20; 10:5.

own plan and action in the story of Israel, his covenant people. His international sovereignty is exercised in relation to his redemptive purposes through this people. Again, this is a perspective that goes a long way back, to the patriarchal stories of Abraham among the surrounding nations, to the great conflict between Yahweh and the Pharaoh at the time of the exodus,[83] to the invasion of Canaan.[84] An ancient poem in Deuteronomy portrays Yahweh as the Most High God, sovereign over the disposition of all nations on earth, yet at the same time choosing to have a special family relationship (inheritance) with Israel.[85]

The clearest articulation of this prophetic understanding of contemporary history (namely, that Yahweh's sovereign control of international history was being exercised in relation to his purposes for his covenant people) is found in Isaiah 40 – 55 – chapters which, like Ezekiel, addressed the situation of the Babylonian exiles. They envisage the rise of Cyrus, the energetic king who united the Medes and the Persians to establish a new empire that would defeat Babylon and release many captive peoples, including the Jewish exiles. But the whole series of world-changing events is ascribed to the plan and control of Yahweh himself. The astonishing paradox of these chapters is that it is the God of one of the tiny captured peoples – the people who in Ezekiel's generation had been dragged off into degrading exile and slavery – who proclaims that he is in complete charge of the seismic shifts of the great empires which appeared to control the destiny of the little peoples.

> He sits enthroned above the circle of the earth,
>   and its people are like grasshoppers ...
> He brings princes to naught
>   and reduces the rulers of this world to nothing.
> No sooner are they planted,
>   no sooner are they sown,
>   no sooner do they take root in the ground,
> than he blows on them and they wither,
>   and a whirlwind sweeps them away like chaff.[86]

Thus Cyrus of Persia has risen to the dizzy heights of his military conquests entirely by the permission and power of Yahweh, God of Israel.[87] In fact, he has been led there by the hand.

> 'This is what the LORD says to his anointed,
>   to Cyrus, whose right hand I take hold of

[83] Cf. esp. the affirmations made in Exod. 9:14–16.   [84] Exod. 15:13–18.
[85] Deut. 32:8–9.   [86] Is. 40:22–24.   [87] Is. 41:2–4, 25.

to subdue nations before him
　and to strip kings of their armour,
to open doors before him
　so that gates will not be shut:
I will go before you ...[88]

But the controlling purpose of Yahweh's instrumental
involvement with Cyrus is entirely centred on the future of Israel,
for it would be Cyrus who would proclaim freedom for the captives
and enable them to return and rebuild Jerusalem and the temple.[89]

For the sake of Jacob my servant,
　of Israel my chosen,
I summon you by name
　and bestow on you a title of honour,
　though you do not acknowledge me.[90]

That in turn, however, reminds us that everything God did in and
for Israel was ultimately related to his own name and glory among
the nations. In fact, Israel only existed at all because of God's
ultimate purpose, declared to Abraham, to bring blessing to all
nations. Thus the irony of God's raising of Cyrus to world
dominance and great fame is that, at the end of the day, the world
would know the name, not of Cyrus, but of Yahweh:

I will strengthen you [Cyrus],
　though you have not acknowledged me,
so that from the rising of the sun
　to the place of its setting
men may know there is none beside me.
I am the LORD, and there is no other.[91]

Now, although we have strayed from Ezekiel somewhat, there is
a dynamic at work here which is entirely consistent with the way
Ezekiel handles the matter of Yahweh's glory among the nations. In
36:16–38 he presents Yahweh as struggling with a terrible dilemma.
On the one hand, the sin of Israel was such that he was left with no
alternative but to punish them and scatter them among the nations
in exile. Yet, on the other hand, the effect of that was to bring
disgrace on his own reputation among those very nations. Thus his
decision to restore Israel and gather them back from the nations
would ultimately be for the sake of his own reputation among the

[88] Is. 45:1–2.　　[89] Is. 44:28.　　[90] Is. 45:4.　　[91] Is. 45:5–6.

nations – not merely for Israel's good. 'It is not for your sake, O house of Israel, that I am going to do these things, but for the sake of my holy name, which you have profaned among the nations where you have gone (36:22).[92] The nations must come to know the glory of Yahweh too, and understand that he alone is the true and living God. That is the long-range purpose behind God's restoration of his people.

The prophets were thus aware of two complementary truths. On the one hand, whatever Yahweh did among the nations was ultimately for the benefit of Israel, his covenant people. Yet on the other hand, what Yahweh did for Israel was ultimately for the benefit of the nations. This double reality is significant, for it preserves the universality of God's sovereignty over all nations, while recognizing the particularity of his unique relationship with Israel. God's providential reign over the nations is related to his redemptive purpose for his people; but his redemptive work among his people is related to his missionary purpose among the nations. The two cannot be separated. They are both beautifully combined in the way Psalm 67 takes the Aaronic blessing of God on Israel and extends it to include the nations, in the context of God's righteous rule over the nations.

> May God be gracious to us and bless us
> and make his face shine upon us …
> God will bless us,
> and all the ends of the earth will fear him.[93]

In the same way, assuming that the God of Isaiah and Ezekiel is still our God and is still on the throne of the universe, we need to look at the world of international affairs and seek to discern what God is doing that impinges upon the life and witness of his people, the church. At the same time, we need to be asking whether the church, in its life and witness, is truly engaging in its biblical mission of bringing the blessing of God to the nations. God runs the world for the sake of the church;[94] God calls the church for the sake of the world. We need to fix our theology and our mission to both poles of this biblical dynamic.

iii. The consistency of God's sovereignty

Thirdly, when we begin to appreciate the balance of these two perspectives, we also come to recognize God's moral consistency in the way he deals both with the nations and with Israel. We pointed

---

[92] See the next chapter for full discussion of this passage.   [93] Ps. 67:1, 7.
[94] Cf. Eph. 1:21–22, speaking of the cosmic dominion of Christ exercised 'for the church'.

out in the introduction to this chapter that the oracles against the
nations are very similar in language, structure and concepts to the
oracles against Israel. We also noted that this was not because
the oracles against the nations were simply reusing the model of the
oracles against Israel, but rather the other way round. If Israel
behaved like an enemy of Yahweh, in her rebelliousness,
unfaithfulness and covenant disloyalty, then she would find herself
spoken to and treated as such. Yet again, we have to say that this
message was already in its old age by the time of Ezekiel. Israel was
warned from the beginning that if they went the way of the
Canaanites, then God would deal with them in the same way –
eviction. The land itself would vomit the Israelites out, with the same
retching disgust as it had vomited out the Canaanites.[95]

In Ezekiel the sins for which the nations fall under God's
judgment are similar to those frequently listed for Israel – pride,
violence, dishonesty, and blasphemous self-aggrandizement (e.g.
28:5, 16–18; 29:3, 9; 31:10). But if anything, the judgment on Israel
was all the more severe, and the description of their sin all the more
specific, because of the immense privilege they had of being the
beneficiaries of Yahweh's saving power, and of being entrusted with
the revelation of Yahweh's covenant demands. As we have already
seen, Ezekiel did not flinch from telling Israel, and especially
Jerusalem, that it was even worse than the worst of the pagan
nations, failing to live even by their standards, let alone by the
righteous standards of Yahweh's law. Like Amos, he insisted that
Israel's unique status as God's elect people, far from granting them
some kind of privileged immunity from judgment, exposed them all
the more to God's punishment.[96] So we must avoid any idea of
divine favouritism in our understanding of the covenant relationship
between God and Israel and its implications for other nations.

But if God could punish Israel just as he punished the nations,
conversely also he could bring blessing and hope to the nations, just
as he did redemptively for Israel. Whether or not *Ezekiel* envisaged
such a future for the nations is a matter we must look at in a
moment. But certainly his contemporary Jeremiah held out such
hope, offering the possibility of restoration on the same basis
(repentance and true worship of Yahweh) as he held it out to
wayward Israel.[97] Isaiah went further still, with words of
eschatological hope and salvation even for Egypt and Assyria,[98] and
calling on 'the ends of the earth' to turn to Yahweh and be saved.[99]
Even for Ezekiel, the least we can say is that he portrays Yahweh as
the God who rules with sovereign freedom and utterly righteous

[95] Lev. 18:24–28; 20:23.   [96] Amos 3:1–2.   [97] Jer. 12:14–17.
[98] Is. 19:19–25.   [99] Is. 45:22–23.

consistency over all nations on earth. His international agenda is connected to the destiny of Israel, but certainly not limited nor bound to it in some ethnocentric way. Ezekiel's little collection of 'oracles against the nations' reminds us of the very important truth: 'our God reigns'.

Walter Brueggemann, in a chapter which, unusually for most theologies of the Old Testament, explores the role of 'The nations as Yahweh's partner', concludes with the following balanced insight. He rightly says that we need to correct

> ... the easy impression that the Old Testament is singularly preoccupied with Yahweh's powerful commitment to Israel. To a great extent it is true that Israel is the singular topic of Yahweh's sovereignty and freedom ... But this claim of centrality for Israel needs to be sharply qualified. Israel does not live in a sociopolitical vacuum. Israel is always in the presence of more powerful nations that impinge on Israel's life in uninvited ways. Moreover, Yahweh has a rich field of engagement with the nations. Some of that engagement is conditioned by the centrality of Israel in this articulation of world history, but much of it is not. According to this testimony, Yahweh's concern with the nations is not shaped or determined simply by the needs and propensities of Israel. Yahweh has Yahweh's own life to live, and it will not be monopolized by Israel.[100]

It seems that the church sometimes needs to be reminded that we worship a God whose interests do not stop, as ours are prone to, at the church door, and whose actions in the world are not determined solely by an ecclesiastical agenda. We need, perhaps to ponder more the implications of the astonishing claim that 'The *earth* is the LORD's',[101] and to remind ourselves that 'God so loved *the world* that he gave his one and only Son ...'[102]

b. The transience of empires as the pattern of human history

'"Who was ever silenced like Tyre ..." shattered by the sea in the depths of the waters' (27:32). 'Dark will be the day ... when I break the yoke of Egypt; there her proud strength will come to an end' (30:18). Ezekiel's portrayal of the fall of these two massive world powers of his day is graphic and sometimes gruesome. His words must also have seemed, at the time, from another planet. We should not forget that both Tyre and Egypt were enormously powerful,

---

[100] Brueggemann, *Theology of the Old Testament*, p. 525.
[101] Ps. 24:1.   [102] John 3:16.

wealthy and influential in the world of Ezekiel's contemporaries. Who could ever have imagined with any claim to be taken seriously that one day Tyre, the greatest maritime trading empire of the Mediterranean world, would be a reduced to a fish market? Who would have believed Ezekiel's prediction that the ancient might of Pharaonic Egypt would one day become 'a lowly kingdom' that would 'never again rule over the nations'? Probably no more than we would have believed at the height of the Cold War that the whole Soviet Union would disintegrate and Russia become a relatively minor player in world affairs; no more than we could envisage the United States of America becoming a Third World country in the twenty-first century. Yet history has vindicated Ezekiel, and the other prophets. The great empires that so dominated the world of their day all came and went, rose and fell, like great waves of the ocean that roll on for miles, but ultimately crash into pathetic little ripples on the shore.

Ezekiel also expresses in his handling of Tyre and Egypt a conviction which is found elsewhere in the prophets: namely, that the rise and fall of empires is a pattern of history directly under the control of God. In both cases, Ezekiel points out that it was God himself who bestowed on these nations their endowments of strength, wisdom and beauty – using, as we saw, the metaphors of Eden to do so (28:11–15; 31:9). There is a positive aspect to human political authority which must be recognized. Daniel acknowledged before Nebuchadnezzar that the king's great power and world dominance at the time was his by the gift and authorization of God.[103] The same perspective was affirmed by Jeremiah.[104] And of course, it is one of the lenses through which the New Testament views the political might of Rome.[105] Power, even great imperial power, can be exercised with God's authority and the legitimacy that comes from it. But not without constraints, and not for ever.

Returning to Tyre and Egypt, Ezekiel describes how they fell from the state of God's blessing and authorization through a combination of arrogance, idolatry, oppression and injustice. They fell under God's judgment and spectacularly disintegrated, like the house built on sand under the onslaught of the storm. No human empire lasts for ever. In biblical history the sequence of Assyria, Babylon, Persia, Greece and Rome is well known. The last four are most probably the sequence envisaged in Daniel's interpretation of Nebuchadnezzar's dream statue with its four metals, and in his own vision of the four beasts from the sea.[106] In both chapters, the

[103] Dan. 2:37; 4:17; etc.   [104] Jer. 27:6–7.   [105] Rom. 13:1–7.   [106] Dan. 2; 7.

successive empires come and go, with authority given from the Most High God, but at the end of the day, it is the kingdom of God alone which is eternal, represented in Daniel's vision by the stone, the saints and the Son of Man.

Walter Brueggemann again helpfully analyses the prophetic interpretation of the rise and fall of the nations, especially the great superpowers. After a survey of what the prophets had to say about Egypt, Assyria, Babylon and Persia, he proposes a four-phase schema which can be seen in each case (though incompletely for Persia):

Yahweh's mandate. Yahweh intends that there should be world powers, and that these world powers should indeed govern, but govern within the bounds of Yahweh's mandate ... The Old Testament witness is explicit in voicing Yahweh's powerful, positive interest in the public process.

Temptation to absolutize power. The seduction to autonomy, which is assigned in this testimony to the first three superpowers [Egypt, Assyria, Babylon], is the temptation to absolutize power that appears to be absolute but is not.

Decisive break in power. In the case of the first three superpowers we have considered, there is a decisive break in their power. In world history great kingdoms rise and fall. What is noteworthy in this testimony ... is that no explanation for the fall of great powers is credited except the governance of Yahweh. Yahweh's sovereignty is partly raw, unchallengeable authority, partly devotion to Israel, and partly intolerance of arrogant injustice ... No power can live defiantly in the face of Yahweh's sovereignty.

Hope for recovery. The recovery of lost power is characteristically an act of hope, not accomplished yet in reportable history. This act of hope, in the largest horizon of world history, is closely parallel to the hope of Israel that is mostly detained and not yet actualized ... Yahweh is the one who intends well-being for all the nations, including the ones formerly defiant and condemned.[107]

It is questionable whether the fourth phase – recovery and hope for the nations – is to be found in Ezekiel (see below), but certainly the first three phases are very clear. The economic power of Tyre and the imperialistic power of Egypt are transient. The Lord gives and

---

[107] Brueggemann, *Theology of the Old Testament*, pp. 518–522.

the Lord takes away. Neither diamonds nor dictators are for ever.

Where, then, in our contemporary world, should such a message give us food for thought? At the level of international politics and the ebb and flow of superpowers, it really needs no elaboration. Within the living memory of those whose lives have spanned much of the twentieth century but survived into the twenty-first, we have seen the amazing demise of the British Empire, on which the sun never set (as they said) as it ruled over a quarter of the world's population; the rise and fall of a Euro-Asian Communist empire; the rise and fall of Germany's Third Reich and of Japan's imperial attempt to dominate Asia and the Pacific; and the ending of several minor dictatorships in Spain, Portugal, Albania and elsewhere; and the dismantling of the monster of apartheid in South Africa. Some of these were predictable; others as surprising as anything in the biblical record.

Reflection on Tyre, however, should direct our thoughts beyond the world of nation states and geopolitical superpowers. The power of Tyre was the power of its wealth and its dominance of regional trade. Ezekiel's metaphor is very telling. Tyre's ship of state was not a warship, but a merchant ship. She did not need to conquer other nations and subdue them by military might. She ruled the waves through economic imperialism. Today, of course, the whole map of world trade is dominated by a very few mammoth players: the USA, the European Union, and some East Asian economies. But increasingly, economic dominance is moving beyond countries and being achieved by companies, some of them controlled by incredibly wealthy individuals who, like the king of Tyre, sit atop pyramids of enormous economic power.[108]

If Ezekiel were bringing his prophetic challenge into the world of the early twenty-first century, what would be the equivalent of his Tyre? It is more likely that it would be a transnational corporation, or brand name, than that it would be any single nation state. For the fact is that in the globalized economic world of hypermodernity, real power has shifted from national political communities to transnational economic giants, frighteningly free from serious political, democratic or moral constraints. 'It is important to remember that of the one hundred largest economies in the world today, fifty-one are corporations. General Motors is bigger than Denmark, Ford than South Africa and Toyota than Norway. Wal-Mart by itself is larger

---

[108] In a recent broadcast on the BBC, Charles Handy pointed out that Cuba is one of the last remaining countries with a centrally controlled economy and a single dictator at the top. But there are seventy large companies in the world today which are financially larger than the total economic output of Cuba, and they also have centrally controlled economies and a single chief executive at the top.

than 161 countries.'[109] The merger of two massive media and Internet companies (Time-Warner and AOL) right at the turn of the twenty-first century produced a gigantic corporation with more economic muscle than several European countries.

The power wielded by such giants is staggering, and certainly qualifies for inclusion among those more-than-human 'principalities and powers' which the Bible identifies as being at work in the world of human history. The social and 'spiritual' power and influence of 'brands' is incalculable, as corporations vie to achieve total global saturation for their designer products. Names like McDonald's, Coke, Nike and Microsoft straddle the globe, not only providing a product but defining a lifestyle, a culture, a clutch of assumed values. Designer labels seduce the young and impoverish their parents. Increasing swathes of the world's economies seem to be controlled by fewer and fewer powerful players, including the dominance in global food supply of large agribusinesses such as Conagra and Monsanto, and the relentless domination of news, information and entertainment media by giants such as Rupert Murdoch's News International, Time-Warner, Disney and Bertelsmann. In addition to the frightening levels of domination and control of so much of the global economy by these giants, there is the sheer obscenity of the wealth of some of the individuals seated on their shoulders. That six of the world's richest men should be individually wealthier than ten of the world's poorest countries put together is a gruesome, distorted reality that would surely have stirred the anger and rhetoric of Ezekiel.[110]

But the message of Ezekiel, as of all the prophets, is: they will not last for ever. This fundamental biblical pattern in the history of human power is both a comfort and a warning and a terrible prospect either way. For the exiles trapped in Babylon it was comforting to be told – even at the height of Babylon's power – that Babylon's time would come.[111] Today, also, the collapse of

---

[109] Tom Sine, *Mustard Seed versus McWorld: Reinventing Christian Life and Mission for a New Millennium* (Crowborough: Monarch, 1999), p. 109. This book is a wide-ranging and staggering exposure of the effects of globalization in almost all areas of life. Its analysis of the social, political, economic and technological revolutions we are living through is sharp and instructive, offering much supporting information to our attempt to bring out the relevance for our own day of Ezekiel's ancient critique of the economic and political power games of his world.

[110] One wonders what invective he might have poured over the fact that each tile in Bill Gates's kitchen costs double the average annual income of people in Africa's poorest countries.

[111] It is noticeable that Ezekiel himself does not include Babylon in his oracles. Yet he must have known of the fierce rhetoric of Jeremiah, predicting Babylon's ignominious fall; he may well have read the letter we now have in Jer. 50 – 51, before it was symbolically weighted with a stone and thrown in the Euphrates to sink like Babylon itself. Perhaps what was safe for Jeremiah to say from the distance of

communism and apartheid gives hope to those still trapped in oppressive regimes. But Ezekiel's predictions also provided a warning for the exiles not to be tempted to put their faith in any other world power, such as Egypt, since all hope placed there would be doomed to disillusion and betrayal. Likewise, today, those whose ultimate faith is placed in the gods of globalized materialism will find that, like all false gods, they will fail and leave their worshippers defenceless. And either way, as Ezekiel so graphically depicted in the case of Tyre, when any of these great economic or political powers collapse, the fallout is devastating. We are alternately assailed by prophets of permanent boom and prophets of a coming world recession. Whichever it may be, Ezekiel's message suggests that as we begin the twenty-first century, the Tyres which rule the waves of world trade, or the Egypts which arrogantly believe they are the makers of their own Nile, will not be there at the end of it.

Yet again, Brueggemann offers a sharp contemporary critique in the light of the Old Testament's portrayal of Yahweh's relentless demand for justice in a world of terror, intimidation and brutality. Reflecting this time on his own home culture in North America, he offers this thought:

> Most readers of this exposition of Old Testament theology will be citizens of the United States, 'the last superpower,' which has survived and prospered until the very 'End of History.'[112] I intend that my analysis of Yahweh and the nations should finally settle in the presence of the United States, which has no viable competitor for power, and which is in an economic, military position to imagine, like Egypt, that it produces its own Nile. The good news is that there is a residue of moral awareness in the ethos of the United States. The threat to that good news is that economic ideology and military self-justification tend easily and eagerly to override that residue of awareness. In such a situation one may wonder: Have we arrived at last at a nation-state that is finally immune to this witness of metapolitics,[113] so that we come to a point in which Israel's witness is seen to be outmoded or

---

Jerusalem would have been too politically dangerous for Ezekiel to proclaim publicly among the captive community in Babylon itself in the early years of their exile.

[112] This term refers to the claim made by Francis Fukuyama that, with the ending of the Cold War, the defeat of communism and triumph of free-market capitalist liberal democracy, we have come to the end of history: *The End of History and the Last Man* (New York: Free Press, 1992).

[113] Brueggemann means by this term the overruling sovereign power of God in human affairs – the 'resilient intention of Yahweh for justice in the world'.

self-deceived rhetoric? *Or is the United States, like every super-power before it, on notice?*[114]

A chilling question to ponder, but one which Ezekiel would probably also have asked – and perhaps disconcertingly answered.

c. The knowledge of God as the goal of God's mission

At the end of the introduction to this chapter and also at the end of section 1, it was pointed out that Ezekiel's favourite expression, 'Then you [or they] will know that I am the LORD', occurs with intense repetition in these chapters of oracles against the nations.[115] It is worth returning to that observation as we draw our reflection on this part of Ezekiel's message to a close. First, an affirmation; then a question.

First of all, it is essential to give full value to this phrase and ponder its implications. For Ezekiel, the glory of Yahweh was at the very core of his existence. As a priest in training, before his exile and his call to be a prophet, that would doubtless have been true of him already, assuming him to have been a devout and believing Israelite. But since the shattering experience by the Kebar Canal, his whole life was dominated by the passion of Yahweh himself which gripped his life like a mighty hand around him. But he lived among a people who had lost touch with that glory of Yahweh, and whose rampant and unrepented sins had finally driven the glory of Yahweh away from the temple and consigned their city to destruction. The first part of his ministry, therefore, had been a massive and costly struggle to make the people of Israel face up to the reality of the God they had abandoned, to recognize his anger, to discern his hand behind the hand of Babylon, to *know* their God in his awesome power and justice. 'Then *you* will know that I am Yahweh your God' applied first of all, then, to Israel. Israel must be restored to the acknowledgment of Yahweh, their covenant God, before history could move forward a centimetre.

But the knowledge of Yahweh as God could not stop short with Israel. For the whole earth belongs to Yahweh. Ezekiel was heir to a rich tradition of worship in Israel, now enshrined in the book of Psalms, in which the universality of Yahweh as the God who must be acknowledged by all the earth is celebrated with all the enthusiasm of faith and imagination combined.[116] As before in our exposition, it would be worth pausing to read the passages from the Psalms in the footnote to feel the weight of this great vision and

---

[114] Brueggemann, *Theology of the Old Testament*, p. 527, italics added.
[115] It occurs fifteen times altogether in Ezek. 25 – 32.
[116] Pss. 22:27; 33:8; 47:7–9; 67:1–7; 72:17–19; 96:1–13; 98:2–4; 117; 148:11.

hope in Israel in relation to the nations and the whole earth. So it is this awareness that feeds Ezekiel's faith as he contemplates the work of Yahweh among the nations. Whatever takes place on the international arena will not only be under the sovereign will of God; it will also serve ultimately to extend the knowledge of Yahweh as God – however mysteriously, and however paradoxically in view of the negative nature of so much of what he anticipates.

The goal of all God's action, and therefore the central passion of his prophet's life and witness, is that God should be known and acknowledged among the nations for who he truly is. And that, surely, must also be the primary and ultimate goal of all mission engaged in by God's people – that the world might know its creator, its Lord and its saviour. This was the prayer of Elijah for Israel: 'O LORD, God of Abraham, Isaac and Israel, let it be known today that you are God in Israel ...'[117] The same longing is echoed in the prayer of Jesus for the world, through his disciples.[118] Israel must *know*, the world must *know*, the glory of the living God. In a sense, the whole earth is already filled with the glory of God.[119] But what is lacking is the universal revelation, recognition and acknowledgment of it. The great prophetic hope is that 'the glory of the LORD will be revealed, and all mankind together will see it'.[120]

Because of poetic scansion, the last line of each verse of the familiar hymn 'God is working his purpose out' does not quite capture all that Habakkuk said in his famous metaphor: 'For the earth will be filled with *the knowledge* of the glory of [Yahweh], as the waters cover the sea.'[121]

Though set very much in the minor key of historical judgment, Ezekiel's insistence that the nations will come to know that Yahweh alone is God fits in with this strong biblical affirmation of God's universal intention that the nations should know him to be truly the living God.

Secondly, then, the question. Did Ezekiel's conviction that the nations would come to know Yahweh as God also include a hope that they would thereby come to a *saving* relationship with God? Is there any *positive* future for the nations in Ezekiel? Can Ezekiel take his place alongside other prophets and psalmists who undoubtedly did entertain such a positive hope, the hope which undergirds the New Testament understanding of mission – God's mission to bring the nations into the sphere of his redemptive grace?[122]

[117] 1 Kgs. 18:36.   [118] John 17:21–23.   [119] Ps. 19:1–4; Is. 6:3.
[120] Is. 40:5.   [121] Hab. 2:14.
[122] I am indebted in the following paragraphs to the work of Rev. David Williams, in his unpublished MA dissertation, '"Then they will know that I am the Lord": the missiological significance of Ezekiel's concern for the nations as evident in the use of the recognition formula' (Ware: All Nations Christian College, 1998).

On the one hand, some scholars have answered the question affirmatively. H. Graf Reventlow[123] explored not only the 'recognition formula' ('Then you/they will know that I am Yahweh'), but also the formula 'in the sight of the nations'. Many of Yahweh's actions would be done before a watching world, with the nations as witnesses.[124] Reventlow argues that the nations, like witnesses in a court case, are not merely spectators, but must make their own response to the events they observe. The nations are witnesses to the events through which Yahweh vindicates his holiness – both in the punishment of Israel and in Israel's restoration. Reventlow believes that it was Ezekiel's hope that, through their observation of what Yahweh was doing, the nations would recognize Yahweh as sovereign God and submit to him themselves.[125]

On the other hand, the majority of scholars believe that such optimism goes beyond what Ezekiel ever actually says. P. M. Joyce, for example, in a careful analysis of all the texts involving the 'recognition formula', classifies them in relation to (a) whether, in each instance, it is Israel or the nations who will know Yahweh, and (b) whether the knowledge of Yahweh will be the result of God's action on Israel or on the nations. He points out that in no case is the recognition formula ('Then they will know that I am Yahweh') used with any prediction that God will *deliver* the nations. Strictly speaking, the nations will know Yahweh only through their witnessing his punishment and his deliverance of Israel, and through their experience of his punishment of themselves. Joyce thus concludes:

> It would seem, then, that the use of the 'I am Yahweh' formula lends no support to the view that there is in Ezekiel a positive hope that the nations will turn in allegiance to the God of Israel; rather reference to the nations here is a rhetorical device, serving to highlight the central concern, which is the revelation of Yahweh.

And likewise:

> In the absence of any clear evidence of a hope that the nations will respond positively to Yahweh, it seems reasonable to understand the words 'in the sight of the nations' in Ezekiel as a similar rhetorical expression.[126]

---

[123] H. Graf Reventlow, 'Die Völker als Jahwes Zeugen bei Ezechiel' ['The nations as Yahweh's witnesses in Ezekiel'], *ZAW* 71 (1959), pp. 33–43.

[124] Ezek. 5:8; 20:9, 14, 22, 41; 22:16; 28:25; 38:23; 39:27.

[125] The same position is taken by Ackroyd, pp. 115–117, following Reventlow.

[126] P. M. Joyce, *Divine Initiative and Human Response in Ezekiel*, *JSOT* Supplement 51 (Sheffield: JSOT Press, 1989), pp. 95, 97.

However, if Reventlow has gone too far in affirming a hope for the salvation of the nations in Ezekiel, Joyce has certainly not gone far enough in regarding the 'recognition formula' and the expression 'in the sight of all nations' as nothing more than a rhetorical device – that is, simply a vivid way of boosting the literary impact of his message, comparable to other prophets calling heaven and earth to hear or witness what they have to say. An expression so frequently used must have meant more to Ezekiel than a rhetorical flourish. In the next chapter, when we examine Ezekiel 36:16–38, we shall see how passionately Ezekiel cared about the reputation of Yahweh that was in tatters among the nations because of the disgrace of the exile. It is Ezekiel's overriding concern that Yahweh's reputation should be restored so that the nations would know the real truth about Yahweh. So his constant affirmation that 'they *will* know' is not just a matter of style, but of real substance. 'Yahweh himself cares passionately about the way the nations perceive him. Yahweh is committed to Israel as the only means by which restoration of his honour can take place.'[127]

Thus while Ezekiel does not go so far as to say that the nations will repent, turn to Yahweh and be saved (other prophets did say that before him and would say it after him), he does say that they will witness both the *justice* of Yahweh in his punishment of Israel and themselves, and the *grace and mercy* of Yahweh in his restoration of Israel. From their witness of these great things, they will know that Yahweh is God. And that much, we have to conclude, was sufficient for this prophet. What the nations would do with such knowledge was beyond his immediate concern. In Israel's case, some would repent and live; others would persist in rebellious wickedness and perish. If Ezekiel extrapolated at all to the wider world of nations, perhaps he may have expected the same differential response and dual destiny there too.

All that really mattered for Ezekiel was that both in Israel and in the world of nations, the glory of God would be revealed, the honour of God's name would be restored, and the truth of God's identity would be known. The universal acknowledgment of Yahweh as God – that alone was Ezekiel's burning ambition. It is a challenge to ask ourselves if our own motivation in mission is as radically God-centred as Ezekiel's clearly was. In the Introduction we observed how Ezekiel's passion for the glory of God is an essential corrective to the plethora of other motivations for mission which focus mainly on human needs and problems – valid and biblical though such concerns are.[128] Here we find the same message

---

[127] D. Williams, op. cit., p. 47.   [128] See above, pp. 24-25.

underlined again. For us who know the richer truth of God's revelation in Jesus Christ, and who look forward to the day when every knee will bow and every tongue confess that Jesus Christ is Lord, to the glory of God the Father,[129] Ezekiel's passion blends with Solomon's prayer in its global mission relevance, 'so that all the peoples of the earth may know that the LORD is God and that there is no other'.[130]

---

[129] Phil. 2:10–11 – a verse in an early Christian hymn which remarkably has inserted the name of Jesus into its quotation of an Old Testament affirmation about Yahweh, Is. 45:23–24.   [130] 1 Kgs. 8:60.

34:1 – 37:28
8. The gospel according to Ezekiel

Introduction

'The old has gone, the new has come!' said Paul, speaking of the new creation that comes into being when anyone is in Christ[1]. But the new creation is not simply a replacement of the old, for there is clearly a continuity from the old to the new. Even for Jesus this was so. In his resurrection body he was still recognizably the Jesus his disciples knew well in the flesh. As the firstfruits of the new creation, then, his resurrection points to the way in which God's re-creating power will redeem and transform the old. Similarly, Ezekiel's vision of the future restoration did not offer a totally new scenario or set of relationships. He still thought in the terms of the primary factors in Israel's worldview: Yahweh, Israel, and the land. And then through this prism, he reflected on Yahweh's relationship with the nations.

Ezekiel envisaged that God's great project of restoration would deal with all these fundamental realities in a comprehensive way and that it would involve change in several different directions or dimensions. The range of material in Ezekiel 34 – 37 can be appreciated when we see that, in those chapters, God promises to bring Israel out of anarchy (34), into the land (35:1 – 36:15), back from disgrace (36:16–38), up from the grave (37:1–14) and together out of brokenness (37:15–28). It is, in modern jargon, a truly holistic gospel. Ezekiel was ministering to a people who were broken and battered in every conceivable way. There were political, economic, agricultural, social, judicial, religious, personal, relational and spiritual dimensions to their sin and their suffering. And God intended to tackle every aspect of that need. Such is the breadth and depth of the biblical gospel. The grace of God reaches the parts that other human solutions cannot reach. People who are involved today in holistic forms of mission, in which evangelism, social action,

[1] 2 Cor. 5:17.

273

economic development and environmental care are combined, understand this glorious, all-embracing scope of the gospel. Indeed, the structure and content of the chapters we are about to study would make a profitable case-study as a paradigm of community transformation at every level. For they describe what God aimed to achieve for a shattered people: he would give them place (their land); political protection; dignity and self-respect again; economic viability; just and competent leadership; religious and spiritual renewal; and practical unity. In short, they would come back from the grave.

1. From tyranny to theocracy (34:1–31)

This chapter begins on the plane of past history, and moves through to future historical restoration, but also, in the way that so many prophetic visions do, seems to transcend anything yet seen in the history of God's people and looks on to an age yet to be fully enjoyed.

a. The removal of the corrupt monarchy (34:1–10)

Ezekiel has never allowed the people to blame anyone else for their misfortunes. To the extent that they were suffering the judgment of Yahweh in all the tragic events of defeat and exile, they were undergoing the just punishment of their own horrendous sins. Ezekiel's work of detailed theodicy (providing justification for the ways of God) had made this point repeatedly. And yet, while holding all his people responsible for their own sin, God and his prophet were well aware that some among them were 'more responsible' than others. Like prophets before him, Ezekiel attacked the leaders of the people for the way they had utterly failed to provide the quality or integrity of leadership that the covenant relationship required. The kings of Judah for the century or more prior to the fall of Jerusalem had, with few exceptions, been moral and spiritual failures whose reigns had led the people further and further into idolatry, injustice and social collapse.[2]

Ezekiel chooses a metaphor for kingship that was well known throughout the ancient Near East, from Babylon to Egypt – the

[2] This was the message, of course, which would soon be written up by those who, during the exile and probably fairly close to the time of Ezekiel himself, compiled the edited history of Israel referred to by scholars as 'the Deuteronomistic History' (because of its strong thematic interpretation of Israel's history in the light of the standards of Deuteronomy). This work includes the historical books from Joshua to 2 Kings (excluding Ruth). The way the later monarchy is portrayed in 2 Kings certainly echoes the evaluation of it offered here by Ezekiel.

shepherd of the flock.[3] He then launches into an attack on *the shepherds of Israel* – meaning the historical kings of the period up to the exile. As we have seen him do before, Ezekiel takes a word from a previous prophet and goes on to quote and expand it in his own way. His favourite, of course, is his own older contemporary Jeremiah. Here it seems most probable that Ezekiel actually had the text of Jeremiah 23:1–6 in front of him as he composed his own indictment and vision of hope, as a quick comparison of the two texts will make clear.

The indictment of Israel's kings shines clearly through the metaphorical language of 34:2–6. Basically, they had served themselves at the expense of their people, rather than serving the people at any cost to themselves. There is no intrinsic harm, of course, in a shepherd using the milk or the wool of his sheep (3), but when this is done without any reciprocal duty of care (4), and, when the shepherds' abuses include slaughtering the best and scattering the rest (3b, 5), clearly we have a picture of ruthless exploitation and self-interest. The picture would be easy to document from the history of the later kings of Israel and Judah. It would also be easy to illustrate in the history of the Christian church right up to the present day. Those who have been entrusted with leading the people of God have always been exposed to the temptation of 'fleecing the flock' for their own advantage in terms of money or status, rather than the genuine and costly work of caring for the lost, the sick, the wounded and the strays. The corruption of political and spiritual power is alike well described by Ezekiel's detailed metaphorical sketch. So is the tragic effect – the pathetic and vulnerable condition of a shepherdless people, scattered and under attack, and with nobody to seek and save them from danger (5–6).

The metaphor slides over into a more literal indication of its target with the expression *My sheep* (6). God is talking about his own people. This is repeated no fewer than five times[4] up to verse 10 alone (and then several times more in the following section). It not only expresses Yahweh's personal concern for the flock that is being so badly treated, but also makes clear where the true ownership lies. The shepherds did not own the flock; they were simply employed to look after it. The kings did not own the people; they were simply entrusted with exercising justice and leadership in their midst. But

[3] For examples and bibliography for the use of the shepherd metaphor for kingship, see Block (2), pp. 279–281. Hammurabi and his successors in Babylon and Assyria all referred to themselves as 'shepherds', usually appointed by a god. An ancient Babylonian proverb prefigured biblical usage in affirming that 'a people without a king is like sheep without a shepherd' (cf. Num. 27:17; 1 Kgs. 22:17).

[4] The variation between *my sheep* and *my flock* is not reflected in the Hebrew, where it is a single expression, *ṣô'nî*, 'my flock'.

the temptation to regard those entrusted to one's care or leadership as one's personal property, a mini-empire, is powerful. It lies at the root of paternalistic patterns of Christian mission and ministry, in which people have used (and abused) their flock as a means of personal power, or a symbol of personal status, or even as a source of personal identity. Against all such attitudes stands this vital reminder that the flock belongs to the Lord, and our accountability is to him for the way we have fulfilled our duty to those who are his.

The verdict on the abusive shepherds is uncompromising (7–10). God says, '*I am against the shepherds.*' This is the same language that we heard in God's denunciation of Jerusalem (5:8), and was typically used against the enemies of Yahweh. The kings of Israel have become as much the enemies of Yahweh as the enemies they themselves had fought against. They will find, however, that Yahweh is an enemy they can neither defeat nor buy off with favours or alliances. '*I will remove them*' (10). These words sound the death knell of the historical monarchy. In spite of the great model of David, the monarchy in Israel was ending as it began, in rebellion and disobedience, and God would tolerate it no longer. Far from defending God's flock, they had become like wolves themselves (10b). The sheep needed rescuing from their own shepherds! So God would act to do so, removing the tyranny and restoring his own divine kingship.

b. The restoration of theocracy (34:11–22)

The shepherds have failed the flock. The kings have failed Israel. But all is not lost, for Israel's true king and shepherd was always Yahweh himself. So these verses picture God taking over from the disgraced human leaders and restoring the true divine kingship – the covenantal theocracy that was meant to have been the distinguishing mark of Israel. This rule of Yahweh would be marked by three things: ingathering (11–13a); tending and feeding (13b–16) and justice (17–22).

First it would include an act of rescue and the ingathering of the scattered flock (11–13a). This was also an achievement attributed to worthy kings in the ancient near-eastern records.[5] As a shepherd gathers his flock together to protect them from danger, so Yahweh will gather his people from their scattering and see to their security. This imagery, here used by Ezekiel in exile where it was particularly relevant, had already been anticipated by Micah.[6] And it would later

[5] Block (2), pp. 290–291. Cf. Yahweh's use of Cyrus, king of Persia, as his 'shepherd', to facilitate the ingathering of Israel from exile (Is. 44:26–28).
[6] Mic. 2:12; 4:6–8.

be used by Jesus himself in describing his own mission 'to seek and to save what was lost' – meaning the 'lost sheep of Israel'.[7]

Secondly, it would involve caring for them properly, by tending their needs and providing good pasture (13b–16). This side of a shepherd's work lends itself naturally to describing the way God cares for his people, collectively and individually. Joseph used it, with plenty of good reason, to portray God's care in his own life.[8] David, of course, immortalized the metaphor with several supporting images of a shepherd's care in Psalm 23. Isaiah 40:11 applies it to the people as a whole, speaking warmly of the tenderness with which Yahweh 'tends his flock like a shepherd'. The language of verse 16 achieves a powerful effect in two ways. It echoes and reverses at each point the failure of the human shepherds (4); and it puts the object before the verb in each case: 'The lost I will seek, the strayed I will bring back, the injured I will bind up, the weak I will strengthen, but the fat and the strong I will destroy.' The emphasis thus falls on the repeated *I will*. All that the oppressive rulers had failed to do, God himself will accomplish. Jesus, likewise, identifying himself as the good shepherd, focused among other things on the role of the shepherd in providing protection and pasture for his flock.[9]

Thirdly, however, the picture is not all one of tender loving care. The flock still needed to be governed, and verses 17–22 point to the necessary work of justice and protection of the weak that needed to go on. Providing good leadership does not necessarily remove all causes of tension and quarrelling in a community. There is probably a hint in these verses of continued wrangling and exploitation even among the exiled community, as people jostled for what little privileges and advantages they could obtain, or struggled to preserve the rank, status and power they had enjoyed before the catastrophe stripped them all. They also point, in a wider way, to the continued need for discrimination within the fellowship of God's earthly people, and the ultimate reality of a judgment that, as Jesus pointed out, will finally separate the sheep from the goats.[10]

In the immediate context, of course, Ezekiel is here giving encouragement to the exiles with the expectation that in the restored community that would return to the land, the rapacious pre-exilic monarchy would be replaced by God's own rule. It would still be the case, however, that the divine rule would need to be earthed through human agents, just as, in the days before the monarchy, Israel's theocratic organization was 'managed' through the human

---

[7] Luke 19:10; Matt. 10:6; 15:24; cf. Luke 15:3–7.   [8] Gen. 48:15–16.
[9] John 10:1–16.
[10] Matt. 25:31–46. Very probably Jesus' imagery in this parable consciously reflects Ezek. 34:17.

judges who ruled temporarily in the name of Yahweh. As it turned out in the history of the post-exilic period, the later rulers of Israel, even though they were not kings in name (with some exceptions later, e.g. the Herods), showed the same mixture of faithfulness and failure as their pre-exilic counterparts. God's leadership of God's people still has to work through fallen human agents.

The same is true for the church. At one level it is right to speak of it as a theocracy, in the sense that our supreme head is Christ, and all authority is given to him. Yet at the same time, there is a place for human leadership, exercising gifts of the Spirit for the benefit and building up of the rest of the community. Such leaders are, as Peter so beautifully put it, 'shepherds of God's flock', but under the overall authority of Christ, 'the Chief Shepherd'. Perhaps with Ezekiel's imagery in mind, Peter sharply warns such under-shepherds to fulfil their pastoral tasks willingly, 'not greedy for money, but eager to serve; not lording it over those entrusted to you, but being examples to the flock'.[11] The theocratic imagery of Ezekiel, then, still has its relevance for the nature and duties of pastoral ministry among God's people.

But finally, it is worth observing that it is this theocratic and eschatological circle of ideas that surrounded the metaphor of shepherding the flock when Jesus made his stunning claim, 'I am the good shepherd' in John 10:11. Unfortunately his saying has been coloured for many Christian readers by a combination of a rather sentimental reading of the individual piety of Psalm 23 and the plethora of Christian paintings of Jesus cuddling a little lamb or carrying one on tender shoulders. But Jesus' claim in John 10 was certainly not merely that he could be nice to poor lost lambs. That was not a claim likely to lead to argument and a charge of demon possession.[12] No, he was standing astride the great vision of Ezekiel. Israel was like a flock of sheep without a shepherd – that is, they had no true king (a dangerous thing to say with the Herods in power). Furthermore, those who were now ruling them were 'thieves and robbers' – just like the rogue shepherds in Ezekiel's indictment. Again, a dangerous charge to make in such company. And against all such impostors, Jesus calmly makes the claim that he is precisely the true shepherd of whom Ezekiel prophesied; the true heir of Israel's theocratic ideal; the one who had said, '*I* myself *will shepherd the flock.*' And who was that? None other than Yahweh, the Lord God himself. Jesus' claim was massive – to be the true king of Israel, the prophesied divine, theocratic shepherd. It is not surprising that shortly afterwards, when Jesus repeated the claim in a different way,

[11] 1 Pet. 5:1–4.   [12] John 10:19–20.

argument turned to anger and the stones that would execute a blasphemer were already in the hands of his opponents.[13]

c. The reign of peace (34:23–31)

In the final climactic section of his vision, Ezekiel wraps the shepherd and flock motif (23, 31) around a portrayal of the new age that relies heavily on earlier texts that had described the blessing that would accompany Yahweh's act of renewal of his people and his covenant with them. There are three main elements in Ezekiel's gathering together of these traditions: a new Davidic ruler (23–24); a new experience of peace and harmony (25–29); and a new affirmation of the covenant relationship between God and his people (30–31).

i. A new Davidic ruler (34:23–24)

The line of kings descended from David had come to an inglorious end with the exile – even though Jehoiachin still survived and even flourished in exile. The monarchy was never restored in its pre-exilic historical state. But God's promises to David constituted a covenant for ever[14] and would be kept, even in a different form. In describing David as the one whom God would appoint to shepherd his people, Ezekiel is connecting with the historical fact that David had, of course, been a literal shepherd before being anointed to the kingship.[15] The messianic hope of a ruler of redeemed Israel from the line of David went deep and is found in various other prophetic passages, before and after Ezekiel.[16] As elsewhere, Ezekiel seems particularly impressed with the prophecies of Jeremiah on this expectation.

Ezekiel highlights several things about this future Davidic ruler. He will be *one shepherd*, which points to the future unity of God's people (a point further developed below in 37:15–28).[17] He will be *my servant*, a term of honour and yet humility which had already been conferred on the historical David. The use of the term here very probably also links to the more developed portrayal of the 'Servant of the LORD' in Isaiah 40 – 55, especially in view of the reference to the role of David in Isaiah 55:3–5. And he *will be prince*

[13] John 10:25–31.
[14] 2 Sam. 7:4–16 (see esp. vv. 13–16). Cf. also Pss. 89; 132.
[15] This is a point which is noted in other places too: 2 Sam. 5:2; 7:8; Ps. 78:70–72.
[16] Amos 9:11; Hos. 3:5; Is. 9:6–7; 11:1; 55:3–4; Jer. 23:5–6; 30:9; 33:15–26; Zech. 12:7–8. Cf. John 7:40–42.
[17] It seems very likely that Jesus also had this verse (Ezek. 34:23) in mind when he claimed that, under himself, there would be 'one flock and one shepherd' (John 10:18).

279

among them. Interestingly, the term 'king' is avoided here,[18] possibly because of the bad odour the word had in the light of such a catalogue of failure and oppression. Also, Ezekiel has stressed that Yahweh himself will be the true shepherd-king of his people, so the role of the human agent of his kingship is slightly downplayed. He will not lord it over the people, but be a 'ruler in their midst'.

There is some mystery as to how we should hold together the idea of God himself being his people's shepherd and the role of a Davidic 'prince' in their midst. Already in historical Israel, of course, there was a strong connection between human royalty and divine kingship, as seen in some of the Psalms.[19] Here Ezekiel is certainly not contrasting the two, but binding them together as two dimensions of the same overall rule. The coming ruler will embody all that the rule of Yahweh himself implies. Like the equally mysterious Immanuel figure, his presence will embody the presence of God himself and all that comes with it.

> Suffice it to know that in him and over him God remains the God of his people and that his divine rule knows no eclipse ... In this 'prince' there exists a shepherd who no longer lives off his sheep and 'looks after himself,' but the shepherd who lives for his sheep, even for those who labor and are heavy-laden (Mt 11:28), the weak and the lost whom he will seek even as the good shepherd does (Luke 15; John 10) ... In all of this, however, there is no question of the establishment of human dominion, but of the event in which God reveals himself as the God of his people. 'Your God – among you.' Such a future is proclaimed to God's people by his prophet.[20]

Ultimately, of course, from a Christian point of view, the combination of the theocratic reign of God himself and the messianic reign of the new David (24) can be understood only in the light of the coming of Jesus, 'great David's greater son'. But this is indeed what the New Testament affirms has taken place. At the time of Jesus' birth Luke records the expectation of the event in a series of encounters which are saturated in language of the restoration of the Davidic kingdom for ever.[21] His Davidic descent was an issue in his lifetime.[22] The Davidic background coloured Peter's speech on the day of Pentecost,[23] and is drawn into the church's theological and scriptural evaluation of the significance of the success of the Gentile mission. James recognizes that if the eschatological expectation of

[18] The term used is *nāsî*, ruler, leader.   [19] E.g. Pss. 2; 45; 72.
[20] Zimmerli, *Ezekiel 2*, p. 223.   [21] Luke 1:27, 32–33, 69; 2:11.
[22] Matt. 12:23; 15:22; 20:30–31; 21:9; 22:41–46.   [23] Acts 2:25–36.

the ingathering of the nations is beginning to take place, then the restoration of the Davidic monarchy has also necessarily happened – which must refer to the resurrection and glorification of Jesus. Accordingly, he quotes from Amos the text which refers to both great events – restoration of the house of David and possession of the nations.[24]

ii. Full and perfect shalom (34:25–29)

The expression *a covenant of peace*[25] means a covenant in which there will be wholeness and harmony. 'Shalom' means much more than absence of strife. Its full biblical dimensions include the welfare of all God's creation, and the enjoyment of joyful freedom from conflict in all the relationships between humanity and nature and between both of those and God. We have seen before that Ezekiel drew deeply on the language and imagery of the covenantal curses in Leviticus 26 and Deuteronomy 28. Here he shows that he has read the rest of the chapters. Ezekiel's portrayal of God's blessing in the restored covenant reality is full of echoes of the promises of Leviticus 26:3–13 and Deuteronomy 28:1–14. In addition he picks up some of the curse language and reverses it. His picture has three main elements: (a) freedom from danger from wild animals (a fear which has lost much of its power in western societies, where the nearest we may get to dangerous animals is in the zoo, but a fear which still afflicts societies where predators have not yet dwindled to extinction); (b) abundant fertility of vegetation and crops; and (c) deliverance from all human oppressors. The combined effect of the repetition and interweaving of all these great reversals in verses 25–29 will be that people can live *in safety* (25); *the people will be secure* (27); *they will live in safety* (28).

The emphasis on security and freedom from fear is significant, and strikes welcome chords in human hearts. So many millions of the human race live in constant fear of everything from natural disasters to the massive violence of state-sponsored genocide and 'ethnic cleansing',[26] to material inadequacies, street crime, old age, unemployment, bereavement, illness, the future in general ...

[24] Acts 15:16; Amos 9:11–12. Paul does not make much of Jesus' Davidic ancestry, but certainly includes it as a factor in the complete gospel account (Rom. 1:3; 2 Tim. 2:8).

[25] The term is first used in God's promise to Phinehas for his demonstration of loyalty to the honour of Yahweh's name during the immorality and idolatry of Israelites at Baal Peor (Num. 25:12).

[26] 'Ethnic cleansing' is one of those euphemisms for either genocide or mass deportation that are particularly obnoxious. Basically, as the metaphor implies, 'ethnic cleansing' means treating people like dirt.

The list is endless. Endless too, however, will be the era of new-covenant blessing in which God's people will live without fear of any kind, for *no-one will make them afraid*. What an exhilarating hope!

Yet again, Ezekiel shows his resonance here with many other prophets who shared this vision of a new era of God's abundant blessing, being enjoyed by a people living in harmony and security in a creation freed from threat and fear. Each prophet has his own delightful angle, but it is worth reading the passages in the next footnote all together, in order to lift up your eyes and heart to our glorious future. The new creation will be a time and a place that will be secure, just, fulfilling, peaceful but busy, productive, non-threatening and environmentally safe.[27]

iii. A full restoration of the covenant relationship (34:25, 30–31)
The precise expression 'a new covenant' is one that is actually used only by Jeremiah (in a text quoted twice in Hebrews),[28] which has unfortunately led many people to the misunderstanding that Jeremiah alone prophesied about a new covenant at all. But as can be seen very clearly here, Ezekiel also envisaged the future of Israel in terms of a renewal of the covenant, as did Isaiah.[29] The most fundamental formulation of the covenant relationship is to be found in the reciprocal phrases 'the LORD [Yahweh] is your God' and 'you [Israel] are his people'.[30] Here, Ezekiel rather cleverly splits them in two, putting the first phrase in with the promise of a new David (24), and the second after the details of the blessings to come (30), before rounding off with an echo of both in the 'shepherd and flock' imagery (31).

So often Ezekiel had uttered the words 'Then they will know that I am Yahweh' in contexts of predicted *judgment*. What a relief and a joy it must have been to utter them again here (31), not with such negative implications, but rather with the wonderful thought that people would truly know the reality of God's character as Yahweh when they live within the perfectly restored relationship of humanity and creation to him. They will not only know that Yahweh is God, but that he is *with them* (30) – no longer 'against them', no longer an enemy. For they too can now be described, no longer as 'the

[27] E.g Is. 11:1–9; 54:9–17 (note, 'covenant of peace in v. 10); 65:17–25; Hos. 2:18–23; Joel 3:17–18; Amos 9:13–15; Zech. 8.

[28] Jer. 31:31–34; Heb. 8:8-13; 10:15–18.

[29] Is. 54:9–10; 55:3. For a fuller discussion of the relationship between the various articulations of the new covenant and the preceding historical covenants between God and, respectively, Noah, Abraham, Moses and David, see Wright, *Knowing Jesus through the Old Testament*, ch. 2, pp. 55–102.   [30] Deut. 26:17–19.

house of rebellion', but by their true covenantal title, *the house of Israel.* The shepherd knows his sheep and they will know him. Yet again, we can clearly see the scriptural source of Jesus' rich imagery for his own enduring and secure relationship to us, his flock.[31]

2. From abandonment to abundance (35:1 – 36:15)

To be a stateless refugee is a terrible plight. At the time of the Kosovo crisis in Europe in the spring of 1999 some of the most moving scenes captured on television were of the victims of the bombing and 'ethnic cleansing' streaming into exile, having lost homes and farms to hostile destruction, and then being forcibly deprived of all personal possessions including passports and identity cards. Apart from the desperate humiliation, the intense anger against the enemy and the agony of multiple bereavements in almost every family, there was also the anxiety about what was happening back home. The land was desolate and devastated, its villages smashed and smoking; and all their property and possessions were at the mercy of looters and carpetbaggers.

With a little imagination it is not difficult to understand the very similar situation of the Judean exiles, except that they had not gone into refugee camps just across the border from their own land, but had walked to the far corners of the earth (as it must have seemed to them), to the pagan, enemy land of Babylon. Their last mental image of the land they had left behind would have been of the systematic destruction being wreaked upon it by Babylonian armies, and the smoke still rising from the fires of Jerusalem. Some of them would have stumbled in captivity past the smoking remains of their own farms and houses. So they arrived in Babylon with a sense of total loss – loss of land and property, but also loss of dignity and identity. All their pride and joy in themselves, their land, their city, their temple, their king, their God, had gone. It would be worth pausing to read through the little book of Lamentations which captures the deep, heartbreaking grief and total loss of self-esteem that gripped the exiles after the fall of Jerusalem.

The work of Ezekiel as pastor after the fall of Jerusalem and the arrival of the last batch of exiles had to include the restoration of this people morally and psychologically, as well as spiritually. The process would take a generation, long before any actual restoration to the land would take place. In chapter 34, as we have seen, Ezekiel addressed their status as a people and promised the restoration of just and godly leadership under God in a renewed covenant. In this

---

[31] John 10:14, 27–29.

section, 35:1 – 36:15,[32] he addresses their anxieties over the land itself, which was an essential part of Israel's sense of identity. They had been living as Yahweh's people in Yahweh's land. Would they ever do so again? Would there even be a land to go back to? If there were ever to be a restoration, God had to deal not just with his own people, but also with external threats to his own land. That is the focus of this section.

a. The land will be saved from the attacks of its enemies (35:1–15)

We can imagine the rumours arriving among the fearful exiles in Babylon. The empty land was being overrun by even more ancient enemies than the Babylonians – the Edomites! And who knows what other nations would join the scramble for the land of milk and honey (36:3; cf. ch. 25)? History was unwinding and the land was reverting to its past. As far as Israel was concerned, even the past was being wiped out, and now there could be no future either. Who or what was Israel without Yahweh's land?

The particular threat came from Edom – the country to the south and east of Judah, inhabited by the descendants of Esau, and inveterately hostile to Israelite governments for many generations. They are referred to here by the personification of *Mount Seir*, a method of addressing them which deliberately parallels the address to *the mountains of Israel* in 36:1. It seems that in the events up to and after the fall of Jerusalem in 587 Edom took every advantage they could from Judah's plight, and did so with venomous enthusiasm and efficiency.[33] This accounts for the feeling against them recorded in Psalm 137:7 and the book of Obadiah. They seem to have boasted that they could take over the whole land of Israel, including the territories of both political kingdoms, north and south (35:10). This was doubtless more a boast than ever a reality, but if news of it reached the exiles, imagine the fear and impotent anger it must have engendered.

The Edomites, however, had not reckoned with the God of the land they were so gleefully carving up in advance (36:5). God has a

---

[32] Although there is a chapter division, it is very clear that 35:1–15 and 36:1–15 are two halves of a single prophetic word. They begin with very similar phrases (35:2; 36:1), and there are many connecting links, including the references to the mountains of Israel and the malicious taunts of Israel's enemies in both halves. For further indications of the unity of the whole section, see Block (2), pp. 309–310. Block helpfully compares the structure of this section with ch. 34. There the hindrances to God's work had to be removed (34:1–11) before God's new order could be established (34:12–31). Here the threat to God's land has to be countered (35:1–15) before God's promised restoration of the land's prosperity can be achieved (36:1–15).

[33] Obad. 10 – 14.

habit of listening in on the boastful threats of the enemies of his people.[34] They don't impress him much. The Edomites' boast was that the lands of Israel *will be ours and we will take possession of them* (35:10); *the ancient heights*[35] *have become our possession* (36:2). But the land still belonged to Yahweh and he would defend it. The close link between Israel as Yahweh's people[36] and the land as Yahweh's land[37] was a fundamental pillar of Israel's faith and identity. Ezekiel reaffirms it here in the face of enemies who threatened it. Clearly, although he had seen the glory of Yahweh leave the temple and city, he now realized that Yahweh had not simply abandoned his land to its fate without a backward look. On the contrary, Yahweh was still, in some sense, *there*[38] and would act to protect his and Israel's inheritance against the aggressor. Yahweh's tenants Israel had been dispossessed temporarily because of their misdeeds, but Yahweh had not thereby surrendered his own title as the ultimate landlord. Here and in chapter 25, therefore, Yahweh hoists a large 'Trespassers will be prosecuted' sign over his land. Paradoxically, having poured out his judgment in the act of driving the people into exile, Yahweh was now acting in their favour against human enemies. This paradox will be explored more in the second half of chapter 36.

It can be seen, therefore, that although chapter 35 looks like just another oracle against the nations, it functions as a word of encouragement for Israel. The tables will be turned. God will ensure that their enemies do not triumph over them for ever and Israel will not lose its identity or patrimony. The sense of reversal is clear even in the language used. The form of God's judgment upon Edom in 35:3–4 echoes almost exactly the words spoken against the mountains of Israel in 6:14, thus confirming the close link between this chapter and 36, where the mountains of Israel are also given the same 'reverse treatment'.

---

[34] Cf. Is. 10:12–19; 37, esp. vv. 3–4; Acts 4:22–31.

[35] There is an irony here; the word used is the same as normally translated 'high places' – the *bāmôt* that were so offensive to Yahweh as places of idolatry. They were the particular focus of the destruction threatened against the mountains of Israel in 6:1–7.

[36] Note the reassuring *my people Israel* in 36:12.

[37] Note *my land* in 36:5, and cf. Lev. 25:23. For a full discussion of this important part of Israel's theology, see Wright, *God's People in God's Land*. See also W. Brueggemann, *The Land* (Philadelphia: Fortress, 1977), and, for a more succinct survey, C. J. H. Wright, *'ereṣ*, in *NIDOTTE* 1.

[38] The Edomites' threat was made against the land, *even though I the* LORD *was there* (35:10). The final phrase (*YHWH šām hāyâ*) is a verbal pre-echo of the final great phrase of the whole book announcing the name of the city of Ezekiel's vision as *YHWH šāmmâ*, 'THE LORD IS THERE'.

b. The people will be freed from the scorn of the nations (36:1–15)

It was not just the fear for their land that gnawed away at the exiles' morale. There was also the shattering blow to their national pride. What possible status among the nations could be held by a decimated remnant of landless refugees? Apart from the sting of military defeat, there was the taunt of landlessness. In the ancient world, as much as today, stateless peoples count for little in the corridors of international power or prestige. For the people of Judah it was a terrible collapse of national self-respect. The once great empire of Solomon, courted by the king of Tyre and the queen of Sheba, was now reduced to this uprooted fragment. Once they had stood astride the major trade routes of the ancient Near East and played a part in the international power games of the great empires of the Nile and the Euphrates. Now they were nothing but the flotsam and jetsam of devastating wars. The earliest prophetic word of Ezekiel in 5:5–17 had come true. From being at the hub of the nations, they had sunk to being a horror to the nations, the target of mockery and abuse. The emotional and spiritual trauma of the experience is poignantly reflected in Lamentations and several psalms.[39]

Ezekiel 36:1–15 addresses such a state of mind. Rhetorically, Ezekiel is told to *prophesy to the mountains of Israel*. This time, however, he is not to set his face against them – the command in 6:2, which has now been applied instead to Mount Seir (35:2). There is clearly an editorial structuring which has placed the positive oracle of 36:1–15 to balance the negative oracle of 6:1–14 (similar to the repetition in ch. 33 of the watchman imagery of ch. 3). The whole section (36:1–15) is addressed to the abandoned mountains, but it is obviously a literary and rhetorical personification; the real listeners are the exiles who felt themselves abandoned in Babylon. 'The desolated land … stands as an objective image of the inner feelings of the exiles.'[40] To the question 'Will Yahweh abandon his land and people for ever?' the answer is a resounding 'No!' The land that lies desolate will be reinhabited and will provide in abundance for the restored community's needs. So 36:2–7 repeats the word of judgment against the enemies who seek to plunder Israel's lost territory, while 36:8–12 predicts the return from exile and the restoration of population[41] and agriculture. This dimension of the restoration will

[39] See esp. Lam. 1:7–10, 17; 2:15–17; 5:1–22; Pss. 79; 89; 137.

[40] Allen 29, p. 174.

[41] The repeated promise to *multiply the number of people* (10), and *increase the number of men* (11), contains another pun. It uses Heb. *'ādām*, the generic word for human beings, which is very similar to, and a deliberate echo of, the word for Edom, *'ᵉdôm*.

be the focus of much more detailed attention in Ezekiel's great final vision (45 – 48, see ch. 9 below). Here, the main point is that the restoration will remove the taunt of the nations against Israel. In addressing the land, therefore, Ezekiel says that its earlier reputation as a place that 'devours' its population[42] will be gone, and with it all *the taunts of the nations* and *the scorn of the peoples* (13–15).

Putting the whole section together, then, we can see that 35:1 – 36:15 constitutes an important piece of 'pastoral reassurance, as damaged self-respect is built up with recourse to faith in a powerful covenant God'.[43] The shattered exiles were given prophetic words that matched so many of the psalms they initially found it impossible to sing: their enemies would not triumph over them for ever; they would not be put to shame for ever; their God would one day lift up their heads again in the sight of the nations. It must have been hard to believe in 587. But it was terribly important that it was said and remembered.

3. From profanity to purity (36:16–38)

A new *word* is introduced at 36:16, but it follows on very appropriately from the preceding section. As we have seen, 35:1 – 36:15 addresses the shattering loss of face that the events of 587 meant for Israel. It is not difficult for us, with our awareness of many similar tragedies that have engulfed nations in our own day, to imagine what it felt like for them. But Israel was not the only party with feelings. Nor was Israel's national pride the only issue at stake. What did the event mean for Yahweh's own reputation? If it was important to look to a future in which *Israel* would no longer suffer the taunts of the nations, how much more important was it that *Yahweh* should have the same expectation?

This new section, then, deals with the same theme as the preceding one: namely, the restoration of Israel; but it does so from the perspective of Yahweh himself. The gospel according to Ezekiel is not just good news for Israel. It is also good news for God. In fact, as we shall see, only for God's own sake is it good news at all. For only that which brings honour and glory to God himself can be

---

[42] This curious expression goes right back to the report of the spies sent out by Moses (Num. 13:32) regarding the dangerous nature of the land. By the time of the exile, after centuries of settlement, it probably does not refer to the harshness of the land itself, but to the number of enemy attacks and deportations that had happened in the northern kingdom and Judea. There may be another echo of the metaphor in Lev. 18:25–28, which speaks of the land 'vomiting out' its inhabitants under divine judgment – though the gastronomical direction has been reversed.

[43] Allen 29, p. 174.

good news for anybody else. So Ezekiel retells the story of Israel's sin and punishment, but from God's point of view; and then paints the most glorious picture of what their restoration will mean – again looking at it from God's point of view.

a. Defiling God's land (36:17–19)

These two verses are as succinct a summary of all Ezekiel's preaching so far as one could imagine. Typically, Ezekiel uses the priestly language of defilement and uncleanness to describe the ugliness of Israel's sin.[44] It is coarse, but not as coarse as Ezekiel was capable of elsewhere. His main point is simply to remind the exiles that their behaviour back in the land had been utterly obnoxious and disgusting to God.[45] But although he uses a ritual analogy, he is not thinking of merely ritual sins. As we have seen from chapters 18 and 22, Ezekiel's understanding of evil is fully moral and social. Here he summarizes their sin in two of its most blatant forms: the wanton shedding of blood and the rampant idolatry. Representatively, each sin encompasses each tablet of the Ten Commandments – offences against God and against fellow human beings. Israel's wickedness had plumbed the depths in both departments. The same summary of the abominations of the people throughout the generations from the conquest is found in the exilic Psalm 106:35–39.

So I poured out my wrath on them (18). Again, this is succinct and summarizes all the horrors of earlier visions in the years before the actual fall of Jerusalem. The moral defilement of land and people demanded a moral response from Yahweh, the God of righteousness and justice. To be consistent with his own nature and name, he had to act in punishment. And those in exile needed no further reminding or explanation of the full extent of that punishment. 'Pouring out my wrath' was quite enough to make the point clear. The judgment was also perfectly just and justified, since it was

[44] A woman's menstrual period rendered her ritually unclean for the week it would normally last; that is, for that time she could not mix with the assembly at worship and needed to perform certain ritual washings. It is very important to remember that in Israelite religious thinking, uncleanness was not necessarily a moral category. Many things caused ritual uncleanness that were not inherently sinful. It is also important to note that the relevant chapter in Leviticus dealing with this form of uncleanness is perfectly gender balanced. Lev. 15:1–18 deals with male uncleanness caused by discharges or emissions (long-term – possibly gonorrhoea – vv. 1–15; and merely nocturnal, vv. 16–18), and then deals with female uncleanness (short-term – the monthly period – vv. 19–24; and long-term menstrual dysfunction, vv. 25–30). The explicit balance is summarized in vv. 32–33. This needs to be said in view of the common misunderstanding that a woman's menstrual uncleanness was another example of gender oppression.

[45] Cf. 'To me their conduct was as filthy as a bloody rag' (NLT).

according to their conduct and their actions. The only glimmer of hope is that the verb, along with those of verse 19 (*dispersed ... scattered ... judged*), is past tense. The judgment had fallen. But could there not also be a future? Not yet – not until the people fully understood the immensity of what their punishment at the hand of the nations also meant to Yahweh their God.

b. Profaning God's name (36:20–21)

These verses are not only crucial to understanding the rest of the chapter; they are central to our understanding of Ezekiel's passion for God. First we must grasp what is meant by *they profaned my holy name* (20). It does not mean that the Israelites began to curse, swear and blaspheme. The popular usage of 'profanity' does not help us here. In Israelite thinking, all of life was divided broadly into two compartments – the holy (*qāḏōš*) and the common (*ḥōl*).[46] Most of life was common, and that was no problem. Ordinary things, ordinary people, ordinary places, were simply common. If they were set apart for sacred use ('sanctified'), then they would become holy. In that theological sense Israel as a whole were a 'holy' people, because they were set apart from the nations to be different, for God's own purpose through them. But otherwise in everyday life, ordinary things could be either clean (normally), or unclean (because of ritual or moral defilement). So the word for 'profane' does not have a necessarily derogatory tone; it simply means common or ordinary – no different from any other object or person in that category. But all holiness ultimately flows from Yahweh himself. His name, above all things, is holy – utterly different and distinctive from all other names and gods. Yahweh could never be 'common', for he was not just one of a class (gods). Rather he was utterly unique – the living, true, holy God. How, then, were the exiled Israelites 'profaning the name of Yahweh'? How were they causing Yahweh to be treated as common and ordinary?

Verse 20b gives the answer. *It was said of them* [the Israelite exiles], *'These are the LORD's people, and yet they had to leave his land.'* Again, we need to engage our imagination. Picture the Israelite prisoners of war arriving in the countries they passed through on the ghastly journey from fallen Jerusalem into exile, and then eventually in Babylon itself. Local people would ask each other, 'Who are these people?'

---

[46] It was a fundamental duty of the priests to teach these distinctions to the people (Lev. 10:10–11). Far from teaching them, Ezekiel charged that they had not even been observing them themselves and had taught that there was no difference anyway – thus 'doing violence to the law' (Ezek. 22:26).

289

'Israelites from the land of Judah. Nebuchadnezzar has captured their city and deported the survivors.'

'What's the name of their god, then?'

'Yahweh, or so I've heard.'

'So, they are Yahweh's people but they've been expelled from Yahweh's land! Yahweh is not much of a god, then, is he? No better than the gods of all the other nations our great king has conquered. Glory to Marduk!'[47]

This was the natural conclusion that was drawn in the ancient world of divine–human international politics. The defeat of a nation meant the defeat of its god. Yahweh was self-evidently defeated. Yahweh was therefore no better than any of the rest of the petty national gods who had succumbed to the might of Babylon and her gods. Yahweh's name would be mocked as just another common loser among the gods. 'What Moses, according to Nu 14:16, held up to Yahweh in prayer as a thing to be feared now became a reality. The nations are speaking of a powerless Yahweh … or, what is far worse, as Moses feared according to Ex 32:12, of a malicious and destructive Yahweh.'[48]

The disgrace of Israel meant the disgrace of Yahweh in the eyes of the surrounding nations. And we can be quite sure that the taunts that would have been heaped on them as hapless prisoners of war would have included taunts about their feeble god and their sad old city.[49] That is what is meant by Yahweh's complaint, *'wherever they went among the nations they profaned my holy name'* (20).[50] Far from being the royal priesthood of Yahweh in the midst of the nations,[51] they were roving profaners of his name. What a tragic reversal!

Yahweh is therefore moved to action. He is moved by deep concern for what is happening to his name in the world. *I had concern* (21) is somewhat weak. The word (*ḥāmal*) actually means to feel deep pity and compassion for someone.[52] It is precisely what God had said repeatedly he would *not* show towards his people in the act of judgment itself. But here, the damage to Yahweh's reputation caused by Israel's crushing defeat actually makes him 'feel

---

[47] More than a century earlier, the Assyrian envoy urged the people of Jerusalem to believe exactly this, that Yahweh would prove no stronger than any of the gods of the peoples already conquered by the Assyrians (2 Kgs. 18:33–35).

[48] Zimmerli, *Ezekiel 2*, p. 247.   [49] Cf. Ps. 137:1–3.

[50] 'They brought dishonor to my holy name. For the nations said, "These are the people of the LORD, and he couldn't keep them safe in his own land!"' (NLT).

[51] Exod. 19:4–6.

[52] E.g. Pharaoh's daughter for baby Moses (Exod. 2:6). The rich man failed to show any such emotion to the poor man and his solitary lamb in Nathan's telling parable about the similar actions of David (2 Sam. 12:6).

sorry for his own name'. The actions which follow, therefore, are not driven by pity for Israel (indeed Israel's claim on any divine consideration is severely relativized below), but by pity for the name of Yahweh that was being dragged through the pagan gutters of Mesopotamia.

c. Defending God's holiness (36:22–23)

God, then, moves to clear his name. The exile had been a moral necessity. But paradoxically it had also produced an intolerable situation. Israel had been created in order to bring glory to Yahweh and to be the agent of the knowledge and blessing of God among the nations. Now they were scattered among the nations, but the effect was the precise opposite. Yet Yahweh's ultimate purpose remained – to be glorified among the nations. As the God and Lord of all the earth, all people must eventually come to recognize him for who he truly is. Accordingly, he must act to reverse the dishonour being caused to his name by the outworking of his own just judgment. He would indeed restore his people.

But what would be the primary motivation of that restoration? Other prophets would make the point, movingly and often, that this restoration would indeed be for Israel's benefit and out of God's loving care and compassion.[53] But through Ezekiel, Yahweh corrects any expectation that his action would be based on mere sentiment. *'It is not for your sake, O house of Israel, that I am going to do these things, but for the sake of my holy name'* (22).[54] So these verses, coming here before the wonderful details of the promised restoration in verses 24–30, are a crucial preface to that expectation and hope. The restoration *will* happen,[55] but its purpose must be seen as dictated by two primary theological considerations: first, the holiness

[53] E.g. Is. 41:8–14; 43:1–4; 54:4–10; Jer. 31; etc. Ezekiel is not in the least denying the mercy of God upon Israel, or his covenant faithfulness, or any of the other great terms for his saving love. His point here is focused exclusively on Yahweh's concern for *himself*, not, in this immediate context, for *Israel*. 'Unlike Isa. 40:1ff., this announcement is not intended primarily as a message of comfort for a broken people; nor is the issue for Yahweh their humiliation and pain huddled in a foreign land. Because they have shamefully trampled underfoot the grace of God, they have forfeited all rights to compassion. When Yahweh begins to work, his concern will be the vindication of his own name, not theirs, among the nations.' Block (2), p. 352.
[54] Probably we should take the form of this sentence as an example of what is sometimes called Hebrew 'relative negation'. In order to indicate the relative priority of one thing over another, you would affirm one and deny the other: e.g. 'I desire mercy, not sacrifice' (Hos. 6:6; the second line indicates that it is a comparison). Thus Ezekiel here does not literally deny that the restoration was for Israel's sake, but affirms that it was much more important to realize that it was primarily for the sake of Yahweh's name.
[55] Note the as yet indefinite *I am going to do these things* (22).

of Yahweh's own name (the reputation of God must be restored); and second, the knowledge of Yahweh among the nations (Yahweh must be known; he must be known for what he truly is; and he must be known universally).

> So it is not sadistic cruelty, with which Ezekiel is sometimes credited, but sincere compassion which leads him at this most decisive of moments, when Israel's restoration is at stake, to insist that the compass must be carefully set in the right direction, since only then can one comprehend the way in which God is acting, and since otherwise he will cease to be the Lord God and be turned into a mere idol ... The clear determination of where the centre of gravity lies ... offers a new hope [to the exiles, and] gives them an indissoluble guarantee of a continued historical existence amidst the chaotic history of the nations ... [namely] God's fidelity to his own intrinsic nature.[56]

There is also a strong missiological current flowing in these lines, as they touch on the ultimate and universal mission of the God of the Bible to be known to his whole creation. Before the exile, that mission had been hampered by the appalling wickedness of Israel which, in spite of all God's intentions, had made Israel even worse than the nations to whom they were meant to set an example (the thrust of Ezek. 5). But now the exile itself, the solution to one problem (Israel's persistent sin), had created another (Yahweh's tattered reputation among the nations). 'What is at stake is not an impressive position for Israel, but the justification of God's claim to reveal himself to the world as its God.'[57] Thus Ezekiel, along with other prophets, argues that God's plan of restoration must do two things: it must provide for a radical change of heart and behaviour among God's people; and it must restore God's own name in the earth. Ultimately, of course, only the final act of God's justice and grace through the cross and resurrection of Christ and the sending of his Spirit would accomplish both.

d. Restoring God's people (36:24–30)

At last the words of pure gospel come pouring forth in one of the most beautiful passages in the whole Bible. The repeated *I will* is emphatic. All that will happen will be the work of God himself. Though the word 'grace' is not used here, the whole passage is a portrait of sovereign grace at work, for it is all founded in the wholly unmerited initiative of God. The catalogue of divine activity

---

[56] Eichrodt, p. 496.   [57] Ibid., p. 497.

encompasses every aspect of Israel's loss and need. It addresses their situation as deportees far from their land (24); the defilement of themselves and their land (25, 29a); their congenital disobedience to the laws of God (26–27); and their disgrace among the nations (28–30). And for each of these desperate realities, it provides an answer, as we shall now see.

i. Gathering the deported (36:24)

The restoration of Israel to their own land[58] is described in terms that echo the original exodus in which God had taken Israel 'out' of Egypt and brought them into the promised land. God will accomplish a new exodus and a new conquest. This double 'exodus from the nations' and 'new entry into the land' motif is found elsewhere in Ezekiel,[59] and is even more common in Isaiah 40 – 55. Hosea may have been the first among the prophets to use it,[60] but it goes back ultimately to the covenant promises found in Deuteronomy 30:3–5. It would not be the generation that went into exile that would return, but even for them, such a promise gave them 'a future and a hope'.[61]

ii. Cleansing the defiled (36:25, 29a)

Answering to the language of defilement and filthiness that had so characterized their lives before (cf. v. 17), this is a beautiful picture of cleansing. It draws its symbolic force from the use of both water and blood in cleansing rituals in Israel's religious system.[62] The action

---

[58] The text is referring, of course, to the expectation of restoration from exile, which historically took place in the following generation. For a variety of reasons, which are explored more fully in ch. 9 below, in relation to Ezekiel's final vision of a restored temple and land, it does not seem appropriate to me to connect this prophecy with the return of Jews to the land of Israel in the twentieth century. Theologically, the New Testament applies the restoration and land language of the Old Testament to the coming of the Messiah and the creation of the new community of extended Israel (believing Jews and Gentiles in Christ), not to a continued territorial centre.

For further discussion of the position I adopt on this controversial issue, see Wright, *Knowing Jesus through the Old Testament*, ch. 2, 'Jesus and the Old Testament Promise', esp. pp. 70–77, and 'A Christian approach to Old Testament prophecy concerning Israel', in P. W. L. Walker (ed.), *Jerusalem Past and Present in the Purposes of God* (Grand Rapids: Baker; Carlisle: Paternoster, 1994). See also the helpful discussion of a whole range of issues related to modern Israel and scriptural prophecy in David E. Holwerda, *Jesus and Israel: One Covenant or Two?* (Grand Rapids: Eerdmans; Leicester: Apollos, 1995), esp. ch. 4, 'Jesus and the land: a question of time and place', pp. 85–112.

[59] Ezek. 11:17; 20:34–38 (where it is combined with judgment in the wilderness); 20:41–42; 28:25–26; 34:13; 37:12–14, 21; 39:27–28.

[60] Hos. 2:14–23; cf. also Jer. 30:1–3; 31; 32:37–38;   [61] Jer. 29:10–14.

[62] Priests and Levites had ceremonial cleansing with water as part of their

described was ritual and symbolic, but the truth it portrayed is very precious indeed. Sin makes us dirty. And dirt is a problem.

In relation to our physical bodies dirt is disfiguring, ugly and repelling. Unless it is very temporary because of unavoidable activity, we regard it as evidence of carelessness or as an offence to others in the vicinity. It is always unhygienic, and sometimes seriously dangerous and life-threatening. Even in ordinary life it can be highly embarrassing – an unnoticed piece of dirt in the wrong place in the wrong company can be a social disaster. To turn up dirty and dishevelled before some human dignitary would be grossly offensive and shameful. Dirt is a major issue for the whole human race. We have exercised enormous ingenuity and creativity in dealing with its accumulation. Indeed, a mark of every civilization has been the effort put into removing dirt, through public water supplies, sanitation and sewage systems. Add to all that the vast expenditure on soaps, gels, disinfectants, cleansers, scrubs, water and air filters and purifiers, deodorants and cosmetics. It seems there are no lengths to which we will not go in order to avoid or get rid of dirt. In some parts of the world, of course, just to have assured clean water would be an inestimable step forward out of the degradation and danger of avoidable dirt.

It does not take much imagination, then, to translate such a category into the moral and spiritual dimension. Our sin creates the same reaction in the presence of God as dirtiness produces among ourselves. It offends and repels *him*, and it ought, at the very least, to embarrass *us*. Indeed, an overwhelming feeling of shame at being dirty in the presence of God's utter cleanness is one of the most profound dimensions of genuine conviction of sin. And when we have sunk to the level of seeing, feeling and virtually smelling our own filthiness, the biblical language of cleansing is unspeakably good news.

Sometimes, God commands his people to wash themselves; that is, to deal with and change the behaviours which make them dirty in his presence.[63] And sometimes it is recognized that people may make superficial efforts to do this, but leave the basic stain of guilt untouched.[64] Much more often, it is recognized that the job of cleaning up the accumulated dirt of our lives has to be done by God himself. In the present context and elsewhere, this cleansing work of

---

consecration (Exod. 29:4; Num. 8:7). The ceremonies for producing 'waters of cleansing' from the ashes of a sacrificial heifer, and using and applying such water in cleansing rituals, are given in Num. 19.

[63] Is. 1:16; Jer. 4:14; 2 Cor 7:1.

[64] Jer. 2:22; cf. how Job feels that all efforts to 'wash', i.e. claim his own innocence, would be frustrated by God's accusation (Job 9:30–31).

God is promised for his whole people corporately.[65] But individual believers, in both Old and New Testaments, knew the intensely personal longing to be clean that comes when we approach God in the consciousness of the dirtiness caused by our sin. David's words have given voice to the heart-cry of millions of contrite sinners:

> Wash away all my iniquity
> And cleanse me from my sin …
> Cleanse me with hyssop, and I shall be clean;
> wash me, and I shall be whiter than snow.[66]

David knew that no animal sacrifice in itself could achieve such cleansing, and threw himself on the merciful compassion of Yahweh. Christians know that the one sacrifice of the Lord Jesus Christ alone has made such cleansing possible, not merely with water, but with the blood of his atoning death. And the same countless millions of repentant sinners have found the breathtaking relief that comes from sinking into the warm cleansing water of this promise: 'If we confess our sins, he who is faithful and just will forgive us our sins and cleanse us from all unrighteousness;'[67] and then walking out again, in the sweet-smelling freshness of a bathed baby.

Among their number are the church members of Corinth, some of whom had been pagan idolaters, heterosexual and homosexual prostitutes and perverts, thieves, drunkards, slanderers and swindlers. In the *church*? Yes, says Paul, 'that is what some of you were. But you were *washed*, you were sanctified, you were justified in the name of the Lord Jesus Christ and by the Spirit of our God'.[68] There is wonder-working power in the cleansing blood of Christ to which the saints in every age bear witness. And because of it, we need not shrink back in embarrassment and shame from the purity of God's presence. Rather we are able – I should say encouraged – to 'draw near to God with a sincere heart in full assurance of faith, having our hearts sprinkled to cleanse us from a guilty conscience and having our bodies washed with pure water'.[69] The language of Ezekiel 36:25 still speaks powerfully today.

iii. Transforming the disobedient (36:26–27)

The ancient saying 'The heart of the human problem is the problem of the human heart' was never better exemplified than in the long history of pre-exilic Israel – itself, of course, a microcosm of the human race. As chapters 16, 20 and 23 have shown, Israel was not

[65] Is. 1:18; 4:4; Jer. 33:8; Zech. 13:1; Eph. 5:25–27.   [66] Ps. 51:2, 7.
[67] 1 John 1:9, NRSV.   [68] 1 Cor. 6:9–11.   [69] Heb. 10:22.

just an occasionally disobedient child, or a sporadically flirtatious wife. They had shown a persistent, wilful and incorrigible determination to disregard the covenant requirements of Yahweh and an unstoppable downward drift towards, and sinking below, the levels of wickedness to be found among the non-covenant nations. The problem lay not just in their behaviour, but in the source of their behaviour – the attitudes and mentality that characterized them. In short, the problem was in their 'heart' and 'spirit'.

The two terms *heart* (*lēḇ*) and *spirit* (*rûaḥ*) describe the inner human person. In Hebrew idiom, the heart is the locus of the mind, not primarily of the emotions. It is in or with the heart that a person thinks, decides and wills. The spirit reflects the inner feelings and aspirations of the person – again, not merely in the sense of emotions, but in terms of the attitude, disposition and motivation which one brings to choices and actions. The two terms are closely related, but not identical. Israel will have to *think* differently, and *feel* differently. Their whole inner world needs to be transformed.

No longer was it enough to expect God to 'circumcise their hearts' in the graphic metaphor of Deuteronomy 30:6.[70] Much more radical surgery is needed now. So, in repetition of 11:19, God proposes a heart transplant. He will remove the *heart of stone*, which has made Israel hard, cold, unresponsive and dead to Yahweh's words of command or of appeal. And he will implant in its place *a heart of flesh* – flesh which is living, warm and soft, and which, in Hebrew idiom, speaks of close kinship and intimate relationship.[71]

---

[70] Jeremiah uses the same metaphor as a command to Israel (Jer. 4:4). He wrestled with the hardness of Israel's heart, and the human impossibility of their changing by themselves any more than they could change their skin colour (Jer. 13:23; cf. 17:9).

[71] It is worth pointing out that Ezekiel's use of 'flesh' here for the new heart is entirely positive. Though in other contexts the Old Testament can use 'flesh' in contrast to 'spirit' to indicate weakness or transience (e.g. Is. 31:3), the word 'flesh' in itself does not have negative or sinful overtones in the Old Testament. The body was never regarded as intrinsically evil, nor compared negatively with the 'soul' (a dichotomy which is simplistic and foreign to Old Testament theology in any case). Paul's common use of 'flesh' (Greek *sarx*) as a shorthand for the sinful human nature in rebellion against God should not be read back into the Hebrew Scriptures. On the other hand, Paul was capable of using 'flesh' in the same positive way as Ezekiel. In 2 Cor. 3:3, speaking of the Corinthian church as his 'letter of recommendation', he comments that this was written 'not on tablets of stone but on tablets of human [lit. fleshy] hearts'. Richard B. Hays regards this passage as a deliberate echo of Ezek. 36, with the added emphasis on the role of the Spirit drawn from Ezek. 37, showing that Paul regarded the church, even the problematic Corinthian church, as the fulfilment of prophetic visions of a new, transformed, eschatological community: R. B. Hays, *Echoes of Scripture in the Letters of Paul* (New Haven and London: Yale University Press; 1989), pp. 125–131.

God will transform Israel's whole mindset and fundamental orientation of will, desire and purpose.

The purpose of such transformation is wholehearted obedience. But that requires a further action of Yahweh upon Israel. '*I will put my Spirit in you.*' In chapter 37 Ezekiel will describe some remarkable effects of this infusion of God's own Spirit, but at this point he is concerned primarily with its effect upon Israel's behaviour in relation to God's law. And that effect will be that Israel will at last be obedient. The twin phrases of verse 27b (*to follow my decrees and be careful to keep my laws*) are identical to the covenantal conditions given in Leviticus 26:3. The paradox here is that God himself, by the gift of his Spirit, will see to it that his renewed people actually will fulfil the condition that he himself sets. The NIV *I will ... move you to follow* is slightly weak. God's intention is stronger than that. He says (lit.), 'and I will make [it happen]' or 'I will work it out, that in my decrees you will walk and my commands you will keep and do them'.

A similar paradox is found in Deuteronomy 30:1–10 (on which Ezekiel may well be reflecting here). There, in verses 2 and 10 (cf. 6:5), the fundamental command that Israel should love God with all their heart and soul is echoed in the condition that they must turn to him and obey him with all their heart and soul. Yet in the centre of the passage (v. 6), God promises that he, the Lord your God himself, 'will circumcise your hearts and the hearts of your descendants, *so that* you may love him with all your heart and with all your soul, and live'. God will do in and for Israel what Israel's history so gloomily demonstrated they could not do for themselves. God's grace will give what God's law requires. The gospel is already breathing through such texts in the law – as it is here in Ezekiel's prophecy.

There is, of course, a tension here (as throughout the Bible) between the role of human will and choice and the role of divine causation. God commands obedience and we must make our free choice to respond and obey – or not. But at the same time, God gives his Spirit and 'makes' that obedience happen. One pole of the tension affirms human freedom. The other affirms divine sovereignty. No amount of theology will ever be able to provide a complete correlation of both truths which does not leave us still conscious of mysteries somewhere beyond our grasp. Ultimately, the proof and the test come through experience. And that seems to be what Paul comes down to when reflecting on the role of the Spirit in relation to the law in actual practical experience of Christian living in Romans 8. The Spirit (whom he significantly calls 'the Spirit of life') sets us free from the law at one level, in relation to sin and death and the inability of our fallen human nature to obey God. Yet the very purpose for which Christ died, and for which we are granted the indwelling Spirit, is 'in order that the righteous requirements of the law might be fully met in us, who do not live according to the sinful human nature ["flesh"] but according to the Spirit'.[72]

iv. Restoring the disgraced (36:28–30)

There is a balance to this whole section (36:24–30), which we can see as Ezekiel now returns from his concentration on the inward working of God upon the hearts and minds of his people to the external realities of their restoration to land and nationhood, with which he had begun in verse 24.

The heart of the covenant with Israel was that they should be Yahweh's people in Yahweh's land, living in harmonious relationship with God and in the midst of the blessing and abundance of the land. In this, of course, as in all else, there is a parallel or analogy between God's dealings with Israel and with all humanity. It was God's desire as creator to live with humanity in the earth he made for that purpose, and for that living together to be blessed in both directions of the relationship – humanity with God and humanity with the earth itself. That same triangle of relationships is here prefigured in the promise of restored Israel: renewed possession of the land (28a – in language which recalls Deuteronomy); renewed covenant relationship (28b); and renewed fertility and agricultural growth. God, people and land would enjoy blessed and harmonious fulfilment.

As so often, Ezekiel seems to be reflecting Leviticus 26 in these verses. In the earlier part of that chapter there is a rich description of what it will be like for an obedient people living under the blessing of God. It would be worth reading Leviticus 26:3–12 in order to feel the background to Ezekiel's hope. The promise noticeably includes rain and fertility, peace and security, agricultural

---

[72] Rom. 8:1–4. Paul's echoes of Ezekiel in this text also include the resurrection language of v. 11, and the metaphor of 'walking' ('living', NIV) in v. 4. Although the New Testament clearly links the gift of the Holy Spirit to God's enabling of believers to live in obedience, it is not necessary to regard Ezekiel's prophecy as exclusively eschatological. That is, in talking about God giving his Spirit to Israel – collectively or to individuals – he was not pointing beyond the horizons of Israel's own understanding and experience to some unprecedented event. The Spirit of God in the lives of believers was not lacking in Old Testament times. And it was certainly linked to moral behaviour, such that David was well aware that the sin in his life threatened the presence of Yahweh's Holy Spirit there (Ps. 51:10–11 – a prayer which, paradoxically, many Christians use in their confessions, while holding strangely negative views about the role of the Holy Spirit in the Old Testament!). On this point, see further Block (2), pp. 360–361.

growth, and the personal, covenant presence of Yahweh among his people. Particularly significant are these words: 'I will put my dwelling-place among you,[73] and I will not abhor you. I will walk among you[74] and be your God, and you will be my people.' In the later part of the chapter (vv. 42–45), when it is envisaged that the people will turn back to God after the curses and the judgment of God have fallen upon them, God promises:

I will remember my covenant with Jacob and my covenant with Isaac and my covenant with Abraham, *and I will remember the land*. For the land will be deserted by them and will enjoy its sabbaths while it lies desolate without them. They will pay for their sins because they rejected my laws and abhorred my decrees. Yet in spite of this, when they are in the land of their enemies, I will not reject them or abhor them so as to destroy them completely, breaking my covenant with them. I am the LORD their God. But for their sake I will remember the covenant with their ancestors whom I brought out of Egypt in the sight of the nations to be their God. I am the LORD.

Almost every phrase of this seems to have influenced Ezekiel, including God's concern for his land, the understanding of the exile as punishment, the assurance that God would not forget his covenant, and the awareness that God's dealings with Israel would be 'in the sight of the nations' – both at the original exodus and in the release from exile. The only place where he differs significantly, for the reasons given above, is in his insistence that Yahweh's action on behalf of Israel would be not (primarily) 'for their sake', but for the sake of defending the holiness of his own name.

e. Shamed by God's blessing (36:31–32)

We need to step back for a moment and survey the flow of argument in the chapter so far. In 36:1–15 we saw that the major focus of attention was the effect of the exile *on Israel*. They had been shamed, plundered and taunted. The promise of God to the mountains of Israel was that all that would be reversed so that 'no longer will you suffer the scorn of the peoples' (15). But in the next verse a major

---

[73] A promise which Ezekiel will elaborate in the great final section of his book.

[74] The Hebrew uses an uncommon form of the verb 'to walk' (*hālak* in Hithpael), which means 'to stroll around' – as one does with a friend or loved one. It is also used for Noah and Abraham 'walking with God' (Gen. 6:9; 17:1), but, more significantly in relation to Lev. 26:12, it is used for God's 'strolling' with Adam and Eve in the garden of Eden. Again it is noticeable how the promises of God to Israel reflect his purposes for humanity as a whole.

shift in focus occurs and Israel is forced to consider the effect of the exile *on Yahweh* (16ff.). He too had been shamed, profaned and taunted, and that was intolerable. So the point is made very strongly in verses 22–23 that the restorative work that Yahweh was about to embark upon would be for the ultimate purpose of restoring the holiness of his own name in the midst of the nations. All the blessings described in the verses we have just been considering (24–30) would obviously be for the inestimable benefit of Israel. But we must not forget their primary purpose that the preface (22–23) set out in advance. It is the reputation of Yahweh in the world that is at stake. Thus even the concluding promise that, with her revitalized agriculture and economy, Israel *will no longer suffer disgrace among the nations* (30) will likewise ensure that neither will Yahweh.

It is with this in mind that we come to what may seem initially to be the somewhat contradictory words of verses 31–32. Israel will have no need to be ashamed in the presence of the nations, for God will have restored them and the time of exile and punishment will be over (36:15). But in the presence of God himself, Israel needs to remember with care. Sins which have been forgiven, and indeed cleansed away, are no longer there to be remembered by God and acted upon for judgment. But they are still there to be remembered by the sinner, as a cause for shame and yet simultaneously as a cause for rejoicing in the grace of God. The wonderful blessings of verses 28–30, far from leading to fresh displays of complacency and a return to pre-exilic forgetfulness and rebellion, should instead produce a salutary sense of shame that such blessings can be enjoyed in spite of such a disgraceful past.

It is actually a mark of true conversion – proof of the 'new heart and new spirit' – that one becomes more concerned for God's reputation and glory than for one's own self-vindicating excuses. It is no burden, then, to acknowledge that what God has accomplished in forgiving and restoring us is for his own sake; in Christian terms, ultimately for the sake and the glory of the Lord Jesus Christ. Verse 32 can be twisted to sound as though God's forgiveness is reluctant and self-interested, while all that is left to humans is shame and disgrace. The truly forgiven sinner, however, has no difficulty responding positively to its truth. The only grounds on which he or she could plead for forgiveness in the first place is the character of God as loving, faithful and consistent to his gracious covenant promises. It is to God's own glory that his response to the repentant is always and everywhere and to everyone the same. It is God's name that is glorified, God's reputation that is enhanced, when guilty sinners like me, who know what it is to be *ashamed and disgraced for* our *conduct*, hear the words of pardon, feel the water of cleansing and long to demonstrate a new heart and a new spirit in fresh obedience through the power of his Spirit. With such emotions in one's heart, the dominant longing is for God to be honoured and praised for his incredible and abundant grace and mercy.

Spiritually and psychologically there is profound insight in this chapter into the proper place of shame in the life of the believer. Israel was *not* to feel ashamed in the presence of the other nations (15), but they *were* to feel ashamed in the presence of their own memories before God (31–32). Similarly, there is a proper sense in which believers who have been forgiven by God for all their sins and offences may rightly hold up their heads in company.

We may have no control over what other people think of us, but that need not destroy the proper sense of dignity and self-respect that comes from knowing the affirmation of God himself. In the Gospels Jesus seems deliberately to have given public affirmation to those who experienced his forgiving and reinstating grace.[75] The strong desire that Yahweh would protect the humble and sin-conscious worshipper from public shame and disgrace is often to be found in the Psalms. A favourite of my own for many years has been Psalm 25:

> To you, O LORD, I lift up my soul;
>   in you I trust, O my God.
> Do not let me be put to shame,
>   nor let my enemies triumph over me.
> No-one whose hope is in you
>   will ever be put to shame ...
> Remember not the sins of my youth
>   and my rebellious ways ...
> For the sake of your name, O LORD,
>   forgive my iniquity, though it is great.[76]

And what relief it is to hear the word of God coming, as it did to Israel in exile, to address that fear with the words of assurance:

> 'Do not be afraid; you will not suffer shame.
> Do not fear disgrace; you will not be humiliated.'[77]

With such a promise, and on the basis of the cleansing and restoring work of Christ, the believer can face the world, certainly not with pride, but equally certainly without shame.

[75] E.g. Zacchaeus, the woman who washed his feet, the woman healed of a menstrual disorder, cleansed lepers, the woman caught in adultery, etc.
[76] Ps. 25:1–3, 7, 11. Cf. Pss. 31; 56; etc.   [77] Is. 54:4.

But on the other hand, the same person, alone with God and the memories of the past, can quite properly feel the most acute inner shame and disgrace. It is not, however, a destructive or crushing emotion. Rather, it is the core fuel for genuine repentance and humility and for the joy and peace that flow from that source alone. When *I* remember my sins I know that *God* does not. From his side they are buried in the depths of the sea, covered by the atoning blood of Jesus Christ, never again to be raised to the surface and held against me. And it is only in the awareness of that liberating truth that I can (or even ought) to remember them. For this is not the memory that generates fresh accusation and guilt – that is the work of Satan the accuser. Satan's stinging jolts of memory need to be taken straight to the cross and to our ascended High Priest, for,

> When Satan tempts me to despair,
> And tells me of the guilt within,
> Upward I look, and see him there
> Who made an end of all my sin.[78]

No, this is the memory that generates gratitude out of disgrace, celebration out of shame. It is the memory which marvels at the length and breadth and depth of God's rescuing love that has brought me from what I once was, or might easily have become, to where I am now, as a child of his grace.

> In the cold mirror of a glass, I see my reflection pass;
> See the dark shades of what I used to be;
> See the purple of her eyes, the scarlet of my lies.
> I said, Love, rescue me.[79]

f. Rebuilding God's reputation (36:33–38)

So this amazing chapter comes full circle. It summarizes the message with which it began: there will be a restoration of Israel to her land. This will not just be a token settlement of a few tenuous survivors. Rather, this will be a major task of complete restoration such as one might see after the ravages of war. Towns will be rebuilt, agriculture will be re-established, the population will begin to increase again.[80]

---

[78] Hymn 'Before the throne of God above', by Charitie Lees Bancroft.

[79] From the song 'Love rescue me', by U2.

[80] It has to be recognized, of course, that there is some distance between Ezekiel's optimistic portrayal of the restoration and the historical reality that faced the returning exiles after the decree of Cyrus in 538 BC (just as there is with the picture painted in Is. 40 – 55 as well). Nevertheless, although the small post-exilic community in Jerusalem and Judah struggled, they did survive, and a restored, viable community was indeed established in the land under Persian protection.

The revival of Israel as a nation in their own land will draw astonished comparisons from the surrounding people – comparing it to the garden of Eden (35).[81]

However, in line with the message of the second half of the chapter, the ultimate purpose of all this is not merely the good of Israel, but the recognition of Yahweh as God among the nations (36, 38). In the immediate historical context, these nations are specified as *the nations around you that remain*. This must refer to the remnants of different ethnic populations that survived the Babylonian predations around the time of the attack on Jerusalem. When those nations see the return of the people of Israel and the rebuilding of their land and nation they will draw conclusions about Yahweh that are the reverse of those they had drawn at the time of Israel's destruction and deportation. In language probably borrowed from Jeremiah, they will see that Yahweh is as capable of building as of destroying, of planting as of uprooting (36).[82]

But in the longer, wider perspective, the chapter ends[83] with the general affirmation that is so central to Ezekiel's whole personality and message – *Then they will know that I am the LORD.* 'They' may include the Israelites of the immediate context, who are now free once again to address God with their prayers and petitions (37), but it probably should be taken in its widest sense. All God's action in relation to Israel in the sight of the nations is so that all of them – Israel and the nations alike – should come to the only final knowledge that really counts: Yahweh alone is God.

4. From *rigor mortis* to resurrection (37:1–14)

It was day-trip time again for Ezekiel. The last time *The hand of the Lord* had lifted him up and set him somewhere, it was to witness the awful abominations going on in the temple in Jerusalem (chs. 8 – 11). The last time he had gone out to the *valley*[84] he had been confronted with the vision of the glory of Yahweh for the second time (3:22–23), and came home unable to speak or leave his house for nearly five years. What atrocious vision or fate awaited him this time? he may have wondered, as the hand of Yahweh took

---

[81] Although this is obviously rhetorical as a metaphor, the use of Eden imagery does hint yet again at the way in which God's dealings with Israel are ultimately part of his universal purpose for the restoration of humanity to that which was lost through the fall.   [82] Jer. 1:10; 31–33; 45:4.

[83] The chapter also returns at the end to the metaphor of sheep and flocks (just as 37:24 also returns to a reference to David as shepherd), which further indicates the structural unity of this whole section of chapters (34 – 37).

[84] The word means a large flat valley, or plain.

him in its familiar grip and transported him *by the Spirit* back to that dread valley.

a. The scene (37:1–2)

Television pictures of the aftermath of war are the nearest we can get to the horror of what confronted Ezekiel in his vision. Unearthed mass graves, bodies in gas-chambers and concentration camps, piles of skulls and skeletons, severed limbs after street explosions, bloated corpses after earthquakes or tidal waves – all modern images which fill us with revulsion and the shudder of witnessing human death on a mass scale. None of these, of course, is quite what Ezekiel saw, but the impact of a whole vast plain covered in unburied human bones must have been equally appalling. As a priest he was not allowed to touch a human corpse. Yet here the hand of God actually takes him for a walk, *to and fro*, through the grisly scene, until he can see for himself two things about these bones. First, that there were *a great many* of them. Later, we learn that there were enough to constitute *a vast army* (10), so this really is the remains of a catastrophic battle in which thousands of people have died. Second, that they were *very dry* – that is, these were not recently slain corpses, but the dry bones of people long dead. Scavenging animals and birds have done their job and the sun has baked and bleached them. Not only is there no trace of life; there is no trace of the recognizable individuals they once were on this earth. Just dry bones in a valley.

What was also very obvious was that they were unburied, and that too was a source of horror greater to Ezekiel than to us. Proper burial was of paramount importance in ancient near-eastern cultures – not just for the sake of the bereaved (as it still is in modern cultures), but for the sake of the deceased also. To be deprived of burial was the final insult, the ultimate degradation. To be unburied meant the perpetuation of suffering into the afterlife. It was a destiny fit only for the truly cursed. Indeed, it was one aspect of the fate decreed for Israel under the covenant curses.[85] These bones, then, are not just evidence of death, but of death under curse. These bones proclaim that their 'owners' had been the victims not only of battle, but also of divine judgment.

b. The question (37:3)

He asked me, 'Son of man, can these bones live?' What a question! There you are, standing in the middle of the biggest accumulation

[85] Deut. 28:25–26; cf. Jer. 34:17–20. Once again, one suspects that meditation on the words of Jeremiah may have influenced Ezekiel's visionary amplification of Jeremiah's vivid rhetoric; in this case the background may be Jer. 8:1–3.

of the deadest bones you can imagine, stretching as far as your eye can see, and God asks you, 'What do you think, then? Could these bones come back to life?' The question is absurd; the answer, surely, is self-evident. But Ezekiel responds with a brilliant answer that returns the ball to God's court: 'Lord Yahweh, only you know the answer to that.'

For indeed, as Ezekiel would have known very well, Yahweh was the Lord of life and death. A fundamental part of Israel's monotheistic creed was the complete rejection of the common idea that there were gods of the world of the living and gods of the world of the dead. No, Yahweh alone was sovereign over both spheres. Life and death were alike subject to his power. One of the earliest poems in the Hebrew Bible proclaims,

> See now that I myself am He!
> There is no god beside me.
> I put to death and I bring to life,
> I have wounded and I will heal,
> and no-one can deliver out of my hand.[86]

The same double affirmation is made by Hannah,[87] and by the psalmist in relation to all life on earth.[88] As well as these liturgical declarations, Ezekiel would have known the stories of those rare occasions in the Old Testament of the resuscitation of the dead through the powerful prayer of Elijah and Elisha,[89] and of the startling revival of a corpse upon contact with the bones of Elisha.[90] So, yes, Ezekiel would have willingly agreed that it was well within the power of Yahweh to revive the dead. However, those stories in the traditions of his people were cases of the resuscitation of recently dead people, people whose bodies were fully intact and scarcely cold. But *bones*? Dry bones of the long dead? Fragmentary remains of people no longer personally identifiable? In what possible way could they 'live again'? It was more than could be imagined, let alone believed. Ezekiel's answer is understandably cautious. 'He had the knowledge not to deny God's ability, but he lacked the faith to believe in it.'[91] So he bounces the question back to God himself.

c. The miracle (37:4–10)

If it was faith he needed, he needed it immediately, for God was speaking again, with a command that made the preceding absurd

---

[86] Deut. 32:39.   [87] 1 Sam. 2:6.   [88] Ps. 104:29–30.
[89] 1 Kgs. 17:17–24; 2 Kgs. 4:18–37.   [90] 2 Kgs. 13:20–21.
[91] Taylor, p. 237.

question seem perfectly sane. *'Prophesy to these bones and say to them, "Dry bones, hear the word of the LORD!"'* Now it is a well-attested anatomical fact that although ears have many bones, bones do not have any ears. To preach to bones is even more futile than preaching to the deaf.[92] It was one thing to have been commanded, in his first encounter with God near this place, to preach God's word to people with stiff faces, hard hearts and bronze foreheads. At least they were alive, with faces, hearts and foreheads of some sort. Now he was confronted with neither faces nor hearts, and the only foreheads were on bleached and broken skulls. 'Preach,' insisted the divine voice; 'Preach to the dead! Preach the promise of breath and life, of flesh and skin, and of the knowledge of Yahweh, the Lord and giver of life!' (5–6).

And so, with a laconic brevity as dry as the bones themselves, Ezekiel describes his simple obedience – *So I prophesied as I was commanded.* That's all. He just spoke aloud with ordinary words. No magic. No secret incantations. No conjuring tricks with bones. Just the living power of the word of the living God invading the valley of the shadow of death. Ezekiel's vision, like his previous ones, now takes on an audiovisual quality that would be censored out if it were ever presented with cinematic realism. His obsession with detail notices every moment of the reconstruction process – bones attaching to each other in precise skeletal correctness, then the sinews, followed by the muscles, and at last the skin. As a priest trained in cutting up animals for sacrifice, he doubtless knew more than most people about anatomy.[93] So it was not difficult for him to visualize the reversal of a process he had probably himself carried out – flaying a cadaver from skin to bone. But suddenly, as the miracle of reconstruction proceeds before his astonished eyes, it all suddenly grinds to a halt. The bones have become nothing but lifeless corpses – a remarkable reversal in its own way, but no great advance on their previous condition. *There was no breath in them* (8b). No breath, no life, no movement. The vultures would have been circling for an unexpected second helping.

Then suddenly, into the continuing silence of death, the divine voice speaks for the third time, to initiate the second and final part of the momentous revival: *'Prophesy to the breath ... "Come from the four winds, O breath, and breathe into these slain, that they may live"'* (9). At this point it is worth noting the dominance of this whole scene by the Hebrew word here translated *breath*. It is the

[92] Even Isaiah rose only to telling the deaf to hear and the blind to see (Is. 42:18), not telling the dead to stand up!   [93] Zimmerli, *Ezekiel 2*, p. 260.

word *rûaḥ*, and it is used ten times in this single section (36:1–14), but with a wonderful variety of significance. At the beginning and end of the section it refers unmistakeably to the Spirit of Yahweh which had lifted Ezekiel and *set* him in the valley (1), and would eventually also lift the whole people and *settle* (same word) them back in their own land (14).[94] But the word also means 'breath' in a literal, straighforward sense, and this is its meaning in verses 5, 6, 8 and 10. *rûaḥ* also means 'wind' – powerfully moving air – and this too is found in verse 9, where *from the four winds* means 'from all directions of the earth'. The central use, in verse 9, *O breath*, which Ezekiel is commanded to summon by prophetic word, has the ambiguity that it doubtless means the Spirit of the living God, but also accomplishes the miraculous act of artificial respiration by which the corpses begin literally to breathe again and stand up alive and vigorous as an army. The whole scene, then, is permeated by the various activities of *rûaḥ* – human, natural and divine: breath, wind and Spirit. And the single total effect of all this activity of *rûaḥ* is life, life out of utter deadness.

There is another event being mirrored here. The picture of the divine breath breathing into inanimate bodies so that they come to life undoubtedly recalls the original creation of humanity as recorded in Genesis 2:7. In that account also there is a two-stage process of divine activity. First God fashioned the human creature[95]out of the lifeless dust of the earth. At a biological level we share the same stuff and substance as the rest of creation, animal, vegetable and mineral. But then, in an act of tender intimacy, God breathed into human nostrils the breath of life[96] so that the human became a living being – living because breathing. So here in Ezekiel's vision, the unique, life-giving power of the creator God once more breathes life into inert human flesh and brings forth a miracle of new existence. The revival of Israel will

---

[94] This device, known as 'inclusion', of using the same words to denote the beginning and ending of a section, is typical of Ezekiel.

[95] *hā-'āḏām* in Gen. 2:7 is used in the generic sense of 'the human', not in the gender-specific sense of 'the man', or the personal sense of 'Adam'. In this sense the account in Gen. 2:7 is complementary to that in Gen. 1:26–27, which concentrates on humanity's creation as the image of God, a term which includes both sexes.

[96] This term uses the expression *nᵉšāmâ*, which is often paralleled with *rûaḥ*. In Gen. 2:7 it does simply mean physical breath, not some kind of immortal soul, which is often mistakenly read into this verse. The expressions 'breath of life' and 'living being' have already been used several times in the preceding context to describe animal life as distinct from vegetation (Gen. 1:20, 24, 28, 30; cf. 6:17, 19; 7:15, 22). Neither term, therefore, refers to anything (such as a 'soul') that humans have which animals do not.

be nothing less than the re-creation of humanity – a thought we must return to.

But first, it is also worth observing the connection between word and spirit here. Perhaps this was another reason for the pause in the proceedings and the command that Ezekiel should speak the word of God again, the word that would release the re-creating Spirit. The combination is powerfully presented in one of Israel's creation psalms.

> By the word of the LORD were the heavens made,
> their starry host by the breath of his mouth.[97]

d. The promise (36:11–14)

At last the whole point of the vision is made clear. Yet again, a popular saying among the exiles has provided the spur to the vision and its application. As we have seen many times before, the mood among the exiles was one of utter despair, once the city had fallen and it became clear that they would not be returning soon – if ever. Exile in the pagan, enemy land of Babylon was a living death. They might as well be in a cemetery. All these feelings are summed up in the lament of verse 11: *'Our bones are dried up and our hope is gone; we are cut off.'*

To such fears, Ezekiel's word of hope now comes. As happens in visions, the scenery changes rapidly. From being in a valley of unburied bones, Ezekiel now pictures Israel as buried in the graves of exile.[98] Ezekiel is not, of course, talking to literally dead people, but to living Israelites whose life in exile was tantamount to being entombed in a cemetery. But *'I am going to open your graves'*, says God – not (as was common) to rob them, or to throw in more bodies, but rather for the miraculous purpose of bringing them up out of them! He would bring them back to life, in the sense of bringing them back to the land and to national restoration. Israel would live again! The dead bones would stand up as a mighty army. And then they would know that it was only by the Spirit of Yahweh that such a national resurrection had taken place.

---

[97] Ps. 33:6. The same psalm significantly draws out the universal implications of this truth, in relation to God's moral demand on all human life and his sovereignty over the world of nations and history.

[98] Some scholars have objected to this sudden change and made it a reason to dissect the oracle more ruthlessly than the original bones themselves. However, given the visionary nature of the event, there is no need to insist on total consistency of imagery and symbolism.

e. The aftermath

Does this text, then, teach the resurrection of the dead? As mentioned above, it was already part of Old Testament belief that Yahweh had the power over life and death, and resuscitation of the dead was not unknown. But there does not seem to have developed a full expectation of resurrection of all people in anything like the New Testament sense, during the major period of the Old Testament itself, and probably not by the time of Ezekiel. The resurrection of Jesus was something unique and unprecedented, and that is what made it such earth-shakingly good news. When people heard the excited proclamation of the disciples that God had raised Jesus from the dead, they did not just say, 'Oh good, another one, then.' It was a new act of God, a powerful demonstration of his ultimate defeat of the power of death altogether and the beginning of a whole new dimension of life.

But when we seek to understand Ezekiel's message in its own context, it is vital to remember that his main point was to bring hope *to Israel as a people.* His vision and its interpretation were not intended to teach a doctrine of bodily resurrection, but to compare the restoration of Israel to the imaginary bringing back to life of the bones of a massive army of slain soldiers. The language is symbolic and metaphorical, and its application was for the still living, not the already dead. That is, Ezekiel's vision promised the exiles that there would be a living future for Israel in the return from exile; it did not promise that those who had died in 587 or those who would die during the exile itself would literally come back to life to share in that return. That kind of resurrection hope seems to have developed later.[99] The main point, then, of Ezekiel's language was to invest the historical events (past and future) of his own day with their true theological significance.[100] On the one hand, this meant accepting the verdict of the exiles on their condition – they were indeed as good as dead, because in covenant terms they had chosen death through disobedience and rebellion. The catastrophe of 587 was indeed national and covenantal death. On the other hand, it meant proclaiming the full significance of what Yahweh was about to do

[99] This depends, of course, on one's dating of relevant texts. The only texts which seem to point unambiguously to individual resurrection include Dan. 12:1–3 and Is. 26:19. Hos. 6:1–2, though quoted in the New Testament in relation to the resurrection of Jesus, in its own context seems to speak of national repentance and renewal by God's power.

[100] On this way of understanding the meaning of prophetic and apocalyptic imagery, and with special relevance to the concept of resurrection as related to Israel's national hope, see N. T. Wright, *The New Testament and the People of God* (London: SPCK, 1992), ch. 10, and pp. 200, 211 and 322.

when he would act to set them free and bring them back. It would be nothing short of life out of death, nothing less than a miracle of resurrection.

Nevertheless, there is no doubt that Ezekiel's vision of dry bones and their revival functions as a very important link in a theological chain to which the full biblical hope of resurrection is anchored. At one end is the connection we have already noted between Ezekiel's vision of God breathing life into the lifeless bodies of Israel's defunct army and the Genesis tradition of God breathing the breath of life into the human-shaped pile of dust that then became a living human being. God's renewal of Israel was like a rerun of creation. Or, to put it the other way round, what God was about to do for Israel would be like the first act in the renewal of humanity as a whole. Here again, as in so many ways, the links between Israel and humanity are apparent. Israel had been called in the first place, through Abraham, to be a blessing to all the nations of the earth. Their election and redemption were for the sake of the rest of humanity. Likewise, therefore, just as their sin and punishment mirrored the fallenness of the whole race, so too their restoration would prefigure God's gracious purpose of redemption for humanity. Resurrection for Israel anticipated resurrection for all.

And at the centre of the chain stands Jesus himself. We have already seen how Ezekiel influenced Jesus in several respects. The most significant echo of Ezekiel 37 comes in a locked room on the very evening of his resurrection, when, we read, 'he breathed on them and said, "Receive the Holy Spirit."'[101] The Lord of life himself, freshly risen to his feet from where he had lain among the bones of the dead, adopts simultaneously the posture of Ezekiel in summoning the breath of God, and the posture of God himself in commanding the breath of the Spirit to come upon the disciples.

But this risen Jesus was the Messiah. And slowly the disciples came to realize that in the resurrection of the Messiah God had done, through Jesus, what they were hoping and expecting that God would do for Israel.[102] The redemption, revival and resurrection of Israel were embodied in the resurrection of Jesus the Messiah. As James would later affirm, the Davidic monarchy was also restored,[103] and as Hebrews would argue in detail, all the great realities of Israel's faith and covenantal security are now embodied in Jesus and inherited by those who believe in him – believing Jews and Gentiles alike.

So the resurrection of Jesus *did* fulfil the vision of Ezekiel through his personal embodiment of the restoration of Israel. But, in line with the thrust of our earlier point, the restoration of Israel through

---

[101] John 20:22.   [102] Luke 24:19–27, 45–49.   [103] Acts 15:16–17.

Jesus was also the first stage of God's wider project of the redemption of the human race. The breath that breathed life into the dead came from *the four winds* – that is, the Spirit of God is at work everywhere in the world, in all directions. That which was focused with tremendous resurrection power on Ezekiel's dead bodies, and then on the dead Messiah, is the same power that is available to the ends of the earth to bring life, salvation and the hope of bodily resurrection to all who trust in the one who sends it. For 'if the Spirit of him who raised Jesus from the dead is living in you, he who raised Christ from the dead will also give life to your mortal bodies through his Spirit, who lives in you'.[104]

5. From enmity to unity (37:15–28)

And so we come to the final scene in this wonderful compendium of the gospel according to Ezekiel. He began with the promise of a restored theocracy: God's people would no longer be badly governed and exploited, but would enjoy the righteous leadership of God himself exercised through the Davidic Messiah (ch. 34). He then moved on to describe the protection of Israel from her enemies. God's people would be restored from the disgrace of landlessness and given back the inheritance that demonstrated their relationship with God (35:1 – 36:15). Yahweh's own point of view then dominated our attention, as Ezekiel ruthlessly portrayed the damage that Israel's sin and punishment had done to the name and reputation of their God. So their restoration would be good news not only for Israel, but also for the name of Yahweh among the nations of the world (36:16–38). But how could all this ever happen to a people as good as dead and buried (or, more poignantly, unburied)? Only by the power of the Spirit of Yahweh and his intention to bring about nothing short of a miracle of resurrection would Israel come back from the dead (37:1–14).

But finally, which Israel? There was one tragic historical fact that stood in the way of full covenantal renewal. The covenant nation had split in two after the reign of Solomon – half a millennium ago, from the standpoint of the exiles. It was an ancient and apparently irreversible cleavage. The northern kingdom of Israel had been wiped off the face of the map in any case, 150 years before the present destruction of the kingdom of Judah. And in spite of some attempts by godly kings like Hezekiah and Josiah to bring about some reunification of the remnants of the north with the people of Judah,[105] it really had not worked out. But Yahweh is not only the God of life;

---

[104] Rom. 8:11.   [105] 2 Chr. 30; 34:6, 9; 35:18.

he is also the God of unity. If death can be reversed, so can division. So Ezekiel's final acted prophecy portrays a future unification of the people of God. There will ultimately be one people of the one God.

Yet again, Ezekiel lays his hands on ordinary objects and turns them into a powerful visual aid to his message. He is told to take (lit.) 'one wood' and write on it; and then to take another 'one wood' and write on it too. The common translation *a stick of wood* (NIV etc.), interprets the term in a possible way: namely, that Ezekiel took two sticks. But the word is general and could mean a piece of wood in almost any shape or form. An ancient suggestion, which is revived and argued for quite strongly by Block,[106] is that the object was a small wooden writing-tablet. These were flat pieces of wood, smoothed with hardened wax, on which rough messages could be written. They were the ancient equivalent of a notepad. This interpretation (cf. REB, 'wooden tablet') makes more sense of the fact that Ezekiel was to write a number of words on each piece of wood. Also, it was common practice to bind or hinge several single tablets together in a kind of double or triple folder – which again, is exactly what Ezekiel was commanded to do – in such a way that the tablets when folded would lie flat on top of each other and could be held in one hand (17). This scenario would seem preferable to imagining Ezekiel writing on thin sticks which were then either spliced end to end or bound side by side.[107] A dynamic-equivalence translation might say, 'Take a single sheet of notepaper and write this on it … Then take another single sheet of notepaper and write this on it … Now glue them together down the middle to make the two sheets into one new single sheet.'

The words to be written on each piece of wood were unmistakable: one represented the kingdom of *Judah*, and the other the northern kingdom which had been dominated by the tribe of *Ephraim* (in fact it was often simply called that). But very significantly, Ezekiel writes the word *Israel* on *both* pieces. Judah is qualified by the words *and the Israelites* (lit. 'children of Israel'), *associated with him*, and Ephraim is qualified by *and all the house of Israel associated with him*. For Ezekiel (and in the sight of God), there never were two Israels. The sad political division could never destroy the fact that there was only one covenant people in God's

[106] Block (2), pp. 399–401.
[107] If sticks were indeed intended, then the possible significance would be that they were meant to symbolize the sceptres of the two royal houses (cf. Allen 29, p. 193). However, as Block argues, something as obvious as royal sceptres would hardly have generated the question of v. 18, and in any case, the prophecy that follows speaks not of a unification of the two schismatic monarchies, but of the two kingdoms under the original Davidic monarchy.

eyes. Even though the northern kingdom had hijacked the name 'Israel' for itself, it was still the case that at a deeper theological level the term still applied to the original ideal concept of the twelve tribes of Israel in covenant with Yahweh and each other. And that is what God now intends to restore.

So the prophecy goes on to envisage a future that will not merely involve the restoration of the survivors of Judah, but will constitute a reconstruction of the original nation. In a literal sense, of course, this did not happen in this way. The dispersion of the northern tribes by the Assyrians after the destruction of Samaria in 721 was never really reversed in the same way that the exiles of Judah returned from Babylon after the edict of Cyrus in 538.[108] But Ezekiel's point, again, is not so much ethnic and geographical, but theological, or perhaps we might say ecclesiological. He is determined to insist that the future of God's people is a future for *one* people. One God, one people, one covenant.

The emphasis on oneness that flows through this passage is less obvious in translation than in the original Hebrew. The word *'ehād* (one) occurs eleven times between verses 16 and 24. Often it is simply translated as 'a', or 'another' or 'together'. But the repetition is emphatic in Hebrew. Verse 17, for example, reads (lit.), 'Combine them one to one into one wood so that they become one in your hand.' The reader is thus well prepared for the final theological thrust of the great panoramic vision with which the chapter concludes, and with it the whole grand message of chapters 34 – 37

Yahweh will create for himself *one nation* (22a), under *one king* (22b), who will reign as *one shepherd* (24). And, with a passion that comes close to saying, 'all lived happily ever after', the oracle piles up together in a grand climax all the themes we have heard already: cleansing from all idolatry (23); righteous rule through the Davidic king (24a); perfect obedience (24b); security in God's land (25); an everlasting covenant of peace (26a); growth (26b); the permanent presence of God in the midst of his people (27); and the perfection of covenant relationship between God and people (23b, 27b). And, as we have now come to expect (for Ezekiel is not one ever to let

---

[108] The view, which is still adamantly held in some quarters, that the 'ten lost tribes' of the destroyed northern kingdom somehow migrated to northwestern Europe and became the ancestors of the Anglo-Saxon peoples (primarily Britain and America) has no basis in reputable historical research (in my opinion), and the theological implication that is then built upon it (namely, that the Anglo-Saxon 'race' has inherited the great privileges of Israel, including the idea that the British monarch sits on the throne of David) flies in the face of the New Testament teaching which affirms Ezekiel's vision of the unity of Israel in the Messiah Jesus, and generates an ethnocentric (and virtually racist) contradiction to the biblical picture of the multinational nature of the people of God in Christ.

us forget), the ultimate goal to be achieved is that the nations will know the truth about who is really God and what he has done for his people (28).

This final note of universality – that God's work in Israel would have implications beyond Israel and affect the rest of the nations – is echoed in another hint that the Johannine Jesus had these texts of Ezekiel very much in mind as he envisaged his own mission. We have already seen how Jesus' claim to be the good shepherd in John 10 is surely a conscious applying to himself of the prophecies of Ezekiel 34. Likewise, in anticipating the spread of his ingathering and unifying work beyond the 'flock' of Israel, he uttered the words that undoubtedly also echo Ezekiel 37:24: I have other sheep that are not of this sheep pen. I must bring them also. They too will listen to my voice, and there shall be one flock and one shepherd.[109]

Such a vision on the one hand anticipates also the insistence of Paul that God's ultimate purpose is 'one new humanity', of believing Gentiles and Jews, united through the cross of Christ and acceptable to God.[110] And on the other hand, it excludes any form of 'two-covenant' theory which wants to suggest that God has somehow got a double agenda running in his saving purposes – one covenant with national Israel, and another with Gentile Christians. As I have argued elsewhere, this 'two-covenant' view 'utterly subverts Paul's claim that the very heart of the gospel was that in it God had created *one* new people ... that through the gospel the Gentiles are heirs *together* with Israel, members *together* of *one* body, and sharers *together* in the promise of the Messiah Jesus (Eph. 3:6)'.[111] Nothing less than this great declaration will satisfy the chords of Ezekiel's great symphonic prophecy of one people under one Lord.

[109] John 10:16. [110] Eph. 2:11–22.
[111] Wright, *Knowing Jesus through the Old Testament*, p. 177.

38:1 – 48:35

9. The glory of God revealed to the world and restored to his people

Introduction

The gospel had been preached in the plains of Babylon; but the glory was still parked on the hills of Judea.[1] The wonderful group of chapters that we have just worked through, 34 – 37, come to their climax with a dual promise in 37:24–28. First, Yahweh would dwell in his sanctuary among his people for ever, in a state of unity, obedience, peace and security. Secondly, the rest of the nations would know that Yahweh is God and would recognize his dwelling-place among his holy people for ever. This dual vision would mean, in each of its parts, a restoration of the glory of Yahweh. In the first place, his glory had been driven from his own sanctuary by the sin of Israel; a cleansed and restored people would enable the return of God's glory. In the second place, the glory of Yahweh had been shrouded by the way the exile had brought dishonour on his name among the nations; the restoration of that name would likewise reveal Yahweh's true glory in the world at large. Thus there are two directions in which God's purposes are flowing as the message of this prophet reaches its climax: God's purpose for God's people; and God's purpose for God's world. And both involve the revelation and restoration of God's glory.

The final, climactic, section of the book of Ezekiel (chs. 38 – 48), takes up these two concerns in reverse order. In chapters 38 – 39 God deals with those who remain implacable enemies of God and his people. The end result of the massive conflict is clear and inevitable: 'I will display my glory among the nations' (39:21). In chapters 40 – 48 Ezekiel portrays the future of God's people with all the rhetorical power of his priestly worldview, sketching the contours of a restored temple, land and people. Again, the key

[1] On the mountain to the east of Jerusalem, to be precise (Ezek. 11:23).

moment in the whole portayal is the return of the glory of Yahweh for permanent residence among his people (43:1–7).

So, although it is tempting to isolate chapters 40 – 48 and to look for an interpretation of them according to some eschatological scheme, and to do the same independently for the mysterious Gog of Magog prophecy in chapters 38 – 39, it is actually quite important to hold them together as negative and positive sides of the same great affirmation. On the one hand, the enemies of God will never finally triumph and will be unable to prevent or disturb the ultimate purpose of God. And on the other hand, the people of God will ultimately enjoy the perfection of their relationship with him and with each other in total and eternal security.

1. The defeat of Gog and the universal acknowledgment of Yahweh (38:1 – 39:29)

In chapter 7 above we listened to Ezekiel's prophecies directed at historical nations of his own day, collected in Ezekiel 25 – 32. We saw that they come from a specific period of Israel's history (mostly having been delivered during or shortly after the siege of Jerusalem), and that they were primarily intended to speak to the exiles themselves. On the one hand they assured the exiles that God would not overlook the cruel and arrogant behaviour of their enemies, and on the other hand they disabused the exiles of any hope that Jerusalem might be delivered by the intervention of Egypt. In these two chapters, 38 – 39, however, we have an undated collection of oracles against an enemy whose identity is deliberately vague and mysterious – Gog, of the land of Magog. We don't know when they were spoken or who the target was.

The editorial position of these two chapters seems at first sight somewhat odd. We might have expected them to be included in the collection of oracles against the nations in chapters 25 – 32. However, the difference is that those prophecies relate mostly to events that took place while the Israelites were in exile, whereas chapters 38 – 39 explicitly envisage Israel having returned to their land and living peacefully there in an unspecified future era (38:8, 11). Another difference is that, whereas chapters 25 – 32 speak of clearly identifiable nations of Ezekiel's own day, the identity of the persons and nations in chapters 38 – 39 is much more mysterious.

We might also wonder why Ezekiel or the final editor of his book allows the grotesque narrative of these chapters to interrupt the flow between the great chapters which promise restoration (33 – 37) and the final vision of that restoration accomplished (40 – 48). The answer probably is that chapters 38 – 39 make the vital point that, when God ultimately restores his people to the perfect relationships described in 37:24–28 and portrayed in a kind of 'virtual reality' in 40 – 48, there will never again be any danger that such peace and blessing could be threatened or destroyed. The destruction of Gog as the final great enemy of Israel and Yahweh thus stands as ultimate reassurance to God's people that their future is secure. No enemy will disturb the peace of God's people in God's earth ever again. In the same way the book of Revelation, making rich use of the resources provided by Ezekiel, describes the final defeat of the hosts of evil (including Gog and Magog),[2] before climaxing with the vision of God dwelling in the midst of his redeemed people in the new creation.[3]

Chapters 38 – 39 show signs of careful structuring such as we also noticed in chapters 25 – 32. On the larger scale, the section is divided into two matching panels (corresponding to the two chapters themselves) in which the destruction of this enemy is twice portrayed in a series of what may be described as cartoon-strip scenarios. At a finer level of detail, we can see that the narrative is broken up into seven sections (which does not surprise us, after observing the frequent literary patterning into sevens in chs. 25 – 32), identifiable by the opening phrase *This is what the Sovereign LORD says*. We shall first summarize the story, and then briefly survey the seven sections.

a. The story

In spite of some unevenness and repetition, chapters 38 – 39 tell a fairly straightforward narrative. Gog, of the land of Magog, chief prince of Meshech and Tubal, will lead an alliance of other nations from the north to attack an unsuspecting Israel living peacefully in her own land. However, behind the scenes Yahweh will be controlling events so that, far from carrying off plunder as they expected, this hostile alliance will be massively defeated and slain, with accompanying cosmic phenomena (earthquake, plague, blood, fire, hail and brimstone). It will take Israel seven months to bury the dead, during which time the scavenging birds and beasts will eat their fill. And the captured weapons of war will provide firewood for seven years. The end result will be that both Israel and all the nations will know conclusively that Yahweh is God and that the historical events of exile and restoration were all his doing. Thus Yahweh's greatness, holiness and glory will finally be fully revealed and vindicated in the earth.

[2] Rev. 20:7–10.   [3] Rev. 21 – 22.

The seven sections of the above narrative, including some repeated material, run as follows.

i. 38:3–9

The grand alliance of *many nations* musters for its invasion. But already the divine sovereignty can be seen at work behind the human machinations: *'I will turn you around ... and bring you out.* The twin expressions *After many days ... In future years* signal to the reader that we are dealing here with an unspecified future. This is an eschatological vision, not a tight historical prediction, except in the sense that it is definitely envisaged as taking place long after the return from exile and the resettlement of the land (8).

ii. 38:10–13

The diabolical evil of Gog's intentions is now made clear. This is not a normal war between equally armed enemies, but a devastating attack upon *a peaceful and unsuspecting people.* The people of God are portrayed as rich in resources and restored to their central place in God's election (*living at the centre of the land,* v. 12, echoes the significant affirmation about Jerusalem's centrality to God's purpose in 5:5), but physically and militarily defenceless. This is not the military state of Judah or Israel of the monarchy, with their fortified cities, standing armies and strategic alliances. Another hint that there is an eschatological element here which does not quite tie in with actual post-exilic history is the description of the people as *living without walls and without gates and bars* (11), whereas 36:35 spoke of the refortification of the settlements after the restoration, and of course the wall of Jerusalem was eventually rebuilt under Nehemiah. Verse 13 envisages the greed of other nations anticipating a good trade in the plunder that Gog and his alliance would carry off.

iii. 38:14–16

The invasion gets under way, with overwhelming numbers and force. The reference to its coming from *the far north*, and being *like a cloud* (cf. v. 9) echoes earlier prophetic predictions of invasion[4] and add to the mysterious eschatological feel of the vision. Also consistent with earlier prophecies, Ezekiel insists that although Gog's evil intentions are fully his own, the ultimate moving force behind his actions is Yahweh himself. Furthermore, the ultimate purpose of this climactic attack and its subsequent defeat is *so that the nations may know me when I make myself holy through you before their eyes* (16). As with Pharaoh[5] and Cyrus,[6] God controls the results of

---

[4] E.g Is. 10:5–11; Jer. 1:13–16; 4:5–6, 11–17.   [5] Exod. 9:16.
[6] Is. 45:5–6. Cf. also God's summoning of the Babylonians, Hab. 1:5–11.

human plans and actions in such a way that God's own name and glory are the final beneficiary in the world.

iv. 38:17–23

This section closes the first main panel of the narrative with the climactic good news for Israel that Yahweh himself will intervene to defend his otherwise defenceless people. Gog and all his hordes will meet more than their match when they face the *hot anger* of Yahweh. The message is reinforced by verbal echoes from the previous sections: '"Great" forces (v. 15) would be met by a "great" earthquake (v. 19) and by proof of Yahweh's greatness (v. 23).'[7] The *many nations* of the invading force (6) would find themselves *many nations* under the torrent of God's destructive judgment (22), which would prove the *greatness* and the *holiness* of God *in the sight of many nations* (23, echoing 16). Furthermore, the textual echoes of earlier prophets become an explicit reference back to them in verse 17. Not only are the future attack and defeat of Gog and his forces entirely under God's control; it was also within God's prophetic foresight. God's defenceless and unsuspecting people may be taken by surprise, but God himself would not be.[8]

The eschatological nature of the portrayal is also reinforced through the highly symbolic language of the means that Yahweh will use to destroy these enemies of his people in verses 19–22. They

[7] Allen 29, p. 207.
[8] There is some dispute over the precise implication of the question in v. 17. As translated in the NIV ('Are you not the one I spoke of …'), the question obviously expects the answer 'Yes', implying that Gog is the fulfilment of all the earlier prophecies about invasions by God's enemies. However, Block argues that the question should be understood as 'Are you the one …?', implying the answer 'No'. On the former understanding, the question implies that Gog will be the climactic fulfilment of all the prophecies of past centuries regarding the enemies that God would bring against his people, thus reinforcing the affirmation that whatever Gog may intend or do has already been fully anticipated by God and is under his control. Block points out, however, that no previous prophet ever mentioned Gog by name. Furthermore, earlier prophecies regarding destructive foes from the north had clearly been historically fulfilled in the Assyrian and Babylonian invasions. Ezekiel would have been calling for a radical reinterpretation of the prophecies of Isaiah and Jeremiah if he were trying to 'recycle' them into a new apocalyptic future. And, most important of all, the previous invaders predicted by the earlier prophets had all been agents of Yahweh's *judgment* on Israel, sent by God to punish them for their wickedness and rebellion. In sharp contrast, Gog is motivated entirely by his own greed and there is no hint whatsoever in Ezek. 38 – 39 that he is an agent of judgment. Rather, his unprovoked and unjustified enmity for the people of God becomes solely the occasion for God to display his own glory by defeating and destroying him. Block, therefore, reads 38:17 as meaning, 'You are *not* the one prophesied in former days, even if you claim to be, for you are not an agent of Yahweh's wrath against his own people. Rather you will be the target of that wrath yourself.' Block (2), pp. 453–456.

include earthquake, environmental disaster, mountains trembling and crumbling, sword, plague, bloodshed, hail, fire and brimstone. This rhetorical catalogue summons memories of the flood, Sodom and Gomorrah and the plagues of Egypt as well as the more recent historical calamities that had befallen Israel. Here, however, it speaks of the total and final defeat of their enemies.

v. 39:1–16

The second main panel takes up the story again and repeats it with some additional detail. We are reminded that the invading army will be fully under the authority of Yahweh, whose purpose is its complete and final destruction (note how 39:1–2 echoes 38:3–4). Mounted archers were fearsome warriors, but verse 3 asserts that Yahweh will simply strike them disarmed and defenceless. We are not told how; it is simply the direct action of God himself. In order to portray that destruction in its totality, Ezekiel envisages that the captured armour and weapons (for which he uses seven different words) will keep Israel in firewood for seven years (9–10),[9] and that the slaughter will be so great that it will take seven months to bury the dead (12–16). Like the threat '*I will send fire*' on the enemies' homelands (6), the triple use of seven is also symbolic and significant in lifting the narrative out of literal expectation into the realm of figurative portrayal of a climactic defeat of God's enemies on *the day I have spoken of* (8 – another eschatological touch). The meticulous and exhaustive care to be taken over the burial of the enemy corpses is in order to *cleanse the land*. The concern comes from the realm of Israel's religious law,[10] but the wider significance will emerge in chapters 40 – 48. If God is to dwell again in full harmony with his people, then his dwelling-place must be clean and holy. No trace of the pollution of his enemies will remain.

The same practical implication of God's holiness in relation to his dwelling among his people is found in the vision of new creation in Revelation 21:1–8.

---

[9] There is clearly here a vivid and imaginative elaboration of Isaiah's picture of the rubbish of war being used as fuel for the fire (Is. 9:5). It also echoes God's own climactic action to end all wars (Ps. 46:9). Ironically, the weapons of destruction would be turned to a use that would spare the natural resources of the land (v. 10), for a sabbatical seven years. This may be Ezekiel's typically colourful way of embellishing the more familiar picture of Isaiah and Micah, that the end of war would mean turning swords into ploughshares and spears into pruning-hooks (Is. 2:4; Mic. 4:3). Our contemporary concern for the ending of war and the armaments trade for the sake of environmental benefit (among other benefits, of course) is not as modern as we might think!

[10] Num. 19:11–22; Deut. 21:1–9.

vi. 39:17–24

We have met Ezekiel's ability to shock before. And we have also encountered his skill in creating grotesque mental pictures with graphic detail, like some wild cartoon. Here we have an example of both. Even if all the corpses of the defeated enemy were to be buried, the length of time it would take would give ample freedom to the scavenging birds and animals. Such is always the horrible reality of war in any age, and it had already been anticipated in 39:4. Here, however, in the command to *Call out*, Ezekiel delivers invitation cards on behalf of God himself to *every kind of bird and all the wild animals*. They are invited to *come together* to a great sacrificial banquet that God has arranged for them. The cartoon not only specifies the gory details of the feast itself, but even pictures the animals seated at *my table* – gorging themselves at the ghastly banquet in the presence of the divine host (19–20). Our response to such a grisly image must first of all recognize that this is deliberately exaggerated and caricatured language, not a literal prediction. 'Comparable to political cartoons, this frame is to be interpreted not as prophetic literary photography but as an impressionistic literary sketch.'[11] Secondly, we must be aware that if it is repulsive to us, it must have been even more so to Ezekiel, who, as a trained priest, would have found the whole image unbearably sacrilegious. Apart from the obvious taboo relating to dead bodies, the picture skewed and violated all kinds of ritual roles in Israel's system. Instead of human beings offering clean animals in sacrifice to God, here was God inviting all kinds of unclean animals (scavengers were all unclean) to a sacrifice that he had arranged, at which the ultimate taboo was violated – the eating of human flesh. It is horrifying imagery, but it conveys a horrifying reality: those who utterly and implacably remain enemies of God and his people will ultimately face utter destruction. New Testament images of worms and smouldering fire may be more familiar, but are no less devastating in their effect.

The destruction of Gog and his hordes is complete, but what is to be learned from these events? In a first reflection (21–24) Ezekiel envisages a double learning – by Israel and by the nations. *Israel* would know the reality and power of Yahweh their God when they witness his judgment of the nations (21–22); *the nations* would know the truth about Yahweh when they understand the reason for his judgment of Israel (23–24). Both 'knowings' would constitute a recognition of Yahweh's *glory*. In this context, appropriately enough after the graphic description of the defeat and destruction of Gog, the emphasis is on God's glory being displayed through the exercise

[11] Block (2), p. 473.

of his justice. The expression *the punishment I inflict* would be better translated 'the justice (*mišpāṭ*) I execute'. Obviously 'punishment' is a correct interpretation of what happened to Gog and his allies for their unprovoked wickedness, but the point here is that Yahweh's justice operates both *on behalf of* his people (by punishing their enemies), and also *against* his own people (by punishing them too). The glory of Yahweh is thus displayed through the recognition of his consistency. And as if to underline the exclusion of any favouritism, the punishment of Israel is emphasized and explained even more thoroughly, using the familiar words of Ezekiel's earlier accusations: they had been exiled for *their sin*, their unfaithfulness, *their uncleanness* and *their offences*. It is worth recalling that these chapters portraying the great final defeat of all their enemies were first directed at the Israelites still in exile, undergoing the wrath of God for their own sin. Any kind of complacent or arrogant gloating over the fate of their future enemies needed to be snuffed out. As God's redeemed people we cannot contemplate the ultimate defeat of evil and the destruction of the wicked with any sense of moral superiority. For we know that apart from the grace of God which has brought us to repentance and restoration, the same fate would justly await us.

vii. 39:25–29

The final section of the great narrative jerks our thoughts back from the apocalyptic portrayal of the distant future and, with the word *now* (25), reminds us that Ezekiel's audience were the exiles whose primary concern was more immediate. Would the exile last for ever? Would Babylon be the grave of Israel? Assuredly not. Israel's future was secure in the promise of God. This passage echoes and summarizes many of the themes and promises we have already met in chapters 34 – 37. Gog and his hordes are left far behind, no longer part of the picture at all. The external threat is gone, and internal peace will reign as the people are restored to a right relationship with their God. One phrase, however, is not an echo of anything else in Ezekiel, for it has not occurred before, except negatively. For the first time in these precise words, though obviously anticipated in chapters 34 – 37, God says, '*I will have compassion on all the people of Israel*' (25). Previously God had only said, in the context of his irrevocable judgment, that he would *not* pity nor have compassion (e.g. 5:11; 7:4; 8:18; 9:10). But now the new era of compassion and restoration is in view, which will (as 36:16–38 had argued) be just as much a vindication of Yaheh's *holy name* as his judgment had been.

Otherwise, these verses repeat the great promises of grace. Even the promise '*I will now bring* Jacob *back from captivity*' carries the implicit reminder of the story of Jacob. For Jacob, a trophy of grace if ever there was one, had also gone into exile in Mesopotamia and had then been brought safely back by God to the land. Also repeated is the recognition that while grace wipes out the sins of the past it does not obliterate their memory. The New International Version unfortunately follows an unnecessary emendation which some scholars make to the Hebrew text by rendering verse 26, *'They will forget their shame.'* The Hebrew, supported by all ancient versions, says, 'They will bear their shame' – meaning that they will bear responsibility for the sin which caused their shame, and accept that they should indeed be ashamed of their conduct. As we saw in our exposition of 36:30–32, there is no contradiction between experiencing God's full restoration and yet at the same time having an acute consciousness of the sin which brought us under his wrath. The effect of such salutary memory is only to increase the gratitude and joy with which we praise our Saviour for his infinite patience and mercy. To remember God's mercy is to remember with grief and shame our terrible need of it. 'Mercy is not a summons to blind forgetfulness.'[12]

The chapter ends with another echo of a much closer text. The exile was a time in which Israel experienced the hiddenness of God. The climax of his judgment upon them has just been expressed in the words *'I hid my face from them'* (23–24). The hiddenness of God's face meant, above all, that worship could not properly be offered.[13] In the new era of God's restoring grace and ingathering protection, however, that barrier will be removed. The frown of judgment is replaced by the smile of blessing in the words *'I will no longer hide my face from them'* (29).[14] And whereas so often in the past Ezekiel had spoken of how God would 'pour out his wrath' upon Israel,[15] the great reversal will witness a very different outpouring – the

---

[12] Zimmerli, *Ezekiel 2*, p. 320.

[13] Other prophets refer to God hiding his face from his people because of their extreme social wickedness, meaning that he would not accept their worship or prayers (Is. 1:15; Mic. 3:4). At a personal level, the experience of the hidden face of God is among the most poignant laments of the psalmists, usually associated with a sense of God's anger, or in some cases with an impatient longing for God to act against oppressors (Pss. 13:1; 27:9; 44:24; 69:17; 88:14; 89:46). For Job, the worst part of his suffering was that he could not 'get through' to God (Job 13:24). Finding that God had hidden his face was tantamount to being treated as God's enemy. Ultimately, all life on earth depends upon God's favour, and one psalmist pictures even the creatures of earth and sea cringing and dying if God should hide his face from them (Ps. 104:29). As a metaphor for exile, then, it portrayed a bleak and terrifying spiritual reality.

[14] When God acts to forgive and restore, he hides his face from the sin but no longer from the sinner (Ps. 51:9).

[15] Ezek. 7:8; 9:8; 20:8, 13, 21, 33, 34; 36:18; etc.

outpouring of God's own self through his Spirit, covering, anointing, flooding and claiming his people for himself: *'I will pour out my Spirit on the house of Israel'* (29).[16] The way is at last clear for God to dwell among his people in renewed worship and eternal fellowship – which is what follows in chapters 40 – 48.

b. The significance

Who, then, is or was this mysterious *Gog, of the land of Magog*? The honest answer is that nobody really knows, but not for want of trying. Certainly, there is no such person known within the rest of Old Testament history. Many scholars reckon that the name may have been a corruption of Gyges, who was a famous king of Lydia in the seventh century BC. Lydia is in Anatolia (modern Turkey), the same region as Meshech and Tubal. The latter seem to have been dreaded foes with a reputation for barbarity (32:26).[17] However, since Ezekiel places the great invasion and defeat in the distant future, it seems most likely that he has simply picked, or created, names for these enemies from a rather vague mixture of terrifying enemies up north.

Subsequent Jewish and Christian interpretation, however, has had an endless fascination with these chapters and their gory *denouement*. Probably Daniel 11:40–45 has been influenced by the story of Gog. Certainly later rabbinic commentaries on the Hebrew Scriptures included the defeat of Gog and Magog in the expected victories of the coming Messiah.[18] With this background it is not surprising that early Christian eschatology also made use of Ezekiel's imagery to portray the great conflict between the forces of evil, both human and satanic, and the reign of God and Christ. Revelation 19:11 – 20:15 envisages a mighty attack by the massed forces of evil, led by Satan, but including 'Gog and Magog',[19] which is comprehensively defeated.

As the centuries of the Christian era passed, different generations have identified Gog with whatever fearsome foe of the day seemed

---

[16] The outpouring of Yahweh's Spirit occurs in four other prophetic texts, all looking forward to the future era of God's restoration of his people. It will be an era of transformation of nature and of justice and peace (Is. 32:15–17); of growth and conversion (Is. 44:3–5); of universal availability of the prophetic gift and of salvation (Joel 2:28–32); and of grace, prayer, repentance and cleansing (Zech. 12:10 – 13:1). On the day of Pentecost, Peter chose one of these (Joel 2:28–32) as scriptural explanation for the outpouring of God's Spirit that inaugurated the new messianic era. He probably could have quoted any of the five texts with equal relevance.

[17] Cf. Ps. 120:5. For detailed discussion of the various nations and places mentioned in Ezek. 38 – 39, see Block (2), pp. 432–444.

[18] Cf. *3 Enoch* 45:5. For discussion of this and other Jewish texts mentioning Gog, see Block (2), pp. 489–490.   [19] Rev. 20:8.

to fit, or needed to be placed under the comforting prospect of God's terrible destruction. Augustine, for example, saw Gog in the faces of the terrible onslaughts of the Goths upon the Roman empire, which seemed to signal the end of Christian civilization as then known. Luther identified Gog and Magog with the dreaded Turks of his day (with some geographical correspondence at least in his favour). In the twentieth century, a popular and influential brand of Christian fundamentalism confidently identified Gog and Magog with the communist Soviet empire. 'Rosh' (the Hebrew word meaning 'head' and translated as *chief prince* in the NIV, 38:2), was obviouly Russia; *Meshech* must therefore be Moscow, and *Tubal* none other than Tobolsk. On this flimsiest of word association (which has no etymological credibility whatever), the Christian world was warned of an impending invasion of the land of the modern state of Israel by the armies of the Soviet empire to the north, which would spark off the final great battle of Armageddon, and other events already plotted on a particular millennialist time-chart. God, as well as Gog, had his marching orders.

Those who were sceptical about the whole scenario were accused of not being prepared to take the Bible literally – to which a sufficient reply seemed to be that, if the foe from the north was to be literally equated with a Russian army invading modern Israel, then presumably we should expect them to be riding horses and fighting with bows and arrows. Even literalists have problems with consistency. And, we might add, literalism of this sort is not noted for its humility either. The collapse of the Soviet empire without a Russian soldier setting foot on the soil of Israel, let alone hordes of them being buried there, has not been marked by a chorus of the prophets of 'Armageddon in our time' saying, 'Thanks for all the money we made out of the books making that prediction, but actually, sorry, we seem to have got it wrong.'

If we allow ourselves to be sidetracked into speculation about the precise identification of Gog and literalistic predictions of exactly how and when the narrative of Ezekiel 38 – 39 will allegedly be played out, we are in danger of ignoring the main point of the chapters. This primary purpose of the whole narrative is the full and final revelation of Yahweh as God and the acknowledgment, by Israel and all the nations, of his true identity and the justice of his ways. In short, whoever or whatever Gog was, is or will be, his sole reason for existence is the display of God's glory. This is repeated throughout both chapters and at their climactic conclusion (38:16, 23; 39:6–7, 13, 21–24, 27–28).

Furthermore, as against all such literalistic attempts to fix the identity of Gog exclusively on to a single historical person or nation,

325

it seems clear that Ezekiel is using figurative language and a range of long-accepted prophetic imagery to make a fundamental affirmation about God's victory and a rock-solid reassurance to God's people about their ultimate security. In the survey of the two chapters above, we have mentioned several features that are clues to the non-literal, symbolic nature of the narrative. These include the vague menace of the 'foe from the north'; the cosmic effects of God's judgment (earthquake, mountains trembling, plague, fire and brimstone, etc.); the repeated use of sevens; the expression 'in that day'; and the personification of animals at God's table.

In view of this, we can see two levels of fulfilment. On the one hand, the symbolism speaks of an ever present reality, namely, human and satanic opposition to God and his people. History is littered with 'Gogs' – those who have thought they would eradicate the people of God. They have not triumphed so far, and this vision affirms that they never will. On the other hand, the extension and application of Ezekiel's vision by John in Revelation leads us to anticipate that the battle between God and his enemies will ultimately come to a climactic finale in which all the forces of Satan and those who have allied with him will be defeated by the power of Christ and then be destroyed for ever.[20] The defeat and destruction of Gog thus offer us prophetic assurance of the ultimate defeat and destruction of all that opposes God and endangers his people.[21] Likewise, just as the picture of comprehensive destruction of evil in chapters 38 – 39 ushers in the prospect of Yahweh dwelling with Israel reconstituted in their land and worshipping him in the perfection of his restored sanctuary (chs. 40 – 48), so the defeat of Satan in Revelation 19 – 20 ushers in the great vision of God dwelling with his people drawn from all nations in a new creation, worshipping the Lamb in the perfection of his presence that will need no temple.[22]

---

[20] In this double application (to continuing historical enemies of God's people, and to a climactic eschatological defeat of the ultimate enemy of God and his people), this interpretation is similar to that adopted by many in respect of the New Testament figure of 'Antichrist'.

[21] As to the precise timing of such a climactic engagement, or the identity of whatever human figures or forces may be involved in it, we do well to be cautious. The Gog narrative speaks of an attack that came as a surprise upon an unsuspecting people. While we are certainly warned in the New Testament always to be on our guard and always to be prepared for the events which usher in the return of the Lord, it is very unlikely that they will proceed in the neat sequence so beloved of certain 'prophetic' schools of thought. His first coming surprised the Bible experts of his day. His second coming is more than likely to do the same.

[22] Rev. 21 – 22.

2. The temple vision and the return of God's glory
(40:1 – 48:35)

And so at last we come to the final climactic vision of this prophet among the exiles. The date in 40:1 places this vision in 573 BC, twenty-five years from the start of the exile and almost twenty years after his first life-changing vision of the glory of God by the Kebar Canal. It was early in those years that the lowest point of Ezekiel's ministry occurred (lowest in theological terms, at least; I daresay he would have cited the night his wife died as the costliest moment in personal and emotional terms). That was when he saw the glory of Yahweh departing from the temple, and the temple itself being consigned to destruction along with Jerusalem in the fire of God's judgment (10:18; 11:22–23). The implication of that divine desertion of the sanctuary in Jerusalem was that God was no longer dwelling with his people. For that was the prime purpose of the temple, as it had been also of the portable tent in the wilderness that preceded it. The temple was not primarily a place of human worship (though of course it was that), but the place of divine presence, where God 'caused his name to dwell'. And, as Moses had so sharply pointed out to God himself, it was the presence of Yahweh their God in the midst of Israel that made them distinctive from the other nations. Take that away and there was nothing left worth having. After the great apostasy of the golden calf, God had at first said that he would permit the Israelites to go on up into the land he had promised them, but he himself would not go with them. Not good enough, said Moses. 'If your Presence does not go with us, do not send us up from here.'[23] Without the presence of Yahweh dwelling in their midst, Israel might as well stay in the wilderness. Now, centuries later, that awful prospect was a reality: Israel was in the wilderness of exile, and Yahweh had abandoned his dwelling-place.

Of course we know, and Ezekiel knew, that Yahweh was sovereign in Babylon also, and his glory could appear there. Nevertheless, Ezekiel must have been haunted by the memory of that vision of the departing glory. And his heart must have slowly filled with hope that all the visions of restoration that had flooded his mind and comforted the exiles (recorded in chs. 34 – 37), would eventually lead up to a fresh vision of the glory returning. Nothing less would do. As in Moses' day, possession (or repossession) of the land would be hollow in itself if Yahweh did not return to dwell among his people. Physical relocation would be nothing more than yet another chapter of migration to add to their national epic, unless it led to the renewal of fellowship with Yahweh through acceptable

[23] Exod. 33:1–5, 14–17.

sacrifices, and the restoration of the people to harmony, justice and peace. And that indeed was the expectation with which those wonderful chapters came to their climax, before being so rudely interrupted by the cacophony of Gog and his hordes.

> I will make a covenant of peace with them; it will be an everlasting covenant. I will establish them and increase their numbers, and I will put my sanctuary among them for ever. My dwelling-place will be with them; I will be their God and they will be my people. Then the nations will know that I the LORD make Israel holy, when my sanctuary is among them for ever (37:26–28).

What sense of awe and anticipation must have gripped Ezekiel, then, as he himself was once again gripped in the mighty hand of God and whisked off in vision to Jerusualem (40:1)? His last visionary day trip there had been utterly terrifying (chs. 8 – 11). But the last time God's hand had lifted and led him in a vision, it was to see a valley full of skeletons become a mighty risen army (37:1–14). If the resurrection power of the Spirit of Yahweh could bring the people of God back from the grave and cause them to live again, what could it do for the city of God and the temple of God? Could they also 'live again'? And most crucially of all, where and when would he see the glory of God again? Would Yahweh come home to stay? The answer comes in 43:1–5, which is the high point corresponding to the low point of 11:22–23; but we have some way to go before we get there.

There are three major themes that are interwoven in these chapters: the temple; the sacrificial system; and the division of the land. Each gets specific attention in some chapters, but there is a mixing of concerns which does not lend itself easily to a straightforward sequence through the material. Fundamentally, Ezekiel is concerned, first, that Yahweh should dwell again among his people in a cleansed sanctuary. So he is granted a visionary tour of a temple of perfectly symmetrical dimensions. Secondly, he is concerned that the people's relationship with Yahweh should from now on be sustained by a full and proper implementation of the sacrificial rituals and priestly duties, through which forgiveness, fellowship and covenant inclusion could continue without threat. So he is given instructions relating to the restoration of the priestly and sacrificial system. And thirdly, he longs to see the unruly and incorrigible wickedness of Israel, which had made the exile so inevitable and so deserved, replaced by a nation living in well-ordered peace and harmony on the land. So his vision pictures the tribes of Israel arranged in perfect balance around the central sanctuary and city, with the land divided equally, and above all, with God himself in the very centre of it all, and the river of life flowing out from his presence to bless, heal, fertilize, feed and give life to the world. We turn now to consider each of these three themes in turn: the return of the presence of God; the restoration of the worship of God; and the reordering of the people of God.

a. The return of the presence of God (40:1 – 43:12)

Ezekiel sets off again on a trip to Jerusalem. The visionary nature of the experience is immediately impressed upon us by the detail that he records: *God ... set me on a very high mountain* (40:2). Only by a well-stretched imagination could Jerusalem fit that description. Ezekiel is, as we might say, being given a bird's-eye view of what *looked like a city*, and within that he is to be given a tour of a virtual-reality temple, complete with a well-equipped tour guide (3). It is important to observe at this point that Ezekiel is told to look at what he is shown and to listen to what he is told so that he can tell his fellow exiles what he has seen (4). Although a great deal of measuring goes on, the impact comes from the mental image of what is seen on his tour, not from a study of blueprints or architect's plans, nor from detailed verbal instructions.[24] The nearest modern analogy that comes to mind is of a three-dimensional, computer-generated, virtual-reality tour of a museum, or some magnificent building. Accompanying commentary with statistical details may well be given *en route*, as it were, but their point is to enhance the scale and majesty of what is being viewed and the impression it leaves on the mind. So what was the central point of that impression? It is important to get our own orientation right before we briefly scan the scenes that Ezekiel so lovingly and longingly describes.

The point, above all, is not to be found in the details themselves, but in the restoration of the dwelling-place of God in the midst of his people. The perfect numerical symmetries and geometric design of the visionary temple provide, in the priestly categories of Ezekiel's whole worldview, an appropriate outworking of the great promise of 37:26–27: 'My dwelling-place will be ... among them for ever.' That was the central and indispensable goal; the concepts and means

---

[24] In fact, the mysterious tour guide is virtually silent throughout. Apart from his meticulous taking of measurements, which he then shows to Ezekiel, he speaks only once at the beginning (40:4), four times during the tour (40:45 – 46; 41:4 – at the central point, the Most Holy Place; 41:22; 42:13–14) and once again at the end (43:10–12 – unless this is a continuation of the speech of God himself from within the temple). This unusual taciturnity adds to the visionary nature of the experience and contrasts with the detailed instructions given to Moses in Exod. 25 – 30.

by which it would be met were of course fleshed out in the only way known to Ezekiel – the temple itself.

i. The tour (40:5 – 42:20)

The tour begins and ends at the same place – the outer wall of the whole temple complex. So the literary structure mirrors the architectural structure, by having the outer wall described in the 'outer' extremities of the text. In the opening paragraph (40:5) the thickness and height of the wall are given: six cubits.[25] In the closing paragraph (42:15–20) the length of the wall is given: five hundred cubits on each side.[26] The final phrase of the description of the wall is also significant in making clear the reason for its existence. Its purpose was *to separate the holy from the common* (42:20). Ezekiel's priestly worldview shines through here, for this distinction was fundamental to Old Testament faith. It was the distinction that ran through the whole of life – human, animal, material and spatial. It was the distinction that the priests were supposed to teach to the people, along with the further division of the common into the sub-categories of the clean and the unclean.[27] Outside the temple area were the ordinary, common realities of life. And of course, beyond the land itself lay the unclean world of the Gentile nations (where the exiles now languished). Inside that wall, however, was the sphere of God's presence.

Even within the temple compound, the holiness of the different spaces and places was 'graded'.[28] This becomes apparent as we follow Ezekiel and his laconic guide around the courts and buildings, with the help of figure 9.2. There was an outer court, immediately inside the wall. Its holiness is marked by being seven steps higher than ground level outside (40:6, 22, 26) Ezekiel enters this through the gatehouse in the middle of the eastern wall, which is described in some detail in 40:6–16. Having arrived in the outer court, he observes the *rooms and a pavement* all around three of its sides (17–19). He then traverses the outer court by visiting the other two outer gatehouses, in the centres of the north and south walls respectively.

---

[25] Approximately ten feet or three metres. Incidentally, this is the only time that the height of any feature of the whole complex is given. Only horizontal measurements are given in the rest of the account.

[26] Thus the whole temple compound was approximately 250 m (850 feet) square. One might like to compare this very approximately with six football pitches arranged in a square.

[27] Lev. 10:10–11.

[28] For a rich and informative exploration of Israel's worldview regarding the 'graded' holiness of space and place, see P. Jenson, *Graded Holiness: A Key to the Priestly Conception of the World* (Sheffield: JSOT Press, 1992).

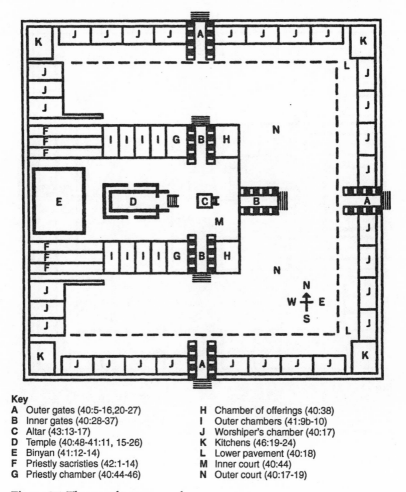

Key

A Outer gates (40:5-16,20-27)
B Inner gates (40:28-37)
C Altar (43:13-17)
D Temple (40:48-41:11, 15-26)
E Binyan (41:12-14)
F Priestly sacristies (42:1-14)
G Priestly chamber (40:44-46)

H Chamber of offerings (40:38)
I Outer chambers (41:9b-10)
J Worshiper's chamber (40:17)
K Kitchens (46:19-24)
L Lower pavement (40:18)
M Inner court (40:44)
N Outer court (40:17-19)

Figure 9.1 The temple compound.

Moving to another level of holiness, closer to the very heart of the temple, he is then led *into the inner court through the south gate* (40:28). This was a court inside the outer court, one hundred cubits from the outer walls on its northern, eastern and southern sides. It has three more gates facing the three outer ones (28–37). Its increased holiness is marked by an increasing height: eight steps up from the outer court (31, 34, 37). Again Ezekiel is impressed with the number of rooms and facilities for the priests which lie on both sides of this inner court (38–47).

Finally, he arrives at the temple building itself, in the middle of

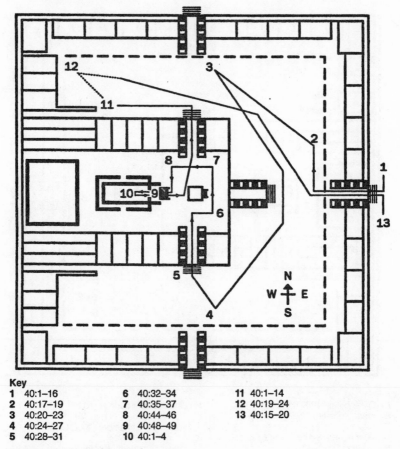

Key
1 40:1–16   6 40:32–34   11 40:1–14
2 40:17–19   7 40:35–37   12 40:19–24
3 40:20–23   8 40:44–46   13 40:15–20
4 40:24–27   9 40:48–49
5 40:28–31   10 40:1–4

Figure 9.2 Ezekiel's temple tour.

the inner court. Its special holiness is represented by its being elevated yet again above the surrounding levels of the inner and outer courts (40:49; 41:8). And internally, just like Solomon's temple and Moses' tabernacle, it is divided into two main rooms: the outer sanctuary, and the Most Holy Place, with a small portico at the eastern entrance. The increasing holiness is also represented by the decreasing size of the entrances; the further in you go, the narrower the entrance becomes: fourteen cubits at the main entrance (40:48), ten cubits at the entrance to the larger sanctuary (41:2), and only six cubits at the entrance to the Most Holy Place (41:3).

At this point on the tour we have obviously reached the climax in spatial terms. Even in a vision Ezekiel is not allowed to go into the Most Holy Place. He stays outside in the *outer sanctuary* while his angelic guide goes into the *inner sanctuary* to do his measuring – and then makes his unadorned declaration, *'This is the Most Holy Place'* (41:1–4). Yes, it certainly was, and that is where Yahweh should have been present in his overwhelming holiness and glory. But the room was empty. Ezekiel knew it. He had seen the glory depart from this very spot years ago. But he also knew that if and when the LORD returned to his temple, this would be his most intimate dwelling-place again. What a moment for the aging[29] priest-prophet to savour, even if only in a vision – to be in the place where he had dreamt of serving God but had probably never stood in physical reality.

Having visited the most central and holy point of the whole scene, the rest of Ezekiel's tour is taken up with viewing various other structures of the visionary temple complex, including rooms for the priests and several other structures along the western wall 'behind' the temple itself. Loving attention is also paid to the woodwork decoration of carved cherubim and palm trees, reminiscent of Solomon's temple furnishings.[30] Much of the text in these chapters is difficult to translate and also difficult to visualize with confidence. Various reconstructions of the arrangement of the buildings have been offered, and it seems superfluous to attempt yet another. The absence of vertical dimensions or anything resembling an 'artist's impression' of the buildings in three dimensions makes any kind of certainty impossible. However, that need not disturb us unduly, since even when the temple was finally rebuilt, they did not feel it necessary to treat Ezekiel's verbal vision report as a blueprint to be followed in detail.

ii. The glory (43:1–11)

At last the moment arrived which Ezekiel must have sensed was so imminent. All the preceding process of inspection and measurement was like a guided tour of an empty palace before the grand arrival of the king himself. The sure-footed guide had brought Ezekiel to the very best vantage point for the spectacle: *the gate facing east.* There, right on cue, he saw again the sight that had launched his ministry – *the glory of the God of Israel coming from the east* (43:1–2). Once again, the overwhelming impression is of engulfing noise like a mighty waterfall, and of a brightness so effulgent that it lit up the earth beneath it. Ezekiel's note of recognition in 43:3 reminds us of his two previous encounters with Yahweh's glory, in his vision of the destruction of Jerusalem, when the glory had moved off towards

---

[29] A relative term, of course. Ezekiel would have been fifty by this time.
[30] 1 Kgs. 6:29.

the east (chs. 8 – 11), and in his call vision by the Kebar Canal, when the glory had come down from the north (chs. 1 – 3). So Ezekiel had seen it all before, but its effect upon him was no less shattering than ever. 'The prophet's physical response, falling down on his face, indicates that neither years of reflection nor decades of divine service have dulled his sense of awe and terror at the sight of the glory of God.'[31] Flat on his face, however, was not the best posture to witness the climactic arrival, so yet again *the Spirit* comes to the rescue and gives him an aerial view from *the inner court* as the *glory of the* LORD proceeds majestically in a dead straight line through the east gate of the outer wall, then the east gate of the inner court, then the great east door of the temple itself, and presumably through the two inner doors, finally into the Most Holy Place itself.[32] The direction of movement is precisely opposite from the line of departure of the glory from the temple and city in chapters 10 – 11 (10:4–5, 18–19; 11:23). From his vantage point Ezekiel sees what he has longed to see since that terrible day – *the glory of the* LORD *filled the temple.* The dark days of divine abandonment are over. The king has come home.

And the king has an announcement to make from his restored residence. His speech falls into two parts: a declaration of his permanent return and its implications (43:7–9); and instructions to Ezekiel about what he is to tell the exiles and why (43:10–11).

The first announcement (43:7–9) begins and ends with words of reassurance, summarizing all the wonderful words of hope that pervaded chapters 34 – 37: *I will live among them forever.* The presence of Yahweh in the midst of his people had always been seen as the fundamental distinguishing mark of Israel even before the construction of the original tabernacle.[33] It remains the ultimate vision of the new creation.[34] Here it is given a particularly royal flavour through the depiction of the temple as God's palace. Earlier Israelite traditions had long portrayed the ark of the covenant as the throne and footstool of Yahweh,[35] both before the building of Solomon's temple and of course after it was placed there in the Most Holy Place. Interestingly, Ezekiel makes no mention of the ark itself, perhaps in agreement with Jeremiah's prediction of the relegation of that particular sacred object in favour of Jerusalem itself as the

---

[31] Block (2), p. 579.   [32] Cf. fig. 9.1, p. 331.   [33] Exod. 33:14–16.   [34] Rev. 21:3.
[35] 1 Sam. 4:4; 2 Sam. 6:2; Pss. 99:5; 132:7; 1 Chr. 28:2. This is an example of the literary figure known as *metonymy*, where an attribute or 'accessory' is used to signify the full reality. 'The pen is mightier than the sword' is a double metonymy, signifying that literature has greater ultimate effect than military power. The throne on which Yahweh was pictured as sitting, and the footstool on which a king would rest his feet, would thus speak of Yahweh reigning as king. The ark, or the temple, or Jerusalem, was thus presented as the focal location of his worldwide dominion.

throne of God in an international eschatological setting.[36] The language of Yahweh's throne and footstool is in any case metaphorical, of course, and, although Ezekiel here locates it in his visionary temple, other voices were aware that a mere house on earth, however symmetrical and beautiful, could not contain the real throne of the sovereign of all the universe. The Israelite historian attributes such an awareness to Solomon himself on the day of dedication of his glorious temple,[37] and Isaiah, anticipating the rebuilding of the temple as Ezekiel did, expands the metaphor to cosmic dimensions and challenges his hearers not to have too lofty a view of any human construction.

> 'Heaven is my throne,
>   and the earth is my footstool.
> Where is the house you will build for me?
> Where will my resting-place be?'[38]

Sandwiched in between the two assertions of God's presence (7a and 9b) come sharp words of ethical imperative. If Yahweh were going to dwell permanently in the midst of his people, there must be correspondingly permanent changes in their behaviour (7b–9a). These verses are a brief echo of the ethical declarations in chapters 34 – 37, where the promise of the restoration of Israel and the return of Yahweh to dwell with them was coupled with the promise of a new heart and a new spirit, perfect obedience, cleansing from impurities and the final rejection of all idolatry. Here, with a historical retrospect, Ezekiel focuses on offences of Israel which had been particularly associated with their kings: *prostitution* (a reference back to Israel's persistent flirtation with other gods and nations, as portrayed in chs. 16 and 23); the cult of royalty (possibly involving statues and worship of dead kings); and the encroachment of human kings into the sacred space that should have belonged to Yahweh alone. These and many other *detestable practices* had led to the terrible destruction under God's *anger*. But now the message was that all such things would be *put away* as the true king takes up permanent residence among them.

The second half of Yahweh's speech from the temple (43:10–11) instructs Ezekiel to *describe the temple to the people of Israel,* with careful attention to detail and probably with drawings as well as verbal reports. These instructions jolt us back to reality. For several

---

[36] Jer. 3:16–17, a passage which has several expectations that are echoed in Ezekiel, including the appointment of shepherds pleasing to God, the removal of stubborn hearts, and the reunion of Israel and Judah.   [37] 1 Kgs. 8:27.   [38] Is. 66:1.

chapters we have been caught up with Ezekiel in his visionary tour of the perfection of the temple and now we are gasping with joy and awe at the visionary prospect of Yahweh's glory taking up residence there again. But Ezekiel-in-the-Spirit will soon be 'sent back' to Ezekiel-in-the-body, and the reality was that he was still an exile, living among exiles in a foreign land, a very long way in time and space from the temple of his dreams. So, in order to appreciate the magnitude of the task ahead for him, we need to remind ourselves again of that context.

The exile had dragged on for a quarter of a century. Weariness and despair must have been the dominant mood. How could Ezekiel rekindle hope? How could the people be assured that their terrible abandonment by Yahweh would one day come to an end? They needed to look forward, not back. The recorded date of this whole vision helped them to do that (40:1). It came in *the twenty-fifth year of our exile*, which was half a jubilee span of fifty years. Jubilee was a time of release from slavery and debt, which Ezekiel later refers to as *the year of freedom* (46:17).[39] Furthermore, the date of the vision locates it at a time of special hope: *at the beginning of the year*, that is, Rosh Hashanah, or New Year's Day. The combined effect was to lift the eyes of the exiles towards their future liberation, rather than their past devastating defeat and present captivity. And then, capitalizing on the symbolic value of the number of years (twenty-five), Ezekiel's temple vision is a veritable patchwork of geometrical shapes, mostly squares and half-squares, made up of twenty-fives, fifties and multiples of those dimensions.

> Chaps. 40 – 42 are a celebration. They harness the wagon of contemporary reality to a star of hope … The account is an architectural symphony, an intricate composition that counterpoints the predicament of exile and the promise of restoration in a grand celebration of God's sure purposes. This theological stylization is presented both as an assurance and as a challenge to the exiles; it ministers pastorally to their needs (40:4; cf. 43:10–11).[40]

The 'assurance' lay in the vision of a restored temple. The 'challenge' lay in the shameful reminder of the old one. The explicit purpose for which Ezekiel was told to report the beauties and perfection of what he saw was to remind the exiles of the shame of their sin. *'Son of man, describe the temple to the people of Israel, that they may be ashamed of their sins. Let them consider the plan, and*

---

[39] Cf. Lev. 25:10.   [40] Allen 29, pp. 235–236.

if [41] *they are ashamed of all they have done, make known to them the design of the temple'* (43:10–11). There is no doubt a deliberate echo here of the last time Ezekiel had toured the temple in a vision. Then (chs. 8 – 11) he had been horrified by the idolatry and blatant pollution of the temple by those who should have been most concerned for its purity. Then too he had told the exiles everything God had shown him (11:25) for the same purpose – to expose to them their own shame and to vindicate the judgment of God upon them. This time, however, the new temple of Ezekiel's vision would be kept pure from all idolatry and sin by the immense walls and the imposing gatehouses, manned by Levites.

But such protection and blessing must always be an incentive for humility. The reminder of their shame, even in the context of salvation and restoration, recalls 16:60–63 and 36:30–32. 'It is characteristic of the preaching of this book that such shame is spoken of not in the context of the judgment sermon but in that of the proclamation of salvation.'[42] In portraying to the exiles the glorious future that God had in store for his people, Ezekiel's purpose was neither to induce obsessive fascination with the temple itself, nor to congratulate the people on their good fortune. As always, his sole concern was to exalt the glory and grace of Yahweh himself and to make clear the implications of a restored relationship with him.

> These people are not the pious congregation which might have coaxed God's mercy down from heaven by the abundance of their good works. They are the people whom God should have 'annihilated' because of their 'faithlessness' ... The vision of the new temple ... is not the vision of a new sacred object or even of a religious treasure which is to be handed over to the people at this period. It is the preparation of the way along which God himself in his majesty will come, of the house in which he himself will take up residence so that his people may come to him at any time, honor him and find shelter in the shadow of his wings.[43]

The fullest experience of such divine residence among a believing and obedient people comes only with the knowledge of the one

---

[41] Probably the LXX reading here 'Then they will be ashamed ...' is preferable, rather than the somewhat inconsistent conditional 'If they are ashamed ...'

[42] Zimmerli, *Ezekiel* 2, p. 418.

[43] Ibid., pp. 420–421. Block makes a similar point: 'This spiritual map of holiness puts them in their place: they are sinners visited by God, and invited to his presence by grace alone. Even in the new order, they do not earn the right to divine favor. Yahweh returns on his own initiative and for his own purposes.' Block (2), p. 589.

through whom God dwelt among us, full of grace and truth. So we must briefly explore how Ezekiel's temple vision relates to the wider context of biblical faith and ethics.

iii. The significance

How, then, as Christian readers of Ezekiel's vision are we to interpret its ongoing significance? How are we to apply it appropriately? In answering this we shall briefly consider it in relation to the later history of post-exilic Israel, the identity and work of Jesus as portrayed in the Gospels and Hebrews, the Christian church considered as God's 'temple', and the climactic amplification of Ezekiel's vision in the book of Revelation.

Did Ezekiel, then, think of his temple in a literal way as something that would one day be built to the specifications of his vision? There can be little doubt that he did indeed expect that the temple would be rebuilt in Jerusalem. It is notable, however, that when they did rebuild the temple, the so-called Second Temple did not follow Ezekiel's precise design. It is often pointed out that in any case there is insufficient detail in his account for it to serve as an architectural blueprint, apart from some outline dimensions (and even they weren't followed). It may also be significant that although Ezekiel was told to convey to the exiles all that he had seen, and especially the symmetrical measurements, the express purpose of that information was to induce shame through the contemplation of his vision's perfection (43:10–11). In other words, the purpose of Ezekiel's vision was not to provide guidance as to *how* the temple was to be rebuilt, but to provide reassurance of the hope *that* it would be rebuilt, and to point beyond the physical temple to the restored relationship between God in his holiness and his humble and obedient people. Nowhere is there any explicit command that they were actually to *build* what Ezekiel described just as he described it. This is in marked contrast to the account of the divine instructions for the original tabernacle in the wilderness,[44] in which the command to 'make' everything according to the pattern given by God is repeated in almost every verse. In Ezekiel's account there is no word at all of any human participation in the planning or building of the whole complex; it is simply presented to him as a divine *fait accompli* in the 'virtual reality', as we said, of his vision.

Nevertheless, of course, they *did* rebuild the temple after the return from exile. So was Ezekiel's vision fulfilled then? Partly, in a physical sense, yes. But an essential part of Ezekiel's vision was not merely a physical temple, but the restored holiness of God and the humble and purified response of his people. Ezekiel envisaged a

[44] Exod. 25 – 31.

people of whom it could be said that they *will never again defile my holy name* (43:7). And sadly this could certainly not be said of the post-exilic community any more than of the pre-exilic nations of Israel and Judah. Indeed, one post-exilic prophet found the lax practices in the Second Temple so offensive to the holiness of God that he wished somebody would shut the temple doors and put an end to the whole charade.[45]

Alongside this record of the failure of the restored temple to live up to the vision of Ezekiel, due to the failure of the people who served and worshipped there, we need to recognize that the Old Testament also had a wider understanding of the fact that God's dwelling was in any case not confined to a temple – old or new. As we saw, the historian of the monarchy recognized this in the account of the dedication of Solomon's temple.[46] Isaiah draws a contrast between the two dwelling places of Yahweh – on the one hand, 'in a high and holy place', and on the other hand (not in the temple but), 'also with him who is contrite and lowly in spirit'.[47] The humble human heart can be God's temple, just as 'a broken and contrite heart' can be the sacrifice that he will not despise.[48] So putting the above two points together, we can see that Ezekiel's temple vision pointed to a more complete fulfilment than simply the physical rebuilding of the temple by people whose human failings continued to defile it in the post-exilic period. And we can also see that the metaphorical use of temple imagery to refer to God's dwelling in or with human beings in a more spiritual sense is a perfectly valid extension of the language, with roots in the Old Testament itself, not merely a case of later Christian 'spiritualizing' tendencies.

The Gospel writers are unanimous that Jesus engaged in some action in the temple of his day which constituted an attack upon its personnel and a temporary disruption of its sacrificial activities. Popularly known as 'the cleansing of the temple', it is widely acknowledged by New Testament scholars that Jesus' action was no mere 'cleansing' of some commercial practices which he thought incompatible with the temple's sanctity. Rather, it was a prophetic sign, which many commentators now take as signifying the coming destruction of the temple itself and the end of all that it stood for in contemporary Jewish theology and politics.[49] It is also widely

[45] Mal. 1:6–13, and esp. v. 10.   [46] 1 Kgs. 8:27.

[47] Is. 57:15; cf. also Is. 66:1–2, which likewise conveys God's 'respect' for the humble and contrite spirit, even though he is king of the universe and cannot be confined to a physical house for a dwelling-place.   [48] Ps. 51:16–17.

[49] Matt. 21:12–13; Mark 11:15–17; Luke 19:45–46; John 2:13–22. For a full discussion of the scholarly debate over the full significance of Jesus' action in the temple, see N. T. Wright, *Jesus and the Victory of God* (London: SPCK, 1996),

agreed that this was the most concrete immediate cause of his arrest and execution. Alongside this negative symbolic portrayal of the coming end of the temple regime, Jesus set the positive message of his own identity as the messianic embodiment of the temple. Apart from the cryptic references to the way his own death and resurrection would constitute an ending of the old temple and its messianic replacement,[50] there are other indirect ways in which he pointed to himself as the true temple. He offered forgiveness directly to sinners on his own authority, bypassing the expected means of obtaining such forgiveness: namely, appropriate procedures in the temple. He brought people restoration to God and their Abrahamic identity (as for Zacchaeus), again without reference to the prescribed temple route for such benefits. He offered streams of living water flowing from the hearts of those who believed in him – most likely a reference to the river of pure water that flowed from the temple in Ezekiel's vision.[51] He placed his own identity as Messiah above whatever physical location for the correct place of worship might be advocated by Jews or Samaritans.[52] So we can clearly see that in the coming of the Messiah, Jesus initiated another level in the fulfilment of Ezekiel's vision. For in Jesus the perfection of God's holiness and beauty did indeed take physical form and 'dwelt [lit. tabernacled] among us', in divine glory, 'full of grace and truth'.[53]

Outside the Gospels, the letter to the Hebrews reflects most fully on the relationship of Jesus to the temple. The overall thrust of Hebrews is that those who have come to believe in Jesus as Messiah have entered into an inheritance that embraces but surpasses all that God had provided for Israel before. This includes entering into a 'rest' that is better than the land, benefiting from a sacrifice that achieves infinitely more than the animal sacrifices ever could, being bound to God in a covenant that fulfils the Old Testament prophecies of a new and better covenant, and being blessed by the ministration of a High Priest whose pedigree and permanence

---

pp. 405–428. While some argue that Jesus intended only a purification and reform of the temple system, Wright and others argue that it was a much more serious symbolic action when taken in the context of all the rest of Jesus' actions and sayings. 'Without the Temple-tax, the regular daily sacrifices could not be supplied. Without the right money, individual worshippers could not purchase their sacrificial animals. Without animals, sacrifice could not be offered. Without sacrifice, the Temple had lost its whole *raison d'être*. The fact that Jesus effected only a brief cessation of sacrifice fits perfectly with the idea of a symbolic action. He was not attempting a reform; he was symbolizing judgment ... The brief disruption which Jesus effected in the Temple's normal business symbolized the destruction which would overtake the whole institution within a generation' (N. T. Wright, op. cit., pp. 423–424).
[50] John 2:18–22.   [51] John 7:37–39; cf. Ezek. 47:1–12.   [52] John 4:19–26.
[53] John 1:14.

outstrip anything known under the Aaronic priesthood. None of this in any way diminishes or belittles what God had done for or given to his people Israel in the centuries before the coming of Jesus. In fact Hebrews affirms that great legacy in his opening verses and in his constant reference back to the Hebrew Scriptures. However, the writer does affirm that in the Messiah, Jesus, believers now have and enjoy a greater reality than was available before. Consistently with all the other realities that 'we have', the writer affirms that in Jesus we have all that the temple signified for Israel, and indeed all that Ezekiel's vision of restoration implied. 'We have confidence to enter the Most Holy Place by the blood of Jesus.'[54] 'You have come to Mount Zion, to the heavenly Jerusalem, the city of the living God.'[55] 'We have an altar ...'[56] If the apostle Peter had been preaching this, as on the day of Pentecost, he might have used his 'this is that' analogy which he applied to a prophecy of Joel.[57] 'This', the Christian believer's enjoyment of access into the presence of God, security in God's dwelling-place, and full atonement for sin, is 'that', the fulfilment of all that Ezekiel longed for in his vision of a restored temple, a resident God and a forgiven people.

The only thing the writer says that we do *not* have is 'an enduring city'.[58] Christians have no territorial centre, no physical land or place that is the focus of faith and worship, because Jesus Christ has taken on the full theological and spiritual significance of all that land, city and temple had held for Israel and opened that significance up to people of all nations. In the light of this it seems to me that Christian interpretations of Ezekiel which insist that there will yet be a literal and physical fulfilment of his vision by the actual building of another temple in Jerusalem, with accompanying miraculous transformations in the geography of Palestine to enable a river to flow down to the Dead Sea, are out of line with the New Testament's own interpretation, which relates the prophetic hope to its messianic fulfilment in Jesus. It is not impossible, of course, that in the days ahead the Jewish community may engage in a project to rebuild a temple in Jerusalem. But such a development would hold no theological, salvific or eschatological significance *for Christians*, for whom experience of God's forgiveness and assurance of God's presence are founded on the person of Jesus (his once-for-all sacrificial death and his continuing priestly intercession at his Father's throne). Indeed, there is a danger that obsession with apocalyptic scenarios involving literal reconstructions of Ezekiel's (and other Old Testament) visions may lead their devout adherents into precisely the kind of devaluing disregard for the complete,

[54] Heb. 10:19.   [55] Heb. 12:22.   [56] Heb. 13:10.   [57] Acts 2:16ff.
[58] Heb. 13:14.

sufficient and final work of Christ that the letter to the Hebrews was written to warn against.

The New Testament goes further, however, in using temple imagery not merely of Jesus himself, but also of the people who are 'in' him. This too ties in with Ezekiel's vision, which was never merely a matter of the restoration of a physical building, but always and essentially included the restoration of the people of God. Paul celebrates the creation of God's new people drawn from Jews and Gentiles and plays on the double Old Testament meaning of 'house' to signify both the household or family of God, and also the temple building in which God would dwell by his Spirit.[59] Peter plunders the Old Testament in similar fashion to mix his metaphors, describing Christians as both the 'living stones' of the new temple in Christ, and also the 'holy priesthood, offering spiritual sacrifices acceptable to God through Jesus Christ'.[60] Significantly, in view of the way Ezekiel linked his vision of the new temple to the moral requirement of holiness among God's people, Paul and Peter both move quickly from their use of temple imagery for the messianic people of God to ethical teaching about the kind of life that was appropriate for those who now constituted the dwelling-place of God.[61] Their challenge was primarily addressed to the corporate community, but it affected each individual believer, and thus Paul can apply the metaphor in a fully individual sense by affirming that the believer's own body is 'a temple of the Holy Spirit'. And since the temple was above all the place where the glory of God should dwell and be visible, Paul can appropriately add, 'therefore honour [lit. "glorify"] God with your body'.[62]

So we can see the New Testament usage of Ezekiel's new-temple vision as applied both to the Lord Jesus Christ himself, and also to the new community of believers in him. However, in the latter case it is as true of the Christian church as it was of the post-exilic Jewish community that we still live as fallen men and women in a fallen world. Although God condescends to dwell among his people and to display his glory through us in many ways, it is far from true yet that God's people have put away all their defilements and their syncretistic mixing of the worship of the living God with the myriad idolatries that surround us. But that day will come. As we have seen before, the book of Revelation offers some profound reflections and refractions of Ezekiel's imagery and message. In John's climactic vision of the new creation, the central focus is on the fact that God will at last dwell with his redeemed humanity, free from all that spoils, grieves or separates us from him or from each other.[63]

[59] Eph. 2:19–22.   [60] 1 Pet. 2:4–5.   [61] Eph. 4:1ff.; 1 Pet. 2:11ff.
[62] 1 Cor. 6:19–20.   [63] Rev. 21:1–4.

Paradoxically, although this wonderful prospect is portrayed as 'the new Jerusalem', John 'did not see a temple in the city, because the Lord God Almighty and the Lamb are its temple'.[64] The perfection and symmetry of Ezekiel's vision of a physical structure are sublimated into the perfection of the unmediated presence of God among his people in a new creation. And in a final echo of Ezekiel's major concern, John sounds the note of moral purity that will for ever characterize the future dwelling-place of God, when he observes that 'Nothing impure will ever enter it, nor will anyone who does what is shameful or deceitful'.[65] Only at one point does John's vision exceed that of Ezekiel's. In the light of the wider Old Testament vision of the ingathering of the nations, and the New Testament's record of the beginning of that great project in the Gentile mission of the church, John includes the nations in his vision of the inhabitants of his new Jerusalem.[66] And in his portrayal of Ezekiel's river of life (which in Revelation flows from the throne of God, rather than from the temple, since there was no temple in John's vision) John adds to Ezekiel's detail that the leaves of the trees would be for healing, the expansion that this would be 'for the healing *of the nations*'.[67] The missiological universality that was only implicit in Ezekiel's passion for the glory of God to be known among the nations here reaches its full affirmation.

b. The restoration of the worship of God (43:13 – 46:24)

As we return now to the text of Ezekiel we need to remind ourselves of two things. First, Ezekiel is still describing all that he saw and heard in his great vision. Though much of the text of these chapters may sound like a list of instructions composed in the midst of post-exilic realities, we are reminded from time to time of their visionary nature by references to the ubiquitous tour guide who was still accompanying Ezekiel in his vision here and there within the temple complex and beyond (cf. 44:1, 4; 46:19, 21; 47:1–2; etc.). Secondly, if our interpretation of the vision of the temple as a whole is on the right lines, then we must apply similar tools to the material which follows. Our understanding of the greater (the temple itself) must govern our understanding of the lesser (the objects, personnel and activities within it). We have just observed that there are several layers of significance to the temple vision: for the exiles themselves (the immediate context of Ezekiel's message, and therefore the right starting-point for all interpretation) it gave reassurance of a future beyond exile in which God would dwell again with his people – a people literally and physically restored to their land and worshipping

---

[64] Rev. 21:22. [65] Rev. 21:27. [66] Rev. 21:24–26 [67] Rev. 22:2; cf. Ezek. 47:12

in a rebuilt temple. But in the New Testament the vision can also be related to the messianic adoption of temple imagery and reality by Jesus, to the ongoing life of the community of believers as the dwelling-place of God through the Holy Spirit, and ultimately to the eschatological vision of God dwelling with his people in the new creation. Similarly, then, when we examine Ezekiel's portrayal of the altar of sacrifice, his arrangements for the temple personnel and his calendar of renewed festivals, we can certainly assume that he anticipated a restoration of these essential aspects of Israel's worship after they had returned from exile. But also, there are aspects of Ezekiel's provisions which we can profitably relate to ministry and leadership within the church, even though, on this side of the cross, we no longer look to the sacrifice of animals by levitical priests on a physical altar.

i. The place of acceptance: the altar (43:13 – 44:4)
On his initial tour of the temple courts the altar drew Ezekiel's attention for just a moment, long enough only to note its location in half a verse: *And the altar was in front of the temple* (40:47b). Now that the glory of Yahweh has returned to the temple, he has time to look around the rest of the inner court where the Spirit had brought him (43:5). And the object which dominates the whole inner court, and certainly now dominates Ezekiel's attention, is the altar. And no wonder; it was massively imposing. From the measurements given in 43:13–17[68] we can visualize the altar as a tiered, square edifice, 10.2 m (approximately 34 ft) square at the base. The top level, which contained the actual hearth for sacrifices, was about 7.2 m (about 24 ft) square on the outside, with an inner space of about 6 m (about 20 ft) square. The whole edifice rose to a height of about 3 m (10 ft), so not surprisingly steps were needed on the east side to enable priests to tend the fire and lay the sacrificial animals on the hearth. The whole thing was probably larger than a peasant's one-storey home. This made it similar in size to the altar in Solomon's temple, but nearly four times larger than the altar prescribed in Exodus 27:1–8 (which was of course a wooden construction designed to be portable).

The week-long programme of sacrifices (43:18–27) was a once-for-all event to decontaminate the altar and reconsecrate it to the holy purpose for which it existed (note the expressions *purify the altar and make atonement for it*, 20; *the altar is to be purified*, 22; *to make atonement for the altar and cleanse it; thus they will dedicate it*, 26). Although this was a new altar in Ezekiel's vision, the

[68] The *long cubit* was a traditional cubit (about 45 cm, 18 in.) plus a handbreadth: i.e. approximately 53–55 cm (20–21 in.).

memories of the defilement of the previous altar by all the detestable practices that had gone on in the temple needed to be cleansed away. Only then could it begin to function as the place where the renewed relationship with God could be enjoyed through ongoing sacrificial ritual as prescribed.

A remarkable feature of this cleansing and inauguration ritual is the part that Ezekiel himself plays in it, in his own vision. After the customary address *Then he said to me, 'Son of man ...'* (18), the *you* (singular) of the following verses must be addressed to Ezekiel himself. He then 'sees' himself (as one often does in dreams) taking part in the procedures along with the priests, procuring the required animals and carrying out blood rites for the purification of the altar. Whether Ezekiel ever hoped that he would personally join in the return from exile to carry out such a ceremony is impossible to know. It would seem virtually impossible that he did. He would have been eighty-five (if he survived) at the time of Cyrus' edict in 538; there is no record of his participation in the restoration of worship in Jerusalem; and in any case it was many years after the edict that the temple was in fact rebuilt. What we have here, then, is not a premonition of an actual future event involving Ezekiel, but rather a visionary 'compensation' to the prophet himself for the fact that he had never been able to serve as a priest in the Jerusalem temple before its destruction. At a deeper level, he is taking on, albeit in visionary terms, the role of a second Moses, inaugurating a fresh start for the worship of Israel, as Moses had done in the purification and consecration of the original altar in Exodus 29:36ff.

The key and climax to the whole passage, however, comes in 43:27. After the week of purification ceremonies, the regular pattern of sacrifices can proceed – summarized in the phrase *your burnt offerings and fellowship offerings*. Though there were other offerings, these two symbolized the vertical and the horizontal of covenant relationship: the burnt offering being wholly given to God, and the fellowship offering being shared as a communal meal among the worshippers. The temple has been rebuilt; the LORD has returned in his glory; covenantal relationship and worship has been restored. And surrounding all this freshly renewed ritual of worship there comes the wonderful promise *'Then I will accept you, declares the Sovereign LORD.'* That, after all, was utterly crucial. It was the persistent sin and rebellion of his people that had forced Yahweh to abandon his temple. He had now returned to his people. But would he allow his people to return to him? Would they be accepted and acceptable? The word of amazing grace was: Yes!

This word also reminds us that behind all the sacrificial ritual described here and in the following chapters, the most important truth being expressed is God's desire to enjoy fellowship with his people. The unfamiliarity and remoteness of the ancient rites may obscure this from view. The emphasis in the temple vision on the walls and gates that protected God's holiness may generate a mental picture of a severe God reluctant to admit anyone into his company. But the words '*I will accept you*' correct that impression. This is the language of love, of welcome, of warmth and invitation. This word smiles at us and greets us with open arms.[69] The altar was the place that actualized that welcome.

> The altar symbolizes the delight Yahweh finds in the worship of his people. He has not returned to his temple to bask in the glory of his new surroundings. He has come to have fellowship with humans. The days of his wrath are far behind, and he reaches out to them, offering a smile and acceptance to those who appear in his divine court.[70]

This affirmation of acceptance is all the more remarkable in view of the repeated message of the pre-exilic prophets that God could not and would not accept the offerings of his people at this very spot because of their persistent wickedness in the religious and social realms.[71] Only the grace of God could reverse that stance. Again we need to remind ourselves that Ezekiel's temple vision as a whole, and this vision of the altar in particular, is all of God's provision. Israel were no more deserving of God's acceptance after the exile than before it. The difference lay in God's own commitment to provide the means of their acceptance – as he had emphatically promised he would do:

> ... there in the land the entire house of Israel will serve me, and there I will accept them ... I will accept you as fragrant incense when I bring you out from the nations ... you will know that I am the LORD, when I deal with you for my name's sake and not according to your evil ways ... (20:40–44).

For us as Christians, of course, the joy of our acceptance into the gracious presence of God is focused on the cross of Christ. Through his sacrifice and the atoning power of his blood, we too, though sinners like the Israelites of old, are cleansed, forgiven and accepted.

---

[69] 'With Yahweh as subject, *rāsâ*, "to accept," represents one of the most hopeful words in the human language.' Block (2), p. 612.   [70] Block (2), p. 612.
[71] Is. 1:11–15; Jer. 6:20; 14:10–12; Hos. 8:13; Amos 5:21–24. Even in the post-exilic restored temple, the sacrifices of the people could be deemed unacceptable when divorced from wholehearted obedience and commitment (Mal. 1:10–13).

As the writer to the Hebrews explains so thoroughly, not only do we have assured access into the presence of God,[72] we also can come regularly to that 'altar' for continual worship and praise in fellowship with him and each other: 'Through Jesus, therefore, let us continually offer to God a sacrifice of praise – the fruit of lips that confess his name.'[73]

Although the chapter division separates 44:1–4 from the account of the altar, it is appropriate to include it here. It brings Ezekiel back to where he had seen the glory of God approaching: namely, the outer gate of the eastern wall (cf. 43:1–4), and then back into the inner court where, yet again, he sees the glory filling the temple and responds with his habitual prostration at the sight (44:4; cf. 43:3, 5). So the geographical and thematic details make a kind of 'envelope' around the whole section dealing with the glory and the altar (43:1 – 44:4), before moving on to the duties of the temple personnel.

The eastern gate, through which in Ezekiel's vision the glory of Yahweh had returned to his temple, was to remain permanently shut (44:2). The explanation given, *because the LORD, the God of Israel, has entered through it*, emphasizes again the holiness of what lay inside the outer wall of the temple courts. Where Yahweh's glory had passed was not to become a place of common traffic. Only the prince (see below) could even enter the gatehouse, only from the other side, and only to eat a sacred meal. There may also be an intentional distinction being made from a practice known in ancient Babylonian religious ritual, which would have been known to Ezekiel, in which the great door of the temple was opened on ceremonial occasions such as New Year to allow a statue of Marduk to be carried through in grand procession.[74] But Yahweh was not a God who needed to be carried anywhere, and he certainly needed no human permission or assistance to enter or leave his sanctuary. Whatever he opened was not to be shut; whatever he shut was not to be opened. The sovereign freedom of Yahweh yet again pervades even a small detail like this. Another possible implication of the closed gate may be that it symbolized his *permanent* return (cf. 43:7, 9). Yahweh had come home and closed the door behind him. He was not about to turn around and leave again. Ezekiel need not fear a repetition of 11:23. The closed

---

[72] Heb. 10:19–22.   [73] Heb. 13:15.

[74] There may be an echo of this ancient custom, in a metaphorical way, in Ps. 24:7–10, where the opening of all ancient gates and doors to the 'King of glory' is based on the prior claim that he has right of entry to any place on earth, since 'the earth belongs to Yahweh' (v. 1).

gate thus proclaims Yahweh's majesty (nobody else could 'walk where he walked'), Yahweh's fidelity (he was not about to leave again), and also 'acquires the character of a "sign" in the strictly biblical sense. It has to be the sign established for ever for the new, definitive turning of God to his people, the constant remembrance of the fact that God has taken up his dwelling in the midst of his people.'[75]

From that point of view it is similar to the New Testament portrayal of Jesus as having 'sat down at the right hand of the throne of God'[76] – a posture that is symbolic of completion and permanence.

ii. The personnel in action (44:5–31)

As we turn to look briefly at Ezekiel's vision of the reformed temple priesthood, we might wonder what the value of this material can possibly be to us, who know that Jesus alone is our great High Priest and that all believers share in the priesthood of God's people. While it is certainly true that the New Testament applies the language of priesthood to the whole people of God in Christ, and that it has no place for a distinct or superior class of priestly 'clergy' within the community, nevertheless the New Testament does recognize a variety of roles and ministries within the church. It also provides for a healthy division of labour among those who serve God's people, and has some challenging things to say about how such servants of the church should be honoured and supported. And in surveying Ezekiel's account of how he saw the levitical priesthood functioning in his restored community of worship, we shall find some interesting antecedents to the New Testament pattern which still speak to us today.

First of all, we may observe *their distinctions* (44:10–16). Ezekiel preserves the distinction within the tribe of Levi between those who were eligible to serve as priests at the altar and in the temple, and those who functioned as assistants to the priests and guardians of the temple courts, premises and furnishings. The former had to be descendants of Aaron; the latter function could be performed by any members of the tribe of Levi. According to Israel's tradition this distinction went back to the history of the establishment of Israel's system of worship by Moses in the wilderness. The background and reasons for it are given in Numbers 18. Some scholars have detected a complicated history of the priesthood in Israel, and regard the claims of the tribe of Levi, and within it the special privilege of the Aaronic lineage, as later developments. However, that issue need not

---

[75] Zimmerli, *Ezekiel 2*, pp. 440–441.   [76] Heb. 12:2; cf. Col. 3:1.

concern us here.[77] Ezekiel has chosen to preserve the distinction, and further to restrict the priesthood to the Zadokite clan.[78] The historical justification he gives (that the Levites had acquiesced in a period of apostasy in Israel, while the Zadokites had remained faithful), is also historically obscure to us, since it is not clear to what event or period he is referring.[79] What is interesting is the division of labour that Ezekiel envisages for the two categories of temple servant.

The Levites were in *charge of the gates of the temple* (44:11), which meant they exercised a kind of policing role among the crowds of worshippers. Beyond that, they functioned primarily in relation to the people. The text emphasizes that direction of their service: *'they may slaughter the burnt offerings and sacrifices for the people and stand before the people and serve them'*. The Zadokite priests, on the other hand, functioned primarily in relation to Yahweh himself: *'the priests ... are to come near to minister before me; they are to stand before me to offer sacrifices ... They alone are to enter my sanctuary; they alone are to come near my table to minister before me and perform my service'* (44:15–16).

So, although the whole tribe was set apart for the service of God, there was a recognition that some of the tasks involved in that service were focused directly on God himself, while other practical and menial tasks were necessary to preserve good order and to facilitate the people in their worship. The early church very quickly realized that a similar division of labour was needed in its own rapidly expanding organization. The people needed to be fed, physically and spiritually. But the same people could not cope with the demands of both tasks. So the apostles wisely commissioned another group of people to take care of the practical needs while they devoted themselves to the ministry of the word. Luke is careful to emphasize that the former group needed to be just as much filled with the Spirit as the latter.[80] Later Paul recognizes gifts of

[77] For discussion of the history of critical scholarship on the priesthood in Israel, and more recent questioning of the earlier consensus, see D. A. Hubbard, 'Priests and Levites', in *New Bible Dictionary* (Leicester and Downers Grove: IVP, 1982), pp. 967–972; and J. G. McConville, 'Priests and Levites in Ezekiel: a crux in the interpretation of Israel's history', *TB* 34 (1983), pp. 4–9.

[78] Zadok was a descendant of Aaron (his genealogical tree is traced in 1 Chr. 6:3–12, 50–53) who rose to prominence in the early years of Solomon. Because of his loyalty to Solomon at the time of the struggle over the succession to David he was appointed by the king to be the chief priest, in place of Abiathar, a descendant of Eli. See 1 Kgs. 1:5–8, 26, 32–40; 2:26–27, 35.

[79] It is usually thought that 44:10–14 implies a continuing punishment of the Levites in the form of a demotion to menial tasks. However, this is probably an exaggeration of Ezekiel's intention.   [80] Acts 6:1–6.

'administration' and 'helping' among the spiritual gifts that the Lord has showered on his church. Alongside the ministry of prophets, pastors, evangelists and teachers, the New Testament endorses the diaconal ministry of that long and worthy line of men and women who continue to serve as churchwardens and sidespersons, vergers, caretakers, stewards, parish secretaries and administrators, cleaners and flower-arrangers.

Secondly, Ezekiel specifies some of *their duties* (44:23–24). The rest of the chapter lists miscellaneous regulations for the priests, which are based on Leviticus 21, with some modifications. Obviously a major part of their time would be taken up with attending to the sacrificial rituals. But verses 23–24 mention another part of the duty of priests which is often overlooked. They had a major role in the teaching and administration of the law. *They are to teach my people ...* Verse 23 is based on Leviticus 10:10–11, which records this teaching function as part of the 'ordination' of Aaron and his sons to the priesthood. Specifically, the content of their teaching was to ensure that ordinary Israelites knew the fundamental differences between *the holy and the common* and between *the unclean and the clean*. These were foundational to Israel's religious worldview. They symbolized within the everyday world of Israelites the holiness of Yahweh and all that was closely associated with him, and the distinction between themselves and the rest of the nations. These were not merely ritual taboos. They were badges of an identity and a mission which called for holiness of life and behaviour as well. In teaching these distinctions, the priests would have taught the rest of the Torah also, with its clear demand for Israel to live out the ethical responsibilities of their election and redemption. The teaching role of the Levite priests is spelled out again elsewhere.[81] Later, part of the complaint of the prophets against the priests was that they were failing so abysmally in this teaching role that the people were falling, untaught and uncorrected, into all kinds of social and religious disorder.[82] Indeed, Ezekiel himself had castigated the priests of his own day for failing to do precisely what he envisages here (22:26). In happier days Nehemiah and Ezra made use of the Levites for teaching and explaining the law in the earliest known example of Theological Education by Extension.[83]

Because of their familiarity with the law, the priests were also to be involved in its administration in the courts: *'in any dispute, the priests are to serve as judges'* (24a). This role in public settling of disputes also rests on much earlier tradition found in Deuteronomy

---

[81] Deut. 33:10; Jer. 2:8a; 18:18.   [82] Hos. 4:1–9; Mal. 2:1–9.
[83] Neh. 8; note vv. 7–8, 11, 13.

17:8–13 and 19:15–21. Jehoshaphat, king in Judah in the ninth century BC, included Levite priests in his appeal court in Jerusalem, set up to judge difficult cases referred to them by local courts.[84] Understandably, if the priests were to teach the law and administer it with integrity, they themselves must be models of obedient living: 'They are to keep my laws and my decrees' (24b).

Putting the three duties together, then, in relation to the law of God, the priests were to be *teachers, conflict resolvers* and *moral examples*. Ezra provides an outstanding example of such leadership, with the added observation that he made the law a matter of personal study as well. An admirable example to all who minister God's word, Ezra's triple commitment to the law was to study it, to do it and to teach it.[85] If only leaders in the Christian church had the same depth and breadth of commitment to the Scriptures! For it hardly needs to be said that these same duties belong to the task of pastoral leadership in the church and are strongly commended in the New Testament. Not only did Paul impress on Timothy and Titus the importance of teaching, careful handling of disputes, and setting an example of personal godliness and integrity; he modelled all three in his own ministry.[86]

Thirdly, attention is given to *their dues* (44:28–30). Ancient tradition also lies behind the opening declaration of these verses. The tribe of Levi was given no allotment of land when Israel entered and settled in Canaan. Whereas the other tribes had a portion of territory which they could describe as their inheritance or possession, Levi's inheritance was to be Yahweh himself, in the sense that they were set apart for his service. Hence the remarkable assertion '*I am to be the only inheritance the priests have ... I will be their possession*' (28).[87] 'They are not granted access to real estate, but to Yahweh himself.'[88] The compensating economic balance was that, although they would not have a share in the land as a productive resource, they would be supported by the prescribed giving of the rest of the tribes of Israel. And it was fully intended that this would be not only adequate for their needs, but actually the *best of all* (30).[89] The Levites would be landless, but not destitute – provided the people were obedient and fulfilled their responsibilities.[90]

[84] 2 Chr. 19:8–11.   [85] Ezra 7:10.
[86] 1 Tim. 4:11–16; 5:17–20; 2 Tim. 1:13–14; 2:1–2, 14–26; 4:1–5; Titus 1:6–9; 2:7–8.
[87] For the tribal territorial division, in which Levi was not included, see Num. 26:52–62. Cf. also Deut. 18:1–2.   [88] Block (2), p. 645.
[89] Full details of the provision that was to be made for the priests and Levites from the offerings of the people are given in Lev. 7:28–36 and Num. 18:8–32.
[90] The potentially precarious economic position of the Levites, being without land, led to their being frequently included along with other vulnerable groups, such as widows, orphans and aliens, in those passages in the Torah where Israel was reminded of their obligations to care for such groups: Deut. 14:28–29; 16:11, 14; 26:11–13.

THE GLORY OF GOD REVEALED

The same double perspective on the dependent status of the priests is expressed in Deuteronomy 18:1–5. The following comments on that passage offer some New Testament and contemporary reflections in relation to Christian ministry:

First of all, it was a bold stroke that consigned Israel's priestly tribe to landlessness. This meant that Israel was not meant to be a nation in which a clerical hierarchy could wield economic power (and all its derivative forms of social influence) as an exploitative, land-owning, elite. In this way Israel was remarkably different from surrounding societies. In Egypt, for example, the temples and priests were major landholders. But in Israel, the priesthood of Yahweh the liberator was not to be a tool of religiously sanctioned oppression. In the history of the Christian church, somehow the 'clergy' sadly forgot this aspect of its biblical roots and pursued economic wealth and power, while re-introducing other, sacerdotal, aspects of Old Testament priesthood that it was meant to have shed in the light of the sacrifice of Christ.

But secondly, the landlessness of Israel's priestly tribe was not intended to impoverish them. They would be *dependent*, indeed. But dependence on an *obedient* people should have meant perfectly adequate provision for their material needs, just as Israel's dependence on their faithful God would include full provision. The principle that those who serve God and teach God's people should be fully provided for by God's people is emphatically re-applied in the NT. Galatians 6:6 applies it to Christian teachers (cf. 1 Tim. 5:17f.). Paul actually makes reference to OT priestly dues, along with many other supporting arguments (including another Deuteronomic law, 25:4, and a command of Christ), in establishing the responsibility of Christian churches to provide for the material needs of those who work for the cause of the Gospel (1 Cor. 9:13). Paul had freely chosen to waive this right in his own personal case, but he explicitly makes himself an *exception* to the principle he insists on for others. Unfortunately, some Christian organizations have turned Paul's exception, rather than his rule, into a policy imposed on their workers. But in view of the teaching of both OT and NT, churches or other Christian groups that fail to pay their workers adequate living wages are not 'living by faith,' but are simply living in disobedience.[91]

[91] C. J. H. Wright, *Deuteronomy*, New International Biblical Commentary (Peabody: Hendrikson; Carlisle: Paternoster, 1996), pp. 215–216.

iii. The pattern of worship (45:13 – 46:15)

The purpose of this whole section of Ezekiel's vision (section b, 'the restoration of God's worship') was to meet Ezekiel's concern for an ongoing relationship between Yahweh and his people. Wonderful though it was to contemplate the return of Yahweh's glory to his temple, what mattered was that the people should have permanent access to him through the sacrificial system, and that their lives should be filled with the festive joy that comes from having every season permeated with grateful worship to God. So these remaining descriptions of the future in Ezekiel's vision portray that reality in the only language available to Ezekiel – the language of Israel's calendar of daily sacrifices, weekly Sabbaths and annual festivals. Though the Christian year has taken over some aspects of the Jewish calendar, much of the detail in Ezekiel's vision is no longer significant for us. Two points of interest may be noted, however.

First, Ezekiel's characteristic eye for small practical details emerges yet again at two points. With large crowds of worshippers thronging the outer court of the temple, doubtless with sacrificial animals and other offerings, how was any semblance of order to be maintained by the harassed Levites? Simple: Ezekiel introduces the first known one-way system and establishes a kind of dual-carriageway traffic flow for the people (46:9–10)! Even the basic principles of crowd control are not too mundane for this most visionary of all the prophets. And what about all the butchery and cooking that accompanied the sacrificial system? The potential dangers of knives, choppers and open fires, not to mention frightened animals with horns, could not be allowed to mix in a haphazard way with the crowds of families and children. So Ezekiel envisages four large kitchen areas, one at each corner of the great outer court[92] where the Levites and ordinary people could do the needful in safety. Meanwhile, to preserve the sanctity of themselves and the holy offerings that constituted their sustenance the priests would have their own separate kitchen and refectory within the inner court (19–24). Once again we are reminded that there is no false dichotomy between the spiritual dimensions of worship and appropriate planning of the practical arrangements that enable it to take place 'decently and in order' – and in safety.

Secondly, Ezekiel frequently mentions the role of the rather enigmatic figure simply called *the prince*. Pointedly, this person is definitely not described as 'the king'. The term *nāśî* describes a leader in a more general sense, not necessarily with any connotation of royalty. Though the figure as described in Ezekiel's vision is clearly

[92] They were substantial enclosures – about 20 × 15 m (about 68 × 50 ft) with built-in barbecue facilities.

some kind of civil authority, there seems to be no explicit connection to the messianic portrayal of a new David that we saw in chapters 34 and 37 – though the use of *nāśî*, the term used in 34:24, might point to such a link. Indeed, nothing is said in these visionary chapters of the 'secular' duties of the prince. He appears rather in the role of a patron and provider for the religious ceremonies taking place in the temple. But although he has a distinct and honoured place within them, there is no exaltation of his status or any separate privileges. Much more is made of his responsibilities than of his status. The following details are recorded about him: he is not involved in any deity-mimicking processions through the outer eastern gate, but he may eat his sacrificial meals there (44:1–3); he is to provide substantial animal and vegetable materials for some of the prescribed sacrifices (45:21–25); on certain days he may enter the eastern gate of the inner court to observe the priests at work there and present his own offerings, but he may not enter the court itself and must adopt a worshipping posture (46:1–8, 12); when he comes to the outer court for other festive occasions, he has no privileged place or time for his entry, but must join the rest of the worshippers as one of them (46:9–10). Apart from these religious dimensions of his function he is given an allotment of land (45:7–8), but he is also severely warned against any repetition of the oppressive practices and exploitative greed of pre-exilic kings and nobles (45:8b–12; 46:18). So this does not appear to be a messianic figure ruling in perfect righteousness. This is a very human figure participating in the rituals, offering sacrifices for his own sins, and susceptible to the perennial temptations that surround those in authority.

The overall impression, however, of all this material is of the resumption of Israel's worship in spite of all previous abuses. There is no assumption of perfection yet in the community Ezekiel envisages after the return from exile. Sins are still being committed and sacrifices are still needed.

> But the glorious fact remains: in his grace Yahweh not only invites the worship·of mortals; he reveals to them activities that guarantee acceptance with him and appoints officials whom he will receive on their behalf. The alienation of the distant past is over. Ezekiel's vision of daily, weekly, and monthly rituals proclaims the continuing grace of a deity at peace with his people.[93]

Christians worship the same deity all over the world with a staggering variety of customs and practices. But the central sacramental significance of our covenantal meal – the eucharist, the

[93] Block (2), p. 677.

Lord's supper, or holy communion – reminds us that in an even greater sense the alienation of the past is over. For whether we celebrate it daily, weekly, monthly or less often, it points unequivocally to the cross of Christ, 'who made there (by his one oblation of himself once offered) a full, perfect, and sufficient sacrifice, oblation, and satisfaction, for the sins of the whole world'.[94] And through that perfect sacrifice we who, like the exiles of Israel and like the Gentiles even more so, 'were once far away have been brought near through the blood of Christ. For he himself is our peace … and … through him we both have access to the Father by one Spirit.'[95]

c. The reordering of the people of God (47:1 – 48:35)

With Yahweh back in residence in his temple and the worship of Israel reinstated, one might have thought Ezekiel's concerns as a priest would have been satisfied. But his vision is not over yet. Yahweh's return to his temple would go along with Israel's return to the land. There would have to be a time of resettlement and of allocating the land again. Furthermore, since the land had been the scene of such rampant abuse until it could bear its defilement no more and 'vomited' the people out into exile,[96] there would need to be a cleansing of the land itself. Then the greed and injustice of the past could be replaced by equality and harmony among the people for the future so that God could continue to dwell among them. Such was Ezekiel's dream. This final dimension of his great vision takes the form, first, of a miraculous *river* – miraculous in its source and flow, and miraculous in its life-giving effects; secondly, of a *land* sliced up with mathematical perfection to symbolize equality and order among the people of God; and thirdly, of a perfectly foursquare *city* in which the 'secular' life of the people went on, but in which the presence of God was as real as in his own sanctuary. So we must look at each of these – river, land and city – in turn.

i. The river (47:1–12)

Our faithful tour guide with his well-worn measuring stick, after his illuminating tour of the temple's cooking facilities, returns for one final splash. Taking Ezekiel back to the entrance of the temple building inside the inner court, he points out, to the prophet's amazement, a trickle of water emerging *under the threshold* from the *south side* of the entrance (the left-hand side as he looked at it, facing west). Before Ezekiel had time to wonder why he had not noticed

[94] From the Order for Holy Communion in the *Book of Common Prayer*.
[95] Eph. 2:13–18. [96] Lev. 18:28.

it before (as one does in dreams), his eager guide whisked him back outside *to the outer gate facing east* (where he had seen the glory approaching), just in time to see the tiny trickle[97] flowing out from under the left-hand side of the gatehouse. Looking around, Ezekiel finds his guide already striding purposefully eastward, either alongside or in the midst of the stream of water. Catching up with him after about 500 metres, Ezekiel splashes into water ankle-deep. Another 500, and he is wading up to his knees. Another 500, and it has reached his waist. At the 2-kilometre mark, he is out of his depth in *a river that no-one could cross*. Returning wisely to the bank, he finds that both banks of the river are now covered with *a great number of trees*, which, he is told, will miraculously fruit every month and perennially be in leaf with healing properties. The guide takes him no further but points eastward down to the great depression of the Dead Sea and tells Ezekiel that the fresh water of the stream from the temple will transform that dead and accursed area into a freshwater lake as rich in fish as the Mediterranean.

Though the visual scenery is very different, there are some similarities with Ezekiel's earlier vision of the valley of dry bones. There is the same surreal, dreamlike sequence, the same attention to sensory detail, the same miraculous transformation, the same dynamic power flowing from God himself. There can be no doubt that, like the earlier vision, the whole account was recognized and recorded as a symbolic vision, not as a literal prediction of any future event. 'No amount of exegetical finesse or insistence on "what the Bible plainly says" can transform the poetry of this passage into a topographically and ecologically realistic account of an event in time.'[98] What, then, does the rich and vivid symbolism of this river of life signify?

First of all, it must be significant that this vision of a life-giving, healing river comes immediately before the account of the boundaries and division of the land. Before the people could settle there again, the land itself needed to be cleansed and healed of all that had defiled it. Through Israel's sin and through the divine judgment of exile the land had become a place of curse and death.

[97] The Hebrew indicates a flow of water no larger than would pour out of the mouth of a bottle or jar. It is this tiny size of the river at its source which highlights the amazing transformation into a mighty river within just over a mile.

[98] Blenkinsopp, p. 231. Among the features which point beyond literal physical possibilities are the source of the river well above the water table; the exponential increase in the river's volume within a short distance with no tributaries; the sudden appearance of orchards full of trees; the ability of the trees to bear fruit every month; the flow of the river directly eastwards from Jerusalem to the Dead Sea; and the purifying effect of the fresh water on the salinity of the Dead Sea, rather than the reverse.

Now it would again become the place of blessing and life, of food and health, that it was always meant to be. There are echoes here that we have heard before, especially in chapter 36, of the pictures of covenant blessing and curse in Leviticus 26. In his promise of restoration after judgment God had said, 'I will remember the land.'[99] This life-giving, fertilizing river keeps that promise in abundance. Now, at a historical level, this vision looked forward to the return of Israel to their land, to their spiritual renewal and to the resumption of the normal tasks of irrigation, fertilizing, ploughing, planting and harvesting. They would once again be God's people in God's land. However, at a deeper level the Bible always links humanity to the earth – the one affecting the other. Because of human sin, the earth came under God's curse.[100] The redemption of humanity will conversely lead to the lifting of that curse and the restoration of God's creation to its original God-intended goodness.[101] Though portrayed in the symbolic language of prophetic vision, the environmental healing depicted in Ezekiel's vision should not be simply spiritualized. There is an ecological dimension to the full biblical understanding of God's saving purpose which should not be overlooked.

Secondly, the most important fact about the river is its source. It comes directly from the presence of God himself. That is why it is capable of giving life and sustenance, for those things are gifts of the living God, as the dry bones also discovered. When combined with the previous imagery, there is added point. As we saw, the permanently closed eastern gate spoke of God's return to his temple, never to leave again. God himself would not retrace his steps eastwards to the exit, but that did not mean that he was imprisoned in his sanctuary. The river of his life-giving blessing was now flowing back through that very gate and on out to the land and the world beyond. As the breath of God had come from the 'four winds' to breathe life back into a dead army (37:9–10), so now the river of God flows *from the sanctuary* (12) to water life back into a dead land and sea. For *where the river flows everything will live* (9). And with life come also *food* and *healing* (12) – among the most celebrated of all God's blessings. It is almost as though God were anticipating the words of his Son, 'I have come that they may have life, and have it to the full.'[102] If there were any suspicion from the preceding texts that God in his sanctuary was there merely for his own benefit, selfishly relishing the offerings and sacrifices of his people, this image dispels it. The flow of benefit is entirely in the opposite direction. It is only because of the life-giving bounty of God that we have anything at all to bring as gifts into his presence. As David put it so

[99] Lev. 26:42.   [100] Gen. 3:17ff.   [101] Rom. 8:18–23.   [102] John 10:10.

perceptively, when he dedicated the abundance of his people's giving
to provide for the building of the original temple,

> 'Everything comes from you, and we have given you only what
> comes from your hand ... all this abundance that we have
> provided for building you a temple for your Holy Name, it comes
> from your hand, and all of it belongs to you.'[103]

Thirdly, we may observe that Ezekiel's river of life is part of a
wider biblical imagery which both preceded and followed him. The
first notable river in Scripture is the one which watered the garden
of Eden and then divided into four great rivers flowing through the
historical world of the ancient Near East[104] Ezekiel has used Edenic
imagery before (28:13; 31:9, 18), so it is likely that his depiction of
this river of life intends to resonate with hints of new creation. The
idea of a river flowing in and from Jerusalem, the city of Yahweh,
appealed to the imagination of some psalmists. In Psalm 46:4 it
symbolizes the joy of living within the security of God's presence.
Psalm 65:9–10 links it to a celebration of the literal gift of rain and
rivers to give fertility to the land of Israel. Since the date of the
prophet Joel is disputed, it is uncertain whether his use of the image
came before or after Ezekiel,[105] but Zechariah undoubtedly owes to
Ezekiel his depiction of a river flowing from Jerusalem. He extends
the imagery, however, to include a flow to the west as well, joining
the Mediterranean to the Dead Sea, and solves the drainage problem
by having the Mount of Olives split dramatically in two.[106]

In the New Testament John portrays Jesus in the temple itself, at
the climax of the Feast of Tabernacles when water was symbolically
poured out, boldly declaring himself to be the source of living water
to all who believe in him.[107] The water-pouring ceremony at the
Feast of Tabernacles in Jesus' day was already interpreted in various

[103] 1 Chr. 29:14–16.   [104] Gen. 2:10–14.   [105] Joel 3:18.

[106] Zech. 14:4, 8. For Zechariah, such geological metamorphoses are a vivid means
by which he depicts the cosmic transformation that will involve the whole earth and
all the nations on the day when Yahweh comes to reign.

[107] John 7:37–39. 'On the seven days of the Feast, a golden flagon was filled with
water from the pool of Siloam and was carried in a procession led by the High Priest
back to the temple ... The water was offered to God at the time of the morning
sacrifice, along with the daily drink-offering [of wine] ... These ceremonies of the
Feast of Tabernacles were related in Jewish thought both to the LORD's provision of
water in the desert and to the LORD's pouring out of the Spirit in the last days.
Pouring at the Feast of Tabernacles refers symbolically to the messianic age in which
a stream from the sacred rock would flow over the whole earth ... The water-pouring
ceremony is ... a foretaste of the eschatological rivers of living water foreseen by
Ezekiel (47:1–9) and Zechariah (13:1).' D. A. Carson, *The Gospel According to John*,
Tyndale Commentary (Leicester: IVP; Grand Rapids: Eerdmans, 1991), pp. 321–322.

Jewish traditions as a symbolic anticipation of the messianic outpouring of the Spirit in fulfilment of various scriptures, including Ezekiel 47:1–9. Jesus seems to have set himself clearly in that context of expectation and to have claimed to be its fulfilment.

But the clearest recycling of Ezekiel's graphic vision comes in the book of Revelation, where the river of life forms part of the depiction of the city of God, the new creation, in which God will dwell with redeemed humanity and in which, above all, 'No longer will there be any curse.' In John's vision there was no further place for a temple or an altar, so the river runs from the throne of God straight down the high street of the city. But the high street has become a boulevard, because Ezekiel's miraculous trees are there too, somehow metamorphosed into one great 'tree of life' which manages to grow on both sides of the river. Ezekiel's river brought blessing to the land and people of Israel; for John, the vision has expanded multinationally, since 'the leaves of the tree are for the healing of the nations'.[108]

As is so often the case with biblical prophetic symbolism, then, Ezekiel's river of living water has several layers of significance. For the exiles, this river spoke of the reversal of the curse, death and barrenness of exile through their return to the land as a people restored to God's blessing and favour. Beyond that, it spoke of the true source of all life and healing – the presence of the living God in his sanctuary. For those who believe in the Messiah, Jesus, the river of living water speaks of the continuing welling up of the Spirit of God which brings life and blessing to the believer here and now and flows out to others. We need to remember that all renewal in the church or in the world flows by God's grace from God's presence and is not something we generate or control. And ultimately the river of life, in Ezekiel and Revelation, anticipates the new creation in which God will have lifted the curse from the earth for ever and will dwell in life-giving abundance with his redeemed people gathered from all nations.

ii. The land (45:1–12, 47:13 – 48:14; 48:21–29)
If Ezekiel considered himself somewhat in the role of a new Moses in the restoration of Israel's sacrificial worship at the altar (43:13–27), there is an even clearer echo of Moses in relation to the land. Just as Moses had described the boundaries of the land and allocated it in advance to the tribes of Israel before the original conquest,[109] so Ezekiel now gives the boundaries of the land again and provides detailed tribal allocations in advance of the return from exile. At a

[108] Rev. 22:1–5.
[109] Num. 33:50 – 34:29. The actual tribal territories are given later, in Josh. 13 – 19.

historical level, Ezekiel's vision at this point serves the same purpose as his vision of a rebuilt temple. It served as a word of encouragement and reassurance for the exiles. The land would be inhabited again. The repopulated mountains of Israel would again rejoice, as he had prophesied in chapter 36.

Ezekiel's purpose, however, is not merely predictive. What kind of restoration would it be when land and people were reunited? How would the vertical dimension of covenant relationship with God and the horizontal dimension of covenant obligation to one another find expression? 'If chaps. 40 – 48 begin with theological architecture [the temple], they end with theological geography [the land].'[110] And it is indeed *theological* geography', for it never did, and arguably never could, take literal shape on the soil of Palestine. As Ezekiel well knew, the exiles who would return were predominantly of the tribe of Judah. The northern tribes had been scattered centuries earlier and the concept of 'the twelve tribes of Israel', though a powerfully resonant spiritual symbol of the unity of God's covenant people, had no extant counterpart in political or territorial reality. And when the exiles did return, the territory they occupied was a rather small and beleaguered province around Jerusalem and Judea. The northern territories had a different status in the Persian administration. So Ezekiel's neat horizontal divisions were never realized, and it is very likely that he never envisaged that they literally would be. Both his virtual-reality presentation of a perfectly symmetrical temple and his visionary portrayal of a perfectly subdivided land served a higher objective than architecture or cartography.

We shall briefly survey the contours of Ezekiel's vision with the help of figure 9.2, and then draw attention to four notable features of it.

The whole section from 47:13 to 48:29, which is concerned with *the land you are to allot as an inheritance to the tribes of Israel* (48:29), falls into two main sections.

First, 47:13–23 specifies the *external boundaries* of the whole land and requires that it be divided up equally among the tribes, with a new and special clause to include resident aliens as well. The boundaries are given in a clockwise sequence – north, east, south, west – and are modelled on Numbers 34:1–12 (which began in the south). On the equal division and inclusion of aliens, see below.

Secondly, 48:1–29 specifies the *internal allotments* of the tribes from north to south. This passage is itself divided into three sections.

(a) 48:1–7. The northern half of the land is described, with the

110 Allen 29, p. 285.

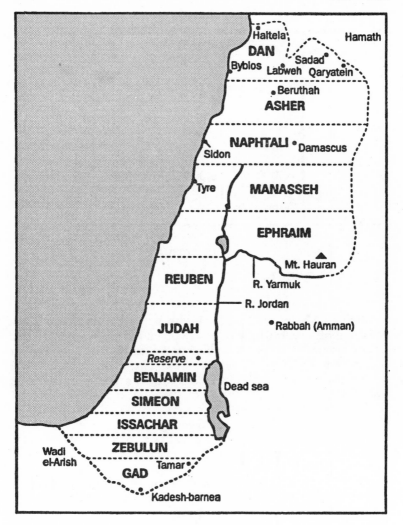

Figure 9.3 Ezekiel's vision of the land of Israel

allotments for seven tribes, given in order from north to south: Dan, Asher, Naphtali, Manasseh, Ephraim, Reuben and Judah.

(b) 48:8–22. The central section of the land is described. This *special portion*, or 'reserve gift' was a unique and unprecedented part of Ezekiel's vision. It has already been mentioned in 45:1–7 (where it occurs appropriately alongside the description of the priests and Levites since they were its primary inhabitants) as the *sacred district*

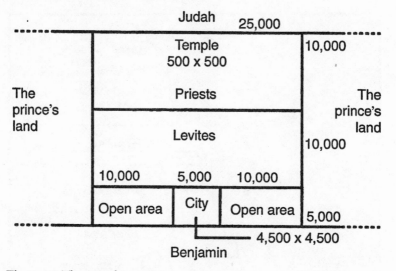

Figure 9.4 The sacred reserve

belonging to Yahweh himself. As can be seen from figure 9.3, it consisted of a central square of 25,000 cubits (8), flanked by two slices of prince's territory stretching to the Jordan in the east and the Mediterranean in the west (21–22). The central square was subdivided into one strip of 10,000 cubits for the priests, with the 500 cubit square temple in the centre (9–12), a second strip of 10,000 cubits for the Levites (13–14), and a third 5,000 cubit strip with *the city* in the centre of that (15–20). Although the Levites would inhabit this central square, it was not counted as a tribal territory like the others; in reality it belonged to Yahweh alone: *it is holy to the LORD* (14).

(c) 48:23–29. The southern half of the land is described, with allotments for the five remaining tribes, starting at the central reservation down to the southern external boundary, in order: Benjamin, Simeon, Issachar, Zebulun and Gad.

The highly schematic nature of Ezekiel's sketch can be seen in several ways. The order of tribes seems to reflect a grading based on their ancestry. The four tribes descended from Jacob's two concubines, Bilhah and Zilpah, are placed furthest from the central sanctuary (Dan, Asher, Naphtali and Gad), while those descended from his two wives, Leah and Rachel, are balanced four on each side of it. This results in a dramatic departure from the historical locations of some of the tribes. The Transjordanian tribes (i.e. Reuben, Gad and half of Manasseh, who originally settled on the eastern side of the Jordan) are brought back across the Jordan, and Gad moves to the far south. Issachar and Zebulun, formerly far-northern tribes, are also relocated to the far south. Placing Judah to the north and Benjamin to the south of the central city reverses their historical positioning relative to Jerusalem. And the straight-line east-to-west orientation of all the tribal territories pays no attention to the natural topographical contours of the physical land. It seems unmistakable that Ezekiel is making a *theological* statement, not providing a functional map.[111] The geometric diagrammatic neatness of his picture bears even less direct correspondence to the physical geography of Palestine than the London Underground diagram does to a street map of that sprawling city. What, then, are the theological affirmations we may detect within it?

First, there is a clear commitment to *equality*. This is a return to the original vision for the settlement of the land by the tribes of Israel. In contrast to the Canaanite system of land tenure in which the land was owned by kings and the bulk of the population lived as tenant farmers, like serfs under the feudal system, the ancient Israelite system attributed to Moses and sanctioned by Yahweh's ownership of the land as a whole was that the land should be divided up in such a way that each tribe had territory proportionate to its size.[112] In the record of the division of land under Joshua, it was further stressed that even internally tribal lands were to be distributed to the clans and families of each tribe.[113] The intention was that every household should have sufficient for economic viability. There was to be a broad and equitable distribution of the land. Ezekiel reaffirms that ideal both verbally and pictorially. The instruction for the land division is that *you are to divide it equally among them* (lit. 'each like his brother', 47:14). And in the 'map' each tribe gets a roughly equal slice of land running east–west, with no tribe grabbing larger or more desirable territories. Within the newly constituted idealized twelve-tribe community of Israel the equality of all the people reflects their covenantal unity.

Secondly, there is a commitment to *security*. Here again is a reflection of the original Israelite pattern of land-holding, in which land was fundamentally inalienable. That is, it could not be simply bought and sold commercially outside the kinship network within which it was held.[114] It was Yahweh's desire that Israelite families

[111] 'One should construe this document not as a literary photograph of the land of Israel but as a cartographic painting by an artist with a particular theological agenda.' Block (2), p. 723.   [112] Num. 33:53–54.
[113] Josh. 15:1; 16:5; 18:11; 19:1; etc. Cf. Judg. 21:24.
[114] The clearest text affirming this principle is Lev. 25:23. The reply of Naboth to Ahab's request that he sell him his vineyard captures the strength of this principle within

should enjoy security of tenure on their land, and mechanisms were devised to restore them to it when they were threatened by poverty and debt.[115] Ezekiel insists that this original ideal must be restored. Tribal lands must be held without threat of loss or dispossession. Historically, the main culprit in causing the distortion and virtual destruction of Israel's system of secure, kinship-based land tenure was the monarchy. Ever since the time of Solomon, it seems that the kings of Israel had indulged their own greed for prime land, and had made grants of it to their favourites, heedless of the original system of tribal inheritance. Wealthy individuals had extended the practice, and over the centuries great numbers of poorer families were dispossessed as land accumulated in the hands of the wealthy few. Along with the religious idolatries of the era, this social and economic evil was a major target for prophetic anger.[116] And just as for the ritual defilements, Ezekiel's word is simple: Yahweh has had enough of it! Let such things have no more place in the restored people of God. Twice Ezekiel makes it clear that the land allotted to the prince is to be sufficient for him. Neither he nor any of those who will wield authority in the new community are to use their status to enrich themselves at the expense of the ordinary people. Greed and rapacity will be replaced by a fresh call for justice: *'My princes will no longer oppress my people but will allow the house of Israel to possess the land according to their tribes ... Give up your violence and oppression and do what is just and right. Stop dispossessing my people'* (45:8–9). The rules of inheritance and jubilee will apply equally to the prince and his family, and he may not bypass them in making any grant to his servants (46:16–18). Above all, he may not encroach on the security of the land of his people: *'The prince must not take any of the inheritance of the people, driving them off their property ... so that none of my people will be separated from his property* (46:18). Thus Ezekiel seeks to put an end to one of the worst abuses of the pre-exilic era.

Thirdly, there is a remarkable call for *inclusivity*. In 47:22–23 Ezekiel calls for land to be given as inheritance not only to Israelites,

---

Israel: 'Yahweh forbid that I should give you the inheritance of my fathers' (1 Kgs. 21:3). As Ahab well knew, Naboth was right. Yahweh did forbid it. Archaeologically the inalienability of land in Israel is well supported, since there is a remarkable dearth of documents recording land sales from Israelite sites, though they are abundant in Canaanite and other ancient near-eastern excavations. For a full account of Israel's theology and practice in relation to land, see Wright, *God's People in God's Land.*

[115] The most important of these were the procedures for redemption of land and debtors, and the jubilee year. Both are described in Lev. 25. See C. J. H. Wright, 'The Jubilee Year', in idem, *Walking in the Ways of the LORD: The Ethical Authority of the Old Testament* (Leicester: Apollos 1995; Downers Grove: IVP, 1996).

[116] Is. 5:8; 10:1–2; Mic. 2:1–2; Amos 2:6.

but also to resident aliens with families living within the tribal boundaries. In the Torah, resident aliens (*gērîm*) were to be treated with care and support.[117] They are often classified along with widows, orphans and Levites, precisely because they did *not* have a share in the land and were therefore economically vulnerable and socially disadvantaged. Although circumcised (*gērîm*) could join the Israelite worshipping community at the Passover,[118] the general rule excluded foreigners from Israel's sacred assembly.[119] All such disadvantages seem to be swept away by Ezekiel's remarkable repeal of the pre-exilic restriction. The resident alien is to share inheritance rights in Israel's most prized possession – the land. Their citizenship is assured. Isaiah 56:3–8 gave much more poetic and rhetorical welcome to the foreigner and the eunuch who committed themselves to joining the people of Yahweh and taking covenantal obligations on themselves. Though more prosaic, Ezekiel's ever practical concern gives concrete expression to the same theological truth. The newly constituted Israel of God will be ritually pure, but it will not be ethnically exclusive.[120] Aliens will be transformed into fellow heirs. Ezekiel anticipates a reality that Paul proclaims as the very heart of the gospel: 'Consequently, you [Gentiles] are no longer foreigners and aliens, but fellow-citizens with God's people and members of God's household ... through the gospel the Gentiles are heirs together with Israel, members together of one body, and sharers together in the promise in Christ Jesus.'[121]

Fourthly, there is a pervading *sanctity* at the very heart and core of the whole nation. It is a God-centred community. Ezekiel expresses this fundamental reality through his central square of holy space – the special reserve that belonged to Yahweh and was permeated by his 'local' presence in a unique way, with the temple at its centre. The repetition of its detailed description (45:1–5; 48:9–14) emphasizes its importance. Israel's land would have Israel's God

---

[117] Lev. 19:33–34 is the classic text. The *gērîm* were to be treated with equality under the law, and indeed, Israelites were commanded to love them as they loved themselves, just as they were commanded to do for their neighbours. However, in the pre-exilic period this did not extend to having a share in the ownership of the land. Ezekiel's proposal is thus radically new.

[118] Exod. 12:48–49.   [119] Deut. 23:1–8.

[120] There is no contradiction between the admission of aliens into the land-tenure system here and the complaint about foreigners having been used as guards and servants in the temple in 44:7–9. In that passage the foreigners are explicitly described as 'uncircumcised in heart and flesh'. That is, they were neither physically circumcised nor living in any kind of covenantal obedience to Yahweh, yet they were employed in his most sacred residence. By contrast, the foreigner and eunuch who are welcomed in Is. 56:3–8 are explicitly said to take upon themselves the prime requirements of covenant membership.

[121] Eph. 2:19; 3:6.

at its geographical centre, portraying that the people of Israel would have God at their spiritual heart. The symbolism is striking and its message unmistakable. The God who had been marginalized by his people and who had finally abandoned his land in destructive judgment had now returned to the centre – the centre of the land, which, as Ezekiel has earlier pointed out, was also 'the centre of the nations' (5:5). And from that centre, sanctifying holiness and life-giving blessing would flow forth as a river to cleanse and to heal the people, and beyond them (though Ezekiel does not say so), the nations and the world itself.

It is not difficult to see how all four theological themes that are wrapped around Ezekiel's portrayal of Israel's reordered land – equality, security, inclusivity and sanctity – have continuing significance within a New Testament portrayal of the realities of Christian fellowship and unity. We too are called to be a people where all are one and equal in Christ, sharing (as is the meaning of fellowship) in all the blessings of our inheritance. We too are called to do justice, within and beyond the church itself, and to refrain from looking after our own interests at the expense of others. We too are definitively a community in which the barriers of 'alienness' are broken down, for the glory of the gospel is that we are 'no longer foreigners and aliens, but fellow-citizens with God's people and members of God's household'.[122] And above all, we are 'saints' – those who have been sanctified by the blood of Christ and are now indwelt, individually and corporately, by the Spirit of God. Our sacred centre is not a little square of earthly cubits, but that temple and throne where God reigns in hearts surrendered to the Lord Jesus Christ.

iii. The city (48:15–20, 30–35)
Ezekiel's final vision had begun with 'some buildings that looked like a city' (40:2). Now that he has had a closer look, it is clear that Ezekiel's description of this city is as artificial and schematic as his description of the land. It is a perfect square which, when its surrounding pasture zone is included, comprises 25,000 square cubits. And it fitted perfectly into the centre of the southernmost strip of the sacred reservation, which itself had 'sides' of 25,000 cubits. Ezekiel is a symbolic theologian, not a futuristic city-planner. We may observe three significant aspects of what he has to say about this city.

First, it was *a place for all the people of God*. The unity and completeness of Israel are focused on this city, for it is the place

[122] Eph. 2:19.

where people from any or all of the tribes may come and work (48:19). And this wholeness is further symbolized in the twelve gates, three on each side, one for each of the twelve tribes of Israel. And this time Levi is included among the gates (for although Levi was not included in the distribution of the land, it was still one of the original twelve tribes). To keep the number of tribes to twelve, the division of Joseph into Ephraim and Manasseh for the purpose of the land distribution is cancelled, and there is a single gate for Joseph. Such an arrangement of gates was never literally achieved at any time in the history of Jerusalem, but it is taken up again, presumably with the same inclusive significance, in John's eschatological vision of the new Jerusalem.[123]

Secondly, it is portrayed as *a place of continuing work and activity.* Ezekiel's vision pictures people living, farming, producing food and working within the city and its surrounding land (48:18–19). At a historical level, it was of course true, as other prophets also foretold, that the city would be rebuilt, land would be cultivated again, and the normal cycles of human life in the city and on the land would be resumed after the exile. This much was certainly envisaged in Ezekiel's vision, and it fits with his equally historical expectation of the restoration of the temple and the sacrificial system which was fulfilled after the return. However, if we allow the vision to speak eschatologically and compare it with other prophetic visions of the future of God's new creation, there is a similar 'earthiness'. The normal activities of human life – enjoying human relationships, working productively with the resources of the earth, producing wealth and cultural achievements – do not evaporate into some spiritual ether in the biblical view of the future. Rather they are to be redeemed and freed from the curses of frustration, decay, danger and death.[124] Even when we draw the significance of Ezekiel's symbolism of the city of God further into the eschatological context that it gains in the New Testament, we note that John's final vision of the city of God also includes work and activity. The Bible does not deal in paradise mythology, but in the sure and certain hope of new creation. And in that new creation the achievements of the kingdoms of this world will be brought – redeemed and purified – into the city of God, and the servants of the Lord will go on serving him.[125] There will be work to be done in the new creation, but it will be work in all its

[123] Rev. 1:10–14. John has added to the twelve gates (symbolizing the twelve tribes of Israel) twelve foundations (symbolizing the twelve apostles), binding together the even greater spiritual unity of God's people, Old and New Testament.

[124] Cf. Isaiah's vision of the new heavens and new earth, Is. 65:17–25; and Zechariah's picture of the new Jerusalem, Zech. 8:4–5.

[125] Rev. 21:26; 22:3.

creation joy, freed for ever from the toil and frustration caused by sin and curse.

Thirdly, and most important of all, it is *the place where God is*. This is the wonderful note with which Ezekiel brings his book to a close. *And the name of the city from that time on will be:* THE LORD IS THERE. It may be significant that he does not give it the name 'Jerusalem'.[126] In some ways, Ezekiel has made it clear that his visionary city is *not* simply a renovated Jerusalem, because he has so deliberately removed the temple from the city, and kept the sacred space of the temple quite distinct from the space allocated to the prince and the territory of the city. The potential for confusion between divine and human kingship, between God's holiness and human glory, that had characterized and compromised the old city was to be avoided in Ezekiel's future arrangement.[127] But although Ezekiel has gone to great lengths to portray the *temple* as the place *par excellence* of God's dwelling, he now wants it to be understood that God's presence was not confined within those protecting walls. The city too, the focal point of the people's ordinary 'secular' working lives, would be the place of God's presence. Not everybody could live in the temple! Not even all the tribe of Levi had access to the inner court and the temple itself. But the concluding message of the book is not merely that God has returned to his temple, but that *God is wherever his people are*. Ezekiel's twelve-gated, foursquare city represents the whole people of God – all the tribes of Israel. And the name of that city speaks the great truth about that people – *THE LORD IS THERE*.

John heard the same truth amplified as a loud voice from the very throne of God himself within the Holy City, 'Now the dwelling of God is with men, and he will live with them. They will be his people, and God himself will be with them and be their God.'[128] And in the meantime we, who live in certain hope of that great day, have the equally certain promise of the Lord's presence in whatever present earthly city we are called to live and witness. 'For where two or three come together in my name, *there am I with them*.'[129]

---

[26] Some scholars suggest that the name in Hebrew, *Yahweh šāmmâ*, may be a deliberate word-play on the Hebrew name of the city, *yᵉrûšālaim*.

[127] The compromise and confusion remained, of course, in the historical Jerusalem. Even in Jesus' day, the temple, Herod's palace and the Roman barracks all jostled together, creating, for Jesus, intolerable theological tensions.

[128] Rev. 21:3.   [129] Matt. 18:20.